Sergei Rachmaninoff

Sergei Rachmaninoff

Cross Rhythms of the Soul

Valeria Z. Nollan

LEXINGTON BOOKS
Lanham • Boulder • New York • London

Published by Lexington Books
An imprint of The Rowman & Littlefield Publishing Group, Inc.
4501 Forbes Boulevard, Suite 200, Lanham, Maryland 20706
www.rowman.com

86-90 Paul Street, London EC2A 4NE

Copyright © 2022 by Valeria Z. Nollan

All rights reserved. No part of this book may be reproduced in any form or by any electronic or mechanical means, including information storage and retrieval systems, without written permission from the publisher, except by a reviewer who may quote passages in a review.

British Library Cataloguing in Publication Information Available

Library of Congress Cataloging-in-Publication Data

Names: Nollan, Valeria Z., author.
Title: Sergei Rachmaninoff : cross rhythms of the soul / Valeria Z. Nollan.
Description: Lanham : Lexington Books, 2022. | Includes bibliographical references and index.
Identifiers: LCCN 2022036893 (print) | LCCN 2022036894 (ebook) |
  ISBN 9781666917598 (cloth) | ISBN 9781666917611 (paperback) |
  ISBN 9781666917604 (ebook)
Subjects: LCSH: Rachmaninoff, Sergei, 1873–1943. | Composers—Biography. | Pianists—Biography. | LCGFT: Biographies.
Classification: LCC ML410.R12 N65 2022 (print) | LCC ML410.R12 (ebook) |
  DDC 780.92 [B]—dc23/eng/20220802
LC record available at https://lccn.loc.gov/2022036893
LC ebook record available at https://lccn.loc.gov/2022036894

Dedicated to the Piven' Family

Contents

Acknowledgments		ix
Introduction		1
1	Rachmaninoff's Origins	13
2	Early Education	41
3	Birth of a Composer-Pianist	55
4	Birth of a Conductor	75
5	The Muses	97
6	Mystery of an Immortal Beloved	125
7	Marriage to Natalia Satina	145
8	Rachmaninoff's Aesthetics	173
9	Rachmaninoff's Religiosity	197
10	Transitions	223
11	The Legendary Virtuoso Pianist	243
12	Rachmaninoff as Humanitarian	263
13	Paradise Regained: The Villa Senar	283
14	The Last Bow: Rachmaninoff and America	303

Afterword: Rachmaninoff's Legacy in the Twenty-First Century	335
Appendix I: Twists and Turns of a Mystery	347
Appendix II: List of Works	355
Selected Discography	361
Selected Bibliography	365
Further Reading	373
Index	375
About the Author and Principal Research Colleagues	385

Acknowledgments

This book is the result of eighteen years of archival research, interviews, travels, writing, and revising connected with Rachmaninoff. It preserves in written form what became a biographical-musicological project of inquiry and discovery about Sergei Rachmaninoff that was shared among a circle of specialists in his multifaceted identity. I was privileged to be among them. The project involved meetings in twos and threes at various museums, long discussions that evolved over meals or walks through Moscow or Tambov or excursions to the Rachmaninoff places in Russia, and travels to Europe and the United States. The main participants in this project, besides myself, were V. I. Antipov, A. S. Bazikov, A. A. Naumov, D. A. Dmitriev, and B. S. Nikitin.

I worked in numerous archives in the countries in which Rachmaninoff spent significant amounts of time, and am indebted to the many individuals who took their time to assist me in obtaining and examining vitally important materials. I wish I could name them all. The archives I consulted were made available to me at the following sites: the Feodor Chaliapin Museum-Estate (Moscow); Russian National Museum of Music (Moscow); Moscow Conservatory Named for Tchaikovsky (Moscow); St. Petersburg Conservatory Named for Rimsky-Korsakov (St. Petersburg); Museum of the Tambov Institute of Music Pedagogy Named for Rachmaninoff (Tambov, Russia); Royal Albert Hall (London); Royal Conservatory of Music (London); Holy Trinity Seminary Archive (Jordanville, New York); Ivanovka Museum-Estate Research Center (Ivanovka, Russia); Kensico Cemetery (Valhalla, New York); Library of Congress (Washington, D.C.); Zentral- und Hochschulbibliothek Luzern (Lucerne, Switzerland); Carnegie Hall Museum (New York); Teatro alla Scala (Milan); Eugene Ormandy Archive, University of Pennsylvania (Philadelphia); Varazze Public Library Archive (Varazze, Italy); and Villa Senar (Weggis, Switzerland).

Among the many persons I interviewed, besides those noted above, whose recollections, reflections, and expertise informed my writing, are: A. I. Ermakov; I. N. Vanovskaia; N. Yu. Tartakovskaia; N. E. Griaznova; E. V. Khokhlova; I. A. Medvedeva; A. G. Kostina; Judith C. Mitchell; Lena Donnelly; Ron and Denise Beech; Gino Francesconi; Elger Niels; Wouter de Voogd; Vladimir Leyetchkiss; Sandro Russo; Margarita M. Anthoine; Scott Colebank; Kevin LaVine; Emilee Pittman; Kate Stimson; Brian Ray; Carole Blankenship; Tim Sharp; Harold Tillek; Robert Threlfall; Henry Z. Steinway; and A. B. Conius Rachmaninoff. The generosity and kindness of all the members of the UK Rachmaninoff Society (now the Rachmaninoff Network) are also deeply appreciated.

Several research grants and an endowed chair position at Rhodes College (Memphis) provided the time and resources for travel to foreign archives and for early drafts of the book's chapters presented at professional conferences. I am indebted to the administrators of the Rhodes College Office of Academic Affairs for their consistent support of my work and their ongoing collegiality. Among them, John Planchon, Mark McMahon, Michael Drompp, and Milton Moreland deserve special thanks. The piano recitals I gave of Rachmaninoff's music in various cities of the United States, Russia, and the United Kingdom helped me to access Rachmaninoff's identity in perhaps the most important way.

Most of all, I am grateful for the love and support of my husband Richard and my son Alex, and for my extended family of the Pivens in Krasnodar Region and Moscow, Russia.

For transliteration of Russian names and words I have used the Library of Congress system (System II in J. Thomas Shaw's *The Transliteration of Modern Russian for English Language Publications*, Madison, WI: University of Wisconsin Press, 1967) for both the text and citations of sources. I omit any indication of ъ (the hard sign) and ь (the soft sign) in the text. In citations of bibliographical material I follow the Library of Congress System consistently. I use transliteration System I only if a Russian name is more readable to speakers of English (such as Vasilievich). In the case of Russian names or words already familiar to a Western audience by a different spelling (such as Tchaikovsky), I retain the spelling familiar to readers. An exception is the last name "Conus," which incorrectly renders the Russian last name in English. I use the correct transliteration "Conius." I have aimed for both consistency and readability.

In referring to Russian persons, I have followed the Russian cultural practice of using the first name, middle name (patronymic, derived from the father's first name), and last name. In the case of a female the middle name would have the suffix -ovna (example: Ivanovna), while a male's middle name would have the suffix -ovich (example: Ivanovich). Female and male last names, if they have Russian or Slavic origins, also differ from each other: a female would have the last name of "Satina," while a male's name would be "Satin." Russians use the polite form of first name plus patronymic, rather than a "Mr." or "Ms." system. Thus, "Sofia Aleksandrovna" would be the polite form, rather than "Ms. Satina."

I retain the translations of the sources I consult but have checked each translation against the original. I indicate each time when a translation from the Russian (or Italian, etc.) is my own. The languages in which I worked are Russian, English, German, French, Italian, Ukrainian, and Church Slavonic.

Figure 0.1 Sergei Rachmaninoff, 1927. Library of Congress, LC-USZ62-100471.

Introduction

Sergei Vasilievich Rachmaninoff was a man of few words who preferred to speak through his music. His cousin Sofia Satina, with whom he felt comfortable sharing his most private thoughts, wrote, "He never—or almost never—uttered words about himself, his tribulations, or his creative work. Only once in my presence in passing did he mention that words were useless, that everything was expressed in his compositions and is expressed in his [piano] playing."[1] He was eloquent and loquacious in his musical compositions, remaining convinced that those who wished to understand his inner world should first and foremost listen to his music. Rachmaninoff could downplay the importance of words because he possessed, to the highest degree, the ability to translate emotion into musical form, along with a dense and passionate inner world that his music revealed to listeners. The philosopher Vladimir Soloviev noted about Pushkin in words that characterize perfectly the relationship between Rachmaninoff the creating artist and the material of his inner life that produced his musical works: "Strong sensuality is the material of genius. As mechanistic movement is converted to heat, and heat to light, so the spiritual energy of creativity in its actual manifestation . . . is a *conversion* of the lower energies of the sensual soul."[2]

Rachmaninoff described himself as being 85 percent musician and 15 percent man.[3] He lived in music as Fyodor Dostoevsky lived in literature. And yet, for us to gain entry to his remarkable life, words *are* needed. Verbal art provides us with the comforting illusion that we are describing a feeling, thought, or experience accurately. We fall short of achieving a completely truthful picture of a particular person's reality, but this realization should not prevent us from seeking the most fitting words for the mental arsenal that will illuminate, however imperfectly, this reality. Rachmaninoff's extraordinary life can be characterized by cross rhythms, one of the most pervasive features of his musical identity, even to the point that he would recommend that pianists practice, not by playing regular scales but by playing twos against threes, threes against fives, fours against sixes as the fingers are advancing up the scales. Devilishly difficult? Indeed. But this process trains the pianist in a rich complexity, making the result emotionally and intellectually satisfying. Concerning the events of Rachmaninoff's life, he negotiated the existential cross rhythms of several cultures, several musical styles, and several women. In music, cross rhythms typically lead to resolution, to a harmonious dénouement—and this was what Rachmaninoff attempted to achieve in all the aspects of his life. What were the movements of the composer-conductor-pianist's soul along the way? The present biography addresses this question.

In Russian culture the understanding of the soul is intrinsically connected with religious, aesthetic, and moral categories bound up with the theology and traditions of Russian Orthodoxy. For Rachmaninoff, as for anyone raised in Russian religious culture, the soul represented the essential center of being, the repository and conveyer of spiritual goodness and beauty—but beauty in a deeper sense. To possess a soul that was active and receptive to spiritual growth and creative self-expression meant that a person was fully alive and in touch with a higher realm of ideas. As the chapters in this biography reveal, Rachmaninoff recognized his musical gifts relatively early and received the best training available at that time in Russia to a young man of the nobility. However, he also carried inside himself an awareness of his place and influence in life, seeking to use these advantages in ethical as well as artistically fulfilling ways. He used the full spectrum of resources available to him to help others, advance the practice of music in Russia and internationally, maintain the highest standards, and avoid entangling himself in any kind of racism, anti-Semitism, or national prejudice.

The idea for a new biography of Rachmaninoff did not come to me naturally or easily. I resisted the notion at first, because I was and still am troubled at the thought that in my effort to portray an *entire* life I can position my subject however I want—and he will not be able to answer, clarify, or object to what I say about him. Because this ethical consideration *is* problematic, I keep in mind my answerability to a human being who died almost eighty years ago. A corollary question arises: Can the artifacts that become representative of an individual's life be accurately read by even a well-informed and careful biographer? A material thing has its own biography and, in the case of the life story of its possessor, is translated by the biographer into an agent affecting the construction of a coherent narrative. The methodology of a biographer includes evaluating the content of personal interviews and archives, but it also involves reading the silences and gaps encountered in those interviews and archives. Silences speak loudest when a life in its totality is examined from a particular perspective. Sometimes what is most important, most representative, is visible, though not immediately apparent.

My overall aim, as a scholar and musician, is to supplement and amend the existing biographies of a major figure in world musical culture whose story is far from being definitively told. Rather than parroting the received account of Rachmaninoff's life, I undertake to correct the historical record on Rachmaninoff—as accurately and sensitively as my research and insights allow. The basic outlines of Rachmaninoff's life and career are well known: one can find in the numerous existing biographies the salient names, places, and dates that form the scaffolding of this life. What is lacking in them, however, is a more complete psychological portrait, an assessment of his character in the context of persons and events of which other biographers have been unaware or which they have neglected, for whatever reasons.[4] One significant area not addressed adequately is that of the women in Rachmaninoff's life whose connection to him informed his compositions. These women—his wife, daughters, musical collaborators, and intimate friends—were fundamentally important to him, and a clearer picture of who they were, both in connection with him and in their own right, may alter our understanding of his musical aesthetics. Biographers have shied away from connecting the composer's intimate, passionate compositions to several remarkable women whom he loved during his lifetime and to whom he openly dedicated major musical works. Thus in my biography the "woman question" represents one of the overarching themes; enhanced knowledge of the role specific women played in Rachmaninoff's inner life surely will sharpen our perception of both the man and his music.

Because Rachmaninoff's music was deeply programmatic and his aesthetics affirmed that music should come from the heart (rather than for the purposes of intellectual experimentation), the connection between his music and his life's experiences becomes even more tightly intertwined and underscores the conclusion that such an approach will yield truer insights into his compositions. My inquiry into the women in Rachmaninoff's life in no way implies, however, that they represent the only category of inspiration for his works; to be sure, the creative process is mysterious and complex. For Rachmaninoff, prevailing musical and intellectual currents, the beauty and majesty of nature, mystery of religion (especially Russian Orthodoxy), and complexity of world events also significantly contributed to the fabric of his compositions.

A "post-hagiographic" biography of Rachmaninoff is needed, not because Rachmaninoff harbored dark secrets in his life and I set out to bring to light some scandalous activities on his part. To the contrary, the most reliable kinds of evidence, even from people who personally did not like Rachmaninoff, consistently underscore his warmth, integrity, humanity, and professionalism. Rachmaninoff was without a doubt a good person, even an exemplary person. His music exudes honesty, sincerity, a strong impulse for emotional harmony, and, as Alexander Ermakov, former Curator of the Rachmaninoff Museum-Estate, has emphasized, goodness. In the twenty-first century the approach to Rachmaninoff's life that is needed is a thorough investigation into the personal side of the composer's identity, and how it connects with the matrix of his compositions and attitudes toward the world around him. Rachmaninoff lived during the apocalypse of the first half of the twentieth century, experiencing firsthand the Bolshevik Revolution of 1917; complete loss of his country, culture, and finances; and reconstruction of his entire identity within a new country, language, and culture. In his personal life the following areas need to be explored further than has been achieved in the existing biographies:

1. Why did Rachmaninoff marry his first cousin, Natalia Aleksandrovna Satina, when there is no evidence at all of any courtship or romantic involvement between them? Biographers have remained confounded about the circumstances surrounding their marriage but have refrained from venturing deeper into this subject. The biography *Sergei Rachmaninoff: A Lifetime in Music* by Sergei Bertensson and Jay Leyda was criticized by Oxford University Press for not developing four aspects of Rachmaninoff's life—the "biographical substance"—sufficiently; one of them was Rachmaninoff's relationship with N. A. Satina and eventual marriage to her.[5] The press expressed an interest in the project but ultimately (for reasons of the market) was unable to accept it for publication. Clearly the account in it of Rachmaninoff's courtship and marriage did not make sense to the editors in terms of its emotional logic.
2. Who is the "mystery person" whose name was crossed out in the dedicatory line of the master score of one of Rachmaninoff's large-scale compositions, and whose identity may be behind the dedicatory reference that appears in the master score of at least one other work?
3. What kind of relationships existed among the members of Rachmaninoff's own family and the large network of his extended family? Reminiscences of some peasant women who worked on the Rachmaninoff-Satin estate of Ivanovka provide new perspectives on these matters.
4. An examination of the extent of Rachmaninoff's humanitarian work sheds light on the people and issues supremely important to him. In addition to his extraordinary career as composer, conductor, and pianist, Rachmaninoff was a committed and active humanitarian. He gave many benefit concerts during both world wars to help those in need in Russia and continued to support his lost homeland throughout his life. For many years he sent large sums of money to Russia through the Soviet Embassy,

as well as organizing the transfer of medical supplies and food parcels for widows, orphans, and others in difficult circumstances in that country.
5. How did Rachmaninoff function within the communities of Russian émigrés of high intellectual and artistic achievement? What were his connections with the lectures of philosopher G. P. Fedotov in New York and with the fate of philosopher Ivan Ilyin? What were his reasons for establishing the publishing company in Paris, TAIR, which produced literature and music by Russian writers and composers who were unable to publish their work in the Soviet Union?
6. How does Rachmaninoff the interlocutor appear in his letters in the original Russian? A livelier psychological portrait reveals the witty and sparkling, rather than the traditionally considered "gloomy" personality that has become the prevailing stereotype in currency today. Instead of keeping his head buried in the well-worn way of life and musical aesthetics of the past, as has been commonly assumed by critics, Rachmaninoff was firmly in step with his cultural origins and the world in which he moved as a towering musical figure.
7. In which ways was Rachmaninoff a seminal figure within the attempts of the devastated Russian Orthodox Church to reorganize itself abroad so that it could minister to the needs of the Russian faithful? What was his role in bringing about stability in Russian Orthodox ecclesial structures? A nuanced portrait of Rachmaninoff must include some discussion of his Russian Orthodox religiosity and his intellectually active personality, because it provides correctives to aspects of his identity that are underdeveloped and poorly understood.

In particular, Rachmaninoff's Russian Orthodox piety is explored and documented in this book as fully as possible. It formed an essential feature of his character, and the present biography provides detailed information about the ways in which this faith tradition informed his way of life and perspectives. He manifested some saintly virtues: he forgave everyone who harmed him and his family, even the Bolsheviks whose violent anti-aristocracy campaign drove him out of his native country and away from the culture that nourished his creative springs and in essence his entire being. As a hugely influential personage internationally, Rachmaninoff lived a fulfilled and complex life that needs to be presented more fully if we are to better understand his compositions and aesthetics. In my study of the existing critical work on the composer I have encountered repeatedly either a complete absence or major misconceptions of Rachmaninoff's Orthodox piety and the profound role this ancient faith tradition plays in the lives of its adherents. Assumptions that Eastern Orthodoxy is similar to the Western Christian confessions of Catholicism and Protestantism are inaccurate and cannot explain the Russian experience; they fail to present Russians in a context in which they can be clearly understood.

The sources of authority of Orthodox Christianity are enormous, traversing chronology and geography over an almost 2,000-year history. The most important ones are monasticism, the saints (with Mary, Mother of God occupying the most honored position), the Bible, Sacred Tradition, the Seven Ecumenical Councils of the first millennium, icons, and the hierarchs of the Council of Bishops. Moreover, the canonical norms of Orthodoxy differ from those of Western Christianity in particular in that Orthodoxy does not problematize the body, the physical self, in ways that have marked the history of Catholicism and Protestantism. As an example, this difference in expressing the reverence toward the sacred is observed in prostrating the entire body in humble prayer (the mystical and physical in Orthodoxy) and, by comparison, bowing only the head (the intellectual in Protestantism and post-Vatican II Catholicism) at the words "let us pray." Rather than the ancient Orthodox individual expression of piety in the open icon-rich spaces of the church, after the Protestant Reformation of the sixteenth century the focus changed to the congregation remaining seated and attentive to the sermon. In ecclesiology it is the difference between a church interior without pews that is adorned with icons, lit candles, and brightly colored walls, and that of a more austere interior with a large crucifix and pews facing a pulpit.[6] In art the difference can be found in the Western perspective that directs the observer to a single point, as opposed to Eastern Orthodox iconography, which in its flat and stylized perspective reaches out to the observer to invite and thereby unite him or her with the saint who is depicted. The image of the icon remembers its original.

Rachmaninoff carried within himself a lived experience of these differences, and this sensibility is expressed consistently in his music. Knowledge of the major features of Orthodox Christianity enables us to develop a better reading of the vocabulary of his compositions and their aesthetics as a whole. This difference has a direct bearing on how Rachmaninoff's passionate, muscular, and compelling music is apprehended in the West.

I have written this biography because my identity and training led inexorably to the project and because the existing biographical and scholarly materials on Rachmaninoff fall short of accurately presenting the composer's identity. My study aims to reveal a Rachmaninoff in his Russianness, the primary and most cherished identity that he worked very hard to conceal from the world outside his immediate family and closest friends (most of whom were themselves Russian). It is an identity immersed in a native culture that was stolen from him; the pain and longing for the Russia he knew were aspects of his inner life that he preferred to keep to himself. He grew to appreciate many aspects of American life and was grateful for the stability and opportunities that the country afforded him—but it goes without saying that one culture and set of ways cannot replace another. It is hoped that the attention given to Rachmaninoff's Russianness will illuminate some differences between Russian and Western culture that will enable readers to better understand the irreplaceability of culture and language, and why Rachmaninoff made the difficult decisions that history and politics forced upon him.

I have played Rachmaninoff's music for over thirty years, undertaking a more formal inquiry into his compositions in 2002. I initially wanted to study his art songs (*romansy*), not only because of their haunting beauty and the composer's masterful craftsmanship, but because of their interconnectedness with Russian poetry—the area in which I am professionally trained. The more I worked on this topic, however, the clearer it became to me that it was not the art songs alone, or even in particular, that fascinated me: it was *all* of Rachmaninoff that engaged my interest, the sum total of his identity. The whole man: the composer-conductor-pianist, husband, father, entrepreneur, philanthropist, intellectual, complex human being. The idea slowly took root and began to grow. The roots became firmly established.

How I have been positioned in life has prepared me well for undertaking this biography. My firsthand knowledge of Russian emigration, with its customs, language, and culture, with its Russian Orthodox worldview, and with its musical sensibilities, gave me valid insights that I did not manufacture artificially. They evolved organically, as an integrated part of my being. My own origins as a child of Russian parents displaced by World War II who emigrated from Germany (where I was born) to the United States represented the cultural soil in which my personality was nurtured, and enabled me to witness what I call "the agony of exile" so familiar to Rachmaninoff and other displaced Russian artists and intellectuals. The hardworking and talented Russians, Ukrainians, Serbs, and Bulgarians whose voices mingled in the spaces of my coming of age longed for the cultures of their homelands. They "sat on their suitcases," as the expression goes, but the changes of government and evolving of better times came too late for them to return.

Many of the life experiences that contributed to the formation of my identity provide me with the access to Rachmaninoff's life that would not be possible for someone who has not lived through these events. I carry within me a specific lived understanding—through my Russian roots, Russian Orthodox practices, and appreciation of European and American traditions—of Rachmaninoff's worldview that I have not encountered anywhere in any language in which publications about him exist. At every opportunity Rachmaninoff emphasized that he was Russian and that his Russianness forged and nourished the features of his identity. I know the meaning of Russianness and understand that this is the critical lens through which Rachmaninoff in his totality must be viewed. To be sure, Rachmaninoff was a citizen of the world, moving smoothly between Western Europe and America after his forced exile from Russia. But his entry to his homeland, Russia, was denied him. In this context I know the meaning of his nomadic existence as well, at least up to the years of the disintegration of the Soviet Union.

A major component of my research involved interviews with those who knew Rachmaninoff and his family personally or who interacted with others who had known him. My interviews took me to Russia, Switzerland, the Netherlands, England, and various cities in the United States. In Russia I traveled to St. Petersburg, Novgorod, Moscow, Tambov (the closest city to the Rachmaninoff-Satin country estate Ivanovka), and Ivanovka (now a museum and research center for the study of Rachmaninoff). Weggis and Hertenstein, both in Switzerland on Lake Lucerne, were the locations of my meetings with the composer's grandson Alexandre Borisovich (Conius) Rachmaninoff. In addition to the many extended conversations I had with Alexandre Borisovich, I also played Rachmaninoff's concert grand piano in his studio at the Villa Senar several times—the same piano that the Steinway family had presented to the composer in the 1930s. I learned later that I was one of the last people to play the Rachmaninoff piano with all of its original parts intact. Without consulting anyone, Alexandre Rachmaninoff had all the original strings and mechanical parts removed and replaced. The piano I played one year later at Senar, notably, did not sound the same as it had originally.

In London I met with the pianist, biographer, and stationer Robert Threlfall, who not only had seen Rachmaninoff in concert *fourteen* times but had also seen in concert many of the other luminaries of the music world of the 1920s and 1930s, including Jan Paderewski, Vladimir Horowitz, Arthur Rubinstein, Josef Lhevinne, and Josef Hofmann. In that same city I also interviewed Harold Tillek, husband of Sofia Vladimirovna Satina, the composer's niece. Twice at Steinway Hall in New York I had leisurely meetings with Henry Steinway, who had known Rachmaninoff and his family personally for many years. Several times I visited Kensico Cemetery in Valhalla, New York, where Rachmaninoff is buried, and conducted interviews and research there on the complex events after the composer's death that affected the location of his funeral and burial. As one can imagine, the fascination and sheer enjoyment produced by these interviews were no less than spellbinding, but the later, more reflective interpretation of their contents and the possible motives of the interviewees proved much more challenging for the purposes of a biography.

In a contemplative mode I worked regularly in Russia at the Russian National Museum of Music in Moscow and at the Rachmaninoff Museum-Estate and Research Center at Ivanovka (neighboring a village population of approximately 300), 300 miles south of Moscow in the fertile black earth region, and I stayed for various periods of time at Tambov, meeting with relevant individuals and carrying out research in the archives of the

Tambov Institute of Music Pedagogy named for Rachmaninoff. I spent many productive hours perusing manuscripts in the Eugene Ormandy archives at the Van Pelt Library of the University of Pennsylvania and in the extensive Rachmaninoff archive at the Library of Congress in Washington, D.C. Among other significant locations to which I traveled, I traced some of Rachmaninoff's movements in Italy, both with his close friend and colleague, the legendary opera singer Feodor Chaliapin, and with his family. My visits to Rome and Varazze, and archival work at Teatro alla Scala in Milan, enabled me to flesh out a viable narrative of Rachmaninoff's activities in this country so significant for classical music.

From my various interviews and archival research, a working narrative of Rachmaninoff's life experiences gradually emerged. My discussion of the women in Rachmaninoff's life is related to the subject of Rachmaninoff's aesthetics, for not only were the women he loved important to him on emotional and practical levels—they were crucial to him *artistically*; they nourished and informed his music. Their significance for him connects directly with the spiritual concept of the "eternal feminine" that originated with Johann Wolfgang von Goethe's *das ewig Weibliche*, resurfacing in an innovative form in Vladimir Soloviev's "eternal feminine" and Alexander Blok's "beautiful lady."[7]

Throughout the approximately fifteen-year period of my travels, archival work, performance of Rachmaninoff's music, and personal interviews (several with nonagenarian eyewitnesses), I worked closely, sometimes intensively in conversations lasting for hours and even days, with the most distinguished Rachmaninoff specialists in the twenty-first century. My and their inquiries, theses, hypotheses, discoveries, questions, and positions were challenged and discussed exhaustively. I firmly believe that the best and most thoughtful positions argued in this biography originated in the crucible of critical thinking in which my colleagues and I found ourselves during this rich period. And yet, there were roadblocks as well.

Two serious problems exist that affect our ability to understand Rachmaninoff more intimately. One concerns the character of the Rachmaninoff archive at the Library of Congress. This archive and the Rachmaninoff archive at the Russian National Museum of Music represent the two most comprehensive repositories of Rachmaninoff materials in the world. The Russian National Museum of Music archive contains mainly the pre-1918 materials, while the Library of Congress houses materials from the period of Rachmaninoff's exile from Russia—1918–1943. Each archive has provided the other with photocopies of major documents and musical scores, although neither archive can be considered complete. The problem with the Library of Congress materials concerns the persons who assembled and organized the archive before it was donated to the Library: Rachmaninoff's wife Natalia

Aleksandrovna Rachmaninoff and his cousin/sister-in-law Sofia Aleksandrovna Satina. The desire of the composer's wife to present her husband's life in the best possible light is understandable. However, adding to this intention is the wish of his sister-in-law, a scientist herself with excellent organizational abilities, to present Sergei Vasilievich in the least controversial light. Not only were Sofia Aleksandrovna and Sergei Vasilievich very close, but many Rachmaninoff scholars (including myself) believe that she was in love with Rachmaninoff all her life and elected not to marry as a sacrificial act in order to remain close to him and his wife (her sister) without any hindrance.

When one considers what it would imply that these two women combed through every item that was to become part of the Library of Congress archive, one may conclude that a whitewashing process could have taken place. Any references to women in Rachmaninoff's correspondence that may have cast a shadow over the image of him that his wife and her sister wished to have preserved for posterity would have been taken out. A curious example that comes to mind is the memoir of her husband that Natalia Rachmaninoff wrote: Her recollections of him begin abruptly with her marriage to him, even though she met him for the first time when she was thirteen years old and interacted with him for long periods of time and in close-knit family activities for many years before their wedding took place. One explanation of this may be that Natalia had written some comments about the period before the wedding, but that, perhaps because of their potentially questionable nature, her sister expunged them from the memoir.[8]

The second problem has to do with the absence of several bodies of Rachmaninoff's letters. The correspondence between him and his mother is missing; the letters he wrote to his teen-age love Vera Skalon were burned; and the correspondence between him and his wife is unaccounted for, as is that between him and both of his daughters. Fortunately for those interested in Rachmaninoff's early years, a segment of Vera Skalon's diary has survived (June–July 1890). It is well known that Vera Skalon was in love with Rachmaninoff in her youth, that she and Natalia Satina (Rachmaninoff) were close friends, and that Natalia dressed for her wedding day at Vera's family home in Moscow (one can imagine how painful this must have been for Vera). Subsequently, just before Vera's own wedding she burned the large packet of the correspondence between her and Sergei (approximately one hundred letters); again, one can only imagine the various emotions contained in it and the reasons why Vera wanted to make sure that no one would ever read that correspondence. However, descriptions of the intense period of Sergei Rachmaninoff and Vera Skalon's young love, the summer of 1890 at Ivanovka, survive in Vera's diary, which has been preserved.[9]

What happened to the other categories of correspondence remains a mystery. It is understandable that the heirs of Rachmaninoff considered these letters personal, but it is also true that Rachmaninoff's identity as someone world-famous had belonged to the international community for many decades and that his heirs were aware that his letters would provide priceless insights into the composer and the man. The question arises: What could the missing letters have contained that would potentially alter the world's prevailing understanding of the composer's life? The unavailability of such artifacts that could definitively shed light on many nuances of the composer's personality, emotions, and convictions hampers research and remains a great tragedy for posterity. And yet, despite the loss of such irreplaceable artifacts, the search for the authentic Rachmaninoff will continue.

Rachmaninoff is surely one of the most maligned and misunderstood major musical figures of the twentieth century, and as such he deserves a better hearing than he has received thus far. The innovativeness and exceptional beauty of his music ought to speak for themselves; and yet, these assessments, so obvious to those who know this corpus of music, have not yet found their way consistently into the major dictionaries and encyclopedias of music, especially those produced in the United States. To be sure, progress is being made in the reception history of Rachmaninoff: his music and reputation continue to be revised in an upward direction. As his work is studied more closely, both on the individual level and as a complete body, he will take his place among the great musical figures of the Western world. From the time of his graduation from the Moscow Conservatory to the present day, Rachmaninoff has retained a distinguished position in the pantheon of Russian composers. His music is much-loved and admired by Russian performers and audiences. Because he is so close to the hearts of Russians, his reception in the future will be broadened, rather than elevated further—he has already attained the highest acclaim possible in Russian musical culture.

If the reader of this book comes away from my foray into Rachmaninoff's life with an awareness of the composer's profound answerability toward art, his highly nuanced relationships with the important women in his life, his Russian Orthodox identity, and his sustained endeavors to defend Russia and her unique civilization to a sometimes-uncomprehending West, then my work will have been vindicated.

Valeria Z. Nollan
Memphis, Tennessee
July 2, 2022

NOTES

1. C.A. Satina, "Zapiska o S.V. Rakhmaninove," in *Vospominaniia o Rakhmaninove*, ed. Z.A. Apetian, 5th ed. (Moskva: Muzyka, 1988), I:115.

2. Vladimir Soloviev, "The Fate of Pushkin," in *The Heart of Reality: Essays on Beauty, Love, and Ethics by V.S. Soloviev*, trans. Vladimir Wozniuk (Notre Dame, IN: University of Notre Dame Press, 2003), 149–50 (emphasis original).

3. See Sergei Bertensson and Jay Leyda, *Sergei Rachmaninoff: A Lifetime in Music* (New York: New York UP, 1956; repr., Bloomington, IN: Indiana UP, 2001), 379.

4. The work of B. S. Nikitin distinguishes itself among existing biographies of Rachmaninoff in its psychological insights and validity. See his *Sergei Rakhmaninov. Dve zhizni* (Moscow: Klassika-XXI, 2008).

5. Bertensson and Leyda, xxxiv.

6. See Valeria Z. Nollan, s.v. "Russian Orthodoxy" and "Russian Orthodox churches," in *The Encyclopedia of Contemporary Russian Culture*, eds. Karen Evans-Romaine, Helena Goscilo, and Tatiana Smorodinskaya (London: Routledge Ltd., 2007).

7. Alexandre Rachmaninoff told me in an interview that Sergei Rachmaninoff stopped composing art songs in the West, because he was deprived of the inspiration and influence specifically of *Russian* women. Personal interview, Senar, Weggis, Switzerland, July 10, 2003.

8. I thank Alexei Alexandrovich Naumov, Senior Researcher at the Russian National Museum of Music, for pointing out this possibility to me.

9. See Nikitin, *Sergei Rakhmaninov. Dve zhizni*, 27–29.

Chapter 1

Rachmaninoff's Origins

(1873–1884)

Abraham begat Isaac, and Isaac begat Jacob.

—Matthew 1:2 (KJV)[1]

The early years of Sergei Vasilievich Rachmaninoff's life in many ways parallel the course of life of the hero of classical Greek tragedy. The hero is born into a noble family, suffers considerably due to circumstances beyond his control, and consequently endures a difficult fall from grace. Rachmaninoff's life was enigmatic and complex, and these attributes apply even to his birth. His entire existence evolved on the boundaries, between two political and musical eras, between Imperial and Soviet Russia, and finally between Europe and the United States. He survived a catastrophic childhood, life-threatening illnesses, political upheaval that threatened him and his family personally, the loss of all his financial assets, and, most deeply affecting, the loss of the entire way of life embedded in his native country and culture: his language, cultural environment, Russian Orthodox religion, and the particular way of life of Russian country estates that defined the identities of generations of aristocrats of Rachmaninoff's social rank. The courage and steely mettle of his personality can best be understood if one bears in mind that he negotiated all of these difficulties and boundary situations, in personal and practical terms, very successfully. He negotiated these crises with grace and dignity as well.

Rachmaninoff was born on March 20, 1873, according to the Julian (Old Style) Calendar that was the official calendar for both the civil and religious communities in Russia until 1917. Considerable confusion has arisen concerning his birthdate; only a knowledge of the Russian Orthodox calendar and early twentieth-century Soviet history can clear up the mistakes that appear in Western biographies of the composer. Russian biographies consistently designate Rachmaninoff's birthdate as March 20, and it is understood that this nineteenth-century date was according to the Julian Calendar, the only calendar that guided Russian life at that time. Some sources further translate the date into the Gregorian (New Style) Calendar, which would locate it on April 1—twelve days later than the Julian Calendar date, because of the Orthodox Church's practice in the *nineteenth* century of adding *twelve* days to the Old Style date. However, in the *twentieth century* the Orthodox Church (governed by the authority of the Moscow Patriarchate) added *thirteen* days to the Julian Calendar date; thus Rachmaninoff's birthday on the Gregorian Calendar in the *twentieth* century appears as April 2. Some Western biographers point out in defense of the April 2 theory that the official birthdate listed in Rachmaninoff's passport is April 2 and that this same date is carved on the tall stone Orthodox cross that marks his grave at Kensico Cemetery in Valhalla, New York. Early Soviet history can provide a fuller explanation of this complex calendar issue.

After the Bolsheviks seized power in Russia in 1917, the decree was promulgated in newspapers and other official sources of the Communist Party that all Soviet citizens were required to change the registration of their birthdates according to the Gregorian (New Style) calendar. This change from the Julian to the Gregorian calendar had been under consideration by the Russian monarchy as far back as during the reign of Tsar Nicholas I (ruled 1825–1855), but was not imposed on the country out of concern that it would bring the state into serious conflict with the Russian Orthodox Church. The issue remained a major item for discussion throughout the nineteenth century, culminating in its final expression in the law signed into effect by Vladimir Lenin on February 14, 1918 (New Style).[2] Lenin's decision was both practical and ideological: he wanted to streamline the new government's relations with the rest of the world, but perhaps more importantly he viewed this change as part of the Bolsheviks' systematic attempts to eradicate the essential features of Russian culture and Imperial Russian ways from public life.

The most reasonable explanation for the April 2 designated birth date would be Rachmaninoff's choice to accept the twentieth century's, rather than nineteenth century's, dating of his birthday by the Russian Orthodox Church—that is, thirteen days' difference between the Julian and Gregorian dates. Since the important date in his mind would remain March 20—the *actual* date of his birth—it would make little difference whether the translated date appeared as April 1 or April 2. For Russian exiles of that time the spiritual significance of their actual birthday was what mattered; as for the differences in the calculations of dates during the turn of the twentieth century, they would be only a tedious exercise at best. Thus of lesser significance than the March 20 date that Rachmaninoff would hold in his mind were the two April dates, if these held any meaning for him at all. His wife and his sister-in-law, who survived him and who planned his funeral, would have held the same views and sensibilities. During that time of violence and extreme instability in his life, the translation of his specific birth date to the New Style calendar would have been of low importance in the overall scheme of the life-altering decisions he was contemplating about his future.

Moreover, at the time of his funeral these two close relatives of his either forgot about the correct dating of his birthday in the terms of the century in which he was born or were so preoccupied with their grief and the other details surrounding the funeral that they allowed the altered date of April 2 to be entered on the permanent marker of the stone Orthodox cross at his grave. Thus, most accurately understood, Rachmaninoff was born on March 20 (Old Style) / April 1 (New Style)—if one uses the nineteenth-century guideline of calculation.

It is widely accepted that Rachmaninoff was born on the estate of Oneg, which is situated on the Vólkhov River to the north of Novgorod, Russia. However, an entry concerning the baptism of the infant Sergei was found in the register of births of the Church of Saints Cosmos and Damian of the village of Starye Degtiari at Semenovo of Staroruss ("Old Russian") District. This would point to Sergei's being born at his father's estate Semenovo, rather than at Oneg, for it would be difficult to imagine that his parents would have taken the newborn infant by horse-drawn carriage to Oneg some two hundred versts (one verst = 2/3 of a mile) away. When one factors into the picture how protective Russians are toward newborn children and new mothers, as well as the typical impassability of Russian country roads in March during unstable spring thaws, it seems highly dubious that Rachmaninoff would have been born in one place and transported to another place far away for his baptism thirteen days later on April 2 (Old Style).[3] Among those present at the baptism was Sofia Aleksandrovna Butakova (1823–1904), Sergei's maternal grandmother, who together with her husband owned the estate Oneg in Novgorod District and who would play a prominent role in his childhood. She was also Sergei's godmother, and he would remain her favorite grandchild. Sofia Aleksandrovna was a strong-willed, wealthy woman who loved her grandson/godson Sergei boundlessly and used the full force of her influence and means to help him throughout the difficult years of his childhood and adolescence. Her attentiveness to his emotional and physical needs would preserve his well-being, lift his spirits, and nourish the wellsprings of his artistic inspiration for many years.

Excerpts from the memoir of composer Nikolay Mikhailovich Strelnikov, a second cousin of Rachmaninoff (Strelnikov was the grandson of Sofia Aleksandrovna's sister Elizaveta Aleksandrovna), illuminate the personality of Rachmaninoff's grandmother Butakova and the daily routines at her estate:

Sofia Aleksandrovna observed a great deal, not forgetting anything, she knew how to help a person not with words, but with action; she liked to be a consummate organizer, the facilitator of what was good and rational. People sensed these traits, valued them, and loved her for them.

It goes without saying, that holidays in the house of S.A. Butakova were the events that regulated the entire course of its measured life. The approach of this or that holiday could be sensed by how, gradually, everything in the house—in which cleanliness and order reigned—was once again cleaned, polished, washed, laundered, and painted.

The attendance of church services, especially on major holidays, constituted an entire ritual, from which no one deviated, not in the daytime, or evening, or late at night, or early in the morning.

People knew very well that Sofia Aleksandrovna loved everything that was culturally Russian, homegrown, made solidly and skillfully. And so she was constantly presented with all sorts of folk crafts, embroideries, a variety of products. It's hard to think of anything she was not given! In these relationships of mutual gift-giving . . . was symbolically embodied that special moral atmosphere of the cult of human labor that connected people in the house of Butakova.

Sofia Aleksandrovna loved her only daughter Liubushka (as she called her) very much. Liubov Petrovna Butakova was a talented, musically gifted person.[4]

Among the many forms of influence that Rachmaninoff's maternal grandmother exerted on him was an introduction to the Russian Orthodox art of bellringing. She was especially fond of the master bellringer nicknamed "Egorka," although she would always respectfully call him by his proper name Egor. Nikolai Strelnikov recalled:

Sofia Aleksandrovna was respected as an expert in [Russian Orthodox] church singing. On this subject she was the single unquestionable authority of her kind, with whom even the entire church hierarchy of Novgorod would consult. The choir directors of Novgorod churches considered Sofia Aleksandrovna a particular unofficial inspector whose word carried a great deal of weight; they often came to her house, considering it a special honor to hear her opinion and receive her advice. Her special favorite also would come to her house—the celebrated virtuoso of church bells named . . . Egor.

. . . [Egor] was a genuine artist in the highest meaning of this term, an artist who deeply impressed me, a boy, with his ecstatic inspiration . . . Egor had his own personally conceived system of ropes and blocks by means of which he in truth virtuosically executed the most complex tones. During the act [of the bellringing] his face, usually having a gloomy expression, would be transformed in inspiration, and he not quite sang, not quite rapturously carried on some kind of dialogue with the resounding bells. In general Egor spoke about his bells as one would speak about living beings, native, beloved, and infinitely dear.

... S.V. Rachmaninoff was also well acquainted with Egor the bell-ringer. It was specifically from Sergei Vasilievich that my father later learned of the death of this marvelous, unique artist.[5]

The way of life directed and organized by Sofia Aleksandrovna at her estate reveals the qualities that were formed in her daughter and her favorite grandchild Sergei: observance of Russian Orthodox religious practices, adherence to a loving yet strict routine, orderliness, and a work ethic based on moral virtues similar to those ensconced in the proverbial Golden Rule.

After Liubov Butakova was married to Vasily Arkadievich Rachmaninoff, and after their son Sergei was born, Sofia Aleksandrovna resolved to prevent her son-in-law from having a detrimental influence on her grandson Seryozha. The young Seryozha became the center of her life and deeply loving heart. "Sofia Aleksandrovna did everything she could to educate him completely free from the impact of V.A. Rachmaninoff's actions."[6] It is entirely plausible that many of Rachmaninoff's personality traits and habits were learned from the way of life that his grandmother led: "an independence of thought, a preference for a measured and orderly routine, a disciplined work ethic, a severe and reserved external manner of behavior, kindness, generosity . . . [and] a boundless love for Russia and everything native to Russia . . ."[7]

A photograph of Sofia Aleksandrovna Butakova that has been preserved shows her seated in an ornate chair with an armrest padded in silk; she is in an elegant noblewoman's dress with a matching elevated hat decorated with ribbons. She possessed fine, regular features and an expression of authority, determination, and intelligence; clearly, this woman was nobody's fool and not to be trifled with. Mme. Butakova had the means to protect what was most precious to her, and, after he was born, the most cherished person to her was her grandson Sergei.

Rachmaninoff lived at the estate of Semenovo until he was almost four. As noted above, the estate belonged to his father Vasily Arkadievich Rachmaninoff (1841–1916). The composer's mother Liubov Petrovna Rachmaninoff, née Butakova (1849–1929), brought four additional estates to her marriage to Vasily Arkadievich as part of her dowry. Her father, General P. I. Butakov, succeeded in keeping his spendthrift son-in-law in check while he was alive, but when he died on January 21, 1877, there was no one left to rein in the ruinous habits of the son-in-law. Semenovo was mortgaged on July 1, 1878, because its owners had accumulated a debt on it of over 4,452 rubles.

Liubov Petrovna's parents were opposed to her marriage to Vasily Arkadievich, but eventually they relented in spite of their better judgment, because, as any good parents, they wanted to see their daughter happily married and they saw that she was deeply in love with him. It is even possible that she was pregnant at the time of their wedding, for the celebration

Figure 1.1   Sofia Aleksandrovna Butakova. Public domain.

was arranged by her parents rather quickly and immediately afterward the newlyweds were taken by Liubov's mother to the countryside to one of the estates owned by Liubov. The Butakovs moved into the estate along with their daughter and son-in-law; their entrance to the main house was from the entryway opposite to that used by Vasily and Liubov. Vasily had counted on a carefree time of social activities in St. Petersburg after being married to a wealthy general's daughter, but instead, he found himself in the depths of the Russian wilderness on an estate with his protective in-laws. He increasingly invented pretexts to go away either to St. Petersburg, Moscow, or Tambov, carousing and accumulating large debts. His irresponsible behavior understandably led to quarrels between his wife Liubov, who continued to love him, and her irate parents.[8] One by one, Vasily would gamble away his wife's estates.

Two years later the newspaper *Novgorodskie gubernskie vedomosti* printed (on May 3, 1880) that the estate of Semenovo, along with its surrounding lands and outbuildings, was scheduled for sale. The property had been appraised at 8,000 rubles. The main house (*barskii dom*) has been described as an extensive one-story wooden structure that was typical for provincial Russian country architecture. The front door was decorated with wooden panels, while in its upper part were glass window panes. Carved wooden moldings decorated the sides of the house's windows; this detail was also characteristic of the architecture of that region, being similar to Scandinavian wooden ornamentation.[9]

Early in 1877 the Rachmaninoffs had moved to the village of Oneg, the only remaining estate of the original four of Rachmaninoff's mother's dowry that had not been squandered by his father.[10] At this time the family consisted of six persons: both parents and their children Elena (b. 1868), Sofia (b. 1870), Vladimir (b. 1871), and Sergei (b. 1873). Aside from the financial problems associated with Semenovo, the reasons for the family's move to Oneg are not clear. One possibility involved the estate's location, which was in Novgorod District and thus closer to the city of Novgorod than Semenovo had been. Oneg was situated about thirty versts from Novgorod, on the left bank of the Volkhov River, which flowed through the city. "The estate consisted of forests, arable land, water-meadows, meadowlands for plowing, pastures, flower gardens, vegetable gardens, and a small park. The old landed estate stood on a high foundation: it had ten rooms and an outside veranda; local peasants called it 'the house with wings,' because of the edges of its roof that extended out quite far from the walls of the house."[11]

In his memoirs Rachmaninoff wrote: "I remember myself from the age of four, and it's strange that all of my childhood recollections, good and bad, sad and happy, in one way or another are without fail connected with music. The first punishments and the first rewards that gladdened my young soul unfailingly possessed a direct relationship with music."[12]

In order for us to understand the particular features making up Sergei Rachmaninoff's personality, we should consider the background and personality traits of his parents. Rachmaninoff's father, Vasily Arkadievich, led the predictable life of a nobleman: he volunteered to join the army in fighting in the Caucasus against Shamil and was subsequently sent to Warsaw for several years in a Guards regiment. When he returned to Russia he married Liubov Petrovna, who came from a wealthy family.[13] Both of Rachmaninoff's parents were talented musicians, and hence they possessed the training and sensibilities to notice his gift for music when he was quite young. His father began tutoring him first, but lacked the discipline and steadfastness to maintain a regular schedule of study with the young Sergei. Consequently Sergei's mother took his musical education into her own hands and began giving him music lessons. Before she married Vasily Arkadievich she had wanted to become a pianist and had received a first-rate musical education. She had studied with the great Anton Rubinstein, which fact alone underscores her musical talent—for such a luminary in the music world would not have taught a mediocre student. She did not finish her studies at the St. Petersburg Conservatory, however. Moreover, Liubov Petrovna possessed an excellent singing voice, which also undoubtedly left an impression on the young Rachmaninoff. In addition to her musical talent, she had been well educated by her parents: she knew several foreign languages and her wide-ranging reading had made her into something of an intellectual among her circle of friends. She was also deeply religious, providing a firm and genuine religious foundation in Russian Orthodoxy for her children.[14]

Liubov Petrovna's extensive family responsibilities and worries soon prompted her to invite her friend Anna Dmitrievna Ornatskaia, a graduate of the St. Petersburg Conservatory, to tutor her son in music. Anna Dmitrievna had also studied with Rubinstein, and she had remained in contact with Rachmaninoff's mother. Both Liubov Petrovna and Anna Dmitrievna noticed in the young Rachmaninoff formidable gifts in music: perfect pitch, a solid memory, large, fine hands with long fingers, and a creative, sensitive mind.

A letter sent to Rachmaninoff's Swiss villa in 1934 by the former governess of the Rachmaninoff children, Madame Defert, describes the incident that prompted the decision to procure a music tutor (Anna Ornatskaia) for the young Sergei. His governess wrote:

> Allow me to prove to you that I was an eyewitness to the discovery of your musical gift. . . . You remember that your mother liked to accompany me on the piano when I sang, but do you remember that day when a stroll had been arranged for your family's guests, but you remained at home under the pretext of not feeling well? I, too, had to remain at home in order to look after you. After a few minutes you came to me and with a sly expression asked for permission to play the wonderful grand piano that you were not allowed to touch without the permission of the adults. When you finally succeeded in convincing me, you surprised me when you proposed that I sing a song that your mother liked to listen to, and you would accompany me. . . . And how amazed I was when I heard the chords that your small hands were able to grasp! . . . in the evening I related all this to your mother. The next morning they told your grandfather, who came to see us immediately [from Tambov] and demanded that your father go to St. Petersburg to invite a good piano teacher from the conservatory to tutor you.[15]

A photo (c. 1882) of Ornatskaia with Rachmaninoff's mother shows the former to be petite, with delicate features and patient, intelligent eyes. A stillness and self-control can also be observed in her extremely pleasant face. Although little information exists concerning Anna Dmitrievna's approach as a teacher of the small child Sergei, the basic characteristics of Russian educational philosophy are well-known in international circles of the arts. This philosophy combines the qualities of strictness with genuine love for each student and his / her well-being, paying particular attention to the student's individual merits. Rachmaninoff himself in an interview about musical training in America ascribes considerable importance to the early educational experiences of a child, concluding that poor instruction at an early age could seriously undermine further education in the given subject:

It is often said that an indifferent teacher will do to start with. Never was there a greater mistake. The child who shows signs of musical aptitude should be given the best teacher it is possible to secure. Do not place a child of even five years old under a poor teacher. Else what is poorly done will have to be done all over again, a difficult matter, for early impressions are the most lasting, as we all know.

It is to be hoped the day will come when there will be no poor teachers, for all will be trained for the great work of teaching and will realize their high calling and wonderful opportunities.[16]

The family's fortunes went from bad to worse, until Oneg as well had to be sold in 1879, only two years after the Rachmaninoffs had moved there. The circumstances surrounding the sale of the estate are not entirely clear, but the available evidence and anecdotes are consistent with each other, pointing to a decline in the family's finances due to the spending habits of Rachmaninoff's father Vasily Arkadievich. As already mentioned, this state of affairs produced constant quarrels and extreme instability in the relationship between Sergei's parents. Paulina Yanovna Avik, the young housemaid for Rachmaninoff's parents while they lived at Oneg, often related the following to her son (whose words follow):

> the young nobleman Sergei Vasilievich as a very young boy would sit at the piano for hours; he was distracted away from music [only] when he was required to do this by his parents. My mother also told me that the [Rachmaninoff] family was large, that its members didn't get along well with each other, and that their daily lives were unstable.[17]

Rachmaninoff himself recalled:

> My parents often quarreled. We, the children, loved our father more. This was probably unfair with respect to our mother, but insofar as father possessed a kind and tender disposition, an amazing kindheartedness, and thoroughly spoiled us, it is not surprising that our hearts were irrepressibly drawn to him. Mother, on the other hand, was characterized by an extreme strictness. For the majority of the time father was absent, and all of the household responsibilities rested on mother's shoulders.[18]

In the face of such an emotionally turbulent childhood, Rachmaninoff's attitudes toward each of his parents were completely understandable. As a young child and adolescent, Rachmaninoff responded to the immediate warmth and gaiety of his father, while shrinking from the discipline and seriousness of purpose that his mother tried to instill into her children's lives. In the absence of any other positive and nurturing structures for her family, Liubov Petrovna desperately sought to give her children a comforting

Figure 1.2   Vasily Arkadievich **Rachmaninoff.** Public domain.

routine and some beneficial habits in preparation for their adulthood. As Rachmaninoff grew older and matured in his perspectives, however, he gained a genuine appreciation and gratitude for what his mother had given him: an understanding of the benefits of discipline and hard work, and a grasp of the accomplishments and inner stability that a regular routine could provide. In this light his assessment as an adult of his parents differed markedly from the ways in which he had viewed their parenting while he was still a child. He remained an attentive and loving son to his parents for as long as they lived.

Photographs of Rachmaninoff's parents reveal two highly sensitive, dignified, and very good-looking individuals. One of the few extant photographs of his father shows Vasily Arkadievich standing in formal dress looking directly at the camera. One can discern in his fine features a similarity to those of his son Sergei: lively, yet calm eyes, a prominent straight nose, and hair that recalls Sergei's before he decided to wear it close-cropped. Sporting a stylish pince-nez, Vasily Arkadievich appears dignified and resolute in his character.

The photographs of Liubov Petrovna all reveal a beautiful, perhaps introverted woman with expressive and sensitive eyes; images of her are permeated with a deep sadness. Her face expresses kindness, devotion, and, at the risk of appealing to stereotypes of Russian women, the quality of longsuffering.

Figure 1.3 Liubov Petrovna (Butakova) Rachmaninoff. Public domain.

On April 14, 1879, at 10 o'clock in the morning, a humiliating public auction of the furniture and other moveable property took place located at Oneg. One can imagine the scene: the Rachmaninoff children were bewildered at the spectacle of strangers wandering among their possessions, while each of their parents experienced slightly differing emotions. Liubov Petrovna possessed a clear understanding of the tragedy that had befallen the family, while her husband Vasily Arkadievich, even at such a distressing time, refused to allow the events around him to unduly dampen his good nature. Bailiffs, appraisers, and creditors stayed at the estate while these events were taking place. Rachmaninoff's maternal grandmother Sofia Aleksandrovna Butakova, not wanting her grandchildren to be traumatized by the public auction, arranged for a trusted servant to take them away by horse-drawn carriage to Borisovo, her own estate in Novgorod, before they could witness that Oneg had fallen into the hands of new owners. The estate itself was scheduled for sale the following year, on May 31, 1880. That same year of 1880 the Rachmaninoff's sixth child, Arkady, was born; the fifth, a daughter named Varvara, had died in infancy at the age of a year and a half.[19]

Toward the end of 1880, when Sergei was only seven-and-one-half years old, the Rachmaninoff family was compelled by its catastrophic financial position to move to St. Petersburg. The years of enduring not only her husband's extravagant wastefulness but his philandering as well took their toll on Liubov Petrovna. Her own dream of becoming a pianist had been ruined, her husband had gambled away the four estates of her dowry, and any chance at a happy marriage with him had withered away. It would be difficult to imagine a more complete downfall for her personally as well as for her family. Moreover, by the end of 1880 she had given birth to six children and had endured the death of one of them, Varvara, in her infancy in 1880 of diphtheria.[20] Liubov Petrovna frantically tried to secure enough funds to care for the remaining five children: Elena (b. 1868), Sofia (b. 1882), Vladimir (b. 1871), Sergei (b. 1873), and Arkady (b. 1880).

In 1882, the year after the Rachmaninoffs' chaotic move to St. Petersburg, the city experienced a diphtheria epidemic that lasted until the spring of 1883. Tragically, a second daughter Sofia died of the disease in 1882. The two oldest boys, Vladimir and Sergei, also fell ill with the disease, but they recovered. After the epidemic had passed and all the surviving children were healthy, their father's visits stopped and he drifted out of the picture of their family life. Sergei missed his father very much; his feeling of loneliness increased when his brother Vladimir had moved to the Cadet Corps and was able to spend only Sundays at home with his family. His sister Elena was too preoccupied with helping their mother with housekeeping and errands to spend much time with her younger brother. The result for Sergei was to bide his time in an environment of disharmony, chaos, and uncertainty. He would wait impatiently each winter for the expected visit of his grandmother Butakova, who would lavish all her love and attention on him and enjoy visiting with him the various cathedrals and churches of St. Petersburg for the services. Sergei made it a habit to play for her on the small family piano, after returning home from church, some of the chants they had heard—thus extending the pleasure they shared of the Orthodox piety conveyed through the music. His grandmother Butakova would give him some money when he was finished playing, thus perhaps without realizing it reinforcing the notion that one could with real joy create and perform music and be paid for doing it.[21] The decline in the family's fortune culminated in new surroundings that were a far cry from the lyrical and refined life they had led in the countryside near Novgorod on a comfortable country estate. The Rachmaninoffs had settled in a rented apartment near the Haymarket District (*Sennaia ploshchad*) in St. Petersburg, the low-income, albeit colorful part of the city immortalized in Dostoevsky's *Crime and Punishment*.[22] The apartment building is located in the heart of the city, on the Fontanka River 133/9.

The Rachmaninoffs lived close enough to the Chevakinsky architectural masterpiece, the St. Nicholas Maritime Cathedral, to be able to attend services there and find comfort in their faith. There were many emotional and financial trials for which they would seek that spiritual comfort. Their apartment consisted of three rooms, not enough to hold the entire family. One child had to be sent away temporarily to live somewhere else, and the lot fell to Sergei. He was dispatched to live with relatives he had never met, the family of his aunt Maria Arkadievna Trubnikova (his father's married sister) in the Kronstadt district of the city. Sergei's *temporary* living situation in this family that, while not his own, turned out to be stable and cheerful enough, lasted from the end of 1880 until the end of the academic year of 1884–1885. After the Rachmaninoffs' oldest daughter Elena was settled at a boarding school nearby and the oldest son Vladimir had entered a military school, Sergei was able to return to live with his family.

It is worthwhile to pause and consider the catastrophic political events taking place in Russia during these years, which formed the backdrop to the crises the Rachmaninoff family was experiencing between the years 1879–1882. On March 13, 1881, Tsar Aleksandr II was assassinated in St. Petersburg by conspirators of the anarchist *Narodnaia volia* (People's Will) Party.[23] The tsar's rule was marked by liberalism and sweeping reforms in all areas of the administration. He sought peace in the Russian empire, and his most important diplomatic achievements include the emancipation of the serfs in 1861 and the sale of Alaska to the United States in 1867. His son Aleksandr III's accession to the throne ushered in a period of drastic reactions and repression, which plunged the country from the liberalization of Aleksandr II into increased censorship and measures to counter his father's reforms. There are no accounts by members of Rachmaninoff's family of the effects these dramatic events exerted on their personal fortunes, but one can only imagine that after the public auction of Oneg, the death of Rachmaninoff's sister Varvara in 1880, the birth by Liubov Petrovna of her and her husband Vasily's sixth child that same year, and the financial troubles in their family that led to the family's move to an apartment in a low-rent district in St. Petersburg—after all of these major events, to add to the instability the Rachmaninoffs were experiencing the national crisis of an assassination and change from liberal to reactionary rule would have only intensified the family's stress at an already vulnerable time. On his numerous forays into various parts of St. Petersburg the young Sergei would have seen the construction site of the Cathedral of the Savior on the Blood many times and surely would have reflected with confusion and fear on the violent challenge to the way of life into which he had been born.

The quarrels between Rachmaninoff's parents increased in frequency, having to do in large part with the future of their children. Vasily Arkadievich had served in the army, and for this reason he wanted both of his sons to follow in his footsteps. Since Liubov Petrovna's father had held the rank of general, Rachmaninoff's older brother Vladimir was expected to enter the exclusive Corps des Pages military school in St. Petersburg. As it turned out, Vladimir was not admitted to the Corps because of the family's altered social position. Concerning Sergei, however, Liubov Petrovna insisted that he continue to be trained by Anna Ornatskaia for admission to the St. Petersburg Conservatory, which took place successfully on September 16, 1882, when Sergei was nine years old, the minimal age required for admission. The difficulties he encountered during the three years he spent at the conservatory (1882–1885) have not been thoroughly examined. During the process of his admission to it, not a single reputable music pedagogue heard him play, and the kindhearted administrator and cellist J. Conius. Davydov —who instituted many positive changes at the conservatory, but who sometimes tolerated lower standards—was out of town at the time and subsequently took a full year's leave of absence in 1882–1883, Rachmaninoff's first year there.

What was Rachmaninoff's level of readiness for entry to the St. Petersburg Conservatory at the age of nine? He was prepared rather well for this step in his education. Both of his parents were musically talented, and his grandfather Arkady Vasilievich was a famous virtuoso pianist who had studied with John Field. The high-level composition and performance of music was all around him, and he clearly inherited musical abilities of his own:

> Music teachers and other educators flocked to his parents' estate. Sergei spoke French well, and knew German and English slightly. His mother, and later Anna Ornatskaia, supervised his musical education, and already at an early age the successes of the young musician were noticed by his famous grandfather.
>
> The accounts of Sergei's childhood improvisations after attending church services in Novgorod and St. Petersburg represent no less than evidence of his first piano compositions. Moreover, he was considerably influenced by Russian folk songs.[24]

Anna Ornatskaia advocated for Sergei's musical training after he was admitted with a scholarship to the St. Petersburg Conservatory by requesting of her former professor Gustav Cross (who had studied with Adolf von Henselt and had become a famous pianist) that he accepted Sergei into his class. However, Cross himself did not teach students as young as Sergei, so the latter's training was transferred to his former student, Professor Vladimir Vasilievich Demiansky (1846–1915)—who was usually given the weaker students aspiring to make their way at the conservatory. If Rachmaninoff had initially studied with Cross, his fate might have taken a different course. Surely Cross would have paid attention to the talents of a nine-year-old boy who could sight read well, was already improvising and composing music, could transcribe a melody and accompaniment by ear, and who possessed absolute pitch. It was at this point that Rachmaninoff's musical education started to be derailed.[25] Demiansky, though a serious pedagogue who was dedicated to his students and hardworking, was not drawn to performing or composing. This combination of qualities in his first professor at the conservatory, however admirable, was not brilliant enough to fire the young Rachmaninoff's imagination at a troubled time in his life.

At the conservatory Sergei's studies with Professor Demiansky included working on the basic techniques of scales, arpeggios, octaves, and development of flexibility and speed gained from the fingers and wrist. Demiansky was kindhearted, adapted his methods to suit the individual student, and in general was loved by his students. The recollections about Demiansky by one of his former students S. M. Maikapar, who auditioned at the conservatory and was accepted in 1885 (three years after Rachmaninoff began his study there), provide an authentic glimpse into their teacher's character:

> As an instructor Demiansky was distinguished first and foremost by his extraordinary conscientiousness in his work with his pupils, his enormous reserves of patience, unusual calmness, and stamina. He never became upset, did not raise his voice, and behaved in a simple, natural, and well-wishing manner. He possessed extensive knowledge and, by that time, many years of pedagogical experience.[26]

Because of Sergei's complicated circumstances at home, which involved as destabilizing a situation as there not being enough room in the family's apartment in St. Petersburg for him, it is not hard to understand why he as a displaced child chose fun and games over the rigors of music study. Sergei avoided his school work as much as he could, preferring to ride the streetcars in the city and wander the streets seeking diversions from his life at the Trubnikovs or at home. He managed to stay in the conservatory for three academic years: fall of 1882 until spring of 1885. During all three of those summers his grandmother Butakova whisked him away to the estate in Novgorod that she had bought just for him. She provided for him boundless love, attention, and the freedom to enjoy the peaceful Novgorod countryside in the summers; she also helped him financially during this period, and, indeed, for as long as she lived. Sergei's "creativity" of this bewildering period extended to falsifying the grades he received at the conservatory before bringing his report book home to his mother. She, for her part, was so preoccupied with her own struggles to care for her children and manage the family's meager finances, that she did not notice.

A fuller understanding of Rachmaninoff's childhood must include some details of his genealogy, his family's high social rank among the Russian nobility, and the family background of his parents. It also must engage the concept of the "clan" (*rod*), for the large extended families of nineteenth-century Russia maintained networks that not only ensured the survival and success of their children but also preserved their status and close connections with the tsar and influential members of the nobility. In these historical, social, and conceptual contexts it is not difficult to understand that Rachmaninoff, with his family's deep roots in the ancient Russian past and genealogical links with such dazzling cultural figures as Aleksandr Pushkin (1799–1837), had a sense of his own nobility and high calling, his "clan's" important place in history, and his artistic sensibilities that were transmitted to him through generations of his musically talented ancestors. In Imperial Russia the cultural and social politics of the clan interacted with identity politics grounded in ethnicity, religion, and class. It is interesting and noteworthy that in Russian society clan and social status determined an individual's destiny, rather than wealth per se. In the way of life on the Russian country estates that formed an archipelago across the plains and steppes, a person could stay at a relative's or friend's estate for many months if that person's rank and social class were acceptable to the hosts. Even if the individual's financial means were modest, this did not matter; what mattered was one's lineage, one's clan, and the connections one had with the tsar and other members of the same privileged class. The family name and its place in the Russian *Register of Nobility* ensured complete legitimacy and acceptance in influential social circles.[27] Each country estate held a special place for its owners: Russians would give their estates names deriving from the first or last names of family members, or would assign an estate a name linked with Russian Orthodox religiosity. One example is the estate of Znamenskoe, whose name comes from the word *znamenie* (sign)—"Mother of God of the Sign." This estate is historically linked with the Rachmaninoffs, which is elaborated below.

The identity and sensibilities of the Russian nobility are inexorably bound up with the way of life particular to Russian country estates. These self-contained enclaves are unique among the landed establishments of the world: they are unlike villas, haciendas, ranches, farms, mansions, or other extended residences of that ilk. Russian country estates remained for over two centuries the residences of landed nobility and their serfs, as well as cultural centers, repositories, foci for the exchange of ideas, and testing grounds for anything new, whether Russian or foreign:

> . . . the art, music, and ideas the cultural world of the estate engendered both set the tone of Russian high culture and transformed it throughout the imperial period . . . A major reason for the resonance of estate culture was that on the estate landowners could replicate, transform, or reject the ruling hierarchical structures of imperial Russia—the autocracy, the bureaucracy, and the family—in any way they found psychologically satisfying . . . [Because of the absolute power of the tsar] in the absence of access to real political power, the landed nobility clung to this vision of estate life as a compensatory way of defining its position.[28]

It is not an exaggeration to state that at least 90 percent of Russian traditional, high culture—the country's literature, music, art, philosophy, etc.—was a product of the life, culture, and resources of the country estates of the nobility.

A specific description of how members of the landed nobility spent their time can be found in a biography of Rachmaninoff's cousin and well-known pianist Aleksandr Siloti [Ziloti]:

> A typical family event occurred in November 1903 at the home of the Pribytkovs, relatives to the Siloti and Rachmaninoff clans. . . . the two were visiting on the same occasion, Siloti having arrived late. When he entered the house, a reading of Fabre's play *Eternal Love* was already underway. At its conclusion, Siloti went to the piano room and began to perform his own arrangement of themes from *Fledermaus*. The second piano in the room was soon taken by Rachmaninoff. "A game of 'catch' began, . . . As though by some magic, the waltz transformed itself into a mazurka, a march, a polka, a fugue, and even a chorale. Leaping from tempo to tempo, from key to key, not once did they get under each other's feet nor lose each other. The improvisation ended to the sounds of general laughter." Later in the evening actress Vera Kommissarzhevskaia [a brilliant actress of that era] gave an impromptu reading of Arensky's "melodeclamation" of poems by Turgenev that she had performed in the Siloti concert earlier that week. This time, Siloti accompanied her on the piano, sight-reading from the manuscript of the full score.
>
> The cousins also enjoyed playing in the children's room at Siloti's home in St. Petersburg. Siloti had bought a magnificent set of toy trains complete with belching locomotives, handsome passenger cars, overpasses, buildings, and scenery. Whenever Rachmaninoff visited, the children fled the train set. Visitors reported seeing Siloti and Rachmaninoff giggling like children themselves as they sent the trains jolting along the tracks.[29]

The complete genealogy of the Rachmaninoff family is recorded in Part Six of the official register of families of the nobility (ancient clans).[30] As all aristocrats in Russia, Rachmaninoff was well acquainted with this register and familiar with his lineage. It is impossible to understand his character without taking into account the clearly delineated class system in Russia and how it shaped the perspectives of the individual.

Rachmaninoff understood well the significance of his noble heritage: in pre-revolutionary Russia he made sure that his family's aristocratic background was properly recorded in various cities, in order to guarantee the privileges to which they were entitled by rank. Not to take this step would have excluded Rachmaninoff and his family from the rights and privileges (some of them crucial for his family's well-being and future success) afforded the nobility at that time. As an adult capable of earning his own living—he had graduated from the Moscow Conservatory and had attained the designation of "Free Artist"[31]—Sergei was officially registered as a member of the Rachmaninoff clan at the age of twenty-two:

> Certificate
>
> By the order of His Imperial Majesty this Certificate of the Tambov Meeting of Deputies of the Nobility, on the authority of p. 276, vol. IX of the Code of Laws of 1876 is presented to the son of Titular Councillor Vasily Arkadievich Rachmaninoff, Sergei, who was born in 1873, in affirmation of the fact that he, Sergei Rachmaninoff, by the decree of this Meeting of 5 June 1895, is entered into the family of Rachmaninoff of Part VI of the register of families of the nobility, certified by the decree of the Governing Senate of the Department of Heraldry on 26 June 1858, № 4360.[32]

Rachmaninoff carried within himself, side by side, both a deep aristocratic sensibility and a democratic worldview. After the tragic events of so-called Bloody Sunday (January 9, 1905, Old Style), during which a peaceful demonstration in St. Petersburg for workers' and various political rights turned violent when some of the protesters who broke through the line of the Imperial Guard were fired upon and killed, Rachmaninoff signed a letter of protest along with many other prominent musicians. The names included major figures in the Russian cultural world: S. Taneev, A. Grechaninov, A. Goldenweiser, F. Chaliapin, A. Kastalskii, Yu. Konius, and K. Igumnov, among others. Their main concern had to do with freedom of expression, especially in, but not limited to, the arts: The letter's core point was articulated as follows: "Freedom of art should not be bounded by anything else in the world, except the inner self-determination of the artist and the basic requirements of social behavior—if art genuinely wants to attain true greatness, true holiness, and be genuinely capable of responding to the most profound stirrings of the human spirit."[33] It was published in the newspaper *Nashi dni* [Our Days] on February 3, 1905; conversations about its contents, however, were circulating among those in Rachmaninoff's circle for several weeks before its appearance.[34] His support for what amounted to more democratic reforms represents a principled and courageous act, only one of many he would carry out throughout his life.

Because Rachmaninoff's professional activities were focused on music, he preferred to keep his political views to himself; hence it is not clear whether he was a monarchist or not. It is worth noting, though, that Rachmaninoff came of age at a time when a more autocratic Russian monarchy, as other European monarchies, was evolving into a constitutional monarchy. Since Muscovite times, the Russian monarchy was benefited by the counsel of advisors and representatives from all strata of society, and this practice contained the seeds of a more democratic form of government as well as the growing presence of a civil society.³⁵ Whatever Rachmaninoff's political leanings happened to be at a given time, he consistently stood on the side of those who were without power and advocated for a freer, rather than more restrictive way of governing.

Rachmaninoff was fair-minded and viewed individuals for their character and accomplishments, rather than because of their social standing—numerous anecdotes and descriptions of his activities in this regard exist to support this claim. However, because of the era in which he was born and raised, he was socialized to take into account the rank of those with whom he came into contact and its relationship to his own family's position. He was both a person of his times and ahead of his times in many ways. He seemed the embodiment of the most positive and progressive aspects of the Russian nobility, which proved especially useful in promoting and preserving culture throughout the territory of Russia. From the early eighteenth century, when under Tsar Peter I (1682–1725) the nobility had to pass a literacy test in order to retain its lands and privileges, to later in that century, when Catherine II (1762–1796) broadened the identity of the nobility to include, in addition to the customary service and loyalty to the Russian tsar or tsaritsa, the promoting of culture throughout the territory of Russia, the nobility's function evolved and expanded until the nineteenth century, when its members began to create literary and artistic works that reflected their country's history, society, and culture.³⁶

Rachmaninoff hailed from the highest ranks of the Moldavian and Russian aristocracy, his familial lineage dating all the way back to Stefan IV (the Great), Ruler (Gospodar') of Moldavia from 1458 to 1504. The ancestral line of nobility of Stefan IV can be traced back to the Moldavian kings (of the family of Dragosh) who ruled that country from 1350 until 1552. Until 1751 the coat-of-arms of the Rachmaninoff clan depicted the head of a bull—this was the official coat-of-arms of the Moldavian State. On November 25, 1751, Russian empress Elizabeth Petrovna established a new coat-of-arms for the Rachmaninoffs, which bore the inscription "For [their] loyalty and zeal." Empress Elizabeth, the youngest daughter of Peter I (the Great) and Ekaterina Skavronskaia, had a specific reason for her gratitude to the Rachmaninoff clan: During the political events of November 24, 1741 that restored Elizabeth (representing the dynastic line of Peter the Great) to the throne, two members of the Rachmaninoff family participated—Gerasim Ievlievich Rachmaninoff and his brother Fyodor Ievlievich Rachmaninoff. The Empress's gratitude was by no means a formality or empty gesture.³⁷ Empress Elizabeth Petrovna gave Gerasim Ievlievich permission to visit his estate in Tambov region, and also to inspect the estate of one of the Empress's favorite courtiers Ustinia Nikitichna Gorelkina that was named Znamenskoe. Upon his return to court, Gerasim Ievlievich purchased Znamenskoe from Ustinia

Nikitichna in 1761. With this acquisition of Znamenskoe, the estate became one of the gathering places of the large Rachmaninoff clan.[38]

Stefan IV, King of Moldavia, by all accounts, was smart, energetic, and possessed tremendous willpower: after years of the country's instability, he succeeded in restoring independence to Moldavia. He also consolidated and expanded the territory of Moldavia. In 1483 Stefan's daughter Elena was married to Ivan Mladoi, the eldest son of Russian Grand Prince Ivan III, thus securing a connection between the two royal dynasties. The family name originated as "Rachmanin" (belonging to Rachman) and evolved to stabilize finally as "Rachmaninoff" (the "–off" at the end further underscores "belonging to").[39] It carried different meanings according to the particular region in which the word was encountered: in the Kostroma and Viatsk regions it meant "cheerful," "talkative," and "sprightly"; in the environs of Moscow and Tver it was associated with the qualities of hospitality, generosity, and extravagance (or even wastefulness); and in the Nizhegorod and Tambov districts the word had the connotation of "lethargic" and "boring."[40] Many of these qualities in an uncanny way would characterize the men of the Rachmaninoff family (less information was recorded about the specific qualities of the Rachmaninoff women).

Each generation of Rachmaninoffs solidified the clan's connection to the ruling aristocracy; moreover, the clan's particular status within the substrata of nobility established it as one that was of "tsar" quality, one that could be tapped to produce candidates for the throne. Thus Sergei Vasilievich Rachmaninoff inherited the socio-political status of the highest ranks of the Russian nobility. He would have had the right to be called "Prince Sergei," but he chose not to use the title; during his life he never attached any particular value to titles.

In addition to inheriting the social position of his ancestors, Rachmaninoff acquired a deep love for music from them. Scholarly writing about him usually foregrounds the musical abilities he inherited from the line of his *male* ancestors, but his musical heritage from his female ancestors is at least as impressive. His mother's musical training and influence on Sergei's childhood impressions has already been noted; anecdotes establish that Sergei was drawn to music and manifested a profound love for it from at least the age of four. That love can be traced back at least three generations, to his great-grandparents Aleksandr Gerasimovich Rachmaninoff and his wife Maria Arkadievna Rachmaninoff (née Bakhmetieva).

By all accounts Aleksandr Gerasimovich was a fine musician whose instrument was the violin. At the family estate of Znamenskoe he organized a choir and orchestra, in which he and his wife participated. Unfortunately, he died before he reached the age of thirty, because of a selfless act of saving a man on the steppes of the Tambov region. He married Maria

Arkadievna Bakhmetieva, who was devoted to instrumental and vocal music, and whose entire family was well known for its musical abilities. Educated in St. Petersburg, Maria Arkadievna was a cultured woman who studied piano with the best teachers available at that time. Sofia Aleksandrovna Satina notes, "One can scarcely doubt that the musical talent that manifested itself so vividly in [Maria Arkadievna's] children, grandchildren, and great-grandchildren was inherited from her."[41] Satina offers a glimpse into Maria Arkadievna's identity through the account of one of the latter's granddaughters, V. A. Satina:

> I remember my grandmother Maria Arkadievna well. She lived at Znamenskoe in the wing quarters and died when I was about seventeen or eighteen years old. She was wonderfully beautiful, and was always elegantly—and, most importantly—neatly dressed. She was extremely strict with us. We were very afraid of her. I often heard her playing the piano. She always sat at the bench unusually straight and played very well. My sister and I in turn would have to go to her and provide her with some amusement, but heaven help us if we leaned against the back of her stool or sat in a hunched-over position. This was considered disrespectful to the elderly. Our heads were filled with many of her observations, and she spoke with us only in French. She died at the age of seventy-six. . . . She was very proud, and many men were in love with her.[42]

Because her husband Aleksandr Gerasimovich died so young, Maria Arkadievna married a second time. Her children from both marriages were very talented musically and passed along to their own children and grandchildren this remarkable legacy of love for music and genuine musicianship (perfect pitch, marvelous singing voices, and a predilection for music) that both she and Aleksandr Gerasimovich possessed.[43] Among their three children was Arkady Aleksandrovich, Sergei Rachmaninoff's grandfather.

Arkady Aleksandrovich was the godson of Tsar Aleksandr I. He married Varvara Vasilievna Pavlova in Orlov District and settled at Znamenskoe, which he had inherited from his father. After he had completed several assignments of military duty, he retired and returned to Znamenskoe in order to attend to the upbringing and education of his eight children. Among them were Vasily Arkadievich, Rachmaninoff's father, and Yulia Arkadievna, who inherited Znamenskoe in 1881 when her father died. She would become the mother of Aleksandr Ilyich Ziloti (1863–1945), Rachmaninoff's famous cousin. Vasily Arkadievich was passed over in the consideration of who would inherit Znamenskoe, because by 1881 he had already squandered the entire dowry of his wife, Rachmaninoff's mother.

During the late nineteenth and early twentieth centuries Znamenskoe emerged as a haven for many prominent cultural figures. The estate was typical for its times:

> . . . it stood on the high bank of the Matyra River (a tributary of Voronezh). Its wide steps of white stone descended from a terrace to a mountain; a short distance away, at the mountain, was a path, while halfway up the mountain one encountered a patio with a gazebo. Near the water stood many acacias and lilac bushes . . . From the terrace there led a lane of lilacs that was so overgrown that one walked along it as through a corridor: not a single ray of light could be seen from the side or above. . . . In the daytime the lives of the inhabitants were spent on that side of the house where an enormous rose garden surrounded by peonies was located . . . Drivers would stylishly come up the carriage drive, rein in their lathered horses at the appropriate place, and then, having discharged their passengers . . . would slowly drive by the far side of the rose garden to the stable.[44]

Rachmaninoff's grandfather Arkady Aleksandrovich was well known as a virtuoso pianist. In his youth he had taken lessons with the internationally known pianist and pedagogue John Field (1782–1837), and he also maintained a correspondence with the legendary Anton Rubinstein (1829–1894). He performed in the best-known salons of Tambov, Moscow, and St. Petersburg and composed pieces for solo piano as well as art songs. Many of his compositions were published, but because of his status as a nobleman it was not socially acceptable at that time for him to pursue music as a profession. The light of Arkady Aleksandrovich's life was his grandson Sergei, whose musical talent manifested itself early in the young boy's life; Sergei in turn was influenced by his grandfather's consuming passion for music and commitment to composing and performing it. Arkady Aleksandrovich's wife, Varvara Vasilievna, was on friendly terms with the poet Vasily Zhukovsky—their correspondence is distinctive in that it was carried out exclusively in verse.

All of the children of Arkady and Varvara inherited from their parents a love and talent for music. This was especially noticeable in Vasily Arkadievich, who would become Rachmaninoff's father, but because of the inconstancy of his personality and lackadaisical attitude toward his responsibilities in life, his musical gifts were never fully developed. He did, however, compose several pieces for the piano and played that instrument extraordinarily well.

At the turn of the twentieth century Znamenskoe was a magnet for prominent cultural figures. Aleksandr Ilyich Siloti, who studied with Nikolai Rubinstein (1835–1881) and was one of the last students of Franz Liszt (1811–1886), lived at the estate for many years. (He would later emigrate to America and teach at Juilliard in New York City.) Siloti was married to Vera Pavlovna Tretiakova, the daughter of the famous founder of Moscow's Tretiakov Art Gallery. The brilliant stage actress Vera Fedorovna Komissarzhevskaia visited Siloti at Znamenskoe and was enchanted both by the beauty of the estate's natural surroundings and by the genuine kindness and hospitality extended to her by the Rachmaninoff / Siloti families. On the occasion of her untimely death of smallpox, Sergei Rachmaninoff would dedicate to her his deeply moving art song "Ne mozhet byt" [It cannot be; Op. 34, No. 7]. He always selected the poems for his art songs very deliberately, connecting their theme with the given dedicatee and sometimes altering the text slightly in order to make it fit the subject matter he had in mind.[45] The granddaughter of Yulia Arkadievna (Rachmaninoff) Siloti, Natalia Konstantinovna Guchkova, married Gustaf Genrikhovich Shpet, one of Russia's preeminent philosophers and publicists. Shpet also spent time working and relaxing at Znamenskoe. Significantly, Znamenskoe was located not far from the church in Tarakanovskoe, in which the major Russian poet and playwright Aleksandr Blok (1880–1921) was married. Rachmaninoff in the early twentieth century would briefly interact with Blok concerning the possibility of setting one of Blok's plays to music (Rachmaninoff decided not to pursue this project).

Sergei Rachmaninoff spent some time each summer at Znamenskoe between 1886 and 1917. His musical, poetic, and philosophical impulses were nourished by the educated and cultured intellectuals with whom he interacted at this estate. Summers were typically spent at the family estates of Znamenskoe and Ivanovka, while the other three seasons were enjoyed in Tambov, Moscow, or St. Petersburg. The Rachmaninoffs, Silotis, and Satins were well received in the highest circles of nobility and kept in step with the latest currents in intellectual and cultural life. Thus Rachmaninoff's worldview and education were cultivated in an environment of Russia's most creative minds—of musicians, artists, actors, and philosophers. The atmosphere was one of traditional, patriarchal Orthodox Russia: the feast days and four major fasting periods were observed, orderliness reigned, and the ties of the clan (*rod*), or family, were enduring and warmhearted.

Throughout his life Rachmaninoff retained fond memories and a deep love for his father, despite the spendthrift habits and philandering that quickly brought the family to financial ruin. Vasily Arkadievich was by all accounts charming, talented in music, lighthearted, irresponsible, and frequently unfaithful to his wife. He loved children, was kind and warmhearted, and could not bear to apply even a mild punishment to his children. Liubov Petrovna, by contrast, was reserved in character, strict with her children, devoutly religious, and somewhat cold in demeanor. However, this enumeration of some of her major character traits should not be misconstrued as cold-heartedness or disinterestedness in her family's well-being. Even after she and her husband separated, she retained her love for him. She advocated vigorously for her children's future, considering specifically the type of education each child would require in order to fulfill his/her talents and abilities. It was she who opposed her husband's desire to send both Sergei and his brother Vladimir to military school. Despite Vasily Arkadievich's own musical talent, he was unable to go against the prevailing social norms mandating that boys of the nobility attend military school; it was Rachmaninoff's mother who, with her musical knowledge and keen sensitivity to Sergei's musical gifts, insisted that he pursue training in music. Rachmaninoff as an adult was a model son to her and helped her financially until the end of her life—but he was not drawn to her and his love seems to have been offered out of obligation, rather than being generated naturally.

From his parents Rachmaninoff inherited several qualities: He developed his mother's abilities in music, her penchant for order and organization, and her attentiveness to the liturgical rhythms and cycles of Russian Orthodoxy; his father handed down to him a genuine talent for music and a love for children. Because of his unhappy family life in his childhood, caused largely by his father's spending and carousing habits, Rachmaninoff retained a protectiveness toward his own family after he was married. The family unit was a bulwark against an unstable world for him, and the emotional stability this unit provided to him was of supreme importance for his well-being. He kept his own life in order, and indeed, due no doubt to the suffering and embarrassment he experienced as a child at the fall in his family's fortunes, he carried within himself all his life a keen sensitivity toward the suffering of his fellow musicians and of his countrymen in general. Rachmaninoff would not repeat the mistakes of his parents: his life would be successful and without financial crises brought on by casual and irresponsible attitudes toward money. He made sure that he could provide for those around him, and at the height of his career was supporting many other families and destitute musicians in the Russian emigration in Europe and America.

NOTES

1. Scripture quotation from The Authorized (King James) Version. Rights in the Authorized Version in the United Kingdom are vested in the Crown. Reproduced by permission of the Crown's patentee, Cambridge University Press.

2. See Robert Williams, "The Russian Revolution and the End of Time, 1900–1940," *Jahrbücher für Geschichte Osteuropas* 43, no. 3 (1995): 364–401.

3. See B.S. Nikitin, *Sergei Rakhmaninov. Dve zhizni* (Moscow: Znanie, 1993), 14–15; and *Ivanovka: Vremena. Sobytiia. Sud'by*, compiled by A.I. Ermakov and A.V. Zhogov (Moscow: Irina Arkhipova Foundation, 2003), 19. This last book lists the information about Rachmaninoff as "Entry No. 9, born March 20, baptized April 2, name Sergei." The entry can be found in the section devoted to April 1873.

4. B.N. Strel'nikov, "Iz vospominaniy N.M. Strel'nikova" (senar.ru, 2006–2022), https://senar.ru/memoirs/Strelnikov/, trans. VZN.

5. Ibid., trans. VZN.

6. Ibid., trans. VZN.

7. Ibid., trans. VZN.

8. L.L. Kovaleva-Ogorodnova, *Rakhmaninov v Sankt-Peterburge* (St. Petersburg: Predpriiatie C.-Peterburgskogo Soiuza Khudozhnikov, 1997), paraphrase of 50–51.

9. The details concerning the sale of the house at Semenovo and architectural particulars are paraphrased from Ermakov and Zhogov, 19–20.

10. Valery Vasilievich Demidov researched the issue of Liubov Petrovna Butakova's estates: He was not able to determine specifically how many estates Rachmaninoff's mother brought with her in her dowry upon her marriage to Rachmaninoff's father. The number commonly found in biographies is four, but it could also have been five. The names of all of the estates have not yet been established. Demidov wrote an article on the topic, titled "Tak gde zhe rodilsia Rakhmaninov?" (March 19, 2003; unpublished). I thank B. S. Nikitin for providing me with this information. Among others, Oskar von Riesemann mentions the estates, and that Vasily Arkadievich squandered four *in toto*.

11. Aleksandr Ermakov, *Sergei Rakhmaninov. Istoki* (Ivanovka: Muzei-usad'ba S.V. Rakhmaninova, 2003), 8, trans. VZN.

12. Ibid., trans. VZN.

13. Sergei Bertensson and Jay Leyda, *Sergei Rachmaninoff: A Lifetime in Music* (New York: New York UP, 1956; repr., Bloomington, IN: Indiana UP, 2001). The information about Rachmaninoff's parents is a paraphrase of 2.

14. Kovaleva-Ogorodnova, paraphrase of 37–38.

15. Boris Nikitin, *Sergei Rakhmaninov. Feodor Shaliapin* (Moscow: ОТиСС, 1998), 24, trans. VZN. A slightly different translation of Mme Defert's letter appears in Bertensson and Leyda, 3.

16. Harriette Brower, "'Beware of the Indifferent Piano Teacher,' Warns Rachmaninoff," *Musician* 30 (February 1925), 12. No translator is listed, but my comparisons of other statements by Rachmaninoff during this period lead to the conclusion that a Russian speaker (perhaps his wife, who learned English more quickly than he) was present and helped with the English wording.

17. Y.F. Netlau, "Vospominaniia Yakova Fedorovicha Netlau," in Ermakov and Zhogov, 20, trans. VZN.

18. *Sergei Rakhmaninov. Vospominaniia zapisannye Oskarom fon Rizemanom*, trans. V.N. Chemberdzhi (Moscow: Raduga, 1992), 16, quoted in *Ivanovka: Vremena. Sobytiia. Sud'by*, 20, trans. VZN. This book was originally published in English as *Rachmaninoff's Recollections Told by Oskar von Riesemann* (London: The Macmillan Company, 1934). The biography should be approached with caution: while it contains many insightful and colorful anecdotes, its author Oscar von Riesemann claimed to have taken notes while interviewing Rachmaninoff (they sometimes took walks together), but neither Rachmaninoff nor anyone else ever saw him with pencil and paper in hand during those walks. Rachmaninoff himself was deeply disturbed at what he read when he received a copy of the completed manuscript from the publisher, with a request for his endorsement. Out of his inbred politeness he requested only a few changes; because von Riesemann was seriously ill at the time and for various other reasons, Rachmaninoff gave the book his approval, despite his

reservations. Hence the direct quotations of Sergei Vasilievich's words at best can be understood as paraphrasing recollected after the interviews. On the other hand, von Riesemann's close acquaintance with the composer lends the biography a certain authority and legitimacy that make its contents extremely valuable.

19. Ermakov, *Sergei Rakhmaninov. Istoki* (Ivanovka: Muzei-usad'ba S.V. Rakhmaninova, 2003), 9–10, paraphrase and trans. VZN.

20. The dates of the six Rachmaninoff children are as follows: Elena (1868–1885); Sofia (1870–1882); Vladimir (1871–1913); Sergei (1873–1943); Varvara—died in infancy (1878?–1880); and Arkady (1880–1945).

21. Bertensson and Leyda, paraphrase of 4–5.

22. The address of this apartment, which is in a building that has been preserved in its entirety, is: Corner of the Fontanka and Nikolskaya Street, Building 133/9, Apt. 60.

23. In 1883 Aleksandr III (son of Aleksandr II) initiated construction of a memorial in his father's honor; the church, Храм Спаса на Крови [Cathedral of the Savior on the Blood], was erected on the site where Aleksandr II had been assassinated. Construction of the church was completed during the reign of Tsar Nicholas II in 1907.

24. Kovaleva-Ogorodnova, paraphrase of 93.

25. Kovaleva-Ogorodnova, paraphrase of 94–96.

26. E.A. Poliakova, "Vladimir Vasilievich Dem'ianskii (1846–1915)—uchitel' S.V. Rakhmaninova," in *S.V. Rakhmaninov i Tambovskii krai v aspekte razvitiia regional'noi kul'tury: Materialy dokladov. III Rakhmaninovskie chteniia*, Nov. 30, 2006, ed. I.N. Vanovskaia (Tambov: Tambovskoe gosudarstvennoe muzykal'no-pedagogicheskii institut imeni Rakhmaninova, 2007), 22, trans. VZN.

27. I am indebted to V. I. Antipov for our discussions in Moscow on the Russian nobility and the abiding importance of "clan" (*rod*) in the Russian mentality.

28. Priscilla Roosevelt, *Life on the Russian Country Estate: A Social and Cultural History* (New Haven, CT: Yale UP, 1995), xiii.

29. Charles F. Barber, *Lost in the Stars: The Forgotten Musical Life of Aleksandr Siloti* (Lanham, MD: The Scarecrow Press, 2002), 92–93.

30. Ermakov and Zhogov, 15, trans. VZN. See also Ivan Ivanovich Rakhmaninov and N. Vasilenko, eds., *Istoricheskie svedeniia o rode dvorian Rakhmaninovykh* (Kiev: G.T. Korchak-Novitskii, 1895).

31. Free Artist—a professional status invented during the reign of Catherine II (the Great), who ruled 1762–1796.

32. Ermakov and Zhogov, 27, trans. VZN.

33. S. Rakhmaninov, Letter of February 3, 1905, in *S. Rakhmaninov. Literaturnoe nasledie. Vospominaniia. Stat'i. Interv'iu. Pis'ma*, ed. Z.A. Apetian (Moscow: Sovetskii kompozitor, 1978), 1: 354, trans. VZN.

34. Ibid., paraphrase 354, 584–85.

35. For a comprehensive analysis of Imperial Russia's currents of representation in the government, see Nicolai N. Petro, *The Rebirth of Russian Democracy: An Interpretation of Political Culture* (Cambridge, MA: Harvard UP, 1997).

36. Priscilla Roosevelt, *Life on the Russian Country Estate: A Social and Cultural History*: 15, 17, 27–28.

37. See Ermakov and Zhogov, 14–17, 30–31.

38. A. Ermakov and A. Zhogov, comp., *Znamenskoe: Rakhmaninovskie mesta Tambovskoi oblasti* (Tambov: TOGUP, 2004), 5, trans. and paraphrase VZN.

39. Ermakov and Zhogov, *Ivanovka: Vremena. Sobytiia. Sud'by*, 15.

40. Ibid.

41. S.A. Satina, "Zapiska o S.V. Rakhmaninove," in *Vospominaniia o Rakhmaninove*, ed. Z.A. Apetian, 5th ed. (Moscow: Muzyka, 1988), I:13, trans. VZN. Satina also notes (in note *** at the bottom of the same page) that she compiled a special genealogy of this generation of the Rachmaninoff-Bakhmet'ev families that traces six generations of their various heirs with respect to their musical abilities.

42. Ibid., 13–14, trans. VZN.

43. Ibid., paraphrased from 14.

44. A. Ermakov and A. Zhogov, comp., *Znamenskoe: Rakhmaninovskie mesta Tambovskoi oblasti*, 7–8, trans. and paraphrase of excerpts VZN.

45. Ibid., 10.

Chapter 2

Early Education
(1885–1892)

Soon after the Rachmaninoff family had relocated to St. Petersburg, Sergei's parents Liubov Petrovna and Vasily Arkadievich became estranged from each other and separated. Since divorce was forbidden in the Russian Orthodox Church, they could resolve their differences only by living apart. Vasily Arkadievich moved to Moscow. Despite her husband's shabby treatment of her, Liubov Petrovna continued to love him for the rest of her life. Tragedy and unhappiness seemed to follow Sergei within the circle of his immediate family during these critical formative years. By the time he was twelve, in 1885, he had experienced the traumatic loss of three of his siblings, all of his sisters: Varvara, Sophia, and Elena. Such shattering losses so early in a life that even without them was extremely unstable must surely have contributed to his deep need for a stable family life in adulthood and his almost mystical fear of death, which would haunt him throughout his life.[1]

Sergei led a largely unsupervised life as a young adolescent in St. Petersburg. Since he was living away from his mother and without those moorings of routine and role models every child needs in order to develop a healthy balance between work and leisure activities, he enjoyed a freedom from routine that served to distract him from the pain of his family's troubles—but it concomitantly hurt his progress in his musical education. Accounts of his riding the streetcars through the city, ice skating with friends, and in general wasting the time he should have used for his musical studies are ubiquitous. His habit of doctoring the bad grades on reports from the St. Petersburg Conservatory that were sent home to his mother did not help matters. Harried from tending to her family's needs and emotionally exhausted, Liubov Petrovna did not notice the altered grades. By the spring of 1885 the situation with Sergei's grades had become critical. He could not continue at the conservatory, and clearly some different steps needed to be taken in order for his musical gifts not to be squandered forever.

Liubov Petrovna sought the advice of Sergei's cousin Aleksandr Siloti (1863–1945), who had trained with the most famous and brilliant pianists of the day: he studied for one year (1881–1882) with Anton Rubinstein and for three years (1883–1886) with Liszt as one of the latter's favorite students.[2] Siloti had returned to St. Petersburg that spring ready to assume a high-profile musical career in Russia. Sergei's mother met with him and asked him to see Sergei in order to assess his younger cousin's musical abilities. After hearing Sergei play and speaking with him about musical matters, Siloti understood that he possessed a natural aptitude for the piano and was at a crucial age for his development into a musician. He recommended that Sergei be sent to Moscow at the end of the summer in order to study with a well-known teacher associated with the Moscow Conservatory, Nikolay Sergeevich Zverev (1832–1893). He would study privately with Zverev and concomitantly take classes at the Moscow Conservatory. That summer Sergei would spend in Novgorod at the haven of his grandmother Butakova's estate. He faced another radical change in his living environment by a move to another city and residence with strangers once again.

In Russian music circles Zverev was famous as a successful pedagogue who not only maintained a busy schedule of private lessons, but also took in to board at his large apartment on Ruzheiny pereulok a small number of gifted students (exclusively males) who would otherwise not have the means to develop their musical knowledge. In part to keep his reputation thriving and in part for his own enjoyment, Zverev would supervise the boys' musical and social education, rarely allowing them visits or vacations with their families. It was in such an arrangement that Rachmaninoff was brought to Zverev, having been recommended by his older cousin Aleksandr Siloti.[3] Rachmaninoff would become such a student, living and studying at Zverev's apartment along with two others: Leonid Maksimov and Matvey Pressman. The three young men became somewhat endearingly known in Moscow circles as Zverev's "cubs" (so-called because in Russian the name "Zverev" is derived from "animal"—loosely connected in Russian culture with "bear"). Rachmaninoff would live at Zverev's for four years, from August 1885 until the fall of 1889, between the ages of twelve and sixteen. Coincidentally, the immensely talented composer and professor Sergei Ivanovich Taneev (1856–1915) was the director of the conservatory during these same years of 1885–1889; he would play a major role in Rachmaninoff's musical development during his last years there. The details of their rewarding interactions will be presented later in this chapter.

We must consider how fragile the twelve-year-old Rachmaninoff was at this point of his life. With his parents separated, his three female siblings deceased, and a new life on his own in Moscow under the supervision of a dedicated but highly emotional music teacher, the young musician could not have felt more destabilized and vulnerable to life's vicissitudes. Sergei's father was not often available to him for visits, and his remaining family members were far away in St. Petersburg; he now found himself in unfamiliar lodgings, largely against his will, with strangers. To be sure, this was not unusual in families of the Russian nobility of the time, but when this change of circumstances for Sergei is taken in the context of his unstable childhood and the tragedies he had faced in his family, one can imagine how difficult this period was for him emotionally. Sergei had always manifested an independence of spirit, a robust constitution that would survive debilitating illnesses and conditions (such as malaria in 1891 and extreme headaches that would last for many years), and an introverted and quiet personality. These features of his emotional and physical being would have to sustain him in his new environment, one in which his every activity was planned and strictly supervised by well-meaning adults, but in which genuine emotional security and nurturing were absent. He understandably developed a close camaraderie with his apartment mates L. Maksimov and M. Pressman; the three boys could share their triumphs in the musical arena and also commiserate with each other when one of them would provoke Zverev's anger by being late for a lesson, playing a piece not up to their teacher's standards, or answering a question in the wrong way.

The austerity of the regimen Zverev established, and complete control he exercised—over the boys' daily routines, behavior, and times of relaxation—can be viewed as excessively controlling and problematic when one considers that these boys were completely powerless and without close relatives in their immediate environment. They were not allowed to see their families for long periods of time; even in the summers they were separated from their relatives, because Zverev would take the boys with him to various country estates and resorts in the south of Russia. On these extended holidays the boys had a chance to relax, but they also continued to be tutored in aspects of music. To be sure, the attention Zverev lavished on his students is praiseworthy and touching, but the degree to which he insisted on controlling the young boys' lives seems unreasonable.

It is worth mentioning that Zverev sought to control the "moral" upbringing of the three boys as well: he took them to brothels in Moscow where they were initiated into experiences with prostitutes (Rachmaninoff took part in such excursions). He also introduced the boys to gypsy singing, both at gypsy camps on the outskirts of Moscow and in the city. It is widely known that Russian music has always been deeply influenced by the melodies and haunting strains of gypsy music. Zverev grasped the significance of this musical influence for the boys' education, but one imagines that some carousing and drinking must also have taken place with the gypsies. Zverev was fascinated by gypsies, and this attraction is by no means unusual, since much of Russian culture (especially music and literature, starting with Pushkin) was influenced by gypsy ways of life and various interpretations of their ethos. One biographer speculated that Rachmaninoff as an adult was always attracted to a certain gypsyish appearance and nature in women.[4] What are some of the attributes of appearance and personality that Russians typically associate with gypsy women? Among other traits, gypsy women had luxurious dark hair and expressive dark eyes, and were considered to possess a mysterious, passionate nature that was attractive to Russian men. Moreover, gypsies were considered to have a natural gift for music that was highly valued in Russian culture in general and Russian musical culture in particular. More will be said about Rachmaninoff's connections with women of gypsy background or appearance in later chapters when his relationships with Anna Lodyzhenskaia and Nina Koshetz will be examined.

One must wonder what psychological effects such an intense and repressive environment would have on an adolescent; after all, the three boys in question were only in their early teens. Even if we bear in mind that such an arrangement was by no means unusual for families during that period in Russia who were seeking a particular kind of education for their children, still the arrangement with Zverev seems in some ways extreme and ethically troubling. Oskar von Riesemann writes:

> One of the conditions under which Zverev accepted superlatively gifted school boys into his home [for instruction] was that they not go home for holidays and that they visited their Moscow relatives as rarely as possible. In insisting on such a condition, Zverev evidently wanted to keep the future artists as far away as possible from the excessive pampering of the home atmosphere with its inflated sentimentality and tenderness [sic]. He especially protected his pupils from the dangerous [sic] influence of premature ecstasy concerning their talents.[5]

This description of Zverev's ostensible motives is unconvincing. Some questions arise. Why did Zverev want to keep his pupils from seeing their relatives in Moscow? Why did he prevent them from going home for the holidays? Were there activities taking place at his house that he wanted to keep hidden from the outside world? It is disturbing to read a justification of keeping children from their families for the reason of "excessive pampering" at home with its "inflated sentimentality and tenderness." Is this not in reality the love and caring that make a developing human being psychologically able to function effectively in his or her life?

Such control over the lives of young and powerless teenaged boys, even if the motives were ones of professional concern, surely was unhealthy and cruel. Even Zverev's sister was described by Rachmaninoff as an extremely unpleasant person, one who did not possess emotional warmth or those nurturing qualities usually associated with women in a position to care for children. When this is added to Zverev's temper and violent outbursts that resulted in some sort of thrashings of the boys or assaults on them with his fists, what emerges is a house in which physical and emotional abuse were taking place. Rachmaninoff attempted to gloss over the physical punishment by praising Zverev for his talents as a pedagogue and his cultured way of life that brought his boys into contact with the most important musical figures and cultural events in Moscow. Indeed, Rachmaninoff's narrative of life with Zverev tells us something about his own personality: Rachmaninoff found it preferable to recall that period of his life in the best possible light. But the education undoubtedly came at a high price.

Matvey Pressman's recollections of Rachmaninoff and their years together under Zverev's supervision provide many vivid details of the daily and nightly routines of the three students and their teacher. One very intimate scene stands out:

> With our combined efforts we settled Zverev into bed and under the covers, and after his comment "Le [Leonid], Se [Sergei], Mo [Matvey]! How pleasant . . ."—and in a chorus we added: "to stretch out the dear little feet after a long day of labor." Then we kissed him on the cheek, blew out the candle, and went to our bedroom.[6]

Even allowing for Russian cultural norms, one feels somehow uncomfortable when reading about the familiarity and physical intimacy experienced by the three teenaged boys as they put their teacher to bed every night, lifting his legs onto the bed, getting him settled under the covers, and kissing him goodnight on the cheek.

Many explanations have been offered for the infamous "quarrel" between the sixteen-year-old Rachmaninoff and Zverev in the fall of 1889, which soon drove Rachmaninoff out of Zverev's apartment and left them estranged from each other until Rachmaninoff graduated from the conservatory on May 7, 1892. Let us consider here Zverev's family background, his activities in the Moscow musical world, and his pedagogical methods.

At the end of the nineteenth century Nikolay Zverev, who would soon reach the age of sixty, was one of the most distinctive and colorful figures in the landscape of Moscow's social and musical life. His coming-of-age musically in some ways paralleled the musical activities of Rachmaninoff's father. Similar to Vasily Arkadievich, Zverev belonged to a prominent Russian family of the landed aristocracy; similar to Vasily Arkadievich, he had squandered several superb country estates; and, similar to Vasily Arkadievich, he was unusually gifted musically. Zverev had studied with Dubuque, Field, and Henselt, among the best pianoforte pedagogues of the 1830s and 1840s.

After he sold his last estate, Zverev received a post in St. Petersburg in one of the government's departments. During a layover in Moscow on his way to start his work in St. Petersburg, he encountered his former teacher Dubuque. The latter was overjoyed to see Zverev, and when he learned what Zverev's monthly salary would be (100 rubles), he offered to match it in Moscow if Zverev would stay and give private music lessons.

Soon Zverev became the most sought-after and well-paid piano teacher in that city. He made his living mainly by teaching students of the wealthy merchant class, the members of which lived in luxurious houses in the best regions of Moscow. In these families, Zverev flourished, in part because of his musical abilities and in part due to his considerable social skills. His presence was mandatory at all society lunches and dinners given by the business and merchant circles of Moscow. There was no equal to him at card games, the usual after-dinner pastime of Moscow's wealthiest families. Zverev preferred the so-called games of chance in cards: whist, Boston, and preference. He was famous at card tables almost more for his elegant and natural manners than for his strategies with the cards. Since Zverev's numerous piano lessons brought in considerable amounts of money, supplemented by his extensive winnings at cards, he was able to live luxuriously. It is interesting and noteworthy that after his dazzling pedagogical career took off, no one was to hear him actually playing the instrument. He seemed to prefer theory to practice; however, judging by the sheer number of his students who became famous, he was a marvelous teacher.

Rachmaninoff's words, as recorded by Oskar von Riesemann, reveal his initial impressions of Zverev:

> I walked into Zverev's house with my heart pounding, frightened by stories of his unimaginable strictness and "liberal fist," and by no means only during practice at the piano. I understood that the golden days and freedom of my childhood were over. A life began that was full of severe discipline and serious studies. The "family" of Zverev consisted of him and his unmarried sister (Zverev was a bachelor), who managed the household. On weekdays we virtually did not see our teacher, because he gave lessons from nine in the morning until nine in the evening—and always away from his home. Since Zverev led an active social life, he rarely came home after work, and by the time that he did arrive home, we, the boys, had long since gone to bed. We [the three boys] shared a bedroom and one grand piano (which often caused little tragedies). Each of us was supposed to practice for three hours a day, which, I think, may have greatly upset the neighbors.
>
> [Zverev] was a person of rare intelligence and enormous goodness, enjoying because of these attributes the greatest respect of the most prominent people of his time. . . . But his explosiveness was just as enormous as his goodness. When he was beside himself in anger, he was capable of attacking a person

with his fists and throwing at the person whatever came into his hands. I could imagine that at such times he could without any hesitation kill his opponent. We, the pupils, more than once had the opportunity to become convinced that Zverev really did have a "liberal fist." I got it from him as well, four or five times, but in contrast to the other boys *not because of a musical matter.* . . . Zverev distinguished himself by his extraordinarily original personality. His brilliant mind and liveliness significantly raised him above the average level of his environment.[7]

In a nutshell, how can Zverev be characterized as an individual? He was an enormously talented pedagogue committed to advancing his students in the field of music. His method of teaching was successful, and he was highly regarded in musical circles. His work ethic was legendary: he taught courses at the Moscow Conservatory, gave private lessons seven days a week at the residences of his students, and also taught the students who lived in his apartment. It is no exaggeration to state that he devoted his entire life to music.

For some of his contemporaries, however, he was too flamboyant. Rumors circulated that he was of homosexual orientation; both anecdotal and scholarly writing often take this possibility as a given.[8] The mysterious, but serious incident between him and Rachmaninoff that led to the latter's departure from Zverev's house might have had something to do with their different sexual orientations. Max Harrison writes:

> A quite different account has survived, however, as to the reason for the parting. According to this version, the problem was not that Rachmaninoff needed a separate room and piano for his composing but that Zveref was a homosexual. Certainly, while he taught the wives and daughters of his patrons in the many Moscow houses he visited, it was notable that he only took boys—never girls, however gifted—to live with him in his own establishment.[9]

What matters here, if Zverev was indeed a homosexual, is whether this orientation played a role in, or even caused, the dramatic rift between him and Rachmaninoff. Zverev took in only male students; this was a well-known fact in Moscow. Since his sister also lived in his apartment and supervised his students, her presence would have made the residence of female students in the house socially acceptable. To be sure, Zverev's decision to take in only male students as lodgers was less complicated than trying to maintain a household of students of both genders. But the single-sex household, combined with Zverev's insistence on keeping the boys in his charge away from their families (was he worried about what the boys might tell their relatives?), remains curious at the very least.

The quarrel between Rachmaninoff and Zverev, as recounted by Rachmaninoff, ostensibly took place because Rachmaninoff requested that he be allowed to work in a room privately at a piano for composing purposes. According to Oskar von Riesemann's conversations with Rachmaninoff, the latter's account of this episode was recorded as follows (in Rachmaninoff's words):

> I asked Zverev if he could help me to buy an instrument [a piano]. Our conversation began calmly and progressed in completely peaceful tones until a point when I uttered some words that instantly enraged him. He jumped up, shouted at me, and threw at me the first object that he laid his hands on. I remained completely composed, but nevertheless added some grease to the fire, saying that I was no longer a child and that I found the tone of his conversation with me unseemly.[10]

This explanation is unconvincing and unsatisfying, because the inner, emotional logic does not follow: it is too simplistic, and Rachmaninoff describes this major feud as if it were ignited by a reasonable request to compose music and purchase a second piano (which should not have upset Zverev). B. S. Nikitin also expresses puzzlement about Rachmaninoff's version of the conflict with Zverev:

> No, some other serious reason was responsible for the quarrel between Rachmaninoff and Zverev. I cannot believe that Sergei could be so ungrateful, and also cannot believe that Zverev, because of a trifling matter . . . could throw his student out of the house.
> It doesn't make sense.
> It is impossible not to think about the simplest matter at hand. Who was preventing Sergei from expressing his creative thoughts musically during the time he had free from his classes? He already was composing freely without a piano, and this included even orchestral scores. Why did he need a separate space so badly? And even if he did need this separate, private space, he could have comfortably composed at the piano [at Zverev's] during the hours designated for his practice or could have composed at the conservatory. It also doesn't connect with reality that Zverev was opposed to [Rachmaninoff's] studies in special theory and composition, because he was preparing pianists [not composers] and considered Rachmaninoff a talented performer, while composition could have distracted him from the main goal [of becoming a pianist].
> In a word, all the known circumstances and explanations explain very little [about this quarrel].[11]

Zverev's fiery outburst and the quarrel that in effect interrupted their relationship for several years are out of proportion with Rachmaninoff's stated reason for the rift. Something else, more fundamental to the emotionally intense and intimate relationship between the older man and his adolescent pupil, may have happened that would better explain the dramatic outcome.

Perhaps Zverev made advances to the young Sergei (who was heterosexual), and the latter rejected them. Such an event would more plausibly have led to the explosion between them that followed and the immediate estrangement that was the result. One can also add to this some accounts by Rachmaninoff's contemporaries which alluded to Sergei's being profoundly uncomfortable with the increasingly immoral atmosphere at Zverev's house. When the point came that he could not bear the atmosphere any longer, he had words with Zverev and the decision was made for him to move out.

A letter Rachmaninoff wrote that was addressed to all three of the Skalon sisters lends further credence to the claim that his quarrel with Zverev was over a deeply intense and personal matter, rather than a mere request to purchase a piano and have time for composing. The letter was written on March 26, 1891, after Rachmaninoff had been living away from Zverev's residence for some time:

> No luck here, either with health, which the Lord doesn't grant me, or with matters at the Conservatory. Imagine, Tata [Natalia], at the student concert I was supposed to play my two-piano rhapsody with Sasha's [Siloti's] pupil, Maksimov, one of Zverev's *inmates*; we had rehearsed, we had matched our playing, everything was going on well, *when suddenly Zverev, who of course remembers that incident with me, decided to create an unpleasantness for me, and meanly refused to allow Maksimov to play with me.* And Sasha also didn't go against Zverev, because he is terribly fond of him, and I was left with nothing but an enormous grief—how much I wanted to play in this concert![12]

This letter underscores the deeply felt animosity and grudge that Zverev was continuing to harbor toward Rachmaninoff for some two years after the rift between them (over Rachmaninoff's request to possibly purchase a piano and do some composing?!). The reaction by Sasha [Aleksandr] Siloti, reported by Rachmaninoff, is understandable: even though he and Sergei were cousins and very close in many ways, Siloti had also been supported by the generosity of Zverev. Starting from 1871 he had lived and studied at Zverev's residence for a period of ten years, returning to his family estate of Znamenskoe only in the summers.[13] He owed Zverev a great deal, and even his relationship with his cousin Sergei could not make him contradict the teacher whose help and kindness enabled him to pursue his musical career. Concerning the capriciousness of Zverev's insistence that Rachmaninoff not perform with Maksimov described in Rachmaninoff's letter, the measure of Zverev's anger and the intensity and length of time of Zverev's reaction are completely out of proportion and against any inner logic that would follow after what, according to Rachmaninoff, was not a disagreement over anything personal whatsoever. Even if Zverev's mercurial temper is factored into the equation, it would not explain the high level of animosity that he continued to carry toward Rachmaninoff. Clearly the argument was over something very personal, perhaps potentially embarrassing, and even compromising.

After Zverev's death of natural causes on September 30, 1893, the three former "bear cubs" who lived and studied together at his house—Pressman, Maksimov, and Rachmaninoff—would remember him with warm feelings whenever they met. As A. S. Pushkin wrote in his poem: "Что пройдет, то будет мило" (what has passed will be remembered fondly).[14] Pressman wrote in his memoir:

> After his [Zverev's] death Rachmaninoff, Maksimov, and I would often get together. The usual topic of our conversations was recollections of our dear old gentleman. The many ways, in which in our childhood we had considered Zverev wrong, unfair, strict, or even cruel, we now perceived as only love and caring for us . . . Our gatherings always ended by fulfilling his covenant: we would each drink a goblet of fine wine to the peaceful repose of his soul.[15]

In Russia at the turn of the twentieth century the topic of homosexuality was a sensitive one not typically brought up in public. It remained a private matter, because of deep-seated, traditional attitudes toward this type of sexual orientation. It was tolerated, and educated, reasonable people did not concern themselves overly about it. In the world of the arts and performance the levels of acceptance and tolerance seem to be greater than in Russian society in general. It was a commonly accepted fact that Tchaikovsky was a homosexual, but the expectation of him was that he be discrete in his behavior. There is some consensus that Zverev was of that orientation as well; anecdotes by his contemporaries point to his having flamboyant and colorful aspects to his behavior, even as he was at the same time impeccable in his manners and bearing in society. Keeping a person's sexual orientation a private matter and out of the public eye was a long-established practice in Russian society, and this fact may explain why, if the rift between Rachmaninoff and Zverev indeed came about because of personal and even intimate differences between them, Rachmaninoff chose to craft a more benign account of why he left Zverev's house. It would spare both him and Zverev a great deal of awkwardness.

Rachmaninoff, embarrassed both at the time and afterward, out of decorum and loyalty to the teacher who had taught him so much, constructed a more ordinary and inoffensive reason for the rift that took place between them. It was not in Rachmaninoff's character to slander anyone, whether friend or foe; he preferred to remain silent or be gracious if he could not speak in a positive way about a colleague or acquaintance. Since the trait of not judging others is intensively foregrounded in Russian Orthodox theology and the writings of the saints, it stands to reason that Rachmaninoff learned and internalized it from his childhood days with his grandmother Butakova, considering it the more humble and spiritually wise way to treat others. If Zverev had indeed wronged Rachmaninoff in any way, the latter chose to make peace with the matter and forgive Zverev, which was not a surprising response for Sergei; forgiveness was one of the qualities most consistently attributed to Rachmaninoff by others he knew throughout his life. Even so, it remains a curious fact that Rachmaninoff, in the course of a long career during which he dedicated 99 percent of his works to either a specific individual or group of individuals (as the Philadelphia Orchestra), did not dedicate a single composition to his teacher Zverev.

Sergei Rachmaninoff's desire to compose was expressing itself firmly when he was between the ages of fourteen and sixteen, before the summer of 1890 when he would first become acquainted with life at the estate of Ivanovka. Not all of his experiments in composition have been preserved, but clearly he was trying out various forms, both instrumental and choral, searching for his own musical voice. Nikitin describes:

> He [Sergei] was fourteen when his three nocturnes [for piano] appeared [1887–88], in which one is struck by the perfection in composition, especially in the third one in C minor; the interesting structure; and the rich harmony—but more than this one is struck by the depth of feeling expressed by the adolescent, a depth that is not found even in adults.
>
> During this same period [1887] he wrote a Scherzo for orchestra [in F major], a very attractive piece, and, although in it there was nothing his own, typical for him, nothing mature in general, this piece is noteworthy because it shows that at fourteen years of age Rachmaninoff was already freely making use of orchestral means of expression. One or two more years, and his progress would bring him to the point of almost the complete maturity of a master. Of course, in possessing knowledge about all the instruments and having a sense of how to compose music, he could not yet handle composing large-format works.
>
> At sixteen he started working on a piano concerto, but, having produced several sketches, decided to leave them for better times [in the future]. Incidentally, within one year he began working on the concerto in all seriousness.[16]

Rachmaninoff was developing his prodigious talents in performing and composing, advancing in leaps and bounds. His reputation at the conservatory also became secure; he was known as one of the finest students, if not the finest, to be making his way among his peers, while his professors already recognized that he would become a giant among them.

Immediately after their argument, Zverev took the sixteen-year-old Sergei to the Satins, the only family relations the latter had in Moscow. On the pretext of an incompatibility of personality, Zverev asked the Satins to take in Sergei to live with them—which they agreed to do. Thus after four years of residing in Zverev's house, Rachmaninoff was moved to his aunt's house (she was his father's sister), a step that marked the beginning of greater independence for him. He did not regret this move, because the Satins' house provided him with the beneficial conditions necessary for studying and composing. The calm, humane, and in general cheerful atmosphere there were a balm for his spirit and a stark contrast to the regimented atmosphere at Zverev's. Despite the fact that he had changed his place of residence and would no longer be studying with Zverev, Sergei could still continue his studies as a student at the Moscow Conservatory.[17]

This preeminent school of music in Russia, which would become world renowned by producing some of the finest musicians and musicologists of the twentieth century, was founded in 1866 by Nikolay Grigorievich Rubinstein (1835–1881) and Prince Nikolay Petrovich Trubetskoy (1828–1900). It was the second oldest institution for higher musical education in Russia, after the St. Petersburg Conservatory, which was founded in 1862 by Nikolay Rubinstein's older brother Anton Grigorievich (1829–1894), the famous conductor-composer-pianist.

Both the St. Petersburg and Moscow conservatories were established in large part because of the prior existence of the Russian Musical Society, which was developed in St. Petersburg in 1859 by Grand Duchess Elena Pavlovna Romanova (an aunt of Tsar Aleksandr II) and the young Anton Rubinstein. One year later a Moscow branch of the Society was formed, and five years after that the city's conservatory would be organized; it was first called the Moscow Imperial Conservatory. Its most prestigious and famous professor was P. I. Tchaikovsky (1840–1893), who taught theory and harmony there from 1866 to 1878. His prominence at this conservatory was paralleled by the importance of N. A. Rimsky-Korsakov (1844–1908) at the St. Petersburg Conservatory; Rimsky-Korsakov was a member of the group of five composers who called themselves the *moguchaia kuchka* (the mighty heap), whose remaining four members were Mily Balakirev, Cesare Cui, Modest Mussorgsky, and Aleksandr Borodin. The atmosphere of creative competition between the Moscow and St. Petersburg composers was sometimes friendly and at other times contentious, but this stimulating musical environment was one from which students studying at both conservatories undoubtedly benefited and which they would remember for the rest of their lives.

NOTES

1. See S.A. Satina, "Zapiska o S.V. Rakhmaninove," in *Vospominaniia o Rakhmaninove*, ed. Z.A. Apetian, 5th ed. (Moscow: Muzyka, 1988), I: 115.

2. Charles F. Barber, *Lost in the Stars: The Forgotten Musical Life of Aleksandr Siloti* (Lanham, MD: Scarecrow Press, 2002), 13. Siloti is buried at the Novo-Diveevo Convent in Spring Valley, NY.

3. The information in this paragraph is paraphrased from Oskar von Riesemann, *Sergei Rakhmaninov: Vospominaniia zapisannye Oskarom fon Rizemanom*, trans. V.N. Chemberdzhi (Moscow: Raduga, 1992), 28–29.

4. See B.S. Nikitin, *Sergei Rakhmaninov. Dve zhizni* (Moscow: Znamia, 1993), 34–43, 96–98. In this context it is noteworthy that his first opera was about gypsies. Rachmaninoff's choice of topic for this opera may have reflected not only his admiration for Pushkin's poem but also his own fascination with the perceived freedom of the gypsies.

5. von Riesemann, 37–38, trans. VZN.

6. M.L. Pressman, "Ugolok muzykal'noi Moskvy vos'midesiatykh godov," in *Vospominaniia o Rakhmaninove*, ed. Z.A. Apetian, I: 178, trans. VZN.

7. von Riesemann, 30–31, trans. and emphasis added VZN.

8. The gifted pianist Vladimir Leyetchkiss, who was one of the last students of Heinrich Neuhaus in the Soviet Union, and who in that context was privy to the musical and cultural narratives Neuhaus had inherited from the early twentieth century, stated matter-of-factly about Zverev's rumored homosexuality: "Это общеизвестный факт." (Trans.: This is a commonly known fact.) Personal interview, New York, September 22, 2007.

9. Max Harrison, *Rachmaninoff: Life, Works, Recordings* (New York: Continuum, 2005), 22.

10. von Riesemann, 52, trans. VZN.

11. Nikitin, 21–22, trans. VZN.

12. Sergei Bertensson and Jay Leyda, *Sergei Rachmaninoff: A Lifetime in Music* (New York: New York UP, 1956; repr., Bloomington, IN: Indiana UP, 2001), 32, emphasis added. Rachmaninoff's musical composition in question is his *Russian Rhapsody in E minor* for two pianos (dated January 12–14, 1891).

13. Barber, 2.

14. Aleksandr Sergeevich Pushkin, from "Если жизнь тебя обманет, Не печалься, не сердись!" (1825). Insightful interpretation of the line by eminent Russian émigré poet I. V. Elagin (1918–1987). The line is in the following stanza: "Сердце в будущем живет; Настоящее уныло: Всё мгновенно, всё пройдет; Что пройдет, то будет мило." Rachmaninoff kept Pushkin's poetry close to him all his life.

15. E. Dmitrievskaia, V. Dmitrievskii, *Rakhmaninov v Moskve* (Moscow: Moskovskii rabochii, 1993), 38, trans. VZN.

16. Nikitin, 25, trans. VZN.

17. This paragraph is paraphrased from Catherine Poivre D'Arvor, *Rachmaninoff: la passion au bout des doigts* (Monte Carlo: Editions du Rocher, 1986), 40–41, trans. VZN.

Chapter 3

Birth of a Composer-Pianist
(1885–1892)

Located on the Bolshaia Nikitskaia, a quiet and narrow, though very scenic street in the heart of Moscow not far from the Kremlin, the Moscow Conservatory in physical size is one of the largest conservatories in the world. The history of its construction and expansion is fascinating, with many of the major dates of renovation coinciding with Rachmaninoff's youth and adult years in Russia. The building on Bolshaia Nikitskaia that would become the initial site of the conservatory was originally constructed as an estate in the 1790s by the renowned architect Vasily Bazhenov for Ekaterina Dashkova, a noblewoman born as Countess Vorontsova. She had owned this land since 1766, and the location for her manor house in the center of Moscow was suitable for her rank and activities. She would rise to become Princess Dashkova, the director of the Russian Academy of Sciences, in 1783 during the reign of Catherine II (1762–96)—the first woman in the world to head a state academy of sciences. In the course of her travels to Europe, Dashkova met Voltaire, Diderot, and even Benjamin Franklin (in 1781). Princess Dashkova died in 1810, after which date her descendants used her estate for various purposes, including renting it. In 1871 the house was rented by the Russian Musical Society of Moscow for development as the Moscow Imperial Conservatory, and in 1878 was purchased by the Society for 185,000 rubles. Its rooms and structures were adapted for musical purposes during the same years that Rachmaninoff was a child discovering his attraction to Russian Orthodox chant and the piano.[1] A photo dated 1894 provides an impression of the manor house-turned-conservatory in which Sergei Rachmaninoff was a music student.

Between the years 1893 and 1902 the construction of a newer and more modern building for the conservatory was completed, which modified some elements of the earlier manor house. These were the years when Safonov was

Figure 3.1 Moscow Conservatory c. 1890. Public domain.

director of the conservatory: the building needed to be expanded, for student enrollments had grown (from 184 to 430 between 1868 and 1894) and the curriculum was developing additional courses. The conservatory's students felt crowded in the stuffy rooms; Rachmaninoff and his peers studying there would have been among those experiencing these growing pains—but in an environment of brilliant professors-musicians. The architect Vasily Zagorsky designed a classical-style architectural complex with three educational facilities and three concert halls with acoustics that are world-renowned. The three concert halls are the Grand Hall, the Small Hall, and the Rachmaninoff Hall (named after the composer in 1986). The building's central ensemble with its two-story-high semi-rotunda and the wall of the right wing are the only parts that resemble the former Bazhenov building.[2] Rachmaninoff's years at the conservatory took place in the original structure, but he visited with students and performed in the new, enlarged, and expanded building many times throughout his years in Russia.

Rachmaninoff was fortunate to embark on his musical training at a time when standards of musical education in Russia had become extremely high, and when he could study with such distinguished teachers as A. S. Arensky (1861–1906) and S. I. Taneev (1856–1915), who were themselves composers and performers. Both the St. Petersburg Conservatory and the Moscow Conservatory had been founded only a few years before Rachmaninoff's birth in 1873; it was serendipitous that his musical gifts could grow and flourish in such fertile soil. The highly respected cultural critic Vladimir Stasov recalled about the musical atmosphere of mid-nineteenth-century Russia: "Before the founding of the [St. Petersburg] conservatory musical education in Russia

Birth of a Composer-Pianist

Figure 3.2 Moscow Conservatory c. 1952. Public domain.

was generally of an amateurish quality. It is true, though, that the dilettantish making of music was very widespread—it was a necessary component of the most cultured kind of home schooling; pupils of gymnasia, institutes, and universities participated in it."[3] Not only was music-making available to Russians with an access to cultural education, but it was also a collaborative activity shared by people in the evenings when the day's work was finished, at celebrations, and as a way for young people to gather and become acquainted. N. D. Kashkin noted that even in the 1850s, "music in its highest forms had not yet become a regular part of our society."[4] Musicologist S. I. Savenko describes:

> Regular concerts did not take place, and in the programs of those that did occur virtuosic shorter genres or instrumental concerti were predominant. . . . The situation changed radically with the founding in 1859 of the Russian Music Society (RMS), headed in Moscow by N.G. Rubinstein. Serious symphonic music, which Moscow had not known before that time, and in which the city had not even been interested, quickly became a necessary staple of cultural life. Conservatories were expected to become a natural base in Russia for professionalism [in music].[5]

The development of Russian musical education and the establishment and evolution of the St. Petersburg and Moscow Conservatories were largely made possible by the activities of A. G. Rubinstein (1829–1894), N. G. Rubinstein (1835–1891), and P. I. Tchaikovsky (1840–1893). The specific identities of these three eminent figures can shed light on the Russian musical standards and education of their times, which laid the foundations for the musical career of Rachmaninoff. The two brothers Anton and Nikolay Rubinstein were closely connected with Petr Tchaikovsky. All three had spent time in Europe, either in formal study with the best music educators of the time or (in Anton's case) as the child prodigy concertizing and seeking further musical growth. All three understood the challenges facing Russian music and desired to establish Western classical music's presence on Russian soil—but reconstituted with the admixture of Russian musical sources and ideas.

The senior figure of this triumvirate chronologically, Anton Rubinstein, was fortunate after much struggle and privation both in Europe and Russia to gain the patronage of Grand Duchess Anna Pavlovna of Russia. During a winter respite from touring Europe as a pianist in 1856–1857 Rubinstein vacationed with the Grand Duchess and members of the Russian Imperial family in Nice. The conversations he held with Anna Pavlovna, who remained devoted to Russia all her life, illuminated a meeting of the minds concerning the raising of musical standards in the country native to both of them. Anna Pavlovna's patronage proved vital to Rubinstein's ability to support his musical work, as well as the formal establishment of the Russian Musical Society (RMS) two years later. The goals of this supremely important initiative were to raise the level of musical performance and literacy among the Russian public and to consolidate knowledge about Western classical music in Russia in order to develop high-quality training for Russian musicians in the native country. Music classes, including in theory, were held in the Mikhailovsky Palace (which now contains the collection of the Russian Museum). Rubinstein personally conducted the concerts of the RMS. Three years later in 1862, with the assistance of the Grand Duchess and the charter of the RMS, he was able to found the St. Petersburg Conservatory. The significance of this act cannot be overestimated, for before this institution of higher learning existed, talented Russian students seeking a musical education had only the two options of seeking a foreign tutor living in Russia or traveling to Europe for formal musical education. Rubinstein was made the conservatory's first director, maintaining oversight especially of the theory and piano curricula while himself teaching instrumentation and composition. He is ranked among the greatest pianists in the history of piano performance. In this context the reminder that Rachmaninoff's mother studied piano with Rubinstein at the conservatory, and what this would signify for the future cultivation of her son Sergei's musical gifts, underscores even further the importance of the conservatory for Russian musicians.

The second luminary, Petr Tchaikovsky, was raised in a somewhat unstable, though educated family and hence experienced an irregular path of musical development. As in many Russian families, he was given musical training at an early age, but also as was the custom in families of the lesser nobility, he was expected to aim for a career in public service. His study at the Imperial School of Jurisprudence in St. Petersburg, from which he graduated, was accompanied by continuing musical education and by attending the opera in the city with his musically inclined friends; in 1861 he had the opportunity to study music theory at the Mikhailovsky Palace with the talented theorist and composer Nikolay Zaremba (1821–1879). One year later, when the St. Petersburg Conservatory opened, Tchaikovsky enrolled in a full course of studies there; he graduated in 1865. This took place eight years before Rachmaninoff was born. As Tchaikovsky's musical knowledge evolved and his reputation as a composer grew, he, as Anton Rubinstein, was aided enormously by the patronage of a prominent noblewoman: in this case, it was Nadezhda von Meck, who remained his close friend and admirer in a relationship-in-correspondence that lasted for many years.[6]

Both Anton Rubinstein and Petr Tchaikovsky were to prove major links for the founding of the Moscow Conservatory in 1866, only four years after the establishment of its counterpart in St. Petersburg. Anton's equally talented brother Nikolay became the co-founder with him of this second Russian conservatory, and their young colleague Tchaikovsky participated in the opening ceremonies:

> On the first of September of 1866 the formal ceremony of the opening of the Moscow Conservatory took place. All of the city's newspapers had published an announcement of this event. One could read in it that the young professor of the new educational institute, Petr Ilyich Tchaikovsky, a recent graduate of the St. Petersburg Conservatory founded four years earlier, gave a salutatory speech and concluded it with the following wish: "May the first music that sounds in this new edifice of art be the music of Glinka." Then, having sat down at the piano, he brilliantly played the Overture to *Ruslan and Ludmila*.[7]

Let us say a few words about Nikolay Rubinstein, the third leading figure in Russian musical education, before resuming the presentation of Russian musical life in the mid- and late nineteenth century as it affected the development of Rachmaninoff. Nikolay Rubinstein, younger than Anton by six years, received fine musical training in Europe and participated along with his brother in the introduction of high-quality musical education into Russia. As a pianist, his style differed markedly from Anton's, and some contemporaries thought that in general he was the superior musician. Nikolay's pianism was more stable, consistent, and accurate—even more in the classical European mode of expression—than was his brother Anton's, which was dynamic, more spontaneous, and powerful. Both, however, possessed the same abiding commitment to improving musical life and education in Russia. At the St. Petersburg Conservatory Tchaikovsky had studied instrumentation and composition with Anton; he became very close friends with Nikolay. It was only natural that, when Anton and Nikolay embarked on the creation of a conservatory in Moscow, Nikolay would offer Petr the position of Professor of Music (specifically, of theory and harmony) there.

The growing professionalization of the practice of music in Russia was informed by two powerful intellectual and artistic currents. An understanding of them will explain in large part the artistic rivalry between the cities of Moscow and St. Petersburg that determined many of the decisions for collaboration and concertizing that Rachmaninoff would be compelled to make during his years in Russia. In the 1840s the immensely erudite and sophisticated debates in public and in writing between the so-called Slavophiles and Westernizers articulated major differences in approach and orientation to patriotism and devotion to Russia. The debates centered around whether Russia's identity should be integrated with Europe's or if Russia should follow her own path, which was organically set by her historical development. In these debates Moscow as the older city (founded in 1147) was frequently cast as more "Russian" than St. Petersburg (founded in 1703), which was artificially created by Peter I (the Great) to be more Western in appearance and sensibilities, and thus the less "Russian" of the two cities. This dichotomy of associations did not translate in its specifics into the field of music, but the belief in the differences between the two cities became canonical and continues to influence the affiliations of Russians to one or the other city to the present day.

In music the debate was framed as one of two recommended directions that Russian music should take: to integrate itself more fully into the older European tradition of classical musical forms and styles, or to evolve a distinctly Russian musical tradition that utilized relevant components of European music theory *in order to arrive at a genuinely native music* that also was bound up with Russian folk music, and Byzantine and Russian Orthodox chant. This split was sharpened with the advent of the St. Petersburg composers, called (by others, not by themselves) the *Moguchaia kuchka* (mighty heap) and led by composer Mily Balakirev (the remaining four consisting of César Cui, Modest Mussorgsky, Nikolay Rimsky-Korsakov, and Aleksandr Borodin). These composers were active from the mid-1850s to 1870, but their influence continued well into the late nineteenth century. All of them were self-taught: Balakirev, Mussorgsky, and Rimsky-Korsakov were noblemen, while Cui and Borodin were commoners. Their musical credo emphasized Russian music's development in line with the culture of the land and village. They advocated for a more native Russian music free of European influences; thus the city of St. Petersburg, the Western city, became associated with a Russian school of music aesthetics. The "mighty heap" desired to extend their compositions in directions away from the Western principles on which the study of music was based at the St. Petersburg Conservatory. Their antipathy to formal Western musical education embodied in both the St. Petersburg and Moscow conservatories opposed them to the main figures advocating a Western-based classical education for Russian musicians and composers—Anton and Nikolay Rubinstein and Petr Tchaikovsky. They were most mistaken about Tchaikovsky, who, though educated in Western musical theory and style, drew from his own childhood impressions of folk and Orthodox liturgical music to create a music that was Russian to the core.

The curriculum of both the St. Petersburg and Moscow conservatories included both music and other liberal arts courses, such as foreign languages (French and German) and Russian literature; the complete course of study lasted for seven to eight years. Even though the official admission age was fourteen, sometimes especially talented students were admitted at ages as young as eight or nine. An example is S. I. Taneev, a fine composer, pianist, and specialist in Bachian counterpoint, who auditioned for Anton Rubinstein at the age of nine and was immediately accepted to the Moscow Conservatory. Taneev would become one of the conservatory's beloved teachers and its director; his tenure there coincided with the years when Rachmaninoff was a student, and the two retained a genuine respect and affection for each other until Taneev's death in 1915.

In the spring of 1888 Rachmaninoff, along with two other excellent students of Zverev's Matvey Pressman and Leonid Maksimov, advanced into the upper levels of the Moscow Conservatory:

> Zverev tried to get [his three students] into Siloti's piano class. He considered that Siloti, himself a Zverev disciple and fresh from his triumphs as Liszt's favored pupil, deserved only the best material. . . . Rachmaninoff would have preferred the piano class of Safonov (where Pressman went) to [studying] with his own cousin, Siloti, but Zverev was in command.
>
> At the end of this school year there was another choice to be made—once more, not *by* Rachmaninoff, but *for* him. In advancing into the senior section of the theory class, students were here divided into those who were to work in "general theory" or in "special theory," and it was clear that anyone recommended for the latter category was considered a potential composer. By the end of his junior course Rachmaninoff had made an excellent impression on his teacher Arensky with the harmonizing of simple melodies.[8]

The final examinations that spring were made even more stressful, but exciting by the announcement that Tchaikovsky would be present and would hear some of the examinations. Rachmaninoff's account of his examination in Arensky's course in harmony, which started at 9 a.m., has been widely publicized; his remarks made to Oskar von Riesemann portray a critical juncture for his career and further solidify the musical and personal bond between him and Tchaikovsky:

When all candidates had turned in their work . . . I alone was left, for I had got entangled in a daring modulation of the prélude and could find no satisfactory solution. At last—by five o'clock—I had finished, and handed my two pages to Arensky. When he glanced at them he did not frown, and this gave me some hope.

On the following day the board was to hear us play our own work. When I had finished my turn, Arensky mentioned to Tchaikovsky that I had written some piano pieces in ternary song form for his class, and asked whether or not he would care to hear them. Tchaikovsky nodded his assent, and I sat down to play my pieces, for I knew them by heart. When I had finished I saw Tchaikovsky go over to the examination record and write something on it.[9]

The examining board of the conservatory had given Rachmaninoff a "5 plus" on his harmony examination, which was the highest grade attainable. What Tchaikovsky had entered into Sergei's record, which Rachmaninoff learned from Arensky not until two weeks later, were three additional plus signs above, below, and beside the "5" assigned by the board. That spring the wife of Tchaikovsky's brother Mme Anatol Tchaikovsky noted that, in reflecting on the accomplishments of some of the young composers whose works he had heard, Tchaikovsky predicted that Rachmaninoff would make a distinguished contribution to music.[10] The bond of respect and affection between the older and younger composers would be unbroken.

By this singular affirmation of Rachmaninoff's budding talents, the most important Russian composer of the Romantic era had anointed his successor. At some of Zverev's gatherings, at which his students-in-residence were expected to play for the guests present, Tchaikovsky had had the opportunity to hear Rachmaninoff play several times. Thus he had followed the young Sergei's progress and very likely had been impressed with his pianism, memory, improvisation, and overall demeanor. Tchaikovsky's act of adding the plus signs to Rachmaninoff's examination grade was not an impulsive or casual one: it was thoughtfully considered and, judging by his subsequent, generous attempts to help Rachmaninoff at the early stages of his career, intended to attract the maximum amount of attention at the conservatory to the potential of Sergei as a composer and pianist. It also guaranteed that in the fall of 1888 Rachmaninoff would be a student in [Sergei Ivanovich] Taneev's first-year counterpoint class—which would represent the starting point on his journey to becoming a composer.

Rachmaninoff would study with the same teachers for a number of years, and in this regard what he was receiving was nothing less than an entire musical legacy of the Romantic era of classical music in Europe and Russia. The content of his courses, especially the upper levels at the Moscow Conservatory, would include polyphony, harmony, counterpoint, the history of notation, analysis of musical pieces, solfège (pitch and sight-singing), orchestration, and instrumentation. His professors were accomplished musicians and pedagogues: they had either studied in Europe themselves or had been students of musicians who had been educated in Europe, and their compositions were being performed regularly in major European cities; if they themselves were also conductors, they were invited to conduct their works in Europe. Authoritative evidence of this activity comes from archival materials at Teatro alla Scala in Milan; a perusal of concert information of the years 1870–1930 reveals a pattern of reoccurring performance of compositions of Tchaikovsky, Arensky, Taneev, Safonov, Siloti, Koussevitsky, and others.[11] Further evidence is provided by concert programs of the period housed in Royal Albert Hall in London.[12] In addition to the aforementioned subjects, Orthodox liturgical music was taught at the Moscow Conservatory by the director of the Moscow Synodal School Stepan Smolensky, and Rachmaninoff attended these classes.[13] Thus his musical training at the Moscow Conservatory would establish his place in a long line of towering figures of classical music; this would set his lineage at the highest levels of the musical aristocracy and become his pedigree, along with the document of his graduation diploma from the conservatory.

Rachmaninoff stayed with each professor for at least two years. With patient Arensky he studied harmony, theory, fugue, and free composition; he was in Arensky's classes for a total of five years. He studied counterpoint in Taneev's famous classes for two years, inheriting from that master teacher and theorist the tradition of precision and deep knowledge of the principles of counterpoint that had come down from the time of Bach. With his enormously talented cousin Siloti he would study piano for two-and-one-half years. Rachmaninoff's study with Siloti took place against the background of a serious rift between Siloti and Safonov that would grow and eventually explode. In the fall of 1888, after his memorable success during the final examinations of the previous spring, Rachmaninoff had decided to have two majors, piano and special theory (for future composers). He was studying harmony with Arensky, counterpoint with Taneev, and piano with Siloti. His quarrel with Zverev had not yet taken place; that would come the following year, in 1889. After the conflict with Zverev, Rachmaninoff tried to reconcile several times with him, but Zverev ceased to speak to him until the time of his graduation. During the academic year 1890–1891 an even more serious event would take place that would directly affect Rachmaninoff's plans at the conservatory. The actors in it were Siloti, Taneev, Tchaikovsky (tangentially), and Safonov.

Aleksandr Siloti was an extraordinary musical figure whose talents were cultivated by Liszt and Tchaikovsky; he had experienced success in his twenties as a concert pianist and conductor in such leading cities of Europe as Berlin, Prague, and Leipzig. In the summer of 1888 Siloti and his wife Vera (the daughter of the wealthy and famous art patron P. M. Tretiakov

[1832–1898]) left Leipzig, where they had been living, and returned to Moscow. They were homesick for Russia, and excellent opportunities awaited them in the musical and cultural world there. In addition to his deep love for conducting and especially arranging music (he became the most trusted arranger and editor of Tchaikovsky's compositions), Siloti was interested in teaching and organizing the concerts of the leading composers of Europe and Russia. The emotional ties the Silotis had with Moscow and the network of professional associates and friends that awaited them there can be glimpsed in the following account:

> [Siloti] had also heard about the final illness of his Conservatory theory teacher Nikolay Hubert and wanted to be there to help him and his family. And, he had accepted an invitation from director Sergei Taneyev to join the senior piano faculty at the Moscow Conservatory, beginning with the fall sessions that year. The other faculty members would be Pavel Pabst (1854–1897) and Vasily Safonov (1852–1918). On July 17 [1888], along with [Konstantin Karlovich] Albrecht, [Petr Ivanovich] Jurgenson, and [Herman Augustovich] Laroche, Siloti attended a party given by Tchaikovsky at his home in Frolovskoe, where congratulations were offered on his new appointment.[14]

Siloti would teach at the conservatory for the last year of Sergei Taneev's expert directorship (1888–1889); his second year there would be spent under its new director Vasily Safonov, whose egotistical and overbearing personality would alienate him and other musical colleagues in a devastating conflict of personalities and musical styles.[15]

Sergei Taneev—an individual of immense erudition, extraordinarily talented pianist, first-rate composer, professor of counterpoint, and with a personality of the highest integrity—had joined the Moscow Conservatory in the fall of 1878 and established himself as a teacher adored by his students, and as a professor admired and respected by his colleagues at the musical institution. His perfect integrity, legendary work ethic, overall broad learnedness, and strong administrative skills made him the obvious choice to succeed the previous director, the unpopular and disorganized Konstantin Karlovich Albrecht (1836–1893). Anton Rubinstein had attempted to persuade Tchaikovsky to accept the post of the new director, but the latter respectfully turned down this offer. Instead, Tchaikovsky enthusiastically endorsed Taneev for the honor of the director's position. Taneev, who had by then worked as a professor at the conservatory for eight years, accepted the offer, although with some legitimate concerns and reservations. He was only twenty-eight at the time, but he would prove an able, principled, and well-organized director who strengthened the curriculum of the conservatory and maintained high standards for both the professorial staff and the students. He served as director from the fall of 1885 to the spring of

1889. During his tenure as director, he was widely admired and respected for his honesty, musical talent, scholarly ways, and congenial personality. The first four of Sergei Rachmaninoff's last five years at the conservatory would coincide with Taneev's directorship there, which resulted in those years being well-ordered and professionally beneficial for him. The assessment by Taneev's famous contemporary Tchaikovsky of the former's first year as director reveals his deep satisfaction at Taneev's accomplishments that year:

> "The first year of your directorship passed not only satisfactorily, but even brilliantly. . . . But I don't know if it was good for you personally to have accepted this burden, and under pressure from me. This is the question before me, and moreover, one that seriously concerns me. I am worried about your health and about the fact that you are torn away from your own studies," wrote Tchaikovsky to Taneev. Tchaikovsky was always sensitive and attentive to the existential and creative feelings of his younger friend.[16]

In May of 1889 Taneev resigned as director of the conservatory, remaining in the position of professor of counterpoint there until 1905.

As noted above, Siloti had worked happily during his first year at the conservatory, which was also Taneev's last. Siloti's personality differences with Safonov started soon after he began teaching there:

> one problem was looming that could not be laughed away. From his first weeks at the Conservatory, Siloti had gradually entered a deep conflict with colleague Vasily Safonov. They disagreed about everything, although initially they tried to keep their disputes private.
>
> When Taneyev decided to resign as conservatory director in 1889 in order to devote more time to composition, he joined with the faculty in choosing the energetic Safonov as his successor. Taneyev called Safonov for a meeting in order to give him the news, and later told pianist Aleksandr Goldenweisser what happened.
>
> "Taneyev invited Safonov to the huge office on the first floor to tell him of his appointment. The telephone on the desk rang, and Safonov picked up the receiver and said, 'Conservatory director speaking.' 'And you know,' Taneyev said, 'it was the first time I realized we had picked the wrong man.'"[17]

Though an extremely talented pianist and conductor, Safonov "had the temper of a wolverine, and was hopelessly addicted to personal power."[18] Even though his initiatives and accomplishments at the conservatory were successful—"[h]e raised funds, improved facilities, and attracted students"[19]—his personality was inflexible and domineering. Safonov was used to getting his own way, lacking the delicacy of manner and tact essential for bringing out the best qualities and loyalty of the sensitive, creative musicians who were on the faculty of the conservatory and dependent on his leadership.

In addition to permanently alienating Siloti, Safonov's manner upset Tchaikovsky to the point that the latter—always the gracious and kind gentleman—decided to resign as director of the Russian Musical Society, which managed the affairs of the Moscow Conservatory. In a letter to Siloti Tchaikovsky, "After praising [Safonov] as a person . . . discloses that he [Tchaikovsky] has many policy and hiring conflicts with him."[20] Tchaikovsky stepped down as director of the RMS in February 1890, "reasoning that the Society needed Safonov more than it needed him and wanting in any case to avoid a public show of friction between the two."[21]

Some of the personality differences between Safonov and Siloti that led to their break, one affecting Rachmaninoff's development as a student, can be viewed in the following description:

> Safonov's reactionary views about administration, teaching, and repertoire were hardened by a tyrannical manner toward subordinates. Siloti, by contrast, tended toward liberal ideas and collegial consultation.
>
> Even more troubling, Siloti and Safonov were incompatible personalities with conflicting agendas. Each wanted the strongest piano students. It was a hard point of antipathy that Safonov had assigned a particularly gifted female student to his own class instead of Siloti's, over her own objections. Safonov also conducted the orchestra, and Siloti wanted podium time, which the director refused to grant. And they differed on pedagogy. Reconciliation proved impossible. Siloti handed in his resignation, effective at the end of the school year in the spring of 1891. Their feud would last for years and would even affect Rachmaninoff's early career.[22]

Because Rachmaninoff planned to graduate with two majors, piano and special theory, and because his piano professor Siloti's withdrawal from the conservatory would take place with one year left before his intended graduation in spring of 1892, he had to consider his options. To spend his final year studying piano with a different professor would prove traumatic and even potentially destructive for a piano student already formed by years of training with a specific method—and his training had cultivated in him the tradition passed from Liszt to Siloti, representing the brilliant pedagogical and piano performance practices of the second half of the nineteenth century. This was not a casual consideration. Thus he arrived at a daring course of action, at some risk to his personal success: he decided to ask Safonov for permission to complete his major in piano in spring of 1891, which would mean that he would finish his studies in this instrument with the same professor with whom he began—Siloti. He petitioned Safonov for permission, and it was granted, in large part because the latter viewed him more as a composer rather than a pianist. For his piano examination Sergei was assigned Beethoven's Sonata in C major (Op. 53, the *Waldstein*) and the first movement of Chopin's Sonata in B minor; both he and Siloti were pleased when they learned that Sergei had passed the examination with honors.[23]

Thus, with his piano major completed and having passed his other examinations in the spring of 1891, Rachmaninoff could look forward to spending a relatively peaceful summer at Ivanovka, his relatives' estate located to the south of Moscow several hours' drive from the provincial city of Tambov. During this summer he would complete his first large-scale work, the First Concerto in F-sharp minor, for piano and orchestra. This was his Opus 1, and it was dedicated with gratitude to his cousin and teacher Aleksandr Siloti. He had begun work on the first movement in the summer of 1890 and had performed this movement as soloist with the orchestra of the Moscow Conservatory, conducted by V. I. Safonov on March 17, 1891. At rehearsals of this first major piece, Rachmaninoff's self-assurance as a composer and enormous talent were made manifest, while his distinction among upper-level students at the conservatory was becoming more noticeable: "At the première of his First Concerto he confidently overruled the conductor, the fearsome martinet Safonov, who happened also to be the conservatoire's Director; twice he was granted special dispensation to bypass graduation requirements, as Scriabin was not; his graduation opera *Aleko* made his name famous overnight . . ."[24] Four days after the première, in the major Moscow newspaper *Moskovskie vedomosti* on March 21 the review of the concert was encouraging:

> The student Rachmaninoff of Arensky's class deserves particular attention: he performed the first movement of a piano concerto of his own composition. Although it is true that in this musical work one can discern echoes of some new composers, still the concerto bears witness to the indisputable and extremely promising talent of its author, who during the current year will complete his studies in composition and thus will embark on the path of independent creative work.[25]

That summer the seventeen-year-old Rachmaninoff finished the concerto at the Satins' estate of Ivanovka, the most inspiring place for him to be creative and experience a sense of well-being. This medium-sized country dwelling (about one hundred acres), with its gardens, outbuildings, and stark, yet beautiful landscape of steppes and occasional stands of oak trees, would grow dearer to Rachmaninoff with the years. He wrote to his friend and fellow musician Mikhail Slonov (composer of art songs and choral works) on July 20, 1891, that his work of composing and scoring his piano concerto was finished. This work proceeded intensively, as Sergei had worked from early morning until late in the evening to bring the whole on July 6 to a satisfying close. Afterward he was exhausted, but felt tremendous satisfaction in composing a first large-scale work in a musical genre for which he experienced a powerful stirring.[26]

Rachmaninoff's letter to Slonov provides evidence of his work ethic, and also of the way in which aesthetic inspiration typically came to him: the concept and flow of each composition would come as a whole, all at once, and he would have to write the musical thoughts down as quickly as possible. He would describe this process more than once in future years. For a young composer to create and write down two entire movements of a concerto in two-and-one-half days, even with the help of an able friend, represents a remarkable achievement by any measure. This concerto would become a permanent part of his repertoire: he would revise it in 1917. For many years the revised version would be the one performed; Geoffrey Norris points out:

> The differences between the 1890–1 and the revised 1917 versions of the concerto reveal much about the composer's development during the quarter-century which separate [sic] them. There is a considerable thinning of the texture, both in the orchestral and in the piano writing, and also the material which tended to make the early version diffuse and episodic is excised.[27]

The thinner texture and tighter piano writing notwithstanding, toward the latter half of the twentieth century increasingly the original was chosen as both the stronger version and as the version most representative of Rachmaninoff's creative genius.

An analysis of the musical elements and gestures of Concerto No. 1 elucidates not only Rachmaninoff's courage and talent in composing a work in such a large-scale form, but also contextualizes his achievement in an environment of a dearth of Russian models from which he could draw inspiration:

> Surprisingly few Russian piano concertos existed before Rachmaninoff's. Tchaikovsky's First Concerto (1874) had been preceded only by Rubinstein's five (1854–1874), of which the Fourth and Fifth were popular items in the concerto repertoire, Rachmaninoff himself performing the first movement of the Fourth in February 1891 at a student concert and again in September the following year at the Moscow Electrical Exhibition. But the Tchaikovsky marked a dramatic advance on Rubinstein's Mendelssohnian lyricism, establishing not only an authentic Russian voice but a new kind of bold grandiloquence . . . Rachmaninoff's teachers, Taneyev and Arensky, disciples of Tchaikovsky, had both tried their hand at writing a piano concerto. Taneyev's, dating from 1876–77, was never completed, but Arensky's, published in 1881 as his Op. 2, was one of the works which had launched him on his career as a composer, and he may well have suggested to Rachmaninoff that he should tackle the same musical form at this early stage of his career; indeed, there may be just a hint of

correspondence between the openings of the slow movements of the Arensky and Rachmaninoff concertos in their melodic lines and scoring.[28]

Since the Mighty Heap in St. Petersburg was composing mainly in the genre of opera, their influence on Rachmaninoff's First Concerto cannot be felt—even though Rachmaninoff maintained to the end of his life that *both* Tchaikovsky *and* Rimsky-Korsakov had affected his musical evolution in equally positive ways.

Interestingly, the concerto that may have influenced Rachmaninoff's first one most of all was the Grieg concerto in A minor (op. 16)—because Siloti was also at Ivanovka in the summer of 1891 and was practicing that concerto regularly. In Rachmaninoff's concerto, "both its [the Grieg concerto] Lisztian rhetoric and elements of its formal design left their mark."[29] It is possible that if Rachmaninoff had not had the Grieg concerto in his ears, with its Lisztian elements discernible in Siloti's playing (and we must recall that Siloti had studied with Liszt), his concerto would have evolved with an entirely different musical content. These influences notwithstanding, because of Tchaikovsky's enormous personal as well as musical impact on the young Rachmaninoff, it would be hard to imagine that he did not also take the Tchaikovsky Piano Concerto No. 1 in B flat minor—a piece to which Siloti was devoted and one he frequently performed—into consideration when working on his own First Concerto. A brief analysis of some of the main features of the concerto's three movements yields the following:

> The concerto opens impressively with an imperious fanfare and a cascade of triplet quavers [eighth notes] in double octaves for the soloist. The idea is not original, for not only the Grieg but also the Liszt in E flat and Schumann concertos open with similar flourishes, but Rachmaninoff's gestures are altogether his own. Nor are they empty gestures, for the descending triplet figure is closely integrated into the movement's fabric, prefiguring . . . the end of the first theme.
>
> The cadenza to the movement is particularly noteworthy. It neatly incorporates all the concerto's main material—the descending quaver figure from the development and the two main themes, in reverse order. It is prophetic of the mature composer in that when the soloist comes to muse over the wistful second theme, the music modulates to the calm of Rachmaninoff's so often favourite key of D flat. . . . the piano writing . . . already demonstrates an intimate understanding of the instrument's possibilities.[30]

Concerning the last two movements:

> The second movement, an *andante cantabile* in D major, is a beautiful nocturne, in mood at least again possibly showing the general influence of Grieg's concerto. The melody is first sung by the piano and then by the orchestra, while the

soloist spins an exquisite decoration in the triplet quavers that so often appear in Rachmaninoff's early works. . . . [In the third and final movement] [a]fter a tentatively quiet introduction in 12/8 time, the piano launches into a wild dance in 9/8, in which added interest comes from the intriguingly disjointed interjection of one bar of waltz rhythm back in 12/8. Two other themes appear in the course of the movement . . . Rachmaninoff uses the lyrical third theme for the final grand climax, creating a precedent for the treatment of parallel themes in the same position in his later concertos.[31]

In this first large-scale composition of Rachmaninoff's there exists a youthful freshness and vitality, even a purposeful playfulness and confidence that would give way in his next concerto—the famous second concerto known all over the world—to melancholy, wistfulness, and sadness, even as the emotional power of its first movement and exquisite beauty of its second would indicate significant growth in Rachmaninoff as a composer.

Rachmaninoff's so-called student works were composed during the years 1887–1892. An examination of their titles and genres reveals much about Rachmaninoff's education in the humanities and Russian / European culture at the Moscow Conservatory. It also establishes the predominant directions into which he was drawn in musical aesthetics, which drew from his ethnic and religious roots as well as European classical music. Rachmaninoff was clearly drawn to Russian and Western literature (of all genres, since his compositions connect with poetry, prose fiction, and drama), Western and Russian opera, Russian folklore, and Russian liturgical chant. He experimented in many forms, as would be expected of a student striving to find his own artistic voice; he composed both instrumental and vocal pieces, writing in large- and small-scale genres. Some examples of his early musical works and their extra-musical origins include: two movements for string quartet—Romance, Scherzo (1889, Western classical music); *Deus Meus*, motet (1890, Western classical choral music); "At the Gate of the Holy Abode," text by Mikhail Lermontov (1890, art song, influenced by Russian Orthodox beliefs); *Manfred*, from poem by Byron (1890, unfinished symphonic work, English literature); Valse and Romance (1890–1891, piano trio, Western classical music); *Prince Rostislav*, from poem by Alexei Tolstoy (1891, tone poem for orchestra, Russian mythology); *Boris Godunov*, from play by Pushkin (undated, vocal work, Russian literature and history); "Grianem-ukhnem," traditional Russian boatmen's song (1891, Russian folklore); *Mazepa*, from poem *Poltava* by Pushkin (undated, vocal quartet, Ukrainian Cossack history); Trio élégiaque for piano, violin, and cello in G minor (1892, Western and Russian classical music); and *Aleko*, from the poem by Pushkin on gypsy culture (1892, Western and Russian opera). The aforementioned musical works, even when examined cursorily, reveal the full range of Rachmaninoff's education in European and Russian music, European and Russian literature (especially of the Romantic period), Russian history, Russian folklore, and Russian Orthodoxy.[32]

Rachmaninoff's musical works of this period, two compositions for orchestra and an opera (his graduation piece), establish his expert handling of orchestral and vocal challenges and also affirm his artistic connections to Russian culture of the past. The first work, a one-movement Youth Symphony, was completed in September 1891. The second was the tone poem for orchestra *Prince Rostislav*; it was finished in December of the same year. The tone poem's subject matter was taken both from an episode in Russia's greatest medieval literary work *Slovo o Polku Igoreve* (The Lay of the Host of Igor, twelfth century) and a poem by Aleksey Konstantinovich Tolstoy (1856) of the same title as Rachmaninoff's composition. The orchestration of this piece sensitively uses the specific musical qualities of each instrument to portray the prince's flight from the enemy and drowning in the Stuhna River, marvelous awakening at the bottom of the river, attempts to call out to his wife and other loved ones, and final resignation to his fate of a watery grave.

In the spring of 1892 Rachmaninoff's father had moved to Moscow and rented an apartment for both of them. With the assistance of some friends, he had found work as a specialist in horses. During this period Sergei's family circumstances affected his peace of mind considerably. He felt somewhat closer to his father, perhaps because of Vasily Arkadievich's cheerful personality, but he also loved his mother deeply and felt comforted when she was nearby as well. The bond between his parents was irretrievably broken: Rachmaninoff's father had entered into a relationship with another woman and had started a new family, while his mother was still struggling with her own basic material needs and providing for her children:

> With some success coming to him Rachmaninoff did not forget about his mother. Liubov Rachmaninova who sometimes did not have money for firewood writes with gratitude in 1890: "Seryozha already helps me from his modest earnings [giving private lessons and recitals]." He also helped his father's new family where his half-brother was growing up.[33]

It was at this apartment that Sergei completed, at lightning speed, his opera *Aleko*, which was the graduation examination assignment in theory. The one-act opera, with a libretto by Vladimir Nemirovich-Danchenko provided for the students on March 26, was due several weeks later. Rachmaninoff finished it on April 13; his strong connection with gypsy culture enabled him to immerse himself in the topic and finish it so quickly. Moreover, perhaps his own secret desire to escape from his own troubles to the perceived life of freedom of the gypsies contributed to his heightened involvement in the composition of its music. The opera came from Pushkin's narrative poem *The Gypsies* (1824). As Claudio Monteverdi before him in Italy in the sixteenth–seventeenth centuries, Rachmaninoff experimented with short vocal works of deep dramatic content—music served the words—and in his compositions gradually expanded this technique to the genre of opera.

The opera's plot is uncomplicated, yet with obvious dramatic possibilities, engaging the universal themes in art of freedom, love, and death. The opera opens with a scene of gypsies settling down for the night near a riverbank. One of the older gypsies relates a sad story from his past: he loved Mariula, who was the mother of their daughter Zemfira, but she left him for another man. Aleko, a man not of the gypsies but who has joined them and is living with Zemfira, is upset by the old man's story. He feels that the old man should have exacted some sort of revenge on Mariula. Zemfira opposes this thought, pointing out that gypsies are free to love whomever they wish—this reveals that she has grown tired of Aleko. Zemfira has fallen in love with a younger gypsy. The following morning Aleko finds Zemfira with her new gypsy lover and kills both of them. The gypsies decide, according to their code of ways, that Aleko should leave their community. The opera ends with heart-wrenching, dark musical motifs as the agonized Aleko reluctantly leaves the gypsies to return to his own "civilized" world.

The final examination for theory took place at the conservatory on May 7, a major event for the music faculty and students at that institution. After Rachmaninoff had finished playing through his opera *Aleko*, Zverev, evidently moved by the music and the momentousness of the occasion, came up to him and warmly congratulated him. He gave Rachmaninoff his gold watch, a gift Rachmaninoff kept and treasured for the rest of his life. Zverev did even more than this: he hosted a postgraduation dinner ostensibly in honor of the graduates, but in reality to celebrate his reconnection with his former student, and he enlisted Tchaikovsky's assistance to help Rachmaninoff land his first contract with the publisher Gutheil.

Rachmaninoff graduated from the Moscow Conservatory on May 29, 1892. It was in this world of competing musical aesthetics and shifting political winds that he would make his way as a future composer, conductor, and virtuoso pianist.

NOTES

1. See Tatyana Klevantseva, "Prominent Russians: Ekaterina Dashkova," https://russiapedia.rt.com/prominent-russians/history-and-mythology/ekaterina-dashkova/, accessed June 14, 2022.

2. See Aleksandr Ivanov, "Istoriia moskovskoi konservatorii" (April 20, 2016), http://moscowwalks.ru/2016/04/20/moscow-conservatorium/; and "The Grand Hall

of the Moscow Conservatory," https://www.mosconsv.ru/museum/english/bzk.html, accessed June 14, 2022.

3. S.I. Savenko, *Sergei Ivanovich Taneev* (Moscow: Muzyka, 1984), 15, trans. VZN. No source is cited for the recollections of the eminent critic V.V. Stasov.

4. Ibid., 15, trans. VZN.

5. Ibid., 15–16, trans. VZN. Russkoe muzykal'noe obshchestvo (RMO).

6. Their absorbing correspondence reveals much about their close bond, as well as life in Catherine Drinker Bowen, *Beloved Friend: The Story of Tchaikowsky and Nadejda von Meck* (Mineola, NY: Dover Publications, 1946; rept., Westport, CT: Greenwood, 1975).

7. S.I. Savenko, 15, trans. VZN.

8. Sergei Bertensson and Jay Leyda, *Sergei Rachmaninoff: A Lifetime in Music* (New York: New York UP, 1956; repr., Bloomington, IN: Indiana UP, 2001), 17, emphasis original.

9. Ibid., 18.

10. Ibid., paraphrase of 19.

11. Author's archival work at La Scala, Milan, June 2014.

12. Author's research in Royal Albert Hall, London, May 2014.

13. See Barrie Martyn, *Rachmaninoff: Composer, Pianist, Conductor* (Burlington, VT: Ashgate Publishing Co., 1990), 254.

14. Rosa Harriet Newmarch, *Tchaikovsky: His Life and Work* (NY: Greenwood Press, 1969), 564, quoted in Charles F. Barber, *Lost in the Stars: The Forgotten Musical Life of Alexander Siloti* (Lanham, MD: Scarecrow Press, 2002), 37.

15. One story about Safonov's appointment as director of the conservatory held that Safonov's family was rich and influential, and the conservatory needed a second floor—which was constructed with various kinds of assistance provided by his family. I thank V. I. Antipov, preeminent Rachmaninoff scholar and graduate of the Moscow Conservatory, for sharing this (at least partial) explanation for Safonov's appointment to the top position of that institution.

16. S.I. Savenko, 75, trans. VZN.

17. Dmitry Paperno, *Notes of a Moscow Pianist* (Portland, OR: Amadeus Press, 1998), 65, quoted in Charles F. Barber, *Lost in the Stars: The Forgotten Musical Life of Aleksandr Siloti*, 47.

18. Barber, 48.

19. Ibid.

20. Barber, 43.

21. Ibid.

22. Barber, 48.

23. Bertensson and Leyda, paraphrase of 33.

24. Martyn, 22–23.

25. E. Dmitrievskaia and V. Dmitrievskii, *Rakhmaninov v Moskve* (Moscow: Moskovskii rabochii, 1993), 34, trans. VZN.

26. Bertensson and Leyda, paraphrase of 36–37.

27. Geoffrey Norris, *Rachmaninoff* (New York: Oxford University Press, 2001), 106–107.

28. Martyn, 49.
29. Ibid.
30. Martyn, 51.
31. Ibid., 51–52.
32. See Bertensson and Leyda, 402–19, for a detailed chronological list of Rachmaninoff's compositions.
33. Natalia Ostrom, Untitled liner notes, *Rachmaninov Plays and Conducts*, Vista Vera VVCD-00023 (1999), vol. 2: 6, compact disc. No further information is available concerning Rachmaninoff's half-brother.

Chapter 4

Birth of a Conductor
(1893–1910)

The end of the nineteenth century and early years of the twentieth were eventful for Rachmaninoff in both professional and personal contexts. He had matured as a musician, having established himself in the music capitals of Russia as a leading pianist and young composer whose creative gifts were more than apparent, and having earned the most prestigious credentials available at that time in Russia—his "document," as the Russians would put it (meaning: his diploma from the Moscow Conservatory, with the highest honors in piano and composition, and the rare award of the Great Gold Medal). He was poised to embark on a magnificent career. He had weathered the death of his much-admired and loved musical mentor Tchaikovsky on October 25, 1893 (Old Style), several months after his graduation, and was testing the waters of his personal life in the form of rewarding connections with people who would remain important to him throughout his life.

This period would represent one of a number of major transitions that Rachmaninoff would be compelled to make in his life. The unexpected death of Tchaikovsky was especially traumatic for him, because of the distinguished composer's loving attention and crucial mentorship in the fledgling stages of Rachmaninoff's career. Tchaikovsky enjoyed a unique authority among Russian composers, being deeply admired, much respected, and generally well-liked. He occupied a special place in Rachmaninoff's inner world; quite simply, Rachmaninoff adored Tchaikovsky and basked in the special attention his mentor had lavished on him when he most needed it. The official narrative of Tchaikovsky's death held that he died from drinking a glass of unboiled water in a reputable restaurant during a cholera epidemic. Differing accounts began to emerge in the months and years after the composer's death that he as a conflicted homosexual had committed suicide or had even been poisoned. The cause of his death continues to be contested to this day.

Tchaikovsky's death prompted Rachmaninoff's creative springs to begin flowing in an outpouring of grief: he composed a *Trio élégiaque* in D minor for piano, violin, and cello, dating its gestation as October 25 to December 15, 1893. He added the inscription, "In Memory of a Great Artist"; by contributing this work to the many memorials in honor of Tchaikovsky, Rachmaninoff also modeled it on Tchaikovsky's own Piano Trio in A minor—which he had composed in honor of his own mentor Nikolay Rubinstein after the latter's death in 1881. The *Trio élégiaque* was first performed on January 31, 1894, in Moscow by Rachmaninoff, Julius Conius, and Anatoly Brandukov. Rachmaninoff wrote to Natalia Skalon on December 17, 1893, describing the upsurge in emotion and creative stirrings he experienced during the process of composing this tribute to his mentor, how carefully he had crafted every phrase of the piece, and how important his solitude was for the compositional process and healing of his emotions.[1] As would be characteristic of Rachmaninoff for the rest of his life, he sculpted and shaped his most genuine feelings into a musical form that expressed what he preferred not to convey in words.

During the years 1900–1902 Rachmaninoff established two major relationships in his life that would provide the emotional stability he had lacked in his childhood and adolescence. His acquaintance with Feodor Ivanovich Chaliapin (1873–1938) through their artistic collaboration, initially at the Private Opera Company of the industrialist and entrepreneur Savva Mamontov (1841–1918) and later in many prominent musical projects, would grow into a deeply rooted friendship that came to an end only because of Chaliapin's death in 1938. The second major relationship is Rachmaninoff's familial connection since his teens with Natalia Aleksandrovna Satina (1877–1951), which would develop into a successful marriage in 1902 that would last a lifetime. Rachmaninoff's relationship with and marriage to Natalia Satina will be discussed in greater depth in the next chapter.

A few words about the entrepreneur Savva Ivanovich Mamontov (1841–1918) are in order, for he served as a magnet for much of the Moscow theater world, and his contributions to musical life in that city not only were innovative but also provided a creative alternative to the more traditional and conservative Imperial Theatres. It was through Mamontov's Private Opera that Rachmaninoff and Chaliapin met and formed the bond that would enrich them and the international world of the arts. Mamontov himself was one of the wealthiest men in Russia due to his business pursuits: he was a railway magnate who built major railroads and roads critical to the country's development—and he was totally devoted to art. He possessed a good singing voice, was well educated in the arts, and had a keen eye for talent in others. Most importantly, he had that rare ability to encourage, even urge others with artistic gifts to develop them further, in part because he also had the financial means to provide anything that was needed for talent to thrive. And he supported not only opera singers and musicians: some of Russia's most important painters, such as Vasily Polenov, Ilya Repin, and Valentin Serov, were hired by Mamontov to produce costume sketches or set designs for his productions.

Theater and music professionals gravitated to Mamontov's independent opera on the outskirts of Moscow to experience complete artistic freedom; if he hired them, they became part of a dynamic collective whose members lived, vacationed, and worked together in ways that helped each one to gain invaluable experience in theater and opera. The opportunity for an artist to explore various creative approaches to an operatic role, or set design, or work of music was understandably a huge relief and source of exhilaration at the same time. By contrast, the approaches to staging a play or opera in the Imperial Theatres remained bound by tradition, by how the given work "was always performed." Mamontov loved the stage and came to life when creating a new production of an opera:

> He was extremely demanding, and could keep the singers on stage for hours, until a scene worked exactly as planned: the dress rehearsal of *Sadko* went on until dawn. At the same time, his charisma, enthusiasm, and brilliant demonstrations inspired the cast, resulting in few complaints.[2]

Mamontov was admired and respected by the arts community in Russia. His abiding passion for all the arts, business acumen, and talents for bringing together the finest artists of the day by means of his vast financial resources were virtually unique in late nineteenth- and early twentieth-century Moscow. Borovsky details:

> He had cultivated his many natural gifts to become an expert in various spheres of creative work. In his youth he had practised sculpture, studied to be a singer and a pianist, written plays and opera libretti. He had tried his hand at acting, taking part in a number of amateur productions. . . . He was chairman of several railway boards and owned factories and banks.[3]

Mamontov's holistic, even revolutionary conception of what stage direction should be involved a thorough preparation for each participant in an opera that included knowledge of the history, culture, and other aesthetic features relevant to the given project. Rachmaninoff's and Chaliapin's own detailed and knowledgeable approach to art would be formed and reinforced by Mamontov's sensitivity to all aspects of the artistic work.[4]

To the occasional frustration of Rachmaninoff, however, Mamontov's kindness and artistic sensitivity to others' opinions could be a negative quality; in a letter to his cousin Liudmila Skalon he provides a vivid description of working with Mamontov:

> Our misfortune is that our main financial supporters are either not particularly intelligent people when it comes to music, or they are not particularly honest. It is also a problem that we are managed not by one leader, but rather ten leaders, and moreover each one states his own opinion, but it differs from the opinion of

another [of the leaders]. But worst of all is that S. Mamontov is himself indecisive and falls prey to everybody's opinions. For example, I had him so excited about the possibility of staging *Manfred* that right on the spot he gave the order to program this opera. Not even five minutes had passed when his friend the artist Korovin, who does not understand anything about music (but who, incidentally, is a very congenial and good person, as is S. Mamontov), talked him out of it. Let's say that I'll try to influence him to look favorably on the project.

If only Chaliapin would agree not to sing, but rather to speak [when necessary in the opera]. Because Chaliapin in *Manfred* would be absolutely magnificent.[5]

The atmosphere of creative freedom and innovation represented the most positive aspect of Mamontov's opera company; however, despite the enormous talents of the individuals involved in his productions, the overall quality varied and standards were not as high as Rachmaninoff and Chaliapin would have hoped. Chaliapin complained in a letter to prominent art and music critic Vladimir Stasov on April 7, 1899, after the Private Opera's first performance of *Boris Godunov*:

Is this a way to behave, for example, towards Mussorgsky? I mean that for all his protestations that an opera as magnificent as *Boris* demands a meticulous production, it seems that Savva [Mamontov] let it go after only two or three rehearsals with the full cast. Really, is it possible? What the hell is this, that by the last rehearsal almost no one knows his role properly. . . . You decide, Vladimir Vasilievich, whether a man sincerely devoted to art would allow this purely so as to hang over the box office the notice "sold out." Eh? Surely not. Isn't that right? But in our theatre they are capable of it. And, of course, we poor artists must, out of pride and most of all out of love for the work to be performed, bend over backwards to avoid ruining the opera.[6]

Feodor Ivanovich Chaliapin and Sergei Vasilievich Rachmaninoff could not have had more unalike childhoods and adolescent lives, which in nineteenth-century Russia were predestined by their social class before birth. They were born in the same year, 1873, only twelve years after the serfs in Russia were legally emancipated by Tsar Aleksandr II (ruled 1855–1881). However, Chaliapin belonged to the peasant class, while Rachmaninoff was of the nobility. Chaliapin's class origins prevented him, even after the emancipation, from enjoying certain rights and privileges, such as in education and career opportunities—while Rachmaninoff's family was registered in the Book of Heraldry and Nobility, guaranteeing its members a specific status, which in turn opened the door to advantages and access in the highest circles that could pave the way for a more fulfilling and prosperous future. The following attempt by Rachmaninoff to help Chaliapin's brother obtain a respectable education illustrates the differences in how the nobility and peasants were treated under the Tsars, and the implications this held for the individual:

Long after Chaliapin had become world-famous, his passport still continued to bear the entry "Origin: peasant". . . a letter from Rachmaninov to the Director of the Moscow Seminary on behalf of Chaliapin illustrates: "The artist Chaliapin wishes to send to your seminary his fourteen-year-old brother who, I must tell you, does not know his notes or his alphabet too well, but in my opinion has an exceptional ear for music and is very gifted. The reasons prompting Chaliapin to seek a place for his brother at your establishment are: first, the boy is insufficiently prepared for music school. . . . [o]ther private boarding schools, such as the Military Academy, are out of the question, since the Chaliapins are peasants."[7]

Chaliapin grew up on the outskirts of Kazan' in extreme poverty in a peasant family: his father was an alcoholic who routinely beat his wife and son Feodor, while his mother was illiterate and meek, working tirelessly to provide for her family and accepting her husband's abuse as her lot. Despite this difficult childhood, Chaliapin remembered his mother's efforts with gratitude: "Thanks to my mother's hard work . . . we always had a clean and tidy home, a lamp burned permanently in front of the ikon, and I often caught the look of sorrow and resignation in my mother's grey eyes when she gazed at the ikon lit by a flickering flame."[8] Her internalizing of both Orthodox humility and forgiveness, along with patience and a strong work ethic, surely imprinted themselves into her son's psyche—for rather than succumbing to crushing circumstances, Chaliapin managed to escape this terrible fate and fulfill himself as an artist. After several attempts to learn a craft by serving apprenticeships (and enduring regular, cruel beatings by those who employed him), Chaliapin wound up learning the trade of bookbinding and dreaming of the theater. He knew only coarseness and brutality in his adolescence, recalling about an apprenticeship at a cobbler's, "I'm surprised they didn't cripple me as a little boy. I think that this wasn't for want of trying on their part, but rather due to the solidity of my bones."[9]

Even though Rachmaninoff's father was irresponsible and squandered his wife's dowry of multiple landed estates, the family did initially possess enormous amounts of money and land. Rachmaninoff had a difficult childhood, but he grew up in a genteel environment on large estates in picturesque natural surroundings; he knew kindness and refinement, and through his aristocratic status and well-connected relatives had every opportunity for the best education. Rachmaninoff was never beaten by family members, and thus did not bear the psychological scars or other effects of such physical violence. As Chaliapin, he was Russian Orthodox, with strong impressions of a mother who was deeply religious, and a loving grandmother in Novgorod who took him to church regularly. Chaliapin, too, all his life remembered the selfless efforts of his mother to keep a clean and tidy house, and her daily prayers before their icons. Both the young Feodor and Sergei had the habit of immersing themselves in Russia's natural beauty—its forests and fields and steppes—in order to escape their very real problems.

What united them was, first and foremost, their compatibility as complementary opposites: Chaliapin possessed a big-hearted personality, was larger than life in many ways, generous and outgoing, at least with those he

Figure 4.1 Rachmaninoff as a Young Man, 1897. Author's collection.

admitted into his inner sanctum. He was known for his directness, occasional emotional outbursts, and a physicality that sometimes manifested itself in his impulsively entering into fistfights against those with whom he disagreed. He had a tall and powerful build, as well as the survival skills acquired from his childhood of brutality and poverty. He understood suffering. By contrast, Rachmaninoff was introverted, kept his emotions well hidden inside himself, and did not express himself in physical ways. His gestures and actions were spare and measured; though exceedingly generous and compassionate, he remained private about the help he gave to others. What the two men had in common was their Russianness—their love for the essential features of Russia, with its Orthodox humility, majesty, and musical sonority of the church bells; their love of humor—for Chaliapin possessed the unfailing ability to make Rachmaninoff laugh—and their broad natures that embraced a depth of spirit, kindness toward others, and the striving for perfection in their art.

The second major source for the lifelong bond between Chaliapin and Rachmaninoff was their abiding commitment to art: for each the muse was enormous, and the creative springs flowed well. Chaliapin discovered theater and later opera, realizing immediately that he had found in the outside world, on the performance stage, what had always been stirring inside him. Initially, when he was quite young, singing and acting served as beautiful escapes from the misery of his reality. However, as he found opportunities to grow in his art, that art became for him the *raison d'être*. He inhabited his roles and served his art fully. By contrast, Rachmaninoff was born into a many-generations-long relationship to music and art. He was steeped in its environment and was able to express his talents for music at an early age. He heard the piano played and art songs sung regularly in the informal salons given by his relatives at their country estates. He was thrilled at the heart-rending sounds of Russian folk singing that took place regularly outside the manor buildings while the peasants (now liberated and working for the Rachmaninoffs-Satins for agreed-upon wages) went about their daily tasks. And he spent many hours of long, standing prayer in the churches hearing the melodious and unexpected modulations of the Znamennyi, Kievan, Novgorodian, and Moscow chants that formed a regular component of Orthodox liturgical services. Music was everywhere in his environment, and, for the most part, he was not hampered in his efforts to apprehend its beauty. His talent for music was encouraged, it was viewed by his relatives as a legitimate and serious activity, and through his familial connections and noble status he received the education that he needed in order to develop that talent.

Throughout their lives Rachmaninoff and Chaliapin maintained an uncompromising attitude toward the art forms they shared and insisted on exerting the maximum control over all possible aspects of composing / creation, rehearsal, and execution / performance of a given artistic work. In these respects the two men were legendary in the musical world. Examples abound of their powerful influence over the artistic process. Rachmaninoff would become one of the greatest conductors and pianists of the twentieth century, with many composed masterpieces to his credit that would take a permanent place in the international musical canon. Chaliapin would not only make his mark as arguably the finest operatic "singing actor," as he put it, of all time, but even more than this, his techniques of creating a character on stage would revolutionize theater itself: the world-renowned actor and theater director Konstantin Stanislavsky (1863–1938), whose far-reaching philosophy of acting was known as "the method" in Hollywood, stated, "Synthesis has rarely been achieved by anyone in the arts, particularly in the theatre. Chaliapin is the only case I can think of."[10] Stanislavsky also acknowledged many times, "My system is taken straight from Chaliapin."[11] His system of acting was inspired by observing Chaliapin on the stage and hearing the latter speak about his approaches to that art. Indeed, Chaliapin's psychological-naturalistic approach to opera made him a unique opera performer and creative genius.

Before being hired by Mamontov, Chaliapin had worked for three concert seasons for the Imperial Theatres, the final year of 1895–1896 being at the prestigious Mariinsky Theatre in St. Petersburg. For the summer of 1896 Mamontov hired him to sing with his Private Opera in Nizhny-Novgorod, and Chaliapin immediately warmed to the freer and more creative environment that Mamontov fostered in his performances. That fall Chaliapin broke his contract with the Mariinsky, choosing instead to move to Moscow for work with the Private Opera. The following musical season of 1897–1898

Rachmaninoff was hired by Mamontov to conduct the Private Opera's orchestra. During the single season that he spent at the Private Opera, he developed his skills as a conductor and was able to refine and have performed his first opera *Aleko*. And he met Chaliapin, with whom he created musical performances of surpassing beauty and whose extraordinary qualities in both artistic and personal spheres would affect Rachmaninoff all his life.

On one occasion, though not the only one, Chaliapin left a detailed memorandum on the desk of the director of the Imperial Theatres, Vladimir Teliakovsky (1861–1924). His authority and audacity as an artist emerge in this memorandum. Because of his enormous and indisputable talent, his striving for perfection, and his drawing power with the public, he tolerated no compromises when it came to art and also knew that his demands would be met:

Conditions Under Which I, Chaliapin, Am Prepared to Work at the Imperial Theatres:

1. All operas in which I appear will be conducted by either [Albert] Coates or [Emil] Cooper.
2. While I am on stage, i.e., during rehearsals or during performances, a fully authorised member of the managerial staff must be present at all times, so that I may at any moment address to him any requests of an artistic nature so that he may deal with any shortcomings in connection with on-stage arrangements.
3. An administrative director to be appointed (abolish the term "principal director" as basically inaccurate).
4. Official notification to all persons taking part in performances or rehearsals in which I sing, to all other artists and the chorus (if necessary) that they are to give serious consideration to whatever remarks I may make pertaining to stage business and to submit to my professional demands as if I were principal director or stage manager.
5. The authority of the so-called principal director to be transferred to me.
6. Application for improvements in the stage lighting of the Bolshoi Theatre must be submitted without delay.
7. I draw the management's attention to the fact that the presence of [Ulrich] Avranek in the theatre as *conductor* [Chaliapin's italics] is not only of no use and no interest to anyone, but is even pernicious since it affects all the artists, even though they may not be aware of it. It is corrupting in musical terms, and therefore his complete removal from the conductor's stand is advisable.

Feodor Chaliapin[12]

Figure 4.2 Feodor Ivanovich Chaliapin c. 1910–1911. Author's collection.

Rachmaninoff was also connected with Teliakovsky during his tenure as conductor of the Bolshoi Theatre: he entered into a contract with the Bolshoi, which was under the jurisdiction of the Imperial Theatres, in the fall of 1904. "Proving himself an energetic administrator, [Teliakovsky] had begun to stir the organization out of its lethargy and was on the look-out for fresh and invigorating talent. His first coup had been to attract Chaliapin away from Mamontov to join the Bolshoi in 1899, and it was perhaps at the singer's suggestion that he subsequently sought Rachmaninoff himself as conductor."[13] His uncompromising attitude toward art and the respect he enjoyed with his colleagues in music can be illuminated by two representative episodes during his time at the Bolshoi. Because of the valuable experience he had gained as a conductor while with Mamontov's Private Opera, as well as his own innate talents for conducting (there were no courses in conducting at the Moscow Conservatory during his years there as a student), Rachmaninoff had quickly risen to the top of the field as one of Russia's most gifted conductors.

The first episode involved Rachmaninoff's debut at the Bolshoi conducting Dargomyzhsky's *Rusalka* (The mermaid), which he knew well from his and Chaliapin's successful collaborations on performances of the opera at Mamontov's. On September 3, 1904, the audience noticed with some surprise that the conductor's chair had been transferred from its traditional position between the stage and orchestra pit, which meant that the conductor kept his back to the performing musicians. Rachmaninoff undertook a first in an Imperial Russian performance hall: to conduct an opera with the conductor's chair on the audience side of the orchestra, facing both the orchestra and singers (a practice that Wagner had debuted in Russia). This bold, yet supremely logical innovation quickly caught on after Rachmaninoff's successful application of it at the Bolshoi.[14] Rachmaninoff had seen the alternative conducting style while on his honeymoon in Bayreuth in the summer of 1902, immediately grasping its significance and practicality. However, in defense of the senior conductor at the Bolshoi whom Rachmaninoff succeeded, Ippolit Altani (1846–1919), the decision to concentrate on the singers had a great deal to do with their artistic level: "it was not Altani's perverse adherence to an obsolete tradition so much as the low level of professionalism among singers, with which Rachmaninoff was already too familiar, that had created and maintained the need for conductors to be in a position where they could give their main attention to the singers rather than to the orchestra."[15] Grasping the essence of the problem with the singers, Rachmaninoff instituted the practice of working with the soloists by accompanying them at the piano while they perfected their roles.

By November 1904, when Rachmaninoff conducted for his cousin Siloti in a concert of works for piano and orchestra in St. Petersburg, his fame as a conductor had skyrocketed and he was already being compared to the finest conductors of the day. In response to Rachmaninoff's conducting of Grieg's *Peer Gynt Suite* on October 22, 1912, the critic Yury Engel affirmed, "Rachmaninoff, a real conductor, by the grace of God (and one who impresses both public and orchestra equally), may be the only Russian conductor to be compared with such names in the West as Nikisch, Colonne, and Mahler."[16] Similar to Chaliapin's regular directives to the management of the Imperial Theatres, "Rachmaninoff's verbal directions to an orchestra were made in an imperious tone which brooked no argument, and contemporaries have suggested that this was acceptable only because of the general recognition of his towering musical authority . . ."[17] Rachmaninoff's own words reveal the depth of his understanding of the conducting process: "To be a good conductor a musician must possess tremendous powers of restraint . . . The full intensity of musical emotion must be there, but at the heart of it is the quietness of perfect mental poise and power controlled."[18]

Mikhail Bagrinovsky, a contemporary of Rachmaninoff's, describes Rachmaninoff's intensive rehearsing with an orchestra in the following words:

> In his rehearsal work Rachmaninoff was greatly helped by his absolute pitch and an astoundingly precise and fine ear. Rachmaninoff really did hear the whole score being performed in its entirety and in all its details. He detected and placed not only the usual kind of mistakes by performers but even the slightest chance inconspicuous imprecisions, no matter how heavy the weight of orchestral sound, tenaciously securing their correction.[19]

The second event that illustrates Rachmaninoff's total commitment to art as well as his musical authority also took place during his tenure as the conductor for the Bolshoi Theatre. Before his assuming of the post, the principal conductor Altani (who remained in that position between the years 1882 and 1906) had for many years tolerated the practice of the orchestra members' creeping out of the orchestra pit through a back door during a pause in their own part in order to smoke a cigarette. This unattractive practice was even noticeable to the concertgoers and clearly affected their concentration during the given musical performance. Appalled at the disservice such a practice did to the music as well as the lack of professionalism it suggested, Rachmaninoff decided to put a stop to it. He understood the sacrifice this would entail for the musicians who smoked, for he himself was a heavy smoker, averaging about two packs of cigarettes per day. He forbade these disruptions to the working atmosphere in the orchestra pit and began to punish the transgressors by imposing a fine on them. In that year of 1905 after the events of "Bloody Sunday," when thoughts of freedom and equality were in the air, such behavior on the part of a conductor offended the members of the orchestra.

In response, the orchestra organized a delegation whose members were sent to meet with Rachmaninoff, as they interpreted it, in order to show this upstart, for whom the consciousness of his own greatness had gone to his head, that they did not wish to tolerate such unfair treatment. The delegates declaimed a passionate speech about freedom and human dignity, concluding it with their words of protest against treatment they were not going to tolerate. Rachmaninoff heard them out in stony silence without a single muscle moving in his face. He replied: "May I ask the gentlemen to tender their request to be released from their position? Their request will be approved without delay." After uttering these words, he turned his back on the delegation and walked out of the room, leaving its members frozen where they stood.[20] How was Rachmaninoff able to withstand such a potential confrontation? Throughout his life he retained a sense of his dignity and stature as an individual, particularly if he was convinced that he was right in a given matter. This, along with his stellar training at the Moscow Conservatory and awareness of his own musical gifts, provided him with the authority to stand his ground. He had no tolerance for mediocrity in art, for, as others in Russian culture before him (such as Pushkin, Dostoevsky, Tolstoy, Levitan, Shishkin, Tchaikovsky, Soloviev, among many others), he consciously and with every fiber of his being served art and was obedient to a classical conception of beauty. He would not tolerate any actions or situation that compromised his vision of the highest possible level of performance. Beauty for Rachmaninoff was intertwined with religious sensibilities and could act as a moral force.

Chaliapin had grown immensely as an opera singer and artist in general while at the Mamontov Opera, but his natural vocal gifts and expressive talent still needed refining. Since he came from humble peasant beginnings, he had had very little education. His voice was "God-given," as Rachmaninoff put it, but it needed much more training in order for him to be successful in the international opera arena—and he also needed to learn the major languages of the operatic repertoire.

In April 1900 Rachmaninoff and Chaliapin accepted an invitation to travel south to Yalta in the Crimea, where many musicians and intellectuals rested from their endeavors or sought treatment for various illnesses in the local sanitoria. As in Europe during these years, tuberculosis was not uncommon in Russia, affecting individuals of all social classes. The warm climate and location on the dazzling shore of the Black Sea made this resort city the ideal antidote to the colder weather and faster pace of life of St. Petersburg and Moscow. Yalta occupied approximately forty-four miles of the southern coast of Crimea, being situated between the sea and hills just south of the Crimean

Mountains. The setting was majestic and inspiring. Rachmaninoff stayed in a guest house on the estate of Prince Lieven. Although he was no longer employed by Mamontov's Private Opera, Rachmaninoff had been invited to accompany Chaliapin in a concert with the opera company, which was on tour. He also found time to interact with the fine actors of the Moscow Art Theatre, who were performing Chekhov's "The Seagull," "Uncle Vanya," and several other plays. It was during this time of opera and theater that Rachmaninoff and Ivan Bunin became acquainted, and their interactions evolved into a close lifelong friendship.

While Rachmaninoff and Chaliapin were enjoying themselves both in performance and interaction with such major cultural figures as Chekhov, a stunning opportunity presented itself: Chaliapin was invited by the prestigious Teatro alla Scala in Milan to appear on its stage the following spring in Arrigo Boito's opera *Mefistofele* (which had premiered at La Scala on March 5, 1868).[21] This would be his first time singing outside of Russia. Chaliapin would be participating in a major revival of the opera and would join a stellar group of performers. Because of his expressive operatic bass voice, Chaliapin would sing the title role and perform with fabled tenor Enrico Caruso (1873–1921) in the role of Faust and soprano Emma Carelli (1877–1928) as Margherita. The opera would be conducted by the distinguished Arturo Toscanini, who had been serving as La Scala's musical director since 1898. (At the end of his life, Toscanini would comment that Chaliapin was the greatest operatic talent with whom he had worked.) One can imagine the scene—Chaliapin hurried to find Rachmaninoff to tell him the news, followed by their celebration of Chaliapin's recognition on the world stage—for such an invitation clearly indicated that word of his Russian operatic success had reached Europe. Chaliapin was excited, nervous, and very uncertain as to whether he could prepare adequately for such a challenging role. If he failed, his career could be shipwrecked in its early stages. But if he succeeded, the world would be in his hands. The temptation was too great, and nervousness was overcome—in large part because Rachmaninoff (whose training represented everything that Chaliapin's lacked) offered to accompany him to Italy and help him prepare intensively for the role.

The trip to Italy was decided: Chaliapin would rent a villa for them in the resort town of Varazze on the coast of the Ligurian Sea and in the mountainous region in the south of Italy, not far from Genoa to the east and farther to the west: San Remo and the border of France. The climate was similar to that of Yalta, although the mountains were not as craggy and impressive as those in the Crimea. Rachmaninoff arrived in Varazze on June 11, as he described in a letter to his friend Nikita Morozov (who had studied at the Moscow Conservatory with him) dated three days later. Chaliapin was delayed in his arrival because of some complications that arose while he was in Paris, which

Rachmaninoff speculated had to do with the "woman problem"—Chaliapin had married the Italian ballerina Iola Tornaghi in 1898 and had some matters to settle with her before joining Rachmaninoff in Varazze. Rachmaninoff wrote to Morozov on June 27, 1900, describing that he had arrived at the resort town on the 11th and that the house in which he and Chaliapin would live was completely disorganized, dirty, and stuffy from the heat. He had managed to obtain paper and ink and had settled into his room preliminarily. But at this early stage of the work he had committed to undertaking with Chaliapin, he greatly regretted even coming to Varazze. His mood was one of total despair.[22]

The task confronting Rachmaninoff and Chaliapin that summer was daunting. The latter recalled later about Rachmaninoff: "[he] was a great artist, a magnificent musician and a pupil of Tchaikovsky: it was he who urged me to study Mussorgsky and Rimsky-Korsakov. He taught me some of the basic principles of harmony. He tried, generally speaking, to give me a musical education."[23] Borovsky characterizes the extraordinary professional connection between Rachmaninoff and Chaliapin thus:

> It would be difficult to decide which of them benefited most from their association. Rachmaninoff, whose [formal] musical culture was greater, helped Chaliapin to polish his performing style. Chaliapin for his part revealed to him that truth of intonation, that secret of combining declamatory expressiveness with the cantilena, "the conversion of recitative into melody" which formed an important part of his vocal talent.[24]

For both musical artists their commitment to attaining the highest levels of art was absolute, along with a zeal and idealism characteristically Russian, to serve art in every way possible. The many connections with art, Russian life, and culture, and what can be described as both a similarity and complimentary oppositeness forged in Rachmaninoff and Chaliapin a powerful personal relationship that lasted all their lives. Each needed the other in order to grow and maintain equilibrium; an account of Rachmaninoff's focus on Chaliapin when they dined with friends is typical:

> "Here he is! He's here!" rang out the voice of Rachmaninov, who was the first to notice the arrival of Chaliapin; every movement, every word of the artist was reflected on his face; he obviously derived aesthetic pleasure from seeing and hearing the famous actor in person, the inflection of his voice and his play-acting. He smiled, laughed, till tears ran down while listening to his jokes and funny stories.[25]

Why did Chaliapin choose Varazze as the location for a summer of preparation for the upcoming opera? The resort town had the advantages of relative isolation and beauty on the Mediterranean; he and Rachmaninoff would be able to accomplish a great deal of work without the usual distractions of a large city. The appeal of being at a seacoast resort for the summer was powerful, as was the reputation of Varazze on the Italian Riviera as a place welcoming to foreign guests. No doubt Chaliapin's Italian wife Iola was able to advise him and recommended this town.

The palm-treed, picturesque resort town had approximately ten thousand inhabitants at that time; it was nestled in a cove and much of its coast had excellent beaches. Its houses and inviting small hotels were painted in pastels that captured the bright sunlight of southern Italy. Varazze was known in northern Italy as an appealing destination for families, having a relaxed and peaceful atmosphere with excellent food. It was not known as a place for singles to meet each other, nor did it have an atmosphere of endless partying. Perhaps less well-known was Varazze's connection to musical culture, and especially to opera, made even stronger by its geographical proximity to Milan—which was only a few hours away by train. The cultural level of the town was higher than usual for a resort, and opera there, as in the rest of Italy, ran in the blood of people of all classes and represented a mainstream form of entertainment. An indicator of Varazze's connection with opera was the composer Francesco Cilea (1866–1950), who was active at La Scala during the turn of the twentieth century and who spent the last years of his life in Varazze.[26] Cilea died in this town; the house in which he lived has become a house-museum devoted to his career.

What kind of routine did Rachmaninoff and Chaliapin follow while in Varazze? Chaliapin had rented a villa not far from the beach in the eastern part of the town, which was closest to Genoa. Rachmaninoff first lived at the rented villa with the recently married Chaliapins, but because he needed more seclusion in order to compose, he decided to rent a room at a boardinghouse. Their routine was as follows: Rachmaninoff and Chaliapin would work on artistic matters of music and opera in the mornings, while in the afternoons Chaliapin would work alone to study the Italian language. They also would have spent time at the beach, taking walks at the water's edge and discussing their musical futures while resting on the sand. The weather was very hot and humid, as one would expect of a resort town in the summer—but in June and even July the water was still extremely cold and thus not conducive for swimming. The beach sand was finely grained, however, good for long walks and standing in the water at least up to the knees. Chaliapin described the rather sober way they lived in order to stay focused on their goal of preparing him for his La Scala debut, but also enabling Rachmaninoff to have ample time for his own composing work.

Whatever was taking place in Rachmaninoff's inner world during the summer of 1900 in those places produced new compositions of tenderness and a wistful longing. By that summer's end he had composed the love duet between Francesca da Rimini and Paolo Malatesta—immortalized in literature in Dante's *Inferno*—for his opera *Francesca da Rimini*. Concerning the Francesca da Rimini story, in his opera Rachmaninoff was contributing to an established tradition of works inspired by the story of the ill-fated lovers that extended far beyond Dante's *The Divine Comedy*; it included Tchaikovsky's orchestral work (fantasia) titled *Francesca da Rimini*, and many other works on the subject in poetry, theater, and painting. After the summer in Varazze Rachmaninoff resumed work on the opera in 1904, completing it in 1906.

Because Chaliapin was recently married and Rachmaninoff was contemplating engagement and marriage to Natalia Satina, the subject of women and relationships with them surely came up often when they were not intensively at work on music and opera. During the 1890s Rachmaninoff had experienced deep affection for the married Anna Lodyzhenskaia, and by 1900 had (according to received accounts) already taken more than a passing interest in Elena Dahl. Besides his feelings of closeness to the woman he would eventually marry, Natalia Satina, he clearly had other emotional entanglements from which he had to extricate himself—if he was to proceed in the events of his life with more or less of a clear conscience and cheerful spirit. Chaliapin, whose own personal situations with women in coming years could not serve as a model for Rachmaninoff, nevertheless would seek to advise Rachmaninoff the best he could. They were the same age, but Chaliapin was already married and thus committed (at least at that moment) to one woman, while Rachmaninoff had several worthy women on his mind. (More will be said about these women in future chapters.) Since Elena, as far as is known, was not married, the question arises: Did she visit Rachmaninoff and Chaliapin in Varazze in the summer of 1900, even for a brief time? It would have been a possibility. Yet, even if she did not, she would have been very much on Rachmaninoff's mind, and this could account for his being drawn to the theme of illicit love in the Francesca da Rimini and Paolo Malatesta story.

A. A. Naumov posits that this period of 1900–1902 represents a mysterious one in Rachmaninoff's life, and that with recent discoveries about the existence of Elena Dahl, a "creative line can be drawn from Rachmaninoff's *Morceau de fantaisie* (Delmo) in G minor for piano (1899, without opus number) to the romantic scene of Paolo and Francesca (1900) and to the Piano Concerto No. 2 in C minor (1900–1901)."[27] During this summer Rachmaninoff made significant progress on the second and third movements of the Piano Concerto, No. 2 (op.18), one of his most important compositions and one he would perform throughout his concertizing career. A full account of the musical features of this major concerto and its possible connection with the material of Rachmaninoff's life is detailed in chapter 6.

Rachmaninoff and Chaliapin worked steadily and painstakingly, for they had a major task ahead of them in preparing Chaliapin for La Scala—but they were also inspired and must have derived much enjoyment (despite the drawbacks of the heat and other distractions of the beach) from evolving their musical art together. The larger part of their work together involved serious consideration of the eternal theme of good and evil, which lay at the center of Goethe's play *Faust* (1806–1831). Using all the knowledge he had acquired during his years at the Moscow Conservatory and subsequent experiences as a conductor and pianist, Rachmaninoff strove to refine in Chaliapin the temperament, musicianship, and interpretive skills needed in order to convey what in Christian cosmology and world literature exists as the ultimate representation of evil—Mefistofele. Originating in German folklore, Mefistofele or Mephisto can be considered either an "assistant" of Satan or his equivalent. With the help of Rachmaninoff, Chaliapin would have to evolve for himself (which he did admirably in the course of his lifetime) an understanding and method of conveying the inner qualities of the characters he would perform in opera. He would develop this art through an almost complete identification with the specific character he was portraying, the outer representation through facial and physical expression and costume of the inner qualities of the character, and throughout the process supreme self-control. As an example of this duality—this self-control and yet complete mastery of the character, Chaliapin opined that an audience does not want to see him, Chaliapin, cry; the audience wants to see Boris Godunov (one of Chaliapin's signature roles) cry.[28]

The synesthesia of understanding and material representation of the inner world of the particular character was produced in part through Chaliapin's thorough understanding of costume and stage make-up (one recalls that in his youth he had been apprenticed to a shoemaker, and in the theater he could sew his own shoes if necessary). In at least one performance of the opera Rachmaninoff would watch as Chaliapin transformed himself, with only a few strokes of stage make-up, into the representation of evil. For Chaliapin the importance of physical gesture, all the lines of the body, were equivalent to what for Rachmaninoff were the musical phrases, themes, and leitmotifs of a composition—as brought into life by performance before an audience.

For their preparation of Chaliapin's role at La Scala, Rachmaninoff and Chaliapin had an enormous treasure trove of the representation of the Devil to draw from in literature, music, religion, and the visual arts. The tradition of representing the eternal struggle between good and evil runs deep in high culture, with the most successful and enduring embodiments of this moral dichotomy being complex and even evoking pity, rather than being two-dimensional. Even in Boito's opera the character Mefistofele reveals various aspects of his inner world in the course of the opera's action:

> In the Prologue in heaven Mephistopheles "is a fatal type, represented as the quintessence of Evil"; in Act I, "in the guise of a gray friar, he is as sinister as a ghost," then, "in the guise of a knight he is elegant, grotesque, bizarre, facetious," "he is violent in the song of the whistle"; in Martha's garden "he is in the honeymoon [depths] of his covenant with Faust, not doubting his triumph--he is as lively and gallant as a Figaro"; on the romantic Sabbath "Mephistopheles is—the Devil," "his infernal nature emerges triumphant, exulting . . ."[29]

Everything turned out as planned and hoped for by the two hardworking musicians. Their efforts in Varazze lasted through June and early July of 1900. After they parted, Rachmaninoff traveled first to Milan, and then returned to Moscow. Chaliapin's debut at La Scala on March 16, 1901 was a triumph: he performed and "inhabited" Mefistofele in eleven performances, a healthy number for such a prestigious opera house with demanding audiences and critics. Borovsky writes, "In Italy—as Chaliapin could not help noticing—all eyes had been on him; people were unable to hide their naive astonishment: a barbarian from Siberia, from some incomprehensible wild land of snows and bears, suddenly turned out to be an artist who eclipsed Toscanini and Caruso."[30]

Both Chaliapin and Rachmaninoff understood well that each of them was made the richer and the more consummate artist as a result of the interactions with the other. The masterful collaboration between them had started with Mamontov's theater but was permanently sealed during the summer in Varazze. Chaliapin loved Russia no less than Rachmaninoff; he felt doubly gratified about his success at La Scala: "'I was in a splendid mood,' he recalled later. 'I felt I had achieved something and not only for myself.'[97] 'I was proud that it had fallen to my lot to have the good fortune of representing Russian art, which still did not have the prestige it deserved in the West.'[98]"[31]

Chaliapin's reputation was sealed with the administrators and audiences of La Scala: he was to perform there again in the years 1904, 1908, 1912, 1929–30, and 1933.

Chaliapin would perform the role of Mefistofele in other foreign cities in the years to come, with dazzling success. His colossal efforts to perfect the role, and Rachmaninoff's sympathetic and expert contributions to his artistic friend's preparations were noticed by everyone, audiences and critics alike. One appreciative review of Chaliapin's performance of the role in London in 1926 in *The Observer* described the range of Chaliapin's expressive means:

> Where Boito had given him anything to sing, he sang into it that world of meaning a composer hopes for, but seldom gets. Where there was . . . nothing to sing,

he declaimed it with a singing or speaking voice, a mutter or roar, as occasion asked. As the singing merged into the speaking, so both merged into acting and the acting into being himself. People sometimes think the devil is an easy part to act: you have merely to let yourself go (in a certain direction) and there you are. But the prince of darkness is a gentleman; although he has a cloven hoof, it is not the cloven hoof of vulgarity and it is because there is not a shadow of cheapness or blatancy that Chaliapin's devil is so great.[32]

The reward for Rachmaninoff's and Chaliapin's prodigious efforts at Varazze was La Scala itself. In the history of various performances that had taken place there during the eighteenth and nineteenth centuries what emerges is the clear presence of Russian music in the opera house's programs. Russian performers and conductors were featured there regularly. Many of them were Rachmaninoff's professors at the Moscow Conservatory, representing a rich cross-fertilization between Russia and Italy of generations of musical giants in opera and instrumental music that hearkened back to the era of Catherine the Great. Rachmaninoff and Chaliapin encountered in Italy in general and Milan in particular the expected deep devotion among Italians to opera, but this genre of high culture also did not forget the vicissitudes of everyday life: On May 22–23 of 1900 (just before they arrived in Italy) at La Scala there was a benefit concert for the sanatoria of Milan ministering to the poor suffering from tuberculosis. An epidemic of this devastating disease was raging in northern Italy at the time. However, everyday life and the schedule of cultural activities would continue despite the epidemic.

In another musical and thematic vein during this remarkable summer Rachmaninoff also completed the sacred a cappella choral work *Panteley the Healer* (inspired by St. Panteley, whose icon would regularly comfort him and his family). By any measure, along with Rachmaninoff's composition in opera form of the duet of Francesca and Paolo, and the major progress made on the two movements of Piano Concerto No. 2, this was an impressive outpouring of musical creativity, produced in the context of distant travels and less-than-ideal living conditions.

The proving ground of Italy would provide both Rachmaninoff and Chaliapin with unforgettable experiences and would catapult them to the world stage in their respective areas of music performance. They had experienced the same intensive and eclectic, yet liberating training in the opera company of Savva Mamontov, and their creative energies and plans were filled to the brim. Their personal lives as well were filled with emotional content: Chaliapin was married by this time, while Rachmaninoff was pondering with his whole heart the outcomes of several different plans for an enduring relationship. Life felt hopeful, and all things seemed possible to these noble-hearted Russian musical giants.

NOTES

1. Sergei Bertensson and Jay Leyda, *Sergei Rachmaninoff: A Lifetime in Music* (New York: New York UP, 1956; repr., Bloomington, IN: Indiana UP, 2001), paraphrase of 63.

2. Olga Haldey, *Mamontov's Private Opera: The Search for Modernism in Russian Theatre* (Bloomington, IN: Indiana UP, 2010), 133.

3. Victor Borovsky, *Chaliapin: A Critical Biography* (New York: Alfred A. Knopf, 1988), 116.

4. Haldey, 134.

5. S. Rakhmaninov, Letter of November 22, 1897, in *S. Rakhmaninov. Literaturnoe nasledie. Vospominaniia. Stat'i. Interv'iu. Pis'ma*, ed. Z.A. Apetian (Moscow: Sovetskii kompozitor, 1978), 1: 272.

6. F.I. Chaliapin, *Literary Works, Letters*, vol. I of *Feodor Ivanovich Chaliapin* (Moscow: Iskusstvo, 1976), 372, quoted in Borovsky, 254.

7. S. Rakhmaninov, Letter, in *S. Rakhmaninov. Literaturnoe nasledie. Vospominaniia. Stat'i. Interv'iu. Pis'ma*, ed. Z.A. Apetian, 1: 278–79, quoted in Borovsky, 33.

8. F.I. Chaliapin, *Literary Works, Letters*, vol. I of *Feodor Ivanovich Chaliapin*, 47, quoted in Borovsky, 33.

9. F.I. Chaliapin, *Literary Works, Letters*, vol. I of *Feodor Ivanovich Chaliapin*, 61, quoted in Borovsky, 34.

10. N. Gorchakov, *Rezhisserskie uroki K.S. Stanislavskogo* (Moscow: Iskusstvo, 1950), 115, quoted in Borovsky, 4.

11. G. Kristi, *Rabota Stanislavskogo v opernom teatre* (Moscow: Iskusstvo, 1952), 59, quoted in Borovsky, 4.

12. V.A. Teliakovsky, *Moi sosluzhivets Chaliapin* (Leningrad: Akademiia, 1927), 159–60, quoted in Borovsky, 27.

13. Barrie Martyn, *Rachmaninoff: Composer, Pianist, Conductor* (Burlington, VT: Ashgate, 2000), 512.

14. Bertensson and Leyda, paraphrase of 105–06.

15. Martyn, 513.

16. Yury Engel, "Symphony Concert," in *Russkie vedomosti*, no. 245 (October 24, 1912): n.p., quoted in Martyn, 517.

17. Martyn, 517.

18. Sergei Rachmaninoff, "The Composer as Interpreter," interview in *The Monthly Musical Record* (November 1934), 201, quoted in Martyn, 518.

19. M.M. Bagrinovsky, "Pamiati S.V. Rakhmaninova," in *Vospominaniia o Rakhmaninove*, ed. Z.A. Apetian, 5th ed. (Moscow: Muzyka, 1988), II: 39, quoted in Martyn, 518.

20. This paragraph represents my translation from the Russian and paraphrasing of Oskar von Riesemann, *Sergei Rakhmaninov: Vospominaniia*, trans. V.N. Chemberdzhi (Moscow: Raduga, 1992), 125–26.

21. The influence of Italian song and opera on Russia date back to the early eighteenth century. La Scala itself was inaugurated in Milan on August 3, 1778, during

the times when Catherine II (the Great)—patroness of the arts par excellence—was Empress of Russia (reigned 1762–1796).

22. Bertensson and Leyda, paraphrase of 93.
23. Borovsky, 207.
24. Ibid., 206–207.
25. Vincent Sheean, "Chaliapin Remembers," *New York Herald Tribune*, December 25, 1932, quoted in Borovsky, 206.
26. I visited Varazze in June 2014 in order to experience the physical place in which Rachmaninoff and Chaliapin worked to prepare the latter for his La Scala debut.
27. A.A. Naumov, "Morceau de fantaisie 'Delmo,'" in *Novoe o Rakhmaninove*, ed. and comp. I.A. Medvedeva (Moscow: Deka-BC, 2006), 177, trans. VZN. The "interview with A.B. Rakhmaninov of two years ago [2004]" refers to my meetings with Rachmaninoff's grandson at the villa Senar in 2003–2004. See Appendix I for additional details.
28. F.I. Chaliapin, *Maska i dush: Moi sorok let na teatrakh* (Moscow: Moskovskii rabochii, 1989), paraphrase by VZN of 130.
29. "[par.] Mefistofele, nel Prologo in cielo, è un tipo fatale, come il Male che rappresenta', nel—l'Atto I, 'sotto le spoglie del frate grigio è *sinistro come un fantasma*', poi, 'sotto le spoglie di cavaliere è elegante, grottesco, bizzarro, faceto', 'è violento nella *canzone del fischio*', nel giardina di Marta 'è Mefistofele Uomo', 'è allegrissimo, è nella luna di miele del suo patto con Faust, non dubita del trionfo, è vivace, galante come un figaro'; nel Sabba romantico 'è Mefistofele-Diavolo', 'la sua natura infernale si sprigiona trionfando, esultando' . . ." [italics original]. Gerardo Guccini, "Spettacolo e visione nella drammaturgia di Arrigo Boito," *Mefistofele* (Teatro alla Scala, Program, Feb. 20–Mar. 18, 1995), 47–48. The quotation is found in the sub-section of the article titled "Strutture figurali performative del *Mefistofele*." Trans. VZN.
30. Borovsky, 300–302.
31. Note 97: F.I. Chaliapin, *Literary Works, Letters*, vol. 1 of *Feodor Ivanovich Chaliapin*, 166; Note 98: M.K. Feodor Ivanovich, *Ocherk ego zhizni i deiatel'nosti* (Moscow: A.V. Vasil'eva, 1903), 63; both references quoted in Borovsky, 302.
32. N.F., "Music of the Week—Chaliapin," *The Observer*, May 30, 1926, n.p., quoted in Borovsky, 298, 300.

Chapter 5

The Muses
(1890–1917)

Childhood impressions and experiences remain with a person for a lifetime, resurfacing at times of nostalgia and taking shape in various forms of self-expression. These memories exert an even greater influence on someone who is especially sensitive and has lived through enormous suffering. The young Rachmaninoff was such a person, carrying the traumas of his early years and adolescence into his adulthood. Later in his life, when already in America, he was asked about the vicissitudes he had experienced. He answered that he had been given his fair share of both sorrow and happiness; among other difficulties, he had lost his homeland and two beloved estates into which he had poured his time and money. Rachmaninoff's answer also stems from a Russian Orthodox understanding of the world, one that acknowledges suffering as an inescapable component of human existence, cultivates patience, and aspires to forgiveness toward others for perceived insults and wrongs. These attitudes are accompanied by "walking around oneself" to develop self-awareness and a conscience, while at the same time appreciating even commonplace features of the world as sources for radiant joy.[1]

The present chapter traces Sergei's connections with three women, underscoring their importance to him for his life and his music. He was attracted to them personally, and they inspired his creative work at a time when he was an established musician, though still relatively young. He would "remember that wondrous moment," as Aleksandr Pushkin's famous poem begins, when each of these women entered and touched his life in ways that he never forgot. As for the women, they all had in common the experiencing of much sadness and even tragedy in their lives. It is thus not surprising that they found their place in Rachmaninoff's art songs (*romansy* [романсы]), a genre in which Rachmaninoff composed prolifically until the end of 1917 when he was forced to leave Russia. In depicting the relationship of Rachmaninoff with the women in question, the Russian country estate of Ivanovka, with its way of life defining how such relationships as these were formed and nurtured, takes center stage. The multifarious activities of a country estate and its complex, yet precise organization of responsibilities and pleasures included the work schedules of the landowners and peasants, music recitals, poetry readings, dinners with discussions of current events, and rehearsals and performances of plays.

Education and the acquiring of various skills were of paramount importance for the participants in this way of life: in the early nineteenth century the Satin family, at its own expense, established a school for the peasants' children. Basic subjects such as grammar, reading, and religion were taught. For children of the landowners a teacher was usually hired to teach music: choruses were created, and home performances staged. New works of literature, music, and plays would arrive regularly, infusing the estate's cultural life with the excitement of taking part in the latest artistic trends. In addition to Russian, French would be taught as well. As a result of these interactions among creative and educated persons, it is not surprising that a large majority of the masterpieces of Russian high culture of the eighteenth to early twentieth centuries came out of these country estates.[2]

The complex relationship between landowners, who were mostly of the nobility, and peasants, who after 1861 acquired the rights to own their own plot of land and work for their previous masters for wages, is captured in the following words:

> All of the splendid Russian culture of the nineteenth century emerged from the landowners' estates. But in light of this we should not forget that behind their gates roared and bubbled violently the ocean of peasant Russia: suffering and celebrating, weeping and singing. [But] if the ear of the landowner was deaf to the sounds of this verbal ocean, if his soul was indifferent and insensitively unresponsive, then from where could Pushkin and Fet, Turgenev and Bunin, Tchaikovsky and Rachmaninoff have originated?
>
> Life on a country estate was contradictory, insofar as its economic basis was routinely built on the labor and suffering of the peasants. But yet, didn't the worldwide glory of Russian culture hold some meaning as well? And it was formed here, among the Russian fields, the legends handed down through the generations, lanes of linden trees, and ancestral memories.[3]

Because the Russian steppes cover vast distances, the country estates became oases: relatives and close friends arrived and stayed for many weeks or even an entire season (mainly summer, but the visits could extend from late spring into early fall as well). Located approximately 330 miles to the southeast of Moscow, Ivanovka until the late nineteenth century was accessible only by horse or coach. The nearest main city was Tambov in Uvarovo

District about 42.5 miles to the north. In the 1890s a new railroad line was constructed from Tambov that included a station about eleven miles away from Ivanovka. By the time that Rachmaninoff came of age, travel between Ivanovka and Tambov, or Tambov and Moscow, had become considerably easier than during the first years of his life in the 1870s. Because Uvarovo District enjoyed a temperate climate and outstanding soil, many noble families chose to develop their estates in this part of Russia. They knew each other and found ways to maintain contact even across the vast distances of hundreds of miles. One example was the breeding and racing of horses, an activity in which Rachmaninoff participated with considerable enthusiasm.

The family estate of Ivanovka was owned by the Satins; it bore the same name of an adjoining village of about one hundred houses. Peasants who worked on the estate lived in this small village. The local parish church that the inhabitants of the estate and village attended was situated five miles away; as was the tradition for owners of Russian country estates, this church had been built by the Satins. It was both the tradition and responsibility of the estate owners to attend to the spiritual well-being as well as physical health and education of their peasants.

In the mid-nineteenth century the estate and village of Ivanovka, both owned by the Satins, consisted of over one thousand acres of land. After the liberation of the serfs in 1861, 564.3 acres of this land (209 desiatinas) were divided equally among the forty-three peasant households attached to the estate. This meant that each household was given approximately 13 acres. Some years after his marriage to Natalia Satina, in 1910, Rachmaninoff purchased the estate, outbuildings, and acreage; the estate with its surrounding lands at that time consisted of about 600 acres. One year after he became the owner of the estate, he gave to the peasants of the village of Ivanovka some additional lands.[4] Thus the estate by 1911 occupied slightly more than 264 acres and was typical for medium-sized Russian properties of this kind.[5] It consisted of two main houses, outbuildings, enclosures for various farm animals, gardens, ponds, large stands of trees, paths for long strolls, and gazebos for reflection and light meals. Its picturesque park was laid out by Baroness Emilia Elisabeth von Krüdener, a relative of Rachmaninoff's wife; the baroness also outfitted the extensive library of Ivanovka.[6] Its fertile soil to this day is a glistening black, part of Russia's *чернозем* (black earth region).[7]

Rachmaninoff lived and worked at Ivanovka for extended periods of time between 1890 and 1917. He especially enjoyed the gardens of lilacs and lilies-of-the-valley (both were his favorite flowers); in the spring and summer the scent of the large, tall lilac bushes lining the road to the main house was intoxicating. Adding to the perfume were the tiny lilies-of-the-valley growing in rows at the feet of the lilac bushes. He laid out his compositions while sitting in his favorite gazebos or walking along the *красная аллея*

Figure 5.1   **Manor House of Ivanovka, 2003.** Author's photo.

(red brick lane) and played the piano in the флигель (smaller house near the main house). Despite the implication of a leisurely life of strolling about and sketching musical notes, Rachmaninoff's routine of composing and practicing the piano for many hours involved strenuous mental toil. As B. S. Nikitin points out:

> 85% of Rachmaninov's compositions were thought of in Ivanovka. His twenty-six years abroad saw only six original pieces, four of which were conceived in Ivanovka. Not everybody knows that Rachmaninov began his fourth concerto in Ivanovka and completed it abroad. Not everybody knows that his *Symphonic Dances* are his Russian project of the ballet "Scythians," also conceived in Ivanovka. . . . Many ideas were conceived, matured, and realized in Ivanovka.[8]

The harmonious way of life and stability of routine of Ivanovka especially appealed to Rachmaninoff, for he could relax but also accomplish a great deal of creative work in this kind of environment. But this work was carried out in an environment of tranquility and restorative beauty. The landscape of the estate was and remains enchanting and conducive to meditation, rest, communing with nature, and engaging in romance.

In some ways the stories of the three women focused on in this chapter intersect. A major trauma of Rachmaninoff's adolescence connected with Ivanovka, a bittersweet episode for the composer, was his first experience of falling in love. The woman's name was Vera Dmitrievna Skalon, one of his

Figure 5.2 Rachmaninoff's "Composing Lane" at Ivanovka, 2003. Author's photo.

cousins. He met her in the summer of 1890. Vera was associated with the time Rachmaninoff spent at Ivanovka, and also with his activities in Moscow. The following fall (1891), when Rachmaninoff was starting what would be his last year at the conservatory, he developed an intense connection with the exotic Anna Aleksandrovna Lodyzhenskaia and her musical family. At Ivanovka in the months preceding and immediately following his marriage to Natalia Aleksandrovna Satina in 1902, Rachmaninoff noticed the beautiful peasant woman Maria Aleksandrovna Ivanova (usually referred to as "Marina"), who eventually became the newly married Rachmaninoffs' house manager.

VERA SKALON

Vera Skalon was the youngest of the three sisters who spent the summer of 1890 at Ivanovka with two other families, the Silotis and the Satins, the latter of which were the owners of the estate. Sergei's family was directly related to the Skalons, Silotis, and Satins, which meant that he had cousins in all three families; the interconnectedness of these clans only intensified the closeness the cousins experienced with each other. Life at Ivanovka involved planning and hard work for both landowners and peasants, but it also included boat rides on the pond, horseback riding, musical performances (most of the cousins played the piano and sang), and conversations over tea and pastries at one of the gazebos that lasted deep into the evening. Various cultural activities and the enjoyment of the well-maintained natural surroundings of the estate were shared by the tight-knit company of cousins in the families of the Rachmaninoffs, Skalons, Satins, and Silotis. Aside from Sergei, they consisted of the three Skalon sisters of Natalia, Liudmila, and Vera (Natalia at twenty-one was the oldest, while Vera at fifteen was the youngest); and the four Satin children of Aleksandr (who was sixteen), Natalia (thirteen years old), Sofia (eleven years old), and Vladimir (eight years of age). Sergei's cousin Aleksandr Siloti, who was ten years older than he, should also be mentioned here as a prominent member of this lively clan.

Vera shared with Sergei (who was two years older) a love of music and poetry, while her outgoing personality helped to bring out his more introverted character. A photograph of her taken in 1897 at the Skalon estate of Ignatovo reveals a stately young woman with delicate features and long, strawberry-blond hair. Rachmaninoff grew close not only to Vera but to her sisters Liudmila and Natalia (the oldest of the three) as well. His relationship with Vera that summer of 1890 was clearly romantic and noticed by others in the family, including Vera Pavlovna Siloti (Aleksandr Siloti's wife) and Vera Skalon's own mother Elizaveta Aleksandrovna. The adults took measures to prevent Sergei and Vera from being alone, and the budding romance seemingly came to an end. However, Vera recorded events and feelings in her diary from June 14 to July 11, 1890, which revealed strong youthful emotions on the part of Sergei, her sister Natalia, and herself that clearly had not been resolved. Many movements of the emotions were at play, and the relationships were complicated. Vera noticed Sergei's attentiveness to Natalia and bore his occasional neglect of her with emotional pain and confusion. On June 8 when Sergei, Natalia, and Vera were together in the house, the latter wrote in her diary:

> In the evening an argument erupted concerning the opera *Mefistofele*, which Tatusha (Natalia) praises so much in her novel [which she had written]. Sergei Vasilievich completely rejects Tatusha's position; they went upstairs with the piano music in question. Tatusha played [the piano] for a long time, but both of them did not change their opinion. I'll be glad when Sergei Vasilievich has finished Tatusha's novel, and hope that he will soon forget it.
>
> Well, whom is he courting? I ask myself this question a hundred times a day, but can't figure out the answer.[9]

On July 9, Vera described a moment of reckoning that took place outdoors:

> After breakfast today they harnessed a horse to the cabriolet, and Sergei Vasilievich because of his seniority drove us around the barn. I waited for my

Figure 5.3 Vera Dmitrievna Skalon, c. 1895. Public domain.

turn in an agitated state . . . I cannot describe my feelings when suddenly he looked at me and said quietly and tenderly: "Oh, with such happiness I'd take away my little Psychopath [Sergei's pet name for Vera] to the ends of the earth." It felt like my heart stopped beating, the blood rushed to my head, and then my heart started beating so rapidly that I almost suffocated. We were both silent. Alas, after several minutes we had already driven around the barn and garden, and once again found ourselves at the front yard. Oh, why can't we in reality go away to the ends of the earth?[10]

On July 10, Vera exulted:

My torments have ended, everything has been clarified. Starting from today I feel paradise in my heart. It may seem strange, but I already had gotten used to the thought that he [Sergei] loves me, but meanwhile I became convinced of it only yesterday. It seems that everyone around me is also happy.

I would like to know if Seryozha has guessed that I love him. I want him to know, but for some reason I also feel ashamed.[11]

Why Vera Skalon would feel "ashamed" is a matter for speculation, but perhaps this reaction can be attributed to her lack of experience with the powerful emotion, and also to having the drama of her feelings play out in full view of her large family. With the passing of the summer, Rachmaninoff returned to Moscow in August for the beginning of the school year at the conservatory. Despite the prohibition put on his direct communication with Vera, Sergei maintained contact with her through correspondence to her two older sisters, particularly with Natalia. This correspondence is filled with polite yet earnest requests, witticisms, awkwardness, and even uneasiness.

B. S. Nikitin describes the connection between Sergei and Natalia Skalon as follows:

Natalia Dmitrievna Skalon because of her age and the particulars of her personality was the dominant one in this company, and even stubborn Sergei in his daily activities and amusements submitted to her authority with pleasure, in jest referring to her as his "Mentor"—a nickname that remained associated with the beautiful and strong-minded girl for a long time. It seemed that in Sergei's pleasure of submitting to the caprices of his "Mentor" was the sense . . . that Natalia Dmitrievna Skalon not only affected him as the oldest sister, but had captivated him as well.

It was very evident that Sergei experienced pleasure in conversing with Natalia Skalon. This is especially noticeable in their correspondence, which served as an extension of their interactions at Ivanovka that summer [of 1890]. Sergei wrote to Natasha often and shared virtually all his thoughts and feelings with her . . . and, if other evidence had not suggested to the contrary, the content of these letters could imply, that during this summer at Ivanovka a longlasting and secure love had been awakened between them.¹²

This "other evidence" consisted of references in the same correspondence between Sergei and Natalia to his feelings of attraction to her younger sister Vera. The liveliness of these letters, as well as the somewhat tangled interactions between Sergei and the three sisters, can be seen in the following excerpts. Sergei clearly had to find ways to communicate with Vera indirectly, through allusions and humor. In a letter to Natalia Skalon of October 9 or 10, 1890, from Moscow, he describes his first teaching experience in a choral society class:

> When I walked into the classroom, externally I was, as should always be the case, completely calm. But, to be honest, in my soul I was somewhat embarrassed, because it was the first time that I found myself in this situation.
>
> All the students stood up. Once again it wasn't possible [for anyone] to discern my inner state—but in my soul I started to laugh and, it seems, right on the spot to myself called them idiots. At their age I would never have stood up in front of a teacher three times younger than they. I sat down and they sat down. It was necessary for me to talk for almost the entire lesson. I spoke badly, but at this point one couldn't expect anything better from me. Judge for yourself. For example, I said: "For you, future teachers of choral singing, is it vital to know this and that," then I started mumbling and thinking at that moment either about how alabaster-skinned the little psychopath [Vera] is, or about how I should construct one passage in the second part of *Manfred*.¹³ On the whole, even here the female generals [the three Skalon sisters] don't allow me to mentally focus the way I should . . .¹⁴

At the end of the same letter Rachmaninoff adds as a postscript: "Please bow to *brikusha* [untranslatable nickname for Vera], and to Tsukina¹⁵ Dmitrievna [Liudmila Skalon] for me."

In another letter that Rachmaninoff wrote to Liudmila Skalon, whose date is established only as the first half of November 1890, he ends with the words "You know . . . the little psychopath [Vera] . . . has such alabaster skin."¹⁶ The following month, in a letter to Natalia Skalon dated December 18, 1890, from Moscow, he writes:

> In her last letter, Vera Dmitrievna, a.k.a. *brikusha*, wrote to me that the three of you are going to a performance of *The Queen of Spades*. I'm not saying for certain, but it's very likely that I, too, will be at that performance; and if I'll be there, I'll take the risk to enter the opera box where the female Skalon generals are seated, in order to remind them of my existence . . . once I enter that space I will have entered into the kingdom of heaven . . . I won't stay with you for more

than five minutes, because I know well that it's not polite to be a bore. That's the ideal of modesty for you, my dear mentor [Natalia Skalon].[17]

In late December Sergei traveled to St. Petersburg to spend some time with his mother and relatives for the holidays. On January 2, 1891, he departed there (as he described in a letter to Natalia Skalon) for Moscow, arriving in the latter city on January 6. He wrote immediately to Natalia from Moscow, and in this letter eagerly, perhaps even anxiously, requested that she send him details about a special meeting that Vera had had with a suitor, Sergei Petrovich Tolbuzin. Vera had known this suitor since childhood. Rachmaninoff wrote to Natalia:

> In your next letter please tell me about your festive ride in the troika. And tell me about the ball you attended. Tell me about the serious conversation between *Brikusha* [Vera] and Sergei Petrovich. Tell me, i.e., write in detail about this last matter. You cannot imagine the extent to which everything concerning *Brikusha* and Sergei Petrovich interests me!!!
>
> Bow to Brikusha for me, and tell her (she probably doesn't know this) that she is "alabaster-white."
>
> S. Rachmaninoff[18]

In the recollections of Liudmila Rostovtsóva (née Skalon), the middle sister of the three Skalon sisters, she provides an anecdote from 1897 that reveals the close interactions of the lively cousins in connection with Sergei. The anecdote also points to the Skalon sisters' teasing acceptance of Natasha Satina's claim on Sergei—when Natasha was twenty years old and Sergei was twenty-four:

> My parents invited Seryozha [Sergei] to our estate Ignatóvo (in what was at that time Nizhegorod Province). Mama kept putting off the day of departure [from St. Petersburg] for Ignatóvo, and my sister Verochka [Vera] even developed a nervous fever due to her agitation and impatience. The fever got as high as 40 degrees C. Finally, it was decided that Tatusha [Natalia Skalon] and I would leave in advance and pick up Seryozha in Moscow. [Natalia and Liudmila arrived at the Satins in Moscow on May 13, 1897, where Sergei was staying, and left with him for Ignatovo on May 15.] When Vera received the telegram stating that all three of us had set out for Ignatóvo, she calmed down and recovered from her fever.
>
> In Moscow we found Seryozha in the most terrible shape. He had grown extremely thin, and every movement on his part produced in him neuralgic pain [in part because of back trouble and in part because of his emotional suffering due to the failure of his Symphony No. 1]. Natasha, his future wife, was deeply concerned about him. While seeing us off at the train, she said, "I give

my treasure into your hands" [emphasis added]. "Don't worry, Natasha," we replied, "we'll try to bring him back to you completely healthy."[19]

Sergei's expansive and introspective letters to Natalia Skalon continued right up to the period immediately preceding his marriage to their cousin Natalia Satina in 1902. Because of the intimate and trusting tone of their remarkable correspondence, the question arises as to whether Sergei entertained more than feelings of Platonic love toward Natalia—and she for him. The ability for him to open his innermost feelings to Natalia resulted in her serving as a kind of confessor who remained very dear to him. With most people he was reserved and introverted, but when he felt close to someone he would reveal to that person an inner world that was broad-ranging in its intelligence, wit, and often self-deprecating humor. His correspondence with Natalia was reflective and honest; he trusted her and felt so emotionally safe with her that he could pour out his feelings in organized form in his letters (some of which are quite long). In a compelling letter of June 26, 1899, Sergei characterizes his nine-year relationship with her as having four significant periods or phases: an immediate meeting of the minds and hearts, a period of estrangement and misunderstanding, a period of mutual compromise in honor of a cherished past friendship, and a return to a solid and mature friendship. He writes:

> In my opinion, dear Tatusha, you and I are now approaching the fourth and at the same time last period of our personal relationship.
>
> Doesn't your sweet letter to me prove this [return to a deep friendship]? Doesn't your phrase, that you think you love me as in the past, also prove this? And the fact that you really regretted having to leave St. Petersburg several hours before I arrived there and your supposition, about which you were correct, that I, too, regretted this—isn't all this, so to say, the first timid breakthrough to our new, renewed, and now already faithful friendship No. 2? Oh! I don't doubt this, at least at the present moment.
>
> For the time being I rejoice in your happiness and weep over your tears and sorrows. I believe that until my death I will be your friend and that now, thank God, we have reached the shore.[20]

The letter in many ways represents an extraordinary outpouring of a perceptive man to whom this woman, though perhaps not consciously the object of romantic, passionate love, meant a great deal and occupied a permanent place in his heart.

Sergei dedicated moving art songs to each of the Skalon sisters; he made sure that the words of the poems he set to music connected with the sensibilities of the given sister.

Throughout his life his music would derive from the emotional content of his interactions with others. This characteristic of his composing was present from his earliest musical works; the relationships with the Skalon sisters, his future wife Natalia, and his closest male friends who were also musicians would give rise to music in a variety of genres during his last student years at the conservatory and first years as a professional musician. Examples include the Romance for cello and piano (August 1890; dedicated to Vera Skalon); the Valse and Romance for piano trio (Valse dated August 15, 1890; Romance dated September 20, 1891; dedicated to Vera, Liudmila, and Natalia Skalon); and the Two pieces for cello and piano (Op. 2, 1892; dedicated to cellist Anatoly Brandukov).

Special consideration must be given here to Rachmaninoff's art songs, a miniature vocal genre much-revered by Russians and produced by most nineteenth- and twentieth-century Russian composers. Tchaikovsky and Rimsky-Korsakov especially inspired Rachmaninoff in this genre, but one must also include Liszt's influence on Rachmaninoff's expansion of the piano's language and prominence in the latter's art songs. The genre's demands, both for the composer and performer, are complex, for each song requires its own mood and subtle dynamics, specific narrative expression, and presentation of an entire, self-contained world within the space of only a few minutes. Moreover, the entirety of each art song consists of the poem whose words attract the composer and express specifically (rather than in the veiled form of musical notes) what he/she has in mind; the musical song setting for the words; the connection that words and music have with a dedicatee; and the creative interpretation of the whole by the vocalist. The hybridity of this genre presents major challenges for those involved in its realization; it is indeed a meaning-laden convergence of poetry and music.

The art song represents one of the most enduring forms of music in Russia, containing in itself the poetry that Russians even in the twenty-first century memorize and love, along with the music that a majority of composers in the classical and popular song traditions craft to align with the spoken words of the poems. It is a truism that Russians love their culture, and that classical forms of musical expression in Russia stay squarely in the mainstream, as opposed to being relegated (as, for example, in the United States) to the edges of musical culture. In Russia, as is the case in Italy with respect to opera, people of all social classes know the art songs of Tchaikovsky and Rachmaninoff (among many other composers). The housekeeper in a hotel, taxi driver, university professor, businesswoman, and receptionist in a dormitory all have a broad familiarity with the well-known art songs of their country.[21] This fact may explain the art song's unintended function as one of the unifying cultural elements of Russia.

Perhaps other explanations can be found for the attachment that Russians have to their tradition of art songs (*romansy*) in the theories of intercultural communication, which categorize countries and regions of the world as more "emotional" (Slavic countries) or more "reserved" (northern countries of Western Europe), which would lead to the conclusion that Russians (whose language is also considered "emotional" in its structures and forms) remain very close to their poetry and music—in themselves art forms that in an unmediated way express the full range of human feelings. Truman Bullard has differentiated in specific ways between Russian classical music—which remains freer in its forms and creates a directness of connection with the listener because it is a relatively young art form—and European classical music—which typically must adhere to centuries of established traditions in form and content and thus does not always seem as free or spontaneous as its Russian counterpart.[22]

Seven characteristics define the way in which Rachmaninoff developed the art song genre and expanded the role of the piano in it:

1. Collaboration between the vocal and piano textures of each song. The skill with which this is accomplished in Rachmaninoff's songs issues from his being a composer who was also a conductor and pianist. The piano participates prominently in the unfolding drama of the given song. This produces a "saturation of beauty" and density of part writing in his musical work.
2. An overtly melodic piano part, sometimes rivaling the beauty of the vocal line. In many of his art songs the piano part is orchestral in its dimensions and can function as a complete artistic work in its own right. As Mozart before him, Rachmaninoff is recognized as a master melodist.
3. Creative exploitation to the fullest of the resources of the human voice and piano.
4. The piano part frames the vocal line, wrapping itself around the body of the song. Typically the first words of the vocal line are introduced by several measures of the piano—and the piano often makes the last statement of the song.
5. A complex emotional content, with an undercurrent of sadness or melancholy.
6. Extensive use of chromatic features influenced by Byzantine and Russian Orthodox liturgical chant.
7. The presence of the so-called *eternal themes* in art as they played out in a Russian composer's mind: the connection between the individual and the Divine; affirmation of Russian Orthodox spirituality; the joy and sadness of love; existential yearning for the homeland; preoccupation with the transitoriness of life and inevitability of death; reverence for the beauty of nature.

The period of Rachmaninoff's life from the late 1880s until 1902, the year of his marriage, saw the composition of art song masterpieces that remain standards in the repertoire of any vocalist working in the Russian Romantic and Late-Romantic traditions. Among the six songs of Op. 4 (1893) "Oh, no! I beg you, don't leave me" (No. 1) is dedicated to Anna Lodyzhenskaia; "In the silence of the secret night" (No. 3) is dedicated to Vera Skalon; and "My beauty, don't sing the songs of Georgia in my presence" (No. 4) is dedicated to Natalia Satina. Moreover, in the fall of that same year Rachmaninoff completed another cycle of six songs, Op. 8, in which "A Dream" (No. 5) is dedicated to Natalia Skalon. Several years later, in 1896, he dedicated his song "I'm waiting for you" (Op. 14, No. 1) to the middle Skalon sister Liudmila. Richard D. Sylvester describes concerning this song: "the images of dark veils and perfumed shadows are effective in suggesting the erotic implications of this rendezvous: a woman . . . is waiting to meet her lover, with passion, longing, and eagerness to surrender."[23] Clearly these women occupied important places in Rachmaninoff's emotional life. The song "In the silence of the secret night" contains intimate words that suggest encounters between the young Sergei and Vera:

I will chase away and summon back
thoughts of the thick locks of your hair
so obedient to my fingers.
I will whisper and repeat the phrases
of my recent talks with you,
full of embarrassment;
and, enraptured, in defiance of reason,
I will awaken the darkness of the night
with your sacred name.[24]

The composer's genuine connection with the song's dedicatee is clear, while its melody is breathtakingly beautiful; it has remained very popular with vocalists programming Russian art songs.

When Vera was married in the fall of 1899 to her longtime friend Sergei Petrovich Tolbuzin, she burned her entire correspondence with Sergei that consisted of over one hundred letters. One can only conjecture the personal content of those letters and regret what was lost in them. The marriage was desired by her parents and she acquiesced to their wishes. This period was difficult for both Vera and Sergei; the accounts of their contemporaries all attest to their continuing strong feelings for each other, and yet respect for the diverging trajectories of their lives. When Sergei was married three years later, in April 1902, Vera helped his bride (and her close friend and cousin) Natalia Satina dress in her wedding gown before the ceremony in Moscow and served as a matron of honor. Again, one can only imagine the pain Vera must have experienced at helping her cousin put on the wedding gown for marriage to the person she herself was unable to attain. Her life became emotionally stressful, very likely due to her new family responsibilities and unresolved feelings for Sergei. She had always been in frail health because of heart trouble, and was fated to die quite young, only seven years later, in 1909, at the age of thirty-four. Rachmaninoff's art song immortalized her and their youthful, undeveloped relationship.

All three of the Skalon sisters retained feelings of love and respect for Rachmaninoff for the rest of their lives. The two sisters who survived Vera's early death, Liudmila and Natalia, were deeply saddened when Sergei and his family left Russia. Years later, upon learning of Sergei's death, Natalia was devastated and outlived "the dearest friend of the happy days of her youth" by only a few months.[25]

ANNA LODYZHENSKAIA

Rachmaninoff's acquaintance and romantic connection with Anna Lodyzhenskaia span the years of 1891–1897. She represents in his life and music the gypsy themes of love, loyalty, freedom, and closeness to nature that captivated Russian creative minds of the nineteenth century and endure in Russian creative expression to this day. One immediately thinks of Pushkin's narrative poem *The Gypsies* (1827), which inspired Rachmaninoff's opera *Aleko* (1892), and even Leo Tolstoy's *The Cossacks* (1853–1862), in which the main character Olenin enters the foreign and exotic world of Cossacks that resembles in some ways the culture of the gypsies.

The young Rachmaninoff dedicated two important works to Anna Lodyzhenskaia: a vividly expressive art song ("Oh, no! I beg you, don't forsake me," Op. 4, No. 1, 1893), and a large-scale musical work (Symphony No. 1 in D Minor, Op. 13, 1895). Interestingly, during this period of composition he also dedicated a lively work to Anna's husband Petr Lodyzhensky (the Capriccio on Gypsy Themes, Op. 12, 1894), perhaps in order to acknowledge respectfully this close relative of Anna's or even out of pity for Lodyzhensky's inability to manage the particulars of his own life successfully. The significance Rachmaninoff attached to his relationship with Anna is underscored by his dedication to her of an entire symphony, his first in that genre. Anna represented a muse to him: her presence occupied both his emotional and composing life. She was several years older than he, and married. A photograph of her that has survived shows a small, delicate dark-haired woman with attractive features. She appears meek, reserved, and refined in the picture. Recollections of Rachmaninoff by his cousins mention that he spent many evenings at her house in Moscow.

In a memoir about Rachmaninoff, Liudmila Skalon recollects:

The entire winter of 1894/95 I lived at the Satins in Moscow near Arbat Street on Serebryanny Lane. Their house was a modest wooden mansion. Downstairs there was a large room with a piano, the bedroom of my uncle and aunt, dining room, and bedrooms of Sasha [the younger brother of Natasha and Sofia] and of Natasha and Sofia. Sofia ceded her place to me, settling herself on the second floor . . . Seryozha [Rachmaninoff] lived at their house once again that winter. His room—a rather spacious and sunny one—was the only one on the third floor. A piano stood in his room, and he practiced and composed on it all day.

Almost every evening Seryozha would go to his friends the Lodyzhenskys.

Anna Aleksandrovna was his passionate platonic love. One could not say that she exerted a good influence on him. She somehow pulled him into her petty, shady interests. Her husband was a dissolute reveller, and she would often ask Sergei to leave the house to look for him. My sisters and I [the three Skalon sisters] and Natasha [Satina] didn't like Anna Aleksandrovna's appearance. Only her eyes were pretty: they were large gypsy eyes. Her mouth was unattractive, with lips that were too full. She had a sister—the well-known gypsy singer N.A. Aleksandrova . . . at Sergei's request, she would sing only songs of the gypsy camps, which made him ecstatic.[26]

Sergei would typically return to the Satins' house from the Lodyzhenskys' at midnight.

During this period of his life, his late teens, Rachmaninoff was experiencing extreme instability: he lacked a permanent place of residence, moving from one country estate to another, felt uncertain about his future career as a musician, and yearned to be in love in a stable relationship with a woman who understood him. He did not have much money, and disliked the necessary task of giving music lessons to children of well-meaning wealthy aristocrats. A telling incident is that in the fall of 1892 he did not have enough money even for the purchase of a new overcoat; the three Skalon sisters took it upon themselves to purchase one and give it to him as a gift—which touched him, but also was slightly embarrassing. It is likely that at this time of emotional fragility and lack of material resources Sergei was introduced to Anna Lodyzhenskaia. He had rented an apartment in Moscow for the academic year of 1891–1892 with his conservatory friend, the talented singer Mikhail Akimovich Slonov, and the latter was acquainted with the Lodyzhensky family. Both Rachmaninoff and Slonov were friends with the young composer Yury Sergeeevich Sakhnovsky, who also spent time at the Lodyzhenskys. Thus either Slonov or Sakhnovsky introduced Rachmaninoff to Anna Lodyzhenskaia, her husband Petr Viktorovich Lodyzhensky, and her sister Nadezhda Aleksandrovna Aleksandrova.

This company of musically gifted and cultured people frequently gathered at the Lodyzhenskys to share meals, recite poetry, engage in long conversations, and perform vocal and instrumental music together. Anna and Nadezhda were of gypsy origins, which added to their appeal for Rachmaninoff and his friends. For his entire life Sergei would retain an intense attraction to gypsy music and culture, a preference of his that was noticed by his contemporaries. Nadezhda Lodyzhenskaia was a celebrated singer of authentic gypsy-camp songs, while Anna's husband Petr played the piano and composed music. As for Anna, no evidence exists of her being musical, but she would have understood and valued the gypsy songs for their soulful melodies and connections to her own heritage. Rachmaninoff accompanied Nadezhda at the piano and played his own compositions as well as those of others for the company. He experienced real solace and pleasure, a feeling of belonging, in such a group of people.

Conflict for Anna came in the form of her husband Petr's too-easygoing and carefree ways. In B. S. Nikitin's words, "Soulful, emotionally responsive, and generous, as many Russians who lacked success in the creation of romantic works of art, he [Petr] gradually became enamored of carousing and began to disappear from gatherings of family and friends."[27] Close friends of Anna were often recruited to look for him and bring him home. Rachmaninoff was among those always willing to help the distraught and somewhat embarrassed Anna in these times of need, and it is likely as a result of their conversations about Anna's personal problems and Sergei's own insecurities that a bond between them was formed. They began to spend extended periods of time together alone: Sergei developed the habit, noticed by his relatives and friends, of visiting her in the evenings and returning home (as his cousin Liudmila Skalon noted) at midnight. Anna evidently was genuine, a good listener, kindhearted, and beautiful in the exotic ways associated with the gypsies. The sadness of her personal life must have made her dark beauty even more attractive to Sergei, while at the same time eliciting in him feelings of injustice and even outrage at her plight. His correspondence of this period is filled with references to her, calling her "my dear relative" (*rodnaia*).

As was the case with Vera Skalon, a powerful and tender art song composed by Sergei captures his conflicted emotions concerning Anna Lodyzhenskaia; it is titled "Oh no, I beg you, don't leave" and is dedicated to her:

Oh no, I beg you, don't leave!
This pain is slight compared to separation,
I'm too happy in this state of torment,
Press me hard against your breast,

Say "I love you." I've come to you again,
Sick, tormented, and pale.

Figure 5.4 Anna Aleksandrovna Lodyzhenskaia, c. 1895. Public domain.

See how weak and pitiful I am,
How much I need your love . . .

New torments lie ahead,
I greet them like caresses, like kisses,
And beg for only one thing in my agony,
Oh, stay with me, don't leave!
Oh, stay with me, don't leave![28]

Rachmaninoff biographer Victor Seroff reflected: "Rachmaninoff in his youth was very different from the portrait that has been painted of him. He was a young man with a very passionate nature, easily carried away, sentimental, spoiled by early success, flattery, and fame, and with none of the strength of will and equilibrium which he fully developed later."[29]

The full complex of feelings that Sergei experienced for this unhappy, irresistible married woman took on additional musical form in the composition of his Symphony No. 1 in D minor. He not only dedicated it to "A.L." [Anna Lodyzhenskaia], but added to the dedication the biblical verse "Vengeance is mine; I will repay, saith the Lord" (Romans 12:19). As is well-known, Tolstoy used the same verse for the epigraph of his novel *Anna Karenina* (1873–1877); Rachmaninoff would have remembered the lines equally from the verse of

Romans and from his acquaintance with the novel. The similarities between Anna Karenina's predicament—an unhappy marriage and illicit relationship—and Anna Lodyzhenskaia's would not have been lost on Sergei, who himself was involved in her family drama. Ultimately, the turbulence of the situation in which he found himself would be expressed in the symphony itself: in its dramatic themes, rhythmic innovativeness, and the dark motifs of the *Dies irae* Latin medieval requiem, the symphony's moods would reflect the panorama of Anna and Sergei's frustrations. Rachmaninoff's famous words concerning artistic creativity come to mind: "Love is certainly a never-failing source of inspiration. Love inspires as nothing else does. To love is to gain happiness and strength of mind. It is the unfoldment of a new vista of intellectual energy."[30]

While Rachmaninoff's experience with the Lodyzhenskys was not a unique one, the performance history of his first symphony emerges as quite remarkable. Word of its completion made its way through the musical circles in Moscow; Sergey Taneev in a letter to M. P. Beliaev written very likely in January–February 1897, awaited its first performance with great anticipation: "I am very happy that Rachmaninoff's symphony will be performed. If Rachmaninoff seemed 'presumptuous,' as you write, it must be attributed to his awareness of his own genuinely outstanding talent for composition . . . On the whole, I expect great things of Rachmaninoff."[31] The awaited première, which took place in St. Petersburg on March 15, 1897, was a disaster that affected Sergei deeply for several years thereafter. Differing versions of what went wrong range from the conductor Aleksandr Glazunov's being inebriated at the performance, to Glazunov's being overly confident about a score that turned out to be more complex and sophisticated than he anticipated (he under-rehearsed it with the orchestra), to the symphony's being of poor quality, badly orchestrated, and overall badly composed. Reviews of the performance, though critical of the conductor and orchestra, were perceptive enough to recognize quality in the composition itself. The words of musicologist Nikolay Fyodorovich Findeisen, who was at the première, can serve as an example: he found the performance unsatisfactory and Glazunov's conducting indifferent to the music. Further, Findeisen notes in the music itself "many new flights of creativity, attempts to find new colors, new themes, new images."[32] Critical assessments of the work after its recovery in the mid-twentieth century only confirmed that Rachmaninoff's first symphony was innovative in many ways. Max Harrison sums up some important aspects of it:

> The score of Symphony No. 1 . . . is a particularly happy hunting ground for motivic analysis and it proves that Rachmaninoff could write genuinely symphonic music rather than the ballets squeezed into sonata shapes written by many composers, from Tchaikovsky to Stravinsky. This suggests that Rachmaninoff,

whatever he thought to the contrary, was descended from Borodin rather than Tchaikovsky. It is, indeed, the first of a number of works demonstrating that rather than being the incontinently 'romantic rhapsodist' he is still often taken to be, Rachmaninoff possessed a sense of large-scale form that was both acute and well focused.[33]

One can imagine the gamut of Sergei's emotions, coupled with the ruination of his desire to present the expression of his lofty feelings for Anna musically in the form of this major symphonic work. It was a public disgrace, a downfall from which the composer did not recover for many years. Rachmaninoff put away his master score of the work and declared that he would not allow it to be performed again during his lifetime. Rumors circulated that he had even destroyed the composition. However, after his death in 1943, a two-piano transcription of the symphony was discovered, and this event led to renewed interest in the work. In 1944 the orchestral parts for the symphony were discovered in the Leningrad Conservatory, and the full score was reconstructed by major Soviet conductor Aleksandr Gauk. The second performance of it took place triumphantly under the baton of Gauk at Rachmaninoff's alma mater, the Moscow Conservatory, after the end of World War II on October 17, 1945. The album notes for the distinguished performance of the symphony in 1967 by the USSR Symphony Orchestra conducted by Yevgeny Svetlanov explain:

> Ironically, with its revival nearly fifty years later in 1945, the First Symphony was hailed by Soviet critics as a turning point in the evolution of symphonic composition. Its polyphonic combinations which earlier caused so much distress now became the acknowledged forerunner of contemporary writing.
> ... here was music akin in its temperament to the writings of Tchaikovsky, Mussorgsky, Borodin and Rimsky-Korsakov—music emerging from a Russian composer who reflected the Russian feeling for lyricism, emotional truth and, above all, tragedy. There are even tender, melancholy Gypsy themes evident in the First Symphony's melodic fabric.[34]

How Rachmaninoff coped with and overcame the depression caused by the symphony's public failure will be discussed in a later chapter—but suffice it to say that he did recover and that during the process of recovery his musical activities did not cease.

Rachmaninoff retained tender feelings for Anna Lodyzhenskaia throughout the 1890s and into the twentieth century. In September 1897, several months after the debacle of the first symphony's première, Rachmaninoff wrote from the Skalons' country estate Ignatovo (where he was staying) to his close friend Slonov that he would soon arrive in Moscow and meet Slonov at the Lodyzhenskys on September 13. In December of that same year Rachmaninoff again wrote to Slonov that Rimsky-Korsakov would be honored at a performance of his opera *Sadko* on the 30th of the month and that the "my dear relative" (Anna Lodyzhenskaia) would be at the performance. In addition to accounts of his contemporaries and the musical works inspired by Anna, evidence of Sergei's feelings for her exists in the inscription he wrote on a photograph he gave her, which he dated May 19, 1892: "May God grant that this photograph will remind my dear, my own Anna Aleksandrovna Lodyzhenskaia as often as possible of the man who was sincerely devoted to her and who will always deeply respect her memory. [signed] The itinerant musician Seryozha R."[35] Indeed, Rachmaninoff always remembered with devotion and gratitude the love he had shared with the meek, beautiful Anna. Even after he was settled in the United States, he sent her money regularly, and after her death continued to give the same assistance to her husband Petr.

MARIA IVANOVA

A different kind of attachment and fate developed in the connections between Rachmaninoff and the peasant woman Maria (Marina) Aleksandrovna Ivanova, who worked as the house manager for the newly married Rachmaninoffs at Ivanovka. Marina was the daughter of Fedosia Dmitrievna, a cook who worked in the kitchen at the estate. By the year of 1885, when Marina was born, twenty-four years had passed since all serfs in Russia had been freed—with just the stroke of the pen of Tsar Aleksandr II, called the "tsar-liberator." Even though this act brought massive dislocation for millions of peasants-serfs, it also increased their rights and gave them freedom of movement from one place to another. Those serfs who were treated well and fairly by their former owners often chose to stay on the land they knew and continue working for their now-employers at agreed-upon wages. Where else would they go? The peasants who lived at Ivanovka during Rachmaninoff's youth and young adulthood were descendants of the serfs who had belonged to the Satins until 1861. After they were liberated, many chose to stay and establish a village just outside the estate's property. They could work on the estate in the daytime and return to their homes on foot in the village in the evening. Marina's mother was either very young at the time of liberation or had not been born yet, but it is probable that her grandmother had been a serf owned by the Satins and bound to the territory of Ivanovka.

Marina was beautiful and talented. A tall, stately young woman with long hair and expressive blue eyes, she was known on the estate for her fine singing voice. She sang Russian folk songs as she worked, and, as Irina Aleksandrovna Brandt (a peasant woman who had worked at Ivanovka with Marina) recollects, her voice could often be heard from various corners of the estate. As the Rachmaninoffs' house manager, Marina carried an enormous amount of responsibility and did her job superbly. Brandt recalls:

> She [Marina] managed to complete many household tasks. She made sure that the clothing of the entire Rachmaninoff family and bed linens were laundered and carefully ironed, made sure that all the rooms of their house were always clean and aired out. She and Yakov [the groom] would ride together to the farmers' market to buy everything needed for the house. She had a beautiful, resonant voice . . . Sometimes she sang to herself, but often she was invited to perform songs in the living room [of the main house].[36]

Marina had a thirst for learning and had largely taught herself grammar, three foreign languages, and to read music.[37] She was one of those peasants who possessed exceptional talents, and whose talents were encouraged by her employers. When one considers her personal and educational attributes, it is easy to understand why Rachmaninoff would have been attracted to her. Both of them shared a love for Russian folk songs and vocal singing.

Rachmaninoff's Song No. 10 of Opus 21 (1902), "Before the Icon," presents a musical reminder of his genuine affection for Marina Ivanova, who was beautiful, smart, musically talented, and so capable that she could manage well the residence of Sergei and Natalia. The song is dedicated to Marina, and thus its connection to her does not have to be surmised. The words by A. Golenishchev-Kutuzov that Rachmaninoff set to music include the lines:

She kept repeating someone's name,
And her gaze was illumined with a prayerful light;
And there was so much love and suffering,
So little hope in this prayer.

But everything was quiet in the silence of the night,
The oil lamp flickered in the gloom so alarming,
And with pity the eyes of the Savior looked down
At the one who had come with an impossible prayer.[38]

The newly married Sergei may have expressed in this song the hopelessness of such a love, selecting poetry with a maximum degree of expressiveness and the powerful image of a woman weeping and prostrating herself in her suffering before an icon. One interpretation of the song's content could surely be the hidden love Marina felt for Rachmaninoff; whether or not her feelings were returned remains an open question.

Irina Brandt was a young woman at the time that Rachmaninoff and his new wife moved into the house next to the main house (*barskii dom*) of the estate. She describes both the attraction that Sergei and Marina had for each other and the possibility of liaisons between the two:

> People said that Sergei Vasilievich and Marina had an affair. I cannot say anything about this, but I don't find anything strange about it, either. One would have to see Marina, in order to understand that not to fall in love with such a girl was practically impossible.[39]

B. S. Nikitin also notes the possibility of a closer relationship between the two than has previously been established:

> In 1922 Rachmaninoff met in Europe with Prof. Samoilov of Moscow State University and asked him to inquire about how Marina was getting along in Moscow. The professor willingly carried out the request and notified Rachmaninoff that Marina received the news about him with great emotional trepidation, and that everywhere in her room there was evidence of [what the professor termed] a "cult of Rachmaninoff."
>
> What can we conclude about this? What can the dedication to a young woman servant of such a sensitive and moving song with the plea for unattainable love tell us?
>
> Well, only what Rachmaninoff himself stated: "A beautiful women, of course, is a source of eternal inspiration."[40]

Marina's association with the Rachmaninoff family continued even after they decided to leave Russia in 1917, and it is significant that he trusted her so completely that he charged her with taking care of all of the family's possessions in their Moscow apartment that they were forced to leave behind (including his musical scores and archive). She carried out his wish bravely, not being willing to sell any of his valuable items even to help with her own material needs in the cataclysmic early 1920s—after the Bolshevik Revolution of 1917, end of World War I in 1918, Civil War of 1918–1922, and ensuing political chaos, violence, and famines that developed in many parts of Russia, including Moscow. Irina Brandt describes:

> I saw Marina for the last time by chance in Moscow. The Rachmaninoffs were already living abroad. . . . Marina told me that she had been able to visit the Rachmaninoffs abroad. She had taken them some of the manuscripts of Sergei Vasilievich. She said that Rachmaninoff had invited her to remain with them, but she turned down the offer. She had a husband and daughter in Moscow and could not leave them. With sadness in her voice she related that all the Rachmaninoffs had become different, that Sergei Vasilievich was working a great deal. As for herself, she was afraid of robbers and the Cheka [secret police].

She feared that she would be robbed, and then what would she say to Sergei Vasilievich? She herself looked sickly . . . Her once large and expressive eyes were dull, in them there was no longer Marina's previous fire and will to live.[41]

Rachmaninoff's enquiries about Marina's well-being and references to her in correspondence are filled with tenderness. As with Vera Skalon and Anna Lodyzhenskaia, Marina's fate was a difficult one. She died in 1925, one month after her husband was arrested and sentenced to five years of prison for supposedly trafficking in contraband—when he tried to send some of Rachmaninoff's personal items abroad to him. The cause of her death is not entirely clear: she was suffering from cancer, but the blow of her husband's imprisonment may have prompted her to commit suicide.[42]

If one considers Rachmaninoff's associations with various women in his life who were important to him both personally and professionally, especially those who remained in his life over long periods of time and to whom he dedicated some of his compositions, it raises the question of whether his relationship with his wife was entirely fulfilling for him. Since he spent his summers at Ivanovka, where Marina Ivanova was associated with him in many ways, and autumns and winters in Moscow where the residence of Anna Lodyzhenskaia and her husband was but a carriage ride away—it is reasonable to conclude that Rachmaninoff had existing emotional ties to at least two women during the period leading up to his marriage to Natalia Satina in April of 1902. It is thus not surprising that Rachmaninoff's future wife intensely disliked both Marina Ivanova and Anna Lodyzhenskaia. Natasha instinctively developed a negative reaction to any person or activity that would interfere with the peace of mind Sergei needed in order to advance his composing and performing projects. Moreover, she as a woman in love with Sergei would sense when another woman posed a threat to her claims on the man with whom she planned to spend the rest of her life. And she kept as close a watch as possible on other women, especially in the arts, who might potentially seek a liaison with her talented and distinctive-looking husband.

Sergei's youthful infatuation with Vera Skalon was characterized by an innocence and playfulness possible only during the time of a person's coming of age. His relations with Anna Lodyzhenskaia played out in an honorable and mutually respectful way, for she was married and there was no expectation that their feelings could develop. The dynamics among Sergei, Marina, and Sergei's wife Natalia were more complicated, however, owing to the proximity in which they functioned together. What remains most striking and most important is the influence these women exerted on him artistically, for he composed musical works of enduring beauty with their images in mind. The touching relationships he had with these young women, and other female figures with whom he would collaborate musically in Russia until 1917, took their place in the pantheon of muses who raised Rachmaninoff's inspiration to its highest level.

NOTES

1. See "Conversations and Exhortations of Elder Zosima" in Fyodor Dostoevsky, *The Brothers Karamazov*, trans. Constance Garnett (New York: Norton, 1976), 298.

2. See Vladimir Soloukhin, *A Time to Gather Stones*, trans. Valerie Z. Nollan (Evanston, IL: Northwestern University Press, 1993); and Priscilla Roosevelt, *Life on the Russian Country Estate* (New Haven, CT: Yale University Press, 1995).

3. V. Petrov, *V mire kruga zemnogo* (Lipetsk: Lipetskoe izdatel'stvo, 2000), 9–10, quoted in A.I. Ermakov and A.V. Zhogov, comp., *Ivanovka. Vremena. Sobytiia. Sud'by* (Moscow: Irina Arkhipova Foundation, 2003), 8.

4. The circumstances of this gift are explained in Chapter 9.

5. To arrive at these dimensions of the estate and its lands, I consulted Ermakov and Zhogov, as well as documents shared with me by I. N. Vanovskaia, Senior Research Associate of Ivanovka, in e-mail messages of July 9–10, 2022. Currently in 2022 the estate proper, which is surrounded by a security fence and patrolled by guards, consists of about 106 acres, with an additional 264 acres outside the fence that belong to Ivanovka as a National Historical Monument and cannot be altered without specific permission. For this data I also consulted an unpublished and untitled article on Rachmaninoff, Ivanovka, and Tambov given to me by B. S. Nikitin. Personal interview, Moscow, June 13, 2007.

6. Ermakov and Zhogov, comp., 36–39.

7. Ivanovka has been completely restored to its original design, according to the drawings of Rachmaninoff's cousin and sister-in-law Sofia Satina. Its restoration was a labor of love lasting many years and involving many people that was coordinated by Aleksandr Ivanovich Ermakov, Curator of the Ivanovka Museum-Estate of Rachmaninoff. It is meticulously maintained by a staff of approximately fifty, which includes research associates, gardeners, security guards, and maintenance workers. My first of three visits to Ivanovka took place in July 2003.

8. B.S. Nikitin, unpublished and untitled article, given to the author in Moscow on June 13, 2007, quote from 11–12.

9. V.D. Skalon, "Dnevnik," in *Vospominaniia o Rakhmaninove*, ed. Z.A. Apetian, 5th ed. (Moscow: Muzyka, 1988), II: 464.

10. Ibid., 465.

11. Ibid., 465–66.

12. B.S. Nikitin, *Sergei Rakhmaninov. Dve zhizni* (Moscow: Znanie, 1993), 28–29.

13. *Manfred*: a symphonic composition by Rachmaninoff, probably unfinished, which has been lost (dated 1890–1891).

14. S. Rakhmaninov, Letter, in *S. Rakhmaninov. Literaturnoe nasledie. Vospominaniia. Stat'i. Interv'iu. Pis'ma,* ed. Z.A. Apetian (Moscow: Sovetskii kompozitor, 1978), 1: 155.

15. "Tsukina" refers to the famous Italian ballerina Virginia Zucchi (1847–1930), who was adored at the time by Liudmila Skalon.

16. Apetian, *S. Rakhmaninov. Literaturnoe nasledie* . . . ,1: 157.

17. Ibid., 161.

18. Ibid., 161–62.

19. L.D. Rostovtsova, "Vospominaniia o S.V. Rakhmaninove," in *Vospominaniia o Rakhmaninove*, ed. Z.A. Apetian, I: 243, 257.

20. E. Yu. Zhukovskaia, "Vospominaniia o moem uchitele i druge S.V. Rakhmaninove," in *Vospominaniia o Rakhmaninove*, ed. Z.A. Apetian, I: 286–87.

21. Richard D. Sylvester observed this same phenomenon during his stays in Russia. See his *Tchaikovsky's Complete Songs* (Bloomington, IN: Indiana University Press, 2004), 283.

22. Truman Bullard, "An Introduction to Russian Music," in *Russia and Western Civilization: Cultural and Historical Encounters*, ed. Russell Bova (New York: Routledge, 2003), 211.

23. Richard D. Sylvester, *Rachmaninoff's Complete Songs* (Bloomington, IN: Indiana University Press, 2014), 63.

24. Translation of lines from "V molchanii nochi tainoi" (Op. 4, No. 3, 1893) by VZN.

25. Nikitin, 31.

26. Rostovtsova, in *Vospominaniia o Rakhmaninove*, ed. Z.A. Apetian, I: 237–39.

27. Nikitin, 34–35.

28. Sylvester, 32.

29. Victor I. Seroff, *Rachmaninoff* (New York: Simon and Schuster, 1950), 65, quoted in Robert Rimm, *The Composer-Pianists: Hamelin and The Eight* (Portland, OR: Amadeus Press, 1985), 147.

30. Basanta Koomar Roy, "Rachmaninoff is Reminiscent," *Musical Observer* 26 (May 1927): 16, accessed at https://www.pianostreet.com/smf/index.php?topic=17183.0.

31. S.I. Savenko, *Sergei Ivanovich Taneev* (Moscow: Muzyka, 1984), 136–37, undated letter, trans. VZN.

32. Nikitin, *Sergei Rakhmaninov. Dve zhizni*, 2nd ed. (Moscow: Klassika-XXI, 2008), 46.

33. Max Harrison, *Rachmaninoff: Life, Works, Recordings* (New York: Continuum, 2005), 80–81.

34. Album Notes, *Rachmaninov Symphony no. 1 in D Minor*, Op. 13, U.S.S.R. Symphony Orchestra, conducted by Yevgeny Svetlanov, recorded by Melodiya, printed by EMI Records, Great Britain, ASD 2471, 1967.

35. Trans. VZN from a view of the photograph.

36. Ermakov and Zhogov, 75.

37. It was not unusual for estate owners to encourage a peasant with marked talents to learn specific subjects, for the mastery of them could produce benefits for life on a given estate. At their own expense, the owners of Ivanovka had established a school for children of the peasant families. The fact that Marina learned foreign languages

also reveals the cultural atmosphere of Ivanovka—the foreign languages especially of French and German, along with some literacy in music, were legitimized in what she observed in the landowners and visitors.

38. "Pred ikonoi," trans. VZN.
39. Ermakov and Zhogov, 75, trans. VZN.
40. Nikitin, *Sergei Rakhmaninov. Dve zhizni* (1993), 91–92.
41. Ermakov and Zhogov, 75–76.
42. I thank A. I. Ermakov for providing me with this information. Personal interview, Ivanovka, July 1, 2005.

Chapter 6

Mystery of an Immortal Beloved

(1897–1902)

Composer, musicologist, and music critic L. L. Sabaneev, who was active in the same cultural circles in Moscow as Rachmaninoff, wrote in his memoir "My Meetings with Rachmaninoff":

> These years (1897–1900) represented the darkest and most troubled time in his biography. Some said that he decided to stop composing, that he had started to drink, that he had fallen in love, and that he had lost his creative gifts and was undergoing treatment at the hypnotist's [sic] N.V. Dahl, in order to restore his creativity. Which of these things was true and which fabricated was hard to tell.[1]

Feodor Chaliapin, who also knew and worked with Rachmaninoff during these years, wrote:

> My acquaintance with Sergei Rachmaninoff belongs among my first and most touching memories of friendships of my youth in Moscow. This took place during my first season with Mamontov [1896–1897]. A very young man was hired by the theatre, and I was introduced to him. . . . Everything I was told about him impressed me. We developed a warm and youthful friendship. We often went to Testov's [restaurant in Moscow] to dine, and talk about the theatre, music, and all sorts of things.
> Then I suddenly started to see him less often. This deep-thinking man with an intense inner life was going through some sort of internal crisis. He stopped appearing in public. He would compose music and tear it up in dissatisfaction. Fortunately, Rachmaninoff by sheer strength of will soon overcame this youthful crisis, and emerged from the "Hamlet" period ready for new [musical] work.[2]

When we consider the instability and turmoil taking place in Rachmaninoff's life in the 1890s and first years of the new century, and ponder accounts of his contemporaries of those years, the conclusion arises that the period immediately preceding his marriage in April 1902 to his first cousin Natalia Aleksandrovna Satina was complex, uncertain, and disjointed. The question arises: Could the emotional life of Rachmaninoff have been linked to another woman besides his future wife, as a result of which he experienced contradictory feelings about his approaching wedding? Underscoring the ambivalent emotions of the composer on the eve of his wedding are the turbulent musical themes of his Piano Concerto No. 2 in C minor (Op. 18, 1900–1901) and the strikingly gloomy poems selected by Rachmaninoff for the settings of his twelve art songs (Op. 21, 1902), such as "Fate" (On Beethoven's Fifth Symphony), "By a Fresh Grave," "Fragment from A. Musset" ("Loneliness"), "On the Death of a Linnet," "Melody" ("I wish I could die"), "Before the Icon," and "How Painful for Me." Details of these themes in Rachmaninoff's Second Concerto and the gloomy subjects of the art songs of Op. 21 are elaborated below.

An intriguing history surrounds Rachmaninoff's Piano Concerto No. 2, the period of whose composition coincides with his well-known creative crisis, which was largely brought on by the fiasco of his first symphony during its première in St. Petersburg. the canonical version of the composer's recovery after such a significant public failure is as follows: The composer's relatives (mainly the Satins) convinced him to seek treatment from the psychotherapist-musician N. V. Dahl, and as a consequence of Rachmaninoff's regularly occurring sessions with Dahl, which included psychotherapy along with fertile discussions about music, the composer was brought out of the state of crisis. However, it is possible that these events did not take place exactly as described herein.

Rachmaninoff may have fallen in love with another woman during this period.[3] The woman's name is Elena Dahl, a possible relative of Dr. Nikolai Dahl, the psychotherapist who purportedly helped Rachmaninoff to recover after the spectacular public failure of the latter's Symphony No. 1 in D minor on March 15, 1897. It was first performed in St. Petersburg under the baton of A. K. Glazunov. In this context some dates of Rachmaninoff's connection with Elena Dahl can be posited. Sergei Rachmaninoff started treatment for depression with Dr. Nikolai Dahl in October 1898 at Dahl's apartment in Moscow. The treatment lasted until December of the same year. The composer's depression came from an understandable source: the public failure of his first symphony. Rachmaninoff's course of treatment of 1898 was followed by a second course with Dr. Dahl in 1900, which is the one recorded in Western biographies.[4]

Thus Rachmaninoff's association with the Dahl family actually began two years earlier, in 1898, than is commonly believed. The second course of treatment took place only months prior to the announcement of his engagement to Natasha in the fall of 1901. Perhaps he was still in love with Elena at the time that he decided to marry Natasha. Apparently, he could not or chose not to pursue the relationship with Dahl, if such a relationship existed, for reasons that have not yet been established. He married Satina instead. There exists only anecdotal evidence of such a relationship, and only in the accounts of Rachmaninoff's grandson Alexandre Conius Rachmaninoff; hence the idea of this relationship must be approached with caution.

What has been pieced together about Sergei Rachmaninoff's posited relationship with the woman Elena Dahl comes from Alexandre Conius Rachmaninoff's personal recollections of a conversation he had with his grandmother Natalia Rachmaninoff; archival research; and hints in several original scores of Rachmaninoff's compositions.[5] According to Alexandre Rachmaninoff's account, his grandfather was in love with Elena (whom he called "Lana") Dahl and they remained in touch in one form or another throughout the composer-pianist's life. The specific nature of their relationship remains unknown, and there is no concrete documented evidence of such a person. Rachmaninoff's grandson's account highlights several important points: (1) there were major obstacles standing in the way of Sergei and Lena's possibly getting married: she may not have been Russian Orthodox, and she was not of the nobility; (2) Sergei stayed in touch with her for the rest of his life; sometimes there were large gaps in time in their being in touch; (3) Natalia Satina knew about this relationship; (4) probably with Sergei's assistance, Elena lived not far from wherever he and his family were living; (5) in the 1930s after the villa Senar was completed, Natalia asked Sergei not to bring Elena there; (6) Elena tried to attend Sergei's concerts whenever she could; and (7) Natalia invited Elena to say good-bye to Sergei at their house in his final days.

Dates and locations that line up with Sergei Rachmaninoff's own whereabouts during his life also place a possible relative of Elena's, Anton-Louis Dahl, in St. Petersburg (where Elena's family lived) and Los Angeles (which could also place Elena in the city of her beloved's final home and the possibility for her to be at his bedside before he died). Anton-Louis Dahl was a pianist who was accomplished enough to be invited to perform at Tsar Nicholas II's court; at some point, very likely because of the Bolshevik Revolution, he made his way to America. Because the Russian emigration at that time was concentrated in both New York State and California, he would have settled in or near New York City, Los Angeles, or San Francisco. His obituary indicates that he died on October 31, 1932, in Los Angeles. His birth date is unknown, but the date of his death could place him as possibly Elena's brother.[6]

Contributing to the possibility of a romantic connection between Rachmaninoff and Dahl are two dedications in his compositions of the given period that remain a mystery; the originals for these scores are located in the

Glinka Museum of World Musical Culture in Moscow. A cryptic dedication occurs in a short piece titled *Morceau de Fantaisie in G minor* by Rachmaninoff that is dated January 11, 1899: the word "Delmo" [Дельмо] appears below the title. The custom of writing one's name in Russian official contexts is in the order of last name, first name, and patronymic (middle name). Thus "Delmo" could be an acronym of an official name: *D* for Dahl, *El* for Elena, and *Mo* for the patronymic Morisovna.[7] On the cover of this musical work was the signature "S.V. Rachmaninoff, 1898." Rachmaninoff may have given this composition to Elena as a gift; it could represent the reawakening of his creative springs because of the positive influence of love. Rachmaninoff scholar A. A. Naumov concludes that a creative thread leads from *Morceau de Fantaisie* (1899) to *Francesca da Rimini* (1900–1904) to Piano Concerto No. 2 in C minor (1900–1901) and that this thematic line of his creativity stems from the feelings he experienced for Elena Dahl.[8]

The master score of his Piano Concerto No. 2 adds to the mystery of this period by showing a second dedicatee line (in addition to the dedication to Dr. Nikolai Dahl) with a name that is crossed out so completely that it is undecipherable.[9] Could this name be that of Elena Dahl? According to Alexandre Rachmaninoff, the crossed-out name is indeed Elena's, and the actual crossing out occurred at some point close to the première of Sergei's Piano Concerto No. 2 in C minor. It was Natalia Rachmaninoff who insisted that her husband eliminate the offending name as a dedicatee of the concerto.[10]

If Rachmaninoff was indeed connected with Elena Morisovna Dahl, it is not known how long their bond lasted. Thus far, precise evidence has not been uncovered. But if E. M. Dahl played an important, perhaps even an essential, role in the inner life of the composer, she could have been a source of his creative inspiration and her presence in Rachmaninoff's life would have influenced his compositions. The matter concerns not merely one or two minor compositions of his, but rather several masterpieces in their originality, large scope, and stunning beauty: the Piano Concerto No. 2, a cycle of art songs, his Symphony No. 2, Symphony No. 3, and perhaps even other compositions whose links with this woman were mentioned by the composer's grandson Alexandre Rachmaninoff.[11] The question of the connection of E. M. Dahl with the creative identity of Rachmaninoff is an important one. If it can be confirmed that their relationship was enduring in some way and that Dahl served as a muse for Rachmaninoff, musicologists will be able to broaden their insights into his complex inner world, and also revise extant information about his compositional process during this period of his life.

Within the spectrum of human emotions there exist endless gradations of love for other persons. If Rachmaninoff's connection with Elena Dahl was as recounted by his grandson, their relationship produces in Rachmaninoff's art a master theme of *love outside of marriage*. For example, his three operas

Aleko (composed as his conservatory graduation project), *Francesca da Rimini* (1906), inspired by the episode in Dante's *Inferno,* and *Monna Vanna* (1908; unfinished, a work that was dear to him) all touch upon this master theme. If we follow this line of inquiry, Rachmaninoff could have been troubled by the situation of his abiding commitment to his marriage and family, and yet concomitant need for a woman of desire and creative inspiration who happened to exist outside of his marriage.

In 2003 Alexandre Rachmaninoff, the composer's grandson, began telling various persons an account of Rachmaninoff's connection with a woman named Elena Dahl. He did not mention, nor (as I found out from him later) did he know Dahl's patronymic. He affirmed, however, that Dahl was the beloved with whom the composer remained in contact throughout his life. He learned about this relationship from his grandmother Natalia Aleksandrovna not long before her death in 1951.[12] Apparently she told no one but her grandson about this relationship, and, according to his account, spent about two hours in an agitated state describing to him her late husband's lifelong connection with another woman. She asked her grandson not to relay these revelations to anyone for a period of fifty years.

Alexandre Rachmaninoff's retelling of his grandmother's deathbed "confession" prompts a revision of some major details of Sergei Rachmaninoff's life and compositions. While it is well known that Alexandre loved and admired his famous grandfather, he made no secret of his rather lukewarm attitude toward his grandmother—he noted that she was "not a warm person."[13] He speculated that his grandmother married and remained with Rachmaninoff because of his wealth and prestige, but this conviction is challenged by the evidence of Natalia Aleksandrovna's devotion to her husband. She met him as a teenager and stayed with him through extremely difficult times: the Bolshevik Revolution of 1917, ensuing period of uncertainty in Europe, and both political and financial instability. She loved him deeply. It is also the case that people who are serious about hiding a relationship can erase virtually all the evidence of that bond, and yet it is curious that no confirmation of even the identity of Elena Dahl has surfaced. However, because of the enormous cataclysms and dislocations that took place in Russia and the Soviet Union during two-thirds of the twentieth century, Russian scholars attempting to piece together the events of a particular life do not find it unusual if the necessary identifying documents are not readily located. The loss of many records confirming a person's existence or whereabouts would not surprise anyone even remotely familiar with the terrible historical events the people of those countries experienced. Moreover, if Elena Dahl was not a citizen of Russia, there would likely not have existed any national identifying records of her birth or whereabouts. One has to decide if the only genuine archival evidence—the dedicatee lines of two compositions—along with some genealogical findings and the account of the composer's grandson suffice for hypothesizing about such an important relationship in Rachmaninoff's life. According to preliminary research, the Dahl family in its genealogy separated into two branches from the original French when they arrived in Russia: a St. Petersburg branch, which had Roman Catholic roots, and a Moscow branch that became Russian Orthodox. N. V. Dahl came from the Moscow branch, but his relative Elena came from St. Petersburg.[14]

It is worth emphasizing that as Alexandre Rachmaninoff's account of this new personage in Rachmaninoff's life made its way to Russia and circulated among major Rachmaninoff scholars, it was taken seriously and discussed in a cautious way. Liudmila Kovaleva-Ogorodnova, for example, describes:

> If there was a person, who, in the words of A.B. Conius-Rachmaninoff . . . all her life followed Rachmaninoff, which resulted in his being torn between her and his wife, was it not also she who over the years created suffering for her beloved, and [as a result] Rachmaninoff in emigration composed so little for this reason as well, besides the usually cited references to his nostalgia [for Russia] and excessive concertizing?[15]

Kovaleva-Ogorodnova logically connects Rachmaninoff's own statement about a beautiful woman's being a perpetual source of inspiration for art and music with the possibility of an elusive yet desirable woman—Elena Dahl—remaining in some way a part of his life.

Lest we dismiss Rachmaninoff's grandson's account as too fantastic or too improbable, it is worth remembering some of the norms of private lives of the turn of the twentieth century in terms of heterosexual male-female relationships. The lives of other creative artists contemporaneous with Rachmaninoff's, some of whom were close friends of his, were at least as complicated as his may have been. His lifelong friend Feodor Chaliapin maintained a separate relationship with a mistress, even buying her a house and having children with her, while being married to Italian ballerina Iola Tornagi. Another friend, writer Ivan Bunin, maintained a mistress while still being married, and at times the two women resided in the same house with him. Musical colleague Igor Stravinsky entered into a complex relationship in Paris with fashion icon Gabrielle "Coco" Chanel. These non-traditional relationships are well-documented.

Rachmaninoff's possible connection with the woman named Elena Dahl is only beginning to come to light. According to what can be pieced together from scant evidence, Rachmaninoff met Dahl at the apartment of her relative, the psychotherapist and musician N. V. Dahl in November or December of 1898, although there has been serious speculation that they may have met earlier, somewhere in the Tambov region. At that time Rachmaninoff was a patient of Dahl's who was trying to cope with the personal and professional crisis of the failure of his first symphony. All accounts of what took place during the "sessions" of Rachmaninoff with Dahl agree that there was no actual "therapy," but rather enlivening and encouraging discussions on music and life. Positive reinforcement on the part of Dr. Dahl lodged itself in Rachmaninoff's consciousness. However, there may have been another stimulus for Rachmaninoff's recovery: he met Elena through Dr. Dahl, and they fell in love.

The unexpected relationship functioned as a resurrection of the human spirit for Rachmaninoff: this love, rather than (or together with) Dr. Dahl's therapy through beneficial and stimulating conversations, returned to him the confidence he needed for composition and performance in general. Rachmaninoff described the process of his sessions with Dahl and recovery thus:

> My relatives told Dr. Dahl that he should use all means available to cure me of my apathy and restore in me the desire to compose. Dahl asked what specifically they wished for me to compose, and received the answer: "A piano concerto." The one I had promised the audience in London, but which in despair I put off writing. As a result, while lying in a dreamlike state in the chair of Dr. Dahl, each day I heard the repeated hypnotic formula: "You will start to compose a concerto. You will work on it with complete ease. The concerto will be beautiful" . . . And while this may seem implausible, the treatment really helped me. Already by the beginning of summer I once again began to compose.[16]

As a result of his nascent relationship with Elena Dahl and the sessions with the psychotherapist and musician (violist) Nikolai Dahl, which no doubt included lively discussions of music as well as talk therapy, Rachmaninoff's creative springs began flowing again. His first successful attempt at composition was represented by the short piece for piano titled *Morceau de fantaisie in G minor* (without opus number), with the aforementioned cryptic dedication "Delmo." Through some genealogical work her patronymic Morisovna was posited, and the acronym of "Delmo" became clear: **D**ahl **E**lena **Mo**risovna. This composition was written on the first page of a music paper album and signed by Rachmaninoff.

It is indeed true that the years of the late 1890s and early 1900s remain one of the most mysterious periods of Rachmaninoff's life. A brief sketch of Rachmaninoff's activities with their corresponding dates is revealing:

March 15, 1897 First performance of Rachmaninoff's Symphony No. 1 in
    D minor (a disaster, most likely due to conductor Aleksander Glazunov's
    failure to understand the complexity and originality of the work's harmonic
    structures). The work was dedicated to Anna Lodyzhenskaia. In 1893,

when Rachmaninoff was twenty years old, he had dedicated to her his song of Op. 4, No. 1, "Oh, no! I beg you, don't forsake me."

1898–1900 Rachmaninoff's two courses of therapy with Nikolai Dahl at the latter's apartment in Moscow, and posited acquaintance with Elena Dahl (probably during the first course of October-December 1898).

August 1900 In Varazze with Chaliapin, Rachmaninoff composed the love duet of Francesca and Paolo for his opera *Francesca da Rimini*, and worked on the second and third movements of Piano Concerto No. 1 in C minor. The Francesca and Paolo story is one of forbidden love, perhaps relevant to Rachmaninoff's own emotional conflict.

Fall 1900 Mysteries surrounding the composition of Rachmaninoff's Spring 1902 Second Concerto in C minor for piano and orchestra (Op. 18), with two dedications: the first dedicatee line to Nikolai Dahl, and a second line that was crossed out but recently recovered—to Elena Dahl. This work was written immediately preceding the period of Rachmaninoff's engagement and marriage to Natalia Satina in April 1902. It is full of passion, tenderness, and a restlessness that until the very end refuses harmonic resolution.

April 1902 The twelve songs of Op. 21 represent some of the most gloomy work Rachmaninoff ever produced.

Summer 1904 Completed his opera *Francesca da Rimini*, from an episode about the star-crossed lovers in Canto V of Dante's *Inferno*.

If we add to this complexity the emotional force with which Elena Dahl entered his life, during a period of dejection following the crash of his first symphony and entry into therapy, then we can imagine the state of his inner life at the time when he and Natasha Satina decided to marry. It is not a foregone conclusion that by the fall of 1901, when their engagement was announced, these other women—Anna Lodyzhenskaia and especially Dahl—were out of his life in psychological terms. He surely retained some residue of his feelings for them and may have even felt sorry for them and himself. Anna Trubnikova writes concerning the ability of Sergei to empathize with others, recalling the occasion of the death of her sister's pet bird, a linnet:

> One morning [after an illness] the linnet lay dead on the floor of the cage. My sister cried bitterly at the death of her beloved bird, and Seryozha, sincerely empathizing with her, wrote the art song "On the death of a linnet" and dedicated it to her.[17]

In the same vein Liudmila Rostovtsova described Sergei's depth of personality:

No one could empathize with another's grief, no one could so delicately and seriously comfort another as Sergei. In every person's character he could find a good quality, could praise it, and no one would take the step of diminishing himself in Sergei's eyes. The tender charm of his person was enormous. His soul often was melancholy and in a state of grief, but this did not prevent him from sometimes being cheerful, joking around, and laughing.[18]

When we consider the sensitivity, religious beliefs, moral values, and highly developed conscience of Rachmaninoff, it would stand to reason that he would experience various conflicting emotions in the face of a less-than-straightforward impending marriage. Could such a sensitive person sustain for many years, even decades, a private, illicit relationship outside of a marriage to which he was committed? It seems unlikely. And yet it is a truism that people can hold several competing, even in some ways compatible, emotions in their hearts. Henry Ziegler Steinway (1915–2008), who knew the Rachmaninoffs in New York in the 1920s and 1930s when he (Steinway) was a teenager and young adult, was asked whether or not Rachmaninoff could have sustained a long-term relationship. He answered "no." But when asked if he thought Rachmaninoff had ever been unfaithful to his wife, he answered immediately, "There was some of that." Steinway continued that people in Rachmaninoff's circle in New York knew that he sometimes visited a woman in Philadelphia, and that Natalia knew about it.[19] Could this woman have been Elena Dahl? Referring to Rachmaninoff's adult married life, his niece Sophia Vladimirovna Satina stated, "there had been women in Rachmaninoff's life other than Natalia."[20]

Notwithstanding the aforementioned, the evidence of Rachmaninoff's life and activities affirms that he was a deeply moral and ethical man, one who considered his actions carefully and who would not have compromised the reputation of his wife or her family. If there were any lifelong connections between him and the person Elena Dahl, he would have kept her at a distance as much as possible. Perhaps there was emotional closeness, but it is difficult to imagine that he could have maintained much more than that and still stay in love with his wife. Considering his deep religious piety, it is also doubtful that Rachmaninoff could have lived with his conscience if he were causing the woman he married, the mother of his children, and co-creator of his entire life this kind of pain and suffering. Both Sergei and Natalia make frequent loving references to each other and the activities of their family in the letters and memoirs available to researchers. Some references are even humorous and witty; in a letter representative of several in which Rachmaninoff mentions his wife, he writes in the postscript of a letter to E. I. Somov from Senar in 1933: "Darling Natasha keeps getting prettier. Her hair is curlier and curlier. Men are swooning [around her], like flies."[21]

Much has been made of Rachmaninoff's "depression" of this period and his subsequent "cure" by the treatment of Nikolai Dahl. To be sure, the composer-pianist was suffering from the failure of his first symphony and experiencing a bout of writer's block. He ceased composing for three years, it is true, but he was too visibly active in musical circles and in his social life to be considered in a state of depression. In the summer of 1898 Rachmaninoff spent two months at the Yaroslavl estate of Tatiana Liubatovich with Chaliapin and the troupe of Mamontov; he tutored Chaliapin in music and studied Shakespeare's *Richard II* in a search for a suitable subject for an opera. His travels and correspondence were frequent and lively. In April 1899 Rachmaninoff conducted the London Philharmonic Orchestra in a performance of his composition the symphonic poem "The Crag" (Op. 7), and also played several of his shorter works (the Prelude in C sharp minor and the Elegy, both from Op. 3). He was invited to perform with the Philharmonic again the following year. Nikitin notes:

> In the memoirs of all his close relatives and friends—Sofia Satina, Liudmila Skalon, Elena Kreitser—of everyone who personally saw Sergei Vasilievich at that time almost every day—there is nothing that could indicate on his part a persistent depression, a nervous illness, or any symptoms of complete dejection.
> . . . his mood over the course of these three years was not a crestfallen one. He experienced the joy of life and was not indifferent to women. He made a successful trip to Crimea, where he accompanied Chaliapin and also performed as a solo pianist.[22]

He finally tried his hand once again at composition: in 1899 he wrote several pieces for piano without Opus number: Morceau de Fantaisie in C minor (January 11, 1899), an untitled, undated piece in D minor, and Fughetta in F major (February 4, 1899). Inspiration was returning to him, and he was actively searching for ideas for new compositions. Even though the search for a new and major composition weighed heavily on him, Nikitin concludes that Rachmaninoff "was happy and moped around to the degree that was typical for his personality, no more and no less."[23]

Both his grandson Alexandre Rachmaninoff and the former curator of the Rachmaninoff Museum-Estate, Aleksandr Ermakov, concluded that his "depression" was a myth. Rachmaninoff was disheartened about his first symphony, but his distress could also at least partially be attributed to the proverbial woman problem. Such a combination of concerns could be a viable explanation for his troubled state of mind, but to describe him as being in a "depression" may be an exaggeration.

Fyodor Dostoevsky's insights into the human soul are well-established. He described his formula for the happiness and well-being of an individual as deriving from equal parts of unhappy and happy experiences across a human lifetime. It stands to reason that he had in mind not only the universal human being but in particular a typical Russian person's psychic make-up. Rachmaninoff read widely in Russian literature and surely knew of Dostoevsky's famous formula; he preferred Dostoevsky's writings to Tolstoy's. In later years Rachmaninoff would describe his life as one characterized by his fair share of unhappiness and suffering.[24] In addition to the devastating times he experienced as a child—growing up in a family marred by arguments between the two parents he loved dearly, the fall of his family from wealth to near-poverty, deaths of his three sisters, and eventual estrangement of his parents from each other—the period of 1897–1902 would be characterized by his deep attachment to more than one woman and search for the best decision to make in order to establish a life of happiness and stability for himself.

If Rachmaninoff was in love with Elena Dahl at the time of his engagement to Natasha, why did he go ahead with the marriage? Elena, a relative of Dr. Dahl's from St. Petersburg, may have been Catholic and this difference between her faith tradition and Sergei's could have been an obstacle to his marrying her. Or the fact that she was a commoner ("из простых," as Alexandre Rachmaninoff recounted[25]), rather than belonging to the nobility as the Rachmaninoffs and Satins, made a marriage between them socially difficult. The two possible reasons together, her being a Catholic and a commoner, may have made a viable union between them extremely difficult. One must also wonder if the situation was even more dire for Sergei: perhaps Elena conceived a child by him, and this accounted for his connection with her of longer duration.[26] Whatever the cause, there is considerable evidence of the fact that Rachmaninoff was tormented during the period immediately leading up to his wedding and that the laws of emotional logic cannot justify such a reaction on his part. He knew his bride and her family thoroughly, and, because her family was financially in reasonably good shape, he could not have been tormented by a future with no financial means.

Thus, in the contexts of the complex period of the turn of the twentieth century in Russia and the vicissitudes of Rachmaninoff's inner life, in the fall of 1901 he and Natalia Satina decided that they wanted to get married.

Scholars and biographers have noted the inexplicably dark and depressed mood of the twelve songs of Opus 21 that Rachmaninoff composed to earn some money for the wedding trip to Europe. He began working on songs Nos. 2–12 of this opus between April 7 and 21 of 1902, just before his wedding to Satina on the 29th of that same month; he finished them very likely during his wedding trip at the Hotel Sonnenberg not far from Lucerne. Harrison writes, "Considering that this was a supposedly happy time, many of the Op. 21 songs have gloomy subjects."[27] It is possible that the composer's inner emotional world was more complex than has previously been assumed, and that Opus 21 reflects a pre-wedding period that was turbulent and anxiety-ridden for him. Only one of the songs, No. 1 ("Fate"), was written on February 18, 1900, two years before the other eleven (April 1902). However, in this song the dark theme of the relentless drive of fate in a person's life connects it with the remaining eleven, and it acquires a larger significance in the context of the other songs of the cycle.

The eventful years of 1897–1902 are immortalized in striking and memorable art songs of Opus 21. The somber mood of *seven* of the twelve songs of this opus makes more sense when we bear in mind the dramatic personal and musical activities Rachmaninoff experienced immediately preceding his wedding to Satina. The songs in question are not superficially or stereotypically "sad" or "depressed"; the intensity and desperation of the emotions in them is shocking and heart-wrenching.[28] In one after the other the situations portrayed are extreme, almost suicidal. B. S. Nikitin provides insights into the songs of Opus 21 that can summarize their contents:

> One could probably expect songs of bright and joyful contents. Composing done in haste? Yes. Rachmaninoff arrived at Ivanovka not later than April 7, and departed from there on April 21. In only two weeks he had written eleven art songs.
>
> But concerning the bright and joyful contents of this song cycle, even if one takes into account the calm and contemplative mood of the superlative songs "Lilacs," "It's So Peaceful Here," and "Twilight," the general impression that remains of the whole is of a completely different kind. *It is simply striking, that six of these art songs are imbued with such a heavy-hearted, even tragic mood, that unwittingly one is forced to contemplate why it was that only a few days before a happy event Sergei Vasilievich could choose to compose music of such a despairingly joyless kind . . .*[29] (emphasis added)

Nikitin finds *unconvincing* the explanation that Rachmaninoff was motivated by financial reasons to write dramatic and effective songs, and that he worked best in the minor keys (as Rachmaninoff admitted in a letter to Marietta Shaginian). He speculates, "Perhaps we shouldn't be surprised if he [Rachmaninoff] chose themes that would tear the soul to pieces. But somehow such an explanation remains unsettling."[30]

When one adds to the seven songs two more, No. 5 ("Lilacs"), about which Barrie Martyn writes, "The poem combines a simple description of nature with the underlying theme of the unfulfilled search for happiness,"[31] and No. 7, in which the mood is wistful, lonely, and sad, this amounts to *nine* of the total twelve. A cursory examination of the contents or representative lines of several of the songs reveals these moods:

No. 1 "Fate"
With her walking crutch,
with her gloomy eyes,
Fate, like a grim sentinel,
Pursues us wherever we go.

No. 2 "By a Fresh Grave"
I'm again alone, and again surrounded
By the same night and gloomy darkness.
Deep and fateful are my thoughts
As I stand over a fresh grave.

What can I hope for, what can I live for,
What can I struggle and strive for?
No longer do I have one to love,
No longer do I have one to pray to.

No. 4 "They Answered"
They asked: "how can we forget for good,
That in this vale of tears there's poverty and trouble,
Malice and sorrow?"
"Sleep"—they answered . . .

No. 6 "Fragment from A. Musset" ("Loneliness")
Why does my sick heart so violently
Beat, and beg, and thirst for peace?
Why am I troubled, afraid in the night?
I'm alone, that was midnight striking . . .
Oh loneliness, oh poverty . . .

No. 8 "Death of a Linnet"
But it can be frightening to love:
A little winged friend was given to him;
Rather than survive his beloved,
He hid in the coffin when he lost her.

No. 10 "Before the Icon"
She kept repeating the name of someone,
Her face glowed with a prayerful light;
And there was so much love and suffering,
So little hope in her prayers.
(Dedicated to Maria Ivanova.)

No. 12 "Sorrow in Springtime"
How painful this is, how I yearn to live . . .
How fresh and fragrant is spring!

No! I can't silence my heart
On this pale blue sleepless night.

If only age would come quickly,
Thread my curls with silver frost,
Make me deaf to the nightingale singing,
To the sounds of the forest murmuring,
So there would not be, in the hushed stillness
This excruciating feeling of sorrow.[32]

Even in Song No. 7, "It's So Fine Here," a song that superficially appears harmonious and calm, the subject matter involves a person alone in the presence of God, experiencing an undercurrent of anxiety. The song's climax on the high note of a "B" that slides down into an "A" evokes a wistful sadness that is inescapable to the listener.

The connection between the themes of the songs and Rachmaninoff's inner world can be further underscored by the composer's own statement about artistic inspiration, that if there is nothing on the inside, nothing on the outside will help. Rachmaninoff's life experiences and emotions are contained in his music. He also made the statement that [spoken, non-musical] words are not needed in order for a person to understand who he was: his music would illuminate everything that was important.[33] But in the art songs we have a saturation of meaning: the poetic words selected with great deliberation by the composer and also his own music interwoven into the mood of the poems, which in turn reflect his state of mind during the time of the compositional process.

Martyn speculates concerning two songs of this opus:

> "Sorrow in Springtime" ["How Painful for Me"], with its black and cheerless theme, much the same as in "By the grave," seems an odd choice with which to finish a group of songs written when Rachmaninoff was in full flight artistically, and when his personal affairs—his marriage was but days away—should have been in their most hopeful and happy state.[34]

Sylvester notes concerning "Sorrow in Springtime":

> It might seem odd that a man on the eve of his wedding would choose a poem so full of anguish as the present one . . . However . . . the theme of the tormenting and conflicting emotions of spring in the Russian [art song] and need not be an expression of the mood of the composer at a given moment, or even of his personal experience. What matters is the sincerity of the music.[35]

These comments have validity and in a general sense ring true, but it is also true in the creative process that the most sincere and effective results in literature, music, etc., come from the wellsprings of deep and authentic feelings, if not actual experience, of the creator.

It goes without saying that Rachmaninoff needed to make these songs effective and attractive to his publisher so that their sale could help to pay for his honeymoon. But the evidence of his life confirms that he never made artistic decisions for commercial purposes. In addition, the speed with which he produced these eleven songs did not compromise their quality at all: as Nikitin notes, at least five of them rank among the best vocal pieces he ever composed: "Lilacs," "It's So Fine Here," "They Answered," "Sorrow in Springtime," and "Fragment from A. Musset" ("Loneliness"). Not only was the quality of the songs not compromised by the limited time available to Rachmaninoff, but instead his creative springs were full of vitality and inspiration—and emotional movement.

When one takes into account that Rachmaninoff's music (by his personal admission) "comes from the heart" and expresses the sum total of his emotions and experiences; that his music was programmatic, rather than intellectualized or "pure"; that almost all of his compositions are dedicated to a person or persons significant to him; and that a profound integrity exists among the poetry, music, and choice of dedicatees for his song settings—then one can make the case that the art songs of Op. 21 have something to tell us about Rachmaninoff's mood prior to his wedding. The markedly dark titles to some of the songs of this opus underscore his feelings of fatalism, gloominess, and utter sadness: "Fate" (No. 1), "By a Fresh Grave" (No. 2), "Fragment from A. Musset" ["Loneliness"] (No. 6), "On the Death of a Linnet" (No. 8), and "Sorrow in Springtime" ["How Painful for Me"] (No. 12).

For Rachmaninoff the period in question, the 1890s and early 1900s, was clearly characterized by attachment to more than one woman. In the end he took a careful, wise, and satisfactory course of action, one almost predetermined by the entirety of his life to that point. His decision for a life with Natalia Satina, a life of stability and predictability over one that was emotionally very risky, indicates how badly he craved the permanent and dependable love Natalia offered him, as well as the family security that had eluded him during the formative years of his childhood and young adulthood.

The situation was extremely complex, and it stands to reason that both Natasha and her sister Sofia (who was extremely close to Sergei) knew something about it. This may even explain why Natasha's memoir written so many years later (which probably was read and edited by Sofia) begins so abruptly with her marriage to Sergei, rather than starting at the point of her acquaintance with him when she was thirteen years old. She fell in love with Sergei almost immediately, spent an entire lifetime with him (including her teenage years), and surely had some memories of their experiences when they were growing up together. Why, then, would she leave out this entire period? A plausible answer would be that the period was too emotionally painful. Did it involve another woman whose presence in Sergei's and her lives was so troubling that Natasha chose not to write about it in her memoir? Moreover, her account of this complication would tarnish the image of her husband that she understandably wished to keep intact.

It is also telling that the people who were in contact with Rachmaninoff during this period and had the opportunity to observe him in his life and at work noted that something seemed to be weighing heavily on his soul. Since the accounts of his contemporaries, even of those who personally did not like Rachmaninoff, almost unanimously praise him for his fine personal qualities—his fairness, work ethic, deep commitment to high musical standards, impartiality in how he treated others, humility, and kindness—it would follow that the pangs of conscience he experienced during these months and years would not stem from a clash with a friend or colleague, but rather be a matter of the heart that was not resolved and for some reason could not easily be resolved.

Out of this turbulent period for Rachmaninoff emerged one of his most remarkable compositions, which has a fascinating composition history: the Concerto No. 2 in C minor for piano and orchestra. Rachmaninoff composed the second and third movements of it in the summer of 1900 at the estate of the Kreutzer family; he was comfortable with them and the conditions for composing were excellent. On December 2 of the same year he performed the two completed movements in Moscow, with his cousin Aleksander Siloti as conductor, at a concert organized by Princess Lieven of the Ladies' Charity Prison Committee. The performance met with enormous success both with musicians and with the general public. In the spring of 1901 Rachmaninoff finalized the composition of the unforgettable, darkly passionate, and tense first movement. Its eight massive opening chords are, along with the first moments of Beethoven's Symphony No. 5 (the percussive da-da-da-dum), among the most recognizable "beginnings" of classical music compositions. The chords successfully evoke the clanging—or tolling—of Russian Orthodox church bells. Barrie Martyn writes:

> Each of the three movements begins with a modulatory preamble. The famous and, be it said, unprecedented opening of the first movement, a sequence of swelling piano chords in F minor punctuated by bass octaves, is like the tolling of a bell, heard distantly at first but with each stroke more penetrating than the last. . . . Rachmaninoff may have derived this opening from his Prelude in C sharp minor by inverting the layout and dynamics of its final bars, where the bass octaves precede and not follow the chords.[36]

Rachmaninoff's teacher, former director of the Moscow Conservatory, and masterful composer in his own right Sergei Ivanovich Taneev was present at the final rehearsal of the second and third movements. The delicate lyricism of the second movement for which Rachmaninoff chose the muted, yet bright key of E major, with his expert handling of the interplay between the orchestra and piano, produced a wistful, unforgettable melody. For the pianist, to play and perform the *a tempo* section (final fifteen measures) of this movement is supremely satisfying: the enormously spread arpeggios in the left hand, along with the glorious chords grasped by the right, bring the movement to a gratifying conclusion. Martyn notes in a widely recorded anecdote, "It is not surprising that the beauties of this movement particularly touched . . . Taneyev, who wept at a rehearsal performance and uttered the single word 'genius', not an expression used lightly by the stern master or by Russians generally."[37]

On October 27, 1901, the entire concerto was performed for the first time, once again under Siloti's baton, by the Moscow Philharmonic Orchestra. Concerning the first movement, which completed the piece but seemingly was composed last in order, it already existed in Rachmaninoff's mind and in some sketches he drafted. Rachmaninoff's music colleague A. B. Goldenweiser recalls,

> In composing the [second] concerto, he [Rachmaninoff] quickly and easily wrote the second and third movements, but for a long time he couldn't settle on the right course for the first one. He had written it down in several variants, but couldn't decide on which to use. As a result, for the day of the designated concert only the second and third movements were ready. . . . Soon after this Rachmaninoff composed his [Second] Suite for Two Pianos Op. 17 and dedicated it to me, as his frequent partner in performing music for two pianos.[38]

The concerto's thematic material is rich, varied, and powerful: its moods evolve from the solemn intensity of the first movement, to the tenderness and wistfulness of the second that establish Rachmaninoff as a master melodist, and finally to the energy and resolution of the third. Michael Steinberg describes:

> Rachmaninoff makes another bridge from the Adagio [second movement] to the finale, beginning with distant, conspiratorial march music in E major, then working his way around to the doorstep of C minor and to the piano's grandly assertive entrance. The march music is now determined and vigorous; for contrast, Rachmaninoff finds the ultimate archetype of his big tunes, the one that Buddy Kaye and Ted Mossman turned into *Full Moon and Empty Arms*. . . . It all moves to a rattling bring-down-the-house conclusion, and when one remembers the biographical background to this Concerto it is pleasing to see that the last tempo mark is *risoluto*.[39]

The concerto boasts a tightly constructed orchestration, with the piano and orchestra alternating in carrying the melodic and accompanying lines.

Particularly in his four concertos Rachmaninoff's composition creates a genuine partnership between the soloist and orchestra, with the melody lines alternating in each "partner." Nikolai Medtner considered the Second Concerto to evoke a broad and dignified Russianness:

> The theme of [Rachmaninoff's] inspired Second Concerto is not only the theme of his life but always conveys the impression of being one of the most strikingly Russian of themes, and only because the soul of this theme is Russian; there is no ethnographic trimming here, no dressing up, no decking out in national dress, no folksong intonation, and yet every time, from the first bell stroke, you feel the figure of Russia rising up to her full height.[40]

Medtner's deep appreciation of Rachmaninoff's concerto also aptly captures Rachmaninoff's brand of patriotism: he loved Russia in all ways, but his devotion to his country was not intentionally expressed in his compositions. Rather, it was a natural upwelling through music of his sensibilities, cultural learnedness, and experiences.

More than any other, this large-scale musical composition bears the imprint of this period, of Rachmaninoff's sorrow, passion, tenderness, vitality, and hope. It is arguably the most popular concerto programmed by U.S. orchestras and one of the most popular performed worldwide in the classical repertoire. The Second Concerto's musical core so clearly suggests unfulfilled love that one of the most famous uses of its music occurs as a leitmotif in the film *Brief Encounter* (1945, dir. David Lean), in which a man and woman, both married, fall in love and meet regularly each week. The list of the concerto's influence on American popular culture is extensive, both in film and vocal music. It indicates beyond a doubt that Rachmaninoff's concerto has established itself as a permanent item in world musical culture. Two noteworthy examples of the concerto's influence in vocal music are Frank Sinatra's song "I Think of You" (1941) and the *Adagio sostenuto* theme of Eric Carmen's ballad "All by Myself" (1975). The direct expression of the internal dilemmas Rachmaninoff was experiencing during the years 1897–1902 resonated with generations of filmmakers and song composers who succeeded him, who grasped the concerto's emotional strength, directness, and universal melodic appeal.

NOTES

1. L.L. Sabaneev, "Moi vstrechi s Rakhmaninovym," quoted in Aleksei Naumov, "V mire muzykal'nykh rukopisei Rakhmaninova," in *Novoe o Rakhmaninove*, ed. I.A. Medvedeva (Moscow: Deka-BC, 2006), 177.

2. F.I. Chaliapin, *Maska i dusha: Moi sorok let na teatrakh* (Moscow: Moskovskii rabochii, 1989), 151.

3. During the years 2003–2004 specialists and admirers of Rachmaninoff's music encountered speculation of a longlasting connection between Rachmaninoff and this unknown woman. This relationship was articulated by the grandson of the composer A. B. Rachmaninoff in conversations with various persons. Personal interview, Senar, Weggis, Switzerland, July 16, 2004.

4. I am grateful to A. A. Naumov for piecing together the sequence of events and dates associated with these courses of treatment.

5. See my account of conversations with Alexandre Rachmaninoff on this matter in Appendix I.

6. See "Anton Luis Dahl: One-Time Pianist to Czar Dies on Los Angeles Street Corner," *The New York Times* (November 1, 1932), 21, https://www.nytimes.com/1932/11/01/archives/anton-luis-dahl-onetime-pianist-to-czar-dies-on-los-angeles-street.html; and "Anton L Dahl (unknown-1932)," Find A Grave, https://www.findagrave.com/memorial/137984530/anton-l-dahl#source, accessed September 13, 2021.

7. The mystery of this dedicatory "word" has also been noticed by Rachmaninoff scholars B. S. Nikitin and Max Harrison. A. A. Naumov theorized the patronymic based on finding in his genealogical research of the Dahls the family member's first name of "Moris" plus the existence of the last two letters of the acronym "Delmo."

8. A.A. Naumov, "V mire muzykal'nykh rukopisei Rakhmaninova. Novye postupleniia, poiski, nakhodki," in *Novoe o Rakhmaninove*, ed. I.A. Medvedeva, 176–77.

9. See Appendix I for more information.

10. Personal interview, Senar, Weggis, Switzerland, July 15, 2004.

11. Ibid.

12. Natalia Rachmaninoff referred to this woman as "Lana Dahl."

13. Personal interview, Senar, Weggis, Switzerland, July 17, 2004.

14. A. A. Naumov conducted genealogical research on the two branches of the Dahl family—one with Western European (probably French) roots and the other with more Russianized roots. Personal interview, Moscow, July 8, 2004.

15. Liudmila Kovaleva-Ogorodnova, *Sergei Rakhmaninov: Biografiia* (Sankt-Peterburg: Vita Nova, 2015), I: 154. See also 141, 155.

16. S. Rakhmaninov, *Vospominaniia Zapisannye Oskarom fon Risemanom*, trans. V.N. Chemberdzhi (Moscow: Raduga, 1992), 116, trans. VZN.

17. A.A. Trubnikova, "Sergei Rakhmaninov," in *Vospominaniia o Rakhmaninove*, ed. Z.A. Apetian, 5th ed. (Moscow: Muzyka, 1988), I: 123, trans. VZN.

18. L.D. Rostovtsova, "Vospominaniia o S.V. Rakhmaninove," in Apetian, I: 239–40, trans. VZN.

19. Personal interview, Steinway Hall, New York, January 9, 2006.

20. Sophia Satina, "Conversations with Sophia Vladimirovna Satina about Her Uncle Sergei Vasilyevich Rachmaninoff," ed. Harold Tillek, unpublished manuscript given to the author of this book in London on June 24, 2005.

21. S. Rakhmaninov, Letter, in *S. Rakhmaninov. Literaturnoe nasledie. Vospominaniia. Stat'i. Interv'iu. Pis'ma*, ed. Z.A. Apetian (Moscow: Sovetskii kompozitor, 1978), 2: 358, trans. VZN.

22. Boris Nikitin, *Sergei Rakhmaninov. Feodor Chaliapin* (Moscow: OTiSS, 1998), 81–82, trans. VZN.

23. Ibid., 82, trans. VZN.

24. My own perusal of Rachmaninoff's library in his studio at Senar confirmed a fine collection of works of Russian prose fiction and poetry, including Pushkin, Nadson, and Chekhov. Visit to Senar, Weggis, Switzerland, July 15, 2004.

25. Personal interview, Senar, Weggis, Switzerland, July 15, 2004.

26. Speculation about a child may seem far-fetched, but Rachmaninoff scholar A. A. Naumov mused that the existence of a child would explain a great deal concerning Rachmaninoff's complex emotional state and would lend support to a more permanent relationship between him and Dahl.

27. Max Harrison, *Rachmaninoff: Life, Works, Recordings* (New York: Continuum, 2005), 105.

28. See B.S. Nikitin, *Sergei Rakhmaninov. Dve zhizni* (Moscow: Znanie, 1993), 90.

29. Ibid.

30. Ibid., 91.

31. Barrie Martyn, *Rachmaninoff: Composer, Pianist, Conductor* (Burlington, VT: Ashgate, 2000), 142.

32. Richard D. Sylvester, *Rachmaninoff's Complete Songs* (Bloomington: Indiana University Press, 2014), trans. Sylvester, 96–123. On p. 97 I translate "Со своими мрачными очами" as "With her gloomy eyes."

33. Paraphrase of S.A. Satina, "Zapiska o S.V. Rakhmaninove" in *Vospominaniia o Rakhmaninove*, ed. Apetian, I: 115.

34. Martyn, 144.

35. Sylvester, 122.

36. Martyn, 126.

37. A.N. Aleksandrov, "Moi vstrechi s S.V. Rakhmaninovym," in *Vospominaniia o Rakhmaninove*, ed. Apetian, II: 162, paraphrased in Martyn, 129.

38. A.B. Goldenweiser, "Iz lichnykh vospominanii o S.V. Rakhmaninove," in *Vospominaniia o Rakhmaninove*, ed. Apetian, I: 415.

39. Michael Steinberg, *The Concerto: A Listener's Guide* (New York: Oxford UP, 1998), 362.

40. N.K. Medtner, "S.V. Rakhmaninov," in *Vospominaniia o Rakhmaninove*, ed. Apetian, II: 350, quoted in Martyn, 127.

Chapter 7

Marriage to Natalia Satina
(1898–1910)

Most people who know something about Sergei Rachmaninoff's life wonder why he married his first cousin Natalia Aleksandrovna Satina. Evidence of any kind of courtship between them is lacking, and their being related by blood seriously concerned their parents. Marriage between relatives was prohibited by Russian law and the Orthodox Church; only special permission from the tsar would make an exception possible. In the face of such major obstacles it remains puzzling and something of a mystery that Rachmaninoff would take such a step. It is unfortunate that the whereabouts of the correspondence between Rachmaninoff and his wife have never been established, for this crucial biographical resource would shed some light on the nature of their relationship. The marriage turned out to be a permanent one, and there was much devotion between husband and wife. A prevailing assessment of Rachmaninoff scholars is captured in the words of Aleksander Ivanovich Ermakov, former curator of the Rachmaninoff Museum-Estate and Research Center at Ivanovka: "The marriage between Sergei and Natalia was a successful one, and a happy one."[1] However, some questions remain concerning the early years of their relationship and Rachmaninoff's possible emotional entanglements even up to the time of their wedding.

Before we consider Sergei's motives and feelings, let us describe Natalia's intentions. Natalia—or Natasha, the customary nickname derived from her given name—fell in love with Sergei probably at the age of thirteen, soon after Zverev brought him to live with the Satins in Moscow in 1890. Her feelings for him by all accounts never wavered; he became the love and project of her life. She was born into one of the most distinguished aristocratic families in Russia: her parents were direct descendants of Prince Mikhail Sviatoy of Chernigov, whose lineage in turn could be traced all the way back to one of the founders of Kievan Rus, the Varangian prince Riurik (d. 879 CE).

Because of her social class and close relations with the Rachmaninoff family, she led the kind of life and received the high level of education that would make her suitable for a match with a nobleman.

In the recollections of Elena Zhukovskaia we encounter a description of her first acquaintance with Natasha and the interests they had in common, which created a lasting friendship between them. During this period Zhukovskaia figured prominently in both Natasha and Sergei's lives: she was close friends with Natasha, and also a talented pianist who received some coaching help in her harmony class from Sergei Rachmaninoff. The activities Zhukovskaia enumerates provide an important glimpse into the type of person Natasha was, which enable us to understand why she was so compatible with Sergei and how her particular personality bonded with his for a lifetime:

> I became acquainted with Natasha and Varvara Arkadievna [Natasha's mother] on November 30, 1893 at a recital of P.A. Pabst, at which, along with other pieces, he performed the Fantasy for Two Pianos of Opus 5 by Rachmaninoff with the composer [at the second piano]. The Fantasy was being performed for the first time, and it met with great success. My acquaintance with Natasha immediately was transformed into a close friendship. We were united by the fact that our tastes and interests were completely identical. Both of us loved music, concerts, the theatre, and books, and we could not abide balls, outings in horse-drawn carriages, and other social amusements.
>
> After we had become acquainted and instantly became close friends, we not only did not seek new acquaintances, but made every effort to avoid them altogether. We were completely satisfied with our little, close-knit circle of friends, and we staunchly opposed the attempts by Varvara Arkadievna to saddle us with new acquaintances.[2]

Zhukovskaia's description of the characteristics and interests she and Natasha shared underscores several qualities that would stand Natasha in good stead as Rachmaninoff's wife and companion in life: Natasha loved music, was of a serious bent, and sought the high culture of which her future husband would become a representative. She was not frivolous, did not seek the diversions of high society (which Sergei also abhorred), and was satisfied with a smaller circle of acquaintances (which was also the preference of Sergei, who was shy and introverted). In their life together there would be many times when Natasha would have to rely on her own inner resources in order to entertain herself, care for their two daughters, and bide her time in unfamiliar surroundings the best she could. She fully understood what demands would be placed on her as Sergei's wife; she accepted them with her eyes wide open and fulfilled her role superbly. In some ways she would become the more dominant one in their marriage, although in major matters she would defer to her husband.

At times one encounters descriptions of Natasha as being a "difficult" person. Her grandson Alexandre Conius Rachmaninoff recalled her as not being a "warmhearted" person.[3] Such generalizations are hard to judge from afar. The extant accounts of her friends, who were also closely acquainted with Sergei, and her own memoir of her life with her husband reveal her as a modest, serious, and hardworking woman who adored her husband and devoted herself to creating the best possible life she could for him and their family. She possessed considerable physical endurance and was well-organized, qualities she needed in order to mastermind their life of *perpetuum mobile*. Natasha would have to coordinate several times each year where the Rachmaninoffs would reside during the concert season of the fall and spring (and school year for their children), as well as where they would spend their summers—according to the time-honored Russian tradition of living outside the city, dacha-like, during that season. And she would have to do this on an international scale. Even with her sister Sofia, who very likely remained in love with Rachmaninoff all her life, Natasha's position was by no means an easy one—and yet, she managed to bear the various burdens placed on her in order to preserve her marriage with Sergei.

One particular burden that may explain Natasha's protectiveness toward Sergei, both before they were married and afterward, had to do with the various other women in Sergei's active schedule of concertizing. His was a professional life in which he was constantly coming into contact with other creative artists, men and women, who came together to perform intense, beautiful, and emotional music. They were often high-strung and eccentric, yet enormously appealing individuals who lived outside the patterns of how people usually set up their personal lives. When Sergei met and worked with these artists, he encountered them in rehearsals and at concerts in which the senses were heightened and all the people presented themselves looking their most elegant and glamorous—and on their best behavior. This was often the nocturnal world, when people and objects appear more mysterious and flattering than they may seem in broad daylight. It was a world of private activity and of secrecy; much was hidden from those on the outside. This was the world in which Sergei and Natasha moved, and Natasha was very aware of the potential for Sergei to become involved with other women. She kept a watchful eye on his activities, managed the complex details of their travels and his concert schedule, and took the lead in raising their children.

Even at Ivanovka, the nest of Natasha's family, life was not easy. Peasant women remembered that she would sometimes complain that Sergei went away too often and did not do his fair share of helping to raise their children. Irina Brandt, a peasant woman who worked at Ivanovka, recalls that in the summer when his family was at Ivanovka Sergei traveled often to Tambov, the city closest to the country estate. Sometimes he went there only with the groom Yakov, whom he knew he could trust. Brandt assumed that he went to Tambov to take care of business associated with Ivanovka, and no doubt this was the case.[4] However, it is also a fact that Sergei enjoyed a freedom afforded him by the constant traveling that could result in relationships with other women. It may be telling that Natasha conceived a dislike for any woman to whom Rachmaninoff may have been attracted, and that she could identify if he seemed to enjoy the company of this or that woman more than was comfortable for her.

Maria (Marina) Ivanova, who became the household manager of Sergei and Natasha's family, provides an example. Natasha disliked Marina intensely, and every person at Ivanovka was aware of her feelings. Something about Marina displeased Natasha, even though she worked tirelessly for the Rachmaninoffs and remained devoted to them until her death.[5] As already noted in a previous chapter, accounts of their contemporaries reveal that Marina was a beautiful woman, that she had a lovely singing voice, that Sergei liked to listen to her sing, and that she enjoyed listening to him play the piano. It is not hard to guess why Natasha disliked Marina, since it seemed likely that Sergei and Marina were attracted to each other.[6]

Natasha's sister Sofia must have posed an extremely complex emotional dilemma for her: Sofia enjoyed a genuine emotional intimacy and intellectual closeness with Rachmaninoff all through their lives, starting from their teenage years. Brandt writes:

> The only person with whom Sofia Aleksandrovna shared a common language was Sergei Vasilievich. I often saw them [at Ivanovka] in the pergola where for a long time they would converse, or they would stroll together along the lanes of the park and pathways of the gardens.
>
> You know, it always seemed to me that Varvara Arkadievna and Natalia Aleksandrovna were dissatisfied with these walks [that they took].
>
> Did Sofia Aleksandrovna and Sergei Vasilievich have an affair, I can't affirm, just as I can't say the opposite. As I already stated, in my opinion, the relations between them were very trusting and close. I think that Sergei Vasilievich trusted Sofia Aleksandrovna more than anyone else. . . . And it also always seemed to me that Sofia Aleksandrovna was consciously sacrificing her life for the sake of her sister's family.[7]

The correspondence between Sergei and Sofia manifests much warmth, soul searching, and liveliness that reveal two people who knew each other well and could share their thoughts on almost any subject. Those who knew the Rachmaninoff and Satin families remained convinced that Sofia Satina selflessly chose to serve her sister's family in order to remain near Sergei. Even some of the Satin family members themselves worried that Sofia's decision not to marry and to remain a part of her sister's family life may have indicated that she was in love with Sergei, who was her first cousin and also became her brother-in-law. And yet, that is how the Rachmaninoffs arranged their lives: Sofia would as much as possible live somewhere nearby, even as Rachmaninoff entreated her to move in with his family.

It must have caused Natasha great pain to see her sister Sofia strolling with Sergei on the grounds of Ivanovka and conversing intimately with him on all sorts of subjects. Natasha and Sofia were very close, and yet she was also aware of her sister's devotion to Sergei. If one examines closely in a single session the 150 or so extant photographs of the Satin and Rachmaninoff families between the years 1880 and 1917, one is struck by the fact that in virtually every photograph taken of the family Sofia has positioned herself right next to Sergei (either behind him, beside him, or bending near him).[8]

The emotional intimacy between Rachmaninoff and his cousin/sister-in-law Sofia Aleksandrovna is manifested clearly in a letter to her that he wrote on May 9, 1927. The letter is quite long, but excerpts from it exemplify the whole:

> My dear Sonechka [endearing diminutive of Sofia],
> I don't know where to start. Actually, I do know... Yesterday evening, upon arriving in Paris, I received your letter, and it made my heart ache. I felt once more how difficult it is for you to live alone and that I was right, in telling you a thousand times, that we, having the possibility... should at least for the last years of our lives live without parting... Together!... And once again I pose the question: what should I do? Concomitantly the question of your workplace worries me. If in conversation with you I externally was at peace with your moving to Washington [DC], it was only because I still hoped that your contract would be renewed. If not, then for the tenth time I repeat: you should not move there. You should live with us and carry out your own work in a laboratory in New York [City] ... and money ... for your personal needs ... you should receive from me.
> How can I prove to you that you are very dear to me, that we all love you so much and are ready to do everything in our power for you with all our heart, even for our own sake?... In summer, if we go to Europe, you must go with us. In winter you must also be with us. Or go to Europe to your mother and brother and live with them and work there in some laboratory. At least I'll know that you are living in peace and that you are with our family.... Like it or not, you must answer this letter and I will be waiting for that answer.[9]

Sofia Aleksandrovna would coordinate the rest of her life with the activities of the Rachmaninoffs, living in the same city as they, or at least not far away from them. She became a widely respected professional woman in her own right, a scientist specializing in biology (especially botany), medicine, and genetics. She would publish numerous scientific papers and would be hired in research positions in the United States (initially in the 1920s at the Carnegie Research Laboratories in Cold Springs Harbor, New York, and in 1943 at Smith College). At Smith College her participation in the important project of growing the fungus *Penicillium* would result in her being awarded an honorary doctorate in science from that institution in 1944.[10]

Throughout her life, even during her teenage years, Natasha protected Sergei's interests, worrying that he was not living in circumstances that would allow him optimal time for composing and practicing. She placed his needs above her own and acted in his best interest even if what she proposed would take him away from her for significant periods of time. She was smart and understood her husband thoroughly: they had grown up together, indeed, had the same relatives and shared a universe of musical interests and acquaintances. And she was able to keep their marriage on firm ground. One can only imagine the peaks and valleys of emotional struggle she endured (for there were no doubt difficult struggles, even if one considers only the logistics of Rachmaninoff's professional activities)—but she and her husband stayed together and maintained a loving and committed relationship to each other. If there was a threat that Sergei would be drawn away from her by another woman, Natasha somehow figured out how to manage the situation—and the threat would be ended. On the question of the women in Rachmaninoff's life outside his marriage, more will be said in later chapters.

Figure 7.1 Sofia Aleksandrovna Satina, c. 1950. Courtesy of Science Photo Library UK.

Natasha's insights into her husband's character as an intense creative artist were accurate and were arrived at because of her perspicacious nature. Simplicity, modesty, perseverance, intelligence, and possessing a substantial inner life—these were the salient character traits of the woman who was to become Rachmaninoff's wife. If she seemed to be a "difficult" person, perhaps she appeared this way in her role as protector of her husband's privacy and coordinator of her family's complex life. At all stages of her relationship with Sergei, Natasha manifested a selflessness to the point of self-effacement that was to provide her future husband with the peace of mind and emotional stability he had lacked in his childhood. There exists no evidence to the effect that Sergei perceived her as difficult; to the contrary, they maintained a congenial bond all their lives.

Natalia's characterization of her husband in her memoir provides a touchstone for understanding him as a person, husband, and creative artist:

> About the personality of Sergei Vasilievich I can say that this was a noble-hearted, kind, and extremely honest man, one who was direct in his judgments. He was very strict towards others, but had the same expectations of himself as of others. Sergei Vasilievich was not afraid to state the most cruel truth to others to their face, which often would make me feel astonished and embarrassed. He was very impatient, and if something needed to be done, he wanted it to be done immediately. Sergei Vasilievich was unusually precise. He never would be late for trains, or to concerts, or visits to friends. He never presented himself as a *grand seigneur* by making others wait for him. He was modest in his conversations and behavior, but carried himself with dignity. I don't think he ever forgot if someone hurt or insulted him, though he never talked about it afterwards.[11]

Two quotations placed side by side reveal the depth of devotion that Sergei and Natasha possessed for each other. The first is found in the recollection of Anna Trubnikova, Rachmaninoff's niece:

> The life that followed was to show that Seryozha did not make a mistake in his choice of a wife. His wife knew how to arrange his life in such a way that his melancholy—which had often tormented him in the past—disappeared. Later in his life he at one point wrote to me from America, when both of his daughters, Tatiana and Irina, were already married: "I'm living now only with Natasha, my faithful companion, the kindhearted genius of my entire life."[12]

The loving emotion Sergei expressed for his longtime wife is palpable, and this revelation, coming from a man of very few words, cannot be dismissed lightly. In light of the whole that is known of Rachmaninoff's life, the conclusion remains that he loved his wife with a quiet feeling that perhaps lacked passion—but that he was touched and grateful to her for her love and devotion to him. The second quotation comes from the concluding section of Natasha Rachmaninoff's memoir: "Thus ended my conjugal life with the most noble-hearted and talented man, the dearest person to me in the world."[13] Her feelings speak for themselves.

Epistolary evidence confirms that Natasha was drawn to her cousin Sergei as early as 1890, when she was only thirteen years old. Her feelings quickly evolved into love for her shy and introverted cousin, and henceforth every act of her life was carried out in order to establish closeness between them and to win Sergei as her husband. In one of his letters to Natalia Skalon, dated September 8, 1890, he politely asks her to tell Natasha that he does like to be "kissed" through letters.[14] This reference implies that in correspondence to him Natasha Satina had sent him kisses via the mail, asking him if he liked for her to do this. She had already developed tender feelings for him.

Natasha Satina possessed musical talent and accomplishments in her own right, and they are important for establishing her abiding love for music, both on its own account and as a vital link between her and Sergei. She was disciplined and hardworking, realizing that through music, Sergei's greatest love, she would be able to stay close to him and win his affection. She was not mistaken in her assumptions. Although she received little active encouragement from her family for her pursuit of music, she persevered in the face of tremendous adversity. In 1895 she was admitted to study at the Moscow Conservatory, where she declared a concentration in music pedagogy. The following description of the circumstances under which Natasha had to practice reveals her difficulties and her perseverance:

> Although Varvara Arkadievna did not hinder Natasha's study of music, she did not create suitable conditions for her to do serious musical work, either. The grand piano stood in a room that provided access into another room, and the Satins often hosted relatives and friends at their house. This meant that in order to work at the piano Natasha had to seize those moments when the room was not being used. This problem, of course, left its mark on her advancement.[15]

In the spring of 1897 Natasha faced a series of difficult final examinations at the conservatory. She was distracted by spring fever and no doubt longed to travel to Ignatovo with Sergei and her two cousins—but her exams prevented her from accompanying them. In a letter dated May 17, 1897 (two days after Sergei, Natalia Skalon, and Liudmila Skalon had left Moscow for Ignatovo), that Natasha wrote to her close friend Elena Zhukovskaia, she described the pain and grief she had experienced at her most difficult examinations:

> On my music theory exam I received only a C+, when I had hoped to earn at least a B; after you left I had studied very diligently, had learned everything perfectly, and had solved even the difficult assignments in melody that Seryozha had given me. All of my unhappiness came about mainly due to the repulsive

Aleksandrovna Ivanovna.[16] I arrived at the conservatory at 9:30 a.m., but I was taken [to be examined] only at 5 p.m. Since the morning we had all been sitting in one room; from agitation and hunger I became so weak that I no longer could concentrate on anything. But this was a trifle compared to what had taken place on the 12th [of May]. I never thought I could be so nervous. My fingers just jumped about on the keyboard. Our class (of S.M. Remizov) was the last one, and we played at 6 p.m.[17]

At the Moscow Conservatory the fifth-level final examinations in pianoforte, for promotion to the sixth level, consisted of a two-day process. On the first day the students of all the professors took a theory examination, while the second day was devoted to the performance of selected pieces from the piano repertoire.[18]

Despite all her fretting, Natasha received a B in pianoforte. Professor Pabst agreed to admit her to his class, and she received from him a list of pieces that she needed to learn over the summer. She was overjoyed at being promoted to Pabst's class, but she soon learned of his untimely death from a heart attack. This news plunged her into despair. Pabst's death contributed to the difficulties Natasha kept encountering in trying to carry out her conservatory studies in an organized and stable manner.[19]

Zhukovskaia describes Natasha's further struggles at the conservatory:

The death of Pabst, a brilliant pianist, marvelous pedagogue, and kindhearted man, really was a genuine tragedy for Natasha and ushered in after it all of her subsequent ordeals. During the entire time of her studies at the conservatory she was plagued by misfortunes, and it took all her tenacity to enable her to graduate from the conservatory. With Pabst's death her enforced wandering from one professor to another began. To replace Pabst, V.I. Safonov invited V.L. Sapelnikov, but the latter was interested only in conservatory performance, and, having squabbled over something with Safonov, left the conservatory at the start of the academic year. After Sapelnikov James Kvast was invited from abroad: he turned out to be an unsuccessful teacher and similarly left soon after being hired. At that point Safonov decided to teach the orphaned class himself. He was an outstanding pedagogue, but was so overloaded with work that of course he could not teach the entire class. The result was that in reality on the sixth and seventh levels Natasha and her classmates virtually did no work; she began to study in a normal fashion only on the eighth level, when she joined the class of K.I. Igumnov. She graduated from the conservatory in his class in 1901, receiving a silver medal.[20]

During the spring and fall of 1901 Sergei and Natalia evolved their relationship to the point of planning an engagement to be married. The news of their intentions shocked everyone who knew them, both those who knew them intimately and those who knew them less well. Rachmaninoff's niece

Anna Trubnikova considered this news to be like a violent explosion.[21] Elena Zhukovskaia writes of Natalia's engagement to Sergei:

> For all of their friends and even close relatives this [impending] marriage was an extremely unexpected event.
>
> I must say that the thought of the possibility of their marriage never entered my mind. I never thought of this possibility probably because Sergei Vasilievich didn't manifest anything even remotely resembling a so-called courtship . . . [The idea of a courtship] was completely incompatible with his personality, with his extreme reticence, and with his dislike of putting his feelings and tribulations on display. Relations between them were of a purely friendly, comradely character. He often teased Natasha. In their teen-age years, when she was very thin and looked much older than her age, he would jokingly say: "You're as thin as a stick, black as a crow, little girl Natalia, I feel sorry for you." Of course, the older she became, the more her appearance improved.
>
> Natasha was constantly concerned about the health of Sergei Vasilievich, about all those small details of everyday life that he was completely incapable of attending to, and she ardently felt both his successes and failures, always encouraging him to maintain a positive frame of mind.
>
> The main thing in his life was musical art, and in order for it to be productive, he needed an atmosphere of the friendship, love, and caring of people who were close to him.[22]

As Zhukovskaia vividly portrayed, the bond between Sergei and Natasha can be explained in several ways that make sense. Sergei knew without a doubt that Natasha was devoted to him. Viewed with these details in mind, his choice of Natasha for his wife was not surprising. Concerning Natasha's understanding of Sergei's feelings toward her, she must have been satisfied with the emotional closeness that existed between them. As for the rest—she cultivated their closeness for the rest of her life, creating for herself and her famous husband a successful marriage that would survive many trials and tribulations in their peregrinations across several continents.

Sergei's unstable and turbulent childhood provides another important key to understanding the adult man and his decision-making. His parents suffered through an unhappy marriage that culminated in a painful separation, as well as a devastating decline in their finances. They lost their entire material wealth as a result of Sergei's father's spendthrift habits. Brandt caustically observed, "I saw Vasily Arkadievich several times, and I can guarantee you that that man could ruin the life of anyone at all."[23] We recall that in St. Petersburg the Rachmaninoffs' apartment was so small that Sergei was the child chosen to go and live with other relatives—this must have intensified his feelings of unimportance, vulnerability, and instability. His major quarrel with Nikolay Zverev also reinforced for him the fact that he had virtually no control over where or with whom he would be living. It makes complete sense that one goal he would set for himself would be the creation of a permanent and secure family haven. Furthermore, Sergei experienced the deaths of his three sisters at a young age, and this, combined with his own intense fear of death, left him with a feeling of profound insecurity and rootlessness. This last has been noticed by many people who wondered at his perpetual nomadic habits as an adult, which cannot be facilely explained exclusively or even partially by his concert schedule of international dimensions.

The Satin family represented for Sergei the stability he lacked in his own family and the emotional conditions he needed in order to fulfill himself as a composer and pianist. They had provided him with a secure haven while he was growing up, and the fact that he was related to them, that he legitimately, by blood and ancestry, *belonged* in this family was vital for his well-being. He had spent many happy summers with the Satins at their estate of Ivanovka, and he continued to love this place until the end of his life. To marry Natasha would even more firmly solidify his attachment to this idyllic and dreamily isolated place in the Russian steppes, the kind of place ideally suited to his temperament. This is not to say, however, that Sergei decided to marry Natasha for financial reasons, or that his decision was a self-serving and coldly calculated one. He and Natasha had become very close by this time; he loved her in ways that he felt were compatible with marriage, and it is clear that she was in love with him.

Thus, Sergei married Natasha Satina because he saw in her the most devoted wife he could wish for, and he knew that she would be the best possible partner for him for the kind of life he sought for himself. For him it was an advantage that she was a relative; that her family the Satins had taken him in many times; that he knew well their habits, personalities, and idiosyncrasies; and that he was fulfilled by their entire way of life as members of the Russian nobility who moved effortlessly and habitually (as was the normal custom for that social class) between their residences in Moscow and St. Petersburg, and their country estate near Tambov hundreds of miles away to the south in a glorious seclusion. Nothing about the Satins or their way of life was unknown to Sergei, and, for their part, they saw in him a worthy relative and talented musician who could provide Natasha with a stable life. At the time that Sergei was ready to marry and establish a home and family for himself, Natasha was the woman foremost on his mind as a candidate. He had no doubts as to her feelings for him and understood that a marriage to her would not involve any risky gambles on his part. But to say that he was passionately in love with her would not present a true picture of his feelings.

Sergei and Natalia had to overcome some major difficulties in order for their wedding plans to go forward. It is very likely that Natasha told her mother, Varvara Arkadievna, soon after she and Sergei had decided on their plans. Zhukovskaia provides a typical description of Natasha's mother: "Varvara Arkadievna was a very active woman whose turbulent energy prompted her constantly to take on projects and organize various events."[24] She had a strong, uncompromising personality, worked very hard at Ivanovka in overseeing the activities of the estate, and maintained a strict, though loving, relationship with her children. She understood that Natasha loved Sergei deeply and would not desist from the desire to marry him, and she also must have viewed Sergei as a suitable match for her daughter. It is not known how Natasha's father reacted to the news, but since her mother was the dominant personality of her parents, she probably convinced her husband of the rightness of the decision. Importantly, the young couple secured the support of the bride's parents. Varvara Arkadievna petitioned Tsar Nicholas II for permission for the couple to marry; her petition would carry considerable weight, because she was a noblewoman of a distinguished lineage.

Rachmaninoff's mother Liubov Petrovna vigorously opposed the marriage, in part because she was religious and the Russian Orthodox Church forbade marriages between first cousins, and in part because she feared for the health of the children Sergei and Natalia would have. It is not known how Rachmaninoff's father viewed his upcoming marriage, but he did not actively stand in the way of the union. Because Liubov Petrovna opposed the marriage, it created a permanent state of animosity between her and her future daughter-in-law. In the 1920s, when the Rachmaninoffs were in exile in Europe and Sergei wrote to his mother to join them permanently, Liubov Petrovna declined the invitation. Sergei was a loving and attentive son to his mother, both while he was in Russia and during his forced exile in Europe and America; he took great care to attend to her needs even from abroad until her death in Novgorod in 1929. Nikolay Georgievich Teiss, a resident of Novgorod who had known Liubov Petrovna personally, affirmed from his contact with her that her son Sergei wanted very much for her to join him and his family in emigration. She always declined Sergei's invitations and entreaties, because her life and friends were in Russia, but more likely because she knew that she and her daughter-in-law would not get along.[25] Sergei surely was relieved at this decision, for if his mother had come to live with them, he would have endured a household in which she and his wife would remain permanently at odds with each other.

Rachmaninoff dedicated two songs to the woman who would become his wife. The first, "Do not sing, my beauty, in my presence" (Opus 4, No. 4; written in summer 1893), is a setting of a poem by Pushkin, Rachmaninoff's favorite poet. When the song was composed Rachmaninoff was twenty years of age, while Natasha was sixteen. He was not interested in her at that time; his thoughts were with Vera Skalon, yet drifting away from Vera as well. Natasha, however, was already very much in love with him. The song describes a man for whom a woman's singing evokes memories of another relationship at another time, in another place:

My beauty, don't sing the sad songs of Georgia in my presence.
They remind me of another life, a distant shore.
Alas! Your cruel melodies remind me
of the steppes, the night, and the features
of a far away, sorrowing maiden.[26]

Judging from the connection Rachmaninoff typically established between a given song and its dedicatee, this song's theme does not focus on the singer (represented by Natalia?), but rather on the memories she brings back for him. Thus Natalia and her family setting remind him of another love. The interpretation seems plausible.

The second song, "Were you hiccupping, Natasha?" (no opus number), is a song-jest, with words by P. Viazemskii that were adapted by Rachmaninoff in a charming scene. It is dated May 17, 1899, and was sent to Natasha—although she was present at the good-natured scene of Rachmaninoff's "declaiming" of the song to several of his female cousins. This song is light-hearted, but lacks the elements of physical attraction and romance that one would expect, considering, by comparison, the sensual details of "In the Silence of the Secret Night" dedicated to Vera Skalon. Rachmaninoff composed this song-jest at the time when he still had some emotional attachment to Anna Lodyzhenskaia and may already have met Elena Dahl. These two songs represent the only pieces Rachmaninoff ever dedicated to his wife.

In the face of his dedications of major pieces of music to other women (whether he was attracted to them or not), the fact that he never again entered her name on the dedicatee line must have caused Natasha discomfort at times when she thought about it. But Sergei was her husband, and what she had of him was far more important than the honor of having one of his major compositions dedicated to her. Natalia understood her importance to Rachmaninoff as his wife, and he valued her opinion as someone highly trained in music. In her memoir written after his death she writes, "I was not allowed to be in the room in which he was composing . . . But even so, since the time when we were young he always played *for me first* each new piece of his [emphasis added]."[27]

Even with the above conclusions, however, the mysteries surrounding this period of Rachmaninoff's life remain. Irina Brandt describes:

> I can only say one thing about the character of S.V. Rachmaninoff: his character was very complex. When I would look at him from the side, it always seemed to me that he was constantly oppressed by something, that some kind of sin was

tormenting his soul. God knows why it seemed that way to me. Even when he laughed, at the corners of his eyes there would always be iciness. And I always felt terrified at this discovery of mine. Even in his music, in many compositions, in the midst of the radiance and happiness I often "heard" this iciness. All this I attributed to the fact that he had a very difficult childhood. After all, how painful and humiliating it must have been [for him] to live as a "poor relative." And Sergei Vasilievich from his early childhood wandered as a stray among houses of "people outside of his immediate family." Later, when I read the recollections of Sergei Vasilievich's relatives, I was amazed at how in their recollections they were all "kindhearted." But if in reality they had been that way, could they have allowed Sergei Vasilievich to wander among people unfamiliar to him? Sergei Vasilievich worked very hard, and it always seemed to me that he labored so much because he was afraid that his children would fall into a state of need.[28]

If one considers Rachmaninoff's associations with various women in his life who were important to him both personally and professionally, especially those who remained in his life over long period of time and to whom he dedicated some of his compositions, it is hard not to conclude that his relationship with his wife was complicated. Since he spent his summers at Ivanovka, where the peasant woman Maria Ivanova was associated with him in many ways, and where the estate of Anna Lodyzhenskaia and her husband was but a horseback ride away—it stands to reason that Rachmaninoff had existing emotional ties to at least two women during the period that led up to his marriage in 1902. And the number could increase to three, if we consider a possible relationship with Elena Dahl.

Concerning Rachmaninoff's musical projects of the period leading up to his wedding, despite this being a complicated time for him, the combination of the tremendous success of his Second Concerto and plans to chart a definite course for his personal life must have brought him some measure of relief. Even with the prospect of an unrealized, lost love, his marriage into the family he had known since his student years at Zverev's would provide a framework within which he could maintain a predictable life and develop himself as a musician. In the fall 1901 Rachmaninoff composed his Sonata for Piano and Cello in G minor (Op. 19), dedicating it to the brilliant cellist and supporter of his early compositional efforts Anatoly Brandukov (1859–1930). Together Rachmaninoff and Brandukov premièred the sonata on December 2 of that year in Moscow. This composition is characterized by a depth of emotion and lyricism, spotlighting the piano somewhat more than the cello—although the cello writing is exquisite and exploits the language of that instrument effectively.

Martyn notes that in Russian music Rachmaninoff, aside from the sonatas of Anton Rubinstein, did not have any models to inform his work on it. The two men's musical association extended at least as far back as 1892, when

Rachmaninoff composed two pieces for his Opus 2 (a prelude and "oriental dance") for cello and piano and dedicated them to Brandukov.[29] Rachmaninoff valued Brandukov's friendship and held him in such high esteem that he asked him to serve (with Alexander Siloti) as one of the best men at his coming wedding several months later.

The marriage between Sergei and Natasha proved more than satisfactory. Regardless of the encounters and relationships Sergei Rachmaninoff maintained with women who mattered to him in his inner world, he and his wife stayed together in a successful marriage until his death—sharing a complex conjugal life characterized by its own harmony and devotion.

The overall relationship between Sergei and Natasha's two families was complex, however, with the Satins' extended family being dominant because of their sheer number of members and also their ownership of the estate on which the newlyweds lived in the summers. Brandt calls into question any account of a harmonious picture of the relations between the Rachmaninoffs and Satins:

> Concerning the arrival of Sergei Vasilievich's mother at Ivanovka, I can say the following: she came to Ivanovka at the end of spring (either in 1912 or 1913, I am not entirely certain).
>
> Sergei Vasilievich drove in his car to pick up his mother at Rzhaks train station. They returned in the early evening. Liubov Petrovna was settled in Marina's room, which was next to mine. Liubov Petrovna was dressed in very plain clothing. She brought with her an icon, which she set on the chest of drawers, and she lit a votive candle beside it. She prayed for a long time in the morning and the evening. Several times Sergei Vasilievich drove his mother to church, to Viazov. And once when she fell ill Sergei Vasilievich brought Fr. Nikolay to her. Fr. Nikolay spent a long time conversing with Liubov Petrovna about something. She spoke in a quiet and, it always seemed to me, sorrowful voice. I was astonished that out of the residents of Ivanovka only Sergei Vasilievich talked with her. The others, in my opinion, simply didn't notice her. Even Sofia Aleksandrovna, who was pleasant to everyone, in the presence of Liubov Petrovna would purse her lips and walk away. Sergei Vasilievich would personally go to Liubov Petrovna's room to call her to a meal or for tea. But more often than not, Marina would bring a tray with the tea kettles, dishes, preserves, and cookies directly to the room where Liubov Petrovna was staying.
>
> And she and Sergei Vasilievich would drink their tea and quietly converse about something for a long time.
>
> During Liubov Petrovna's visit to Ivanovka the feeling was in the air that relations among everyone had become strained. Varvara Arkadievna and Natalia Aleksandrovna, in my opinion, even did not hide the fact that they were displeased about the arrival of Liubov Petrovna. It seemed as if Sergei Vasilievich had invited his mother to Ivanovka without the approval of his relatives.

Figure 7.2 Sergei and Natalia Rachmaninoff, 1907. Public domain.

The weather that spring was warm. Liubov Petrovna came just in time for a garden still in bloom. In the daytime she would stroll in the garden, sit on a bench under the blossoming apple trees, or sit right on the grass under the trees.

It seemed to me, that she tried not to be a burden on anyone. Even her smile was somehow very sad. And sorrow streamed from her sunken eyes. What she prayed about, no one knew, for she prayed in a whisper or noiselessly moved her lips in prayer. Sometimes Sergei Vasilievich in the evenings would take Liubov Petrovna for a ride in his automobile. Very likely Sergei Vasilievich did everything so that Liubov Petrovna would like Ivanovka. Often one could see Liubov Petrovna by the blooming flower beds. Probably she wanted to tend the flowers, but was afraid that this would displease her hosts. Sergei Vasilievich took Liubov Petrovna to the train station himself. The driver sat at the wheel, while Sergei Vasilievich and Liubov Petrovna sat in the back seat. Only Marina and I came to say good-bye to her.

After the departure of Liubov Petrovna, Sergei Vasilievich walked about frowning for a long time and for several days didn't talk to anyone. Liubov Petrovna had stayed at Ivanovka for about a month. Later I heard Varvara Arkadievna blaming her for the break-up of her [Liubov Petrovna's] family. In my opinion, this accusation was unfair. Several times I had seen Vasily Arkadievich. . . .

In remembering Liubov Petrovna, I can say only kind words about her. Her meekness and piety impressed me. She wished only goodness for everyone. After all, it wasn't her fault that Vasily Arkadievich had squandered her property. And I felt sorry for Sergei Vasilievich, that he, because of the prejudices of his wife's relatives, was not able to pay enough attention to his mother.[30]

One artifact that adds to the puzzlement concerning the match between Sergei and Natasha is Sergei's last extant letter to Natalia (Tatusha) Skalon, with whom he had maintained an intimate and confessional correspondence for many years. Written at the train station of Chudovo, where Sergei had been waiting for an express train to Moscow for three hours and used the time to compose a missive to her. It is dated April 1, 1902, and portrays his turbulent state of mind in the weeks leading up to his wedding.

My dear Tatusha,
 . . . On my last trip I hurt your feelings very likely because I wasn't able to stop by to see you, and I want to talk to you about this injury to your feelings and ask your forgiveness for it. Not to see you was my deliberately thought-out intention, notwithstanding the fact that I very much wanted to see you and love you very much (on my word of honor). But my new future relatives placed me in a vise, insisting that if I visited you, then I must visit everyone else. . . .

Forgive me! And, for your part, do start cursing my wife's family, because you shouldn't curse me, but besides them there is no one to curse, and, moreover, someone has to be cursed for this act . . . Ask your mother and father to forgive me as well for not stopping by. I'm worried that they, too, may have gotten angry at me. . . .

... At the end of this month I will abandon all caution and shall get married. Without fail I expect a present from you, as fine and expensive as befits you to give me. I don't expect you to come [to the wedding]. For God's sake, I implore you, don't come. The fewer people there will be, the better. I say this to you in all seriousness. Concerning the present, whatever you come up with, you can ... send it even on the day of the wedding. ...

I am so terribly tired, Tatusha. Not from being on the road today, and not from writing this letter, but from the entire winter—and I don't know when I will be able to rest ... [In] summer I must, without laying down my hands, write ... like a fiend so as not to go broke. And I, as I have told you, am already so terribly tired now, and am so worn out, and weakened. I really don't know what the future will bring.

Farewell, Tatusha. And thus, the résumé of my letter: forgive me and send me a present, and have pity on me.[31]

Your S. Rachmaninoff

Many astonishing revelations from Sergei Rachmaninoff emerge in this letter. It reveals his deep intimacy with Natalia Skalon: it may be that both of them felt the stirrings of a mature love for each other. Sergei considered her a trusted confidante and we see the workings of his inner world revealed in what he communicates to her only a short time before his wedding. Most curious are Rachmaninoff's entreaties for Natalia to forgive him, and his sensitivity to her feelings and concerns about the slightest perceived failing on his part. Perhaps most cryptic are his final words to her: "Farewell ... and have pity on me." For what in particular did he want Tatusha to pity him? Rachmaninoff's letter to her is filled with a strange sadness and wistfulness that the events of that time in his life cannot satisfactorily account for. After all, the period immediately preceding a wedding is a happy, albeit busy and stressful, time for a young couple. Something was not quite right about the contours of Sergei's emotions before his wedding. He may have had mixed feelings about getting married in general—or there may have been some unfinished business in his life concerning another woman that would explain his sadness and confusion.

Max Harrison provides some insights into this memorable letter:

Rachmaninoff's announcement that [he and Natasha] were to marry was a surprise to all. It was presumably most of all a surprise to Natalia Skalon, with whom he had exchanged confidences for over a decade. Certainly his casualness in telling her is remarkable ... Rachmaninoff said that he expected a fine, expensive wedding present from her, ended by saying how exhausted he was, repeating his request for a present and asked her to have pity on him. What present, if any, Natalia Skalon sent him cannot be guessed, but their long correspondence apparently ended then and there.[32]

The wedding of Sergei Rachmaninoff and Natalia Satina took place on April 29, 1902. It was raining and the events that ultimately sealed their wedding vows were quite dramatic. Natalia's mother Varvara Arkadievna had secured the approval of the priest Fr. Amfiteatrov of the Archangelsk Cathedral in Moscow for the ceremony. However, the petition to allow the first cousins to marry had to be sent to the tsar, according to protocols, on the day of the ceremony itself—for it would be impossible for a priest to perform the ceremony without permission of the tsar. To the relief of Sergei and Natalia, as well as the small number of attendees, the permission was granted. Aleksandr Siloti and Rachmaninoff's close friend from the conservatory, cellist Anatoly Brandukov, served as best men. For the couple's wedding trip they would travel to various cities in Europe for sightseeing and to attend musical performances. From Lucerne, Switzerland, Rachmaninoff wrote to another conservatory friend Nikita Semenovich Morozov (who would in the future become a professor of theory at the Moscow Conservatory), who was also traveling in Europe. After a month of touring Europe he had grown weary of seeing historic buildings, palaces, cathedrals, and the various sights of the major cities. He was experiencing a mental and cultural fatigue, longing instead for a quiet room and contemplation instead of constant movement. He did appreciate the beautiful scenery of Lucerne, with its pine forests and mountain views. He and Natasha rented two rooms in a pension, also arranging to have a piano delivered there so that he could work on his music. He was reviewing the songs of Opus 21, concluding that they had been written too quickly and even seemed unfinished in some ways.[33]

As it turned out, Morozov was able to join the Rachmaninoffs for a trip to Bayreuth to attend the Wagner Festival; Aleksandr Siloti had generously given the couple tickets to the festival as a wedding present. They attended performances of the *Ring* cycle, *The Flying Dutchman*, and *Parsifal*. This somewhat lavish and extended wedding trip would provide Sergei and Natalia not only with fond memories but also cherished locations for future stays and a residence in Europe.

Despite his rewarding though exhausting travels, Sergei fretted over the state of readiness of his cantata *Spring* (Op. 20), which was a major compositional undertaking involving baritone solo, mixed chorus, and orchestra. Dedicated to his close friend Nikita Morozov, the cantata was set to the poem of Nikolai Nekrasov *The Verdant Noise*. The plot of the poem is straightforward: a peasant decides to kill his wife, who has been unfaithful—but at the arrival of spring he relents because of the associations of hope and renewal with that season (traditional associations for art and literature as well). Rachmaninoff had conceived it and worked on it intensively in January and February of 1902, but had to set it aside because of the upheaval of his wedding and the extended wedding trip in Europe. Once again Rachmaninoff treats the theme of illicit love, potential revenge, and forgiveness—a profoundly Christian inner journey for the suffering peasant. We are reminded of the epigraph to his Symphony No. 1: "Vengeance is mine; I will recompense." Moreover, since these were years during which Rachmaninoff was in all likelihood settling for himself some emotional upheavals he had experienced in the 1890s and right up to his marriage, it is not surprising that this theme would be uppermost in his mind when "speaking" through his music. Martyn describes a concern about the work's orchestration:

> Although Rachmaninoff was later to agree with Rimsky-Korsakov's criticism of the work's orchestration that "there is no sign of spring in the orchestra," and to profess a desire to "alter the whole instrumentation," the orchestral palette is nevertheless used with considerable subtlety, though the colouring is predominantly sombre, perhaps suggesting that the composer's prior interest in the text was not spring but the agonizing predicament of the peasant.[34]

The cantata was first performed on March 11, 1902, in Moscow, conducted by Siloti, for Rachmaninoff was still abroad. The baritone solo was sung by Dmitry Smirnov, later being taken up by Chaliapin for whose voice Rachmaninoff surely intended that vocal part.

The Rachmaninoffs returned to Russia during the latter part of that summer, joining Natasha's family and Aleksandr Siloti at Ivanovka. In October 1902, with the coming of colder weather that would make the country estate not possible for habitation, Sergei and Natalia moved to Moscow and rented an apartment at 11 Vozdvizhenka St., where they would live during the fall and winter seasons until 1905.

Inspired by his musical impressions from his wedding trip in Europe, Sergei began to work on a new composition, the *Variations on the Theme of Chopin's Prelude in C minor* (Op. 22). He worked on these variations between August 1902 and February 1903, performing them for the first time in Moscow on February 10, 1903. This new composition was published that same year. Along with his two later works of the *Corelli Variations* (Op. 42, 1931) and *Rhapsody on a Theme of Paganini* (Op. 43, 1934), the *Chopin Variations* would constitute Rachmaninoff's three forays into the variation genre. Throughout his career Rachmaninoff was especially drawn to the music of Chopin, both for its intricate melodic meanderings and for the latter's masterful creation of miniatures (which Rachmaninoff stated were for him more difficult to compose than large-scale works). For his *Chopin variations* Rachmaninoff selected a well-known, stately, and hauntingly beautiful prelude by that composer. Its memorable melody aside, Rachmaninoff was also attracted by the structural possibilities of the prelude and its potential for demonstrating various techniques of pianism. In twenty-two variations on the theme Rachmaninoff explored those possibilities and pianistic techniques, providing the pianist with a rich array of crafting the basic theme.

During this same productive year of 1903 Rachmaninoff composed a set of ten preludes (Op. 23). Even though he initially had no plan to compose a complete set of twenty-four preludes, in 1910 he wrote another set of thirteen preludes, strategically avoiding the Prelude in C sharp minor, which already existed (Op. 3 No. 2, 1892)—and which completed the twenty-four for the set. Dedicated to Aleksandr Siloti, the preludes of Op. 23 were all composed in 1903, except for the G minor prelude (No. 5), which had been conceived and written in 1901. Rachmaninoff first performed the Opus 23 preludes on February 10, 1903, in Moscow. These pieces have remained among his most popular works, performed by many pianists worldwide. In addition to each being in a different key, the preludes project various moods and emotions. The G minor prelude—with its tripartite structure that begins in a march rhythm, evolves into a lyrical middle section, and then gradually quickens its pace to an expansive and thrilling ending that repeats the basic melody of the piece—is extremely effective in performance. Rachmaninoff's acoustic recording of it of 1920 fortunately has been preserved, showing his characteristic rhythmic snap and daring dynamics especially in the final measures. The D major prelude (No. 4) with its undulating melody and delicate voicings has also remained among the most popular of the set.

On May 14, 1903, the Rachmaninoffs' first child, named Irina, was born at Ivanovka. After she was born and he had assured himself that both mother and daughter were in good health, peasants on the estate remember Sergei playing the piano for hours afterward in a celebratory mood. The arrival of this child heralded for him new feelings of fatherhood and family contentment, with an even greater attachment to the land as the bulwark against the poverty he always feared. Although he rarely revealed the programs for his works, he disclosed that he composed a particular prelude on the memorable day of the birth of his daughter. Rachmaninoff's Prelude in E flat major (Op. 23, No. 6) provides a rare example of one of his compositions about which the program is known. In its peaceful character, freshness of expression, and harmonic resolution the prelude provides some insights into the composer's coming to terms with the complexity of his personal life and his acceptance of the course he had set for himself in the early 1900s. A consideration of personal circumstances in an analysis of a musical work is especially appropriate for Rachmaninoff's compositions because of their direct and honest communication of his emotional state to the listener. His and Natalia's second child, a daughter who was named Tatiana, was also born at Ivanovka under equally favorable circumstances four years later, on June 21, 1907.

Rachmaninoff maintained a serious interest in composing for opera, prompted by the early success he experienced with his conservatory graduation work of *Aleko*. The appeal of that one-act opera, even though a required assignment, stemmed from its direct association with Pushkin—who is at the heart of Russian culture, and who remained Rachmaninoff's most loved poet throughout his life. Two of his subsequent operas of this same period, *Monna Vanna* (1904, unfinished) and *Francesca da Rimini* (1900–1905, Op. 25) are connected in their themes of illicit love, although they diverge on the outcome for the female main characters. They are discussed elsewhere in the present book. The same years of 1903–1905 witnessed Rachmaninoff's return to Pushkin, specifically one of his masterful *Little Tragedies*, *The Covetous Knight*. Once again composing a one-act opera and drawing from his favorite author, Rachmaninoff in the libretto stayed as faithful as possible to Pushkin's original drama in verse.

The *Covetous Knight* treats the well-established theme of the seductive power of money and its fatal connection with sin. Its primary male characters-singers exhibit a differing attitude toward money, ranging from Albert's complete submission to it, to his father the Baron's objectifying love for it, to the Duke's moderate approach, to the Moneylender's use of it for exploitation of others (the fifth character is Ivan, a servant). The opera was performed in a two-opera program with *Francesca da Rimini* at the Bolshoi Theatre in Moscow on January 11, 1906, with Rachmaninoff as conductor. Rachmaninoff had intended for Chaliapin to sing the role of the Baron, but for various reasons the latter did not stay in the production. This is an unfortunate irony, since Chaliapin had urged Rachmaninoff to take up the composition of the opera so that he could perform the role of the Baron.

During the years of 1906–1909 the Rachmaninoff family would alternate its residence between Dresden in the fall and winter, and Ivanovka in the spring and summer. Sergei was very prolific in his composition work, with conducting and performance opportunities abounding as well. He was to produce the major works of his Symphony No. 2 in E minor (1907), Piano Sonata No. 1 in D minor (1907), and the symphonic poem *Isle of the Dead* (1909). These compositions are discussed elsewhere in the present book. In addition, Rachmaninoff's third piano concerto was stirring within him even while he was at work developing the aforementioned massive musical ideas.

Rachmaninoff's life entered a period of perhaps the greatest stability and happiness he had known to that point. His creative output was large and significant: Among the many works associated with Ivanovka, he produced in 1909 the magisterial Piano Concerto No. 3 in D minor (Op. 30), which would be considered for many decades of the twentieth century the most difficult work of its genre. It was dedicated to Josef Hofmann, who never played it, perhaps due to his small hands and the piece's wide arpeggios. Or, he may have found the monstrously challenging concerto somewhat intimidating. This third composition of Rachmaninoff's in a large-scale genre expressed

Marriage to Natalia Satina

Figure 7.3 Sergei Rachmaninoff with Daughters Irina (left) and Tatiana (right), 1923. Courtesy of Carnegie Hall Rose Archives.

the mature man: Rachmaninoff had more than established himself as a formidable musician in Russia and would only expand that reputation further in Europe and America. He was married with two charming daughters, secure in his family life, and fulfilled in his development of the estate of Ivanovka. Unknown to him, his rise in the musical world would be accompanied by the gradual rending of the cultural fabric of the traditional Russia that was familiar and dear to him, until it was violently torn apart first by World War I and ultimately by the Bolshevik Revolution of 1917.

Rachmaninoff began serious work on his Piano Concerto No. 3 in D minor in May 1909 at Ivanovka. He slaved over it, as he described, for the entire summer, finishing it for the most part on October 2 that same year. With the possibility of an American tour spotlighting his third concerto in the offing since June, on July 15 he mused humorously in a letter to Morozov:

> It wouldn't be a bad idea for me to have a secretary, if only the salary would correspond with the amount of business correspondence I get. But before that, I'd like to buy an automobile. I can't tell you how much I want one! That's all I lack now—an automobile and a secretary!
>
> What is *not* consoling is that I'm going to America after all. Devil take it! I think I'd even give up the secretary if I could get out of going there. That's how

much I don't want to go. But then, perhaps, after America I'll be able to buy myself that automobile. So it may not be so bad!³⁵ [emphasis original]

He had accepted an offer to tour in America for two-and-one-half months—from November 4, 1909, to January 27, 1910—and was still finalizing the details of the concerto as he began his journey across the Atlantic Ocean. He practiced on a silent "dummy" piano while crossing the ocean on a steamship, in order to set the concerto in his mind and his fingers.

Rachmaninoff's third piano concerto in its opening differs from the second concerto in his use of the orchestra with respect to the piano: the orchestra sets a dotted rhythmic motto at the beginning of the piece for two measures before the piano enters with simple octaves. Whereas in the second concerto the piano opens the piece with a series of massive chords before becoming the accompaniment to the orchestra's playing of the first movement's main theme, in the third concerto the orchestra briefly starts the piece with the piano taking on the melody. In both concertos the opening themes are structured as a weaving around the tonic note, producing strikingly simple yet memorable melodies. While his second concerto is stately, wistful, and darkly majestic, the third concerto emerges as bursting with confidence, muscular, and glittering with an almost explosive beauty. It does not run too much of a risk to suggest that the program of the third concerto relates to Ivanovka and Rachmaninoff's exuberant love for this estate and the life on it. The driving, pulsating rhythm and high energy of the first and third movements are unified by many elements, one of them being the dotted rhythmic motto—which V. I. Antipov identified as Rachmaninoff's "galloping rhythm" connected with his love of horseback riding in the environs of Ivanovka.³⁶ While the Intermezzo representing the second movement contains passages of genuine sadness, they are eclipsed by the overall affirming moods of the first and third movements (which are thematically related to each other).³⁷

As Patrick Piggott sums up concerning the concerto's third movement:

> The finale is one of the most dashing and exciting pieces of music ever composed for piano and orchestra. Every possibility of the modern piano is exploited in it: the impetuous opening theme in D minor; the rhythmically urgent theme in C and its variant, the happy, soaring melody in G—all are carried forward on wave after wave of dazzling passage-work, backed by an ever-widening range of pianistic resonances, by Rachmaninov's characteristic rhythmic verve, and by effective orchestration. The most difficult structural problem of the movement (how to provide relief and contrast to such an opening without allowing the interest to sag) is solved with skill.
>
> The themes of the first section then reappear, all of them a tone lower than before and all presented in entirely different ways. The happy G major theme,

now in F, is extended until the key of D minor has been re-established; and then, with an ever-increasing excitement, a long and percussive coda on a dominant pedal leads, via tempestuous cascade of piano octaves, to a final ecstatic outburst of melody from both piano and orchestra . . . Into this long and effective coda Rachmaninov put all that he had in reserve of glamour and excitement, for the summing-up of so brilliant and so emotionally high-powered a concerto was in itself a challenge not to be shirked.[38]

Fortunately recorded for posterity are Rachmaninoff's own performances of his second and third concertos with the Philadelphia Orchestra.[39] In both concertos he plays at the highest speed the music can tolerate, but without sacrificing his musicality and lyricism where needed. At these tempi he "heard" his own music, indicating that within the dense textures of his compositions the notes of the main themes had to be strung as closely together as feasible so that the melodic lines would be maximally audible. There is deep emotion in both concertos, but not a trace of sentimentality. One is reminded of Michael Steinberg's assessment of Rachmaninoff's performance of his music, which provides crucial clues about how the latter envisioned his compositions: "Nor should one forget Rachmaninoff's own fiercely rugged, boldly limned, tough, anti-pathetic playing even of his own most pathos-drenched music."[40] Many fine pianists have performed and had recorded Rachmaninoff's third piano concerto. Among those who were his contemporaries, he admired Walter Gieseking's performance of the piece. Concerning Vladimir Horowitz, who had a special personal and musical relationship with Rachmaninoff and the Russian School of Piano, Rachmaninoff stopped short of praising Horowitz too lavishly, for he noted in Horowitz's playing both masterful talent and a lack of musicality.

Barrie Martyn raised a perceptive consideration about the third concerto in the context of Rachmaninoff's entire musical trajectory:

It [the concerto in its last movement] grandiloquently climbs one last emotional peak before Rachmaninoff brings his most elaborate work in concerto form to a triumphant and exhilarating conclusion. However, in developing for his Third Concerto the characteristic features of its predecessor, and pushing them to the very limits of expressive and virtuoso possibility, the composer may in a sense be said to have created a problem for himself: along this route he had reached a point beyond which he could not go. That, surely, is the reason why his fourth and final concerto, conceived only five years later, was necessarily to be so different in style.[41]

Martyn pays Rachmaninoff a supreme compliment in alluding to the near-perfection of Rachmaninoff's third concerto in musical terms, but rightly wonders if its peaks created for Rachmaninoff's compositional expectations that were difficult, if not impossible, to realize.[42] It also may be the case that in his fourth concerto Rachmaninoff, in observing some of the features of the Russian Silver Age of art and literature, chose to participate in that age to some extent by thinning the texture of this concerto.

Rachmaninoff played the Third Concerto for the first time with the New York Symphony Orchestra under the capable baton of Walter Damrosch during his American tour. The tour also included major performances with the Boston Symphony, the Philadelphia Orchestra, and the New York Philharmonic (this last with conductor Gustav Mahler, whose skill and musicianship Rachmaninoff greatly admired). Critical assessments of Rachmaninoff's music were mixed, though the critics were impressed with his technique as a pianist and the nuances and precision he drew from the various orchestras in which he served as guest conductor. It frustrated him that his Prelude in C sharp minor (Op. 3, No. 2) continued to attract both audience and critics' attention out of proportion (he maintained) to its intrinsic musical worth, but he felt compelled to perform it whenever it was requested. Rachmaninoff's own impressions of American audiences were far from flattering. From America he wrote to his young cousin Zoya Pribytkova,[43] in answer to a letter she had sent him, that Americans were consumed by the practice of "doing business" and their efforts to involve him in various aspects of business activity had become tiresome to him. In contrast to what he felt was a dry and fast-paced life all around him, Rachmaninoff was touched by the charm and sweet Russianness of Zoya's letter.[44] In an interview that he gave to the Russian magazine *Muzykalnyi truzhenik* after returning to Russia, he noted that the tour had been very tiring, since he performed almost every day for three months. He played only his own compositions and enjoyed genuine success but remained critical of American audiences, who he felt were cold, spoiled, and merely seeking novelty in their appraisal of new artists.[45] Overall, however, the tour was an immense success, and it set the stage for important future collaborations that Rachmaninoff would undertake both in Europe and the United States.

NOTES

1. Personal interview, A. I. Ermakov, Ivanovka, July 1, 2005. V. I. Antipov had originally assessed the marriage between Sergei and Natasha as a happy one. In recent years, however, he revised his thinking in order to accommodate the hypothesis of a beloved in Rachmaninoff's life—which would call into question the notion of a "happy" union. Personal interview, Moscow, June 5, 2015.

2. E.Yu. Zhukovskaia, "Vospominaniia o moem uchitele i druge S.V. Rakhmaninove," in *Vospominaniia o Rakhmaninove*, ed. Z.A. Apetian, 5th ed. (Moscow: Muzyka, 1988), I: 255–56, trans. VZN.

3. Personal interview, Senar, Weggis, Switzerland, July 15, 2004.

4. Irina Aleksandrovna Brandt, "Pis'mo 2," in *Ivanovka: Vremena. Sobytiia. Sud'by*, compiled by A. I. Ermakov and A. V. Zhogov (Moscow: Irina Arkhipova Foundation, 2003), paraphrase of 77–78.

5. When the Rachmaninoffs left Russia in December of 1917, they left many of their belongings in Moscow with Marina Ivanova, who took care of them and refused to sell them even when she was in financial need. Personal interview, Aleksandr Ermakov, Ivanovka, July 2, 2005.

6. Brandt, "Pis'mo 1," in Ermakov and Zhogov, 75.

7. Ibid., 79, trans. VZN.

8. Other researchers into Rachmaninoff's life besides myself (such as V. I. Antipov and A. A. Naumov) have noticed this very obvious feature of the photographs—and have reached the same conclusions about Sofia's feelings. I examined this large body of photographs at the Russian National Museum of Music in Moscow.

9. Letter of S.V. Rakhmaninov in Ermakov and Zhogov, 71–72, trans. VZN.

10. "Dr. Sophia Alexandrovna Satina: 1879–1975," Find a Grave, https://www.findagrave.com/memorial/104618748/sophia-alexandrovna-satina, accessed June 20, 2022.

11. N.A. Rakhmaninova, "S.V. Rakhmaninov," in Apetian, II: 317, trans. VZN. Even when speaking about her husband, Natalia refers to him by using the polite form of his name (first name and patronymic), which etiquette is still common in Russia today.

12. L.D. Rostovtsova, "Vospominaniia o S.V. Rakhmaninove," in Apetian, I: 247, trans. VZN.

13. Rakhmaninova, in Apetian, II: 332, trans. VZN.

14. See Sergei Bertensson and Jay Leyda, *Sergei Rachmaninoff: A Lifetime in Music* (New York: New York UP, 1956; repr., Bloomington, IN: Indiana UP, 2001), 27.

15. Zhukovskaia, in Apetian, I: 257, trans. VZN.

16. Aleksandra Ivanovna Gubert was the "right hand" of the conservatory's director V. I. Safonov. She was exacting, pedantic, and generally considered unpleasant by the students studying there. See Zhukovskaia, in Apetian I: 259.

17. Zhukovskaia, in Apetian, I: 267, trans. VZN.

18. Ibid., paraphrase, I: 267.

19. Ibid., paraphrase, I: 267.

20. Ibid., I: 268, trans. VZN.

21. See Bertensson and Leyda, 97.

22. Zhukovskaia, in Apetian, I: 311–12, trans. VZN.

23. Ermakov and Zhogov, 77, trans. VZN.

24. Ibid., 256, trans. VZN.

25. Personal interview, B. S. Nikitin, July 15, 2007, Moscow. Nikitin referenced N. G. Тейсс of Novgorod, who had researched the life of Rachmaninoff's mother.

26. Translation of lines from "Ne poi, krasavitsa, prim ne" (Op. 4, No. 4, 1893), VZN.

27. Rakhmaninova, in Apetian, II: 314, trans. VZN.

28. Ermakov and Zhogov, 74, trans. VZN.

29. See Martyn, 67, 136.
30. Ibid., 76–77.
31. Bertensson and Leyda, 97–98, trans. Bertensson and Leyda, edited by VZN.
32. Max Harrison, *Rachmaninoff: Life, Works, Recordings* (New York: Continuum, 2005), 103.
33. Bertensson and Leyda, paraphrase of 98–99.
34. Barrie Martyn, *Rachmaninoff: Composer, Pianist, Conductor* (Burlington, VT: Ashgate, 1990), 138. The quoted matter of Rachmaninoff comes from Oskar von Riesemann, *Rachmaninoff's Recollections* (London: George Allen & Unwin Ltd., 1934), 144.
35. Bertensson and Leyda, 159.
36. Personal interview, V. I. Antipov, Moscow, July 16, 2007.
37. I omit a discussion of the two cadenzas that Rachmaninoff wrote for the first movement of the third concerto, which is a fascinating musicological topic in and of itself.
38. Patrick Piggott, *Rachmaninov: Orchestral Music*, BBC Music Guides (Seattle, WA: University of Washington Press, 1974), 53.
39. All four concertos were recorded with the Philadelphia Orchestra. Leopold Stokowski conducted two performances of the second concerto (1924, 1929), while under Eugene Ormandy's baton Rachmaninoff recorded performances of his first, third, and fourth concertos (1939–1941).
40. Michael Steinberg, *The Concerto: A Listener's Guide* (NY: Oxford UP, 1998), 360.
41. Martyn, 214. Patrick Piggott reaches the same conclusion concerning the pianistic "peak" Rachmaninoff had reached with his third concerto. See Piggott, 53.
42. See Martyn, 214.
43. In some sources the family name Прибыткова is transliterated as "Pribitkova." This is incorrect: in the Russian original the vowel in the second syllable is equivalent to "y" in transliteration. Hence "Pribytkova."
44. Bertensson and Leyda, paraphrase of 163–64.
45. Ibid., paraphrase of 165.

Chapter 8

Rachmaninoff's Aesthetics
(1906–1918)

From the year of his marriage until he and his family left Russia in 1917, Rachmaninoff's places of residence would alternate among an apartment on Strastnoi Boulevard in Moscow, the family estate of Ivanovka, and extended stays in Europe (mainly in Dresden, Germany). These were years of hard work yet tremendous fulfillment for him.

Along with the peaceful way of life on Russian country estates and significant cultural encounters in major cities of Europe, Rachmaninoff inherited the intellectual and aesthetic traditions of nineteenth-century Russia. He was born and educated at a time when his native country had already established itself in the arenas of literature, painting, sculpture, and music. To be sure, the training and proving grounds for those areas of artistic creation remained in Western Europe, especially Italy, Germany, England, and France—but what was learned and assimilated in Europe was metamorphosed into intrinsically Russian themes and styles. Rachmaninoff received the best education in the humanities available in Russia in the latter part of the nineteenth century. He was tutored in French and German, and read widely in French, German, and Russian literature. Because of his family's aristocratic social status, he interacted with Leo Tolstoy, Petr Tchaikovsky, Anton Rubinstein, Anton Chekhov, Vera Komissarzhevskaia, Aleksandr Blok, Marietta Shaginian, Ivan Bunin, Feodor Chaliapin, Maksim Gorky, and many other leading cultural figures of that time. Chaliapin was close friends with writer and political activist Gorky; in an anecdote involving Rachmaninoff, Chaliapin writes:

> I remember that the first time I heard Gorky's name was from my dear friend S.V. Rachmaninoff. This took place in Moscow. Seryozha Rachmaninoff once came to my place on Leontiev Lane and brought me a book.

"Read it," he said. "What a marvelous writer has appeared in our midst. He's probably young."

It seems to me, that the book was the first collection of Gorky's: "Malva," "Makar Chudra," and other stories of his first period. As it turned out, I really liked the stories. They exuded something very close to my soul.[1]

As a participant in Savva Mamontov's private opera, Rachmaninoff very likely would also have rubbed shoulders with some of the leading nineteenth- and early twentieth-century painters, such as Valentin Serov, Vasily Polenov, Mikhail Vrubel, and Konstantin Korovin. In his married life—he married into a similarly aristocratic family related to his own—he even interacted with the Russian court: he and Natalia Satina maintained a close friendship with the brother of Tsar Nicholas II, Grand Duke Mikhail Aleksandrovich, and his beloved Natalia Sergeevna Sheremetevskaia during the years of 1909–1916.[2]

By the time Rachmaninoff was born, the identity of Russian music was firmly established: its Byzantine and European origins, along with its Russian folkloric heritage, had already begun to produce that unique melodic quality, directness, and beautiful sadness one associates with Russian music. Rachmaninoff remained a composer in the Late Romantic style, but within that style he evolved his own musical and pianistic idiom throughout his life. His music reflects the crossroads of the artistic currents of Romanticism, Symbolism, Modernism, and Russian Orthodox Spiritual Realism; all of these influences produced a music that for him was above all *personal* and genuine. Russia's path in history was fraught with difficulty and torment, and yet Russian creative thinkers and musicians in the material and musical forms of their cultural production never lost sight of the essential radiance of life, love of nature as represented by the Russian countryside, yearning for philosophical truth, and belief in the attainability of paradise in the earthly world.

By the early nineteenth century, when Mikhail Glinka (1804–1857) was composing, the tuning system known as "equal temperament"—twelve chromatically equidistant notes, with equal tones for each octave—had already been established. The temperament known today as the standard was in place during Rachmaninoff's childhood, which meant that throughout his composing life the musical assumptions he made about scales and keys were the same as they are today. He felt most comfortable composing in the minor keys; he noted that his compositions were more successful in those keys. The musical advantages he possessed included a thorough understanding of the composing process, collaboration with numerous talented and well-educated musicians and pedagogues, and relatively favorable circumstances for creative work, especially during his Russia years of 1892–1917.

Rachmaninoff spent long periods of time in Europe, especially in Italy and Germany. He traveled abroad in 1900 when Chaliapin received the offer to sing the title role in Boito's *Mefistofele* at La Scala. In 1902 he and Natalia had spent their honeymoon in Germany and Switzerland. Because Natalia's grandmother was German, the Satin family maintained close ties with their German relatives' home city of Dresden. During the period of 1906 until April 1909 Sergei and his wife spent three seasons living abroad in Dresden (where the Satin family had a villa on Sidonienstrasse), but they made sure to spend each summer in Russia at Ivanovka. Rachmaninoff badly needed to withdraw himself from his many musical responsibilities in Moscow, for he felt powerful creative stirrings to compose. Dresden offered relative isolation and continuous, uninterrupted time for writing down the music inside him. His compositional output was impressive: in particular, his Symphony No. 2 in E minor (Op. 27) demonstrates the confidence of a master, with luxurious and undulating melodies that evoke the architectural beauty and rich culture of that German city.

Rachmaninoff crafted the long symphony—it had four movements—even more carefully than usual, because he did not want to repeat the catastrophe that had befallen his first symphony (through no fault of his). He began work on the symphony in Dresden in October 1906, although he may have sketched the idea and some fragments of it as early as 1902 during his wedding trip; he finished the first draft of the score on January 1, 1907. He continued rewriting some sections and started serious work on the orchestration at Ivanovka in the summer of 1907, with the intent of premièring it in Russia at the beginning of 1908. In a letter to Morozov written from Dresden on December 31, 1907, Rachmaninoff described the length of time he spent on each of the four movements: "1st movement—three months; 2nd movement—3 ½ weeks; 3rd movement—2 weeks; Finale—about 4 weeks. This means 2 months for the last three movements and three months for the first. I should add, too, that the first movement was written in Russia."[3] Rachmaninoff's reference to the first movement being written in his homeland may have had something to do with its relationship to his so-called Youth Symphony of 1891: the opening section of his Second Symphony is very similar to that of the earlier student piece.[4] Thus the symphony has origins at both Ivanovka and in Dresden. To avoid a disaster similar to what took place at the première of his First Symphony, Rachmaninoff conducted the Second Symphony himself for its first performance in St. Petersburg at one of Aleksandr Siloti's concerts on February 8, 1908.

Rachmaninoff's Second Symphony remains one of his finest compositions and one of the finest symphonies of the Late Romantic period. The Second Symphony shows his continuing maturation as a composer, one who intensified the symphony's appeal over the First in the naturally-flowing and breathtaking beauty of its lyricism; in the masterful, confident handling of its orchestration; and in the [intellectual satisfaction of] its organic growth.[5] Ken Meltzer summarizes the four movements:

The first begins with an extended slow-tempo introduction (*Largo*), opening with a motif that will appear in various guises throughout the work. The principal quick-tempo section (*Allegro moderato*) follows. The second movement is a vibrant scherzo (*Allegro molto*), culminating in the brass's chorale transformation of the Symphony's opening measures. The beautiful third movement (*Adagio*) is based upon two melodies, presented at the outset. The finale (*Allegro vivace*), recalling music from previous movements, propels to an exuberant close.[6]

What remains memorable about the Second Symphony, in addition to its surpassing beauty and extended length (about one hour) appropriate to a full development of its major themes, is Rachmaninoff's genius as a melodist. The third movement (*Adagio*), as Patrick Piggott describes,

> opens with a short but very beautiful *ritornello* in which rising thirds, treated sequentially, play an important part . . . But the principal theme itself, announced by the solo clarinet, is the very epitome of Rachmaninoff's most typical melodic style . . . It is a very long melody, moving mostly be step and never straying very far from the dominant of the scale—the note on which it begins. But though beautiful in itself it owes most of its poetic effect to the shifting and subtly organized harmonic web that underlies it.[7]

Rachmaninoff's Second Symphony was an immediate success and continues to be an important part of his repertoire that is performed worldwide by major orchestras. In December 1908 he learned that this symphony had won the Glinka Award in Russia, specifically the symphonic prize of 1,000 rubles. Rachmaninoff was vindicated in his efforts to compose another symphony, and whatever unpleasant feelings may have lingered from the debacle of the First Symphony were for the most part dispelled.

This extremely productive period of Rachmaninoff's work saw not only the Second Symphony coming into being, but also the noteworthy compositions of his Sonata #1 in D minor based on Goethe's *Faust* (Op. 28, 1906–1907), the unfinished opera *Monna Vanna* (1907), "Letter to K.S. Stanislavsky" (1908), *Isle of the Dead* (Op. 29, 1909), and Piano Concerto No. 3 in E minor (Op. 30, 1909). These works are discussed below, except for *Isle of the Dead*, which because of its thematic connections with life, death, and immortality is analyzed in chapter 9 along with Rachmaninoff's religion-inspired works.

Rachmaninoff's months spent in Dresden proved artistically fruitful in many ways. One of the products of this period was his Sonata No. 1 in D minor (Op. 28). Between December 1906 and February 1907 Rachmaninoff undertook work on a piano sonata, while still involved with details of his Second Symphony. After his return to Moscow he played a draft of the sonata at a gathering that included Oscar von Riesemann, Vladimir Wilshaw, Leo Conius, Konstantin Igumnov, and Nikolai Medtner. The response of these musically gifted men was overwhelmingly positive, but Rachmaninoff determined to polish the sonata some more before it could be published. On May 26, 1907, Rachmaninoff traveled to Paris to perform the sonata in Diaghilev's "Russian Season," which enabled him to evaluate its structure even further. Only by April 1908 did he consider the sonata completed and in its publishable form. Igumnov premièred the sonata in Moscow on October 17, 1908; Rachmaninoff performed it three weeks later in Leipzig. At this point the composer revealed that Goethe's *Faust* was the inspiration for the sonata. The intensive work that Rachmaninoff and Chaliapin had carried out in Varrazze to prepare the latter for his La Scala debut, along with Rachmaninoff's artistic fascination with the struggle between good and evil, surely contributed to his choice of inspiration for his first piano sonata.

Martyn points out that in his First Sonata Rachmaninoff adheres to the same structural concept as in Liszt's "Faust" choral symphony (S.108), which he knew well: the music does not present the entire plot of Goethe's tragic play, but instead offers three portraits of the main characters. The sonata's first movement gives an impression of Faust himself, the second imagines Gretchen (Margareta), and the third dramatizes the flight to Brocken and image of Mephistopheles.[8] The first and second movements correspond in mood and conflicting impulses: in the first movement, "[t]he juxtaposition of abruptly contrasting dynamics and of doubt and certainty seems to reflect the struggle of opposing aspirations that goes on in the mind of Faust. . . ."[9] The second movement's gentle melody suggests Margareta's purity, but it becomes more complex and troubled, "perhaps reflecting the agitation in Margareta's heart, until it is resolved at last by an exquisite *veloce* flourish over the keyboard."[10] The third and final movement is dazzling in pianistic language, bringing to life the intensity and terror of the witches' flight to the Brocken Mountain and Walpurgis Night, as well as the complex demonism of Mephistopheles. In its opening moments the movement demonstrates the stirring dynamism and rhythmic drive that exemplify Rachmaninoff at his best. However, these very strengths are achieved at the expense of any discernible melodies, and thus Rachmaninoff's sonata may have ushered in a practice for the composer of combining precisely these qualities (absence of clear melody, yet strong dynamism and rhythmic drive) in the last movements of some of his succeeding works. Examples include his Third Concerto, Second Sonata, Fourth Concerto, and Third Symphony.[11] All things considered, Rachmaninoff's first piano sonata is a musically impressive composition and one that contains his thematic handwriting: In its focus on the religious struggle in the soul of humankind, the temptation of evil that can be resisted (expressed in the *Dies irae* phrase occurring at key moments), the expansion to the fullest of the resources of the piano (and pianist), and ultimate affirmation of faith in God this major piece expresses some of the composer's most cherished artistic ideas. Even without the program from Faust, the sonata can be enjoyed exclusively for its sonic and technical richness.

Rachmaninoff's opera *Monna Vanna* remained dear to him and a personal favorite for his entire life. The reasons for this attachment remain unclear, since he never completed it and stopped composing in the opera genre after ceasing work on this project. Originally a play by Maurice Maeterlinck (1862–1949), *Monna Vanna* had been successfully staged in Moscow during the years 1902–1904, with the distinguished actress and theater manager Vera Komissarzhevskaia in the title role. Rachmaninoff very likely attended one of the performances, since he had a lifelong attachment to Russian theater and at this point in his creative work was exploring the dramatic possibilities of various plays for adaptation to opera. He finished work on the vocal score of Act 1, but subsequently had trouble securing the copyright for the whole; this led to his suspending composing work on the opera. He took the unfinished score with him when the Rachmaninoffs felt compelled to leave Russia in 1917. It was only in 1984 that a world première took place in New York with Tatiana Troyanos, Sherrill Milnes, and John Alexander performing with the Philadelphia Orchestra.[12]

Maeterlinck's play and Rachmaninoff's projected opera have a satisfying happy ending, in narrative and moral terms. Heroism and sacrifice triumph over jealousy and treachery. What remains intriguing about this opera is Rachmaninoff's attitude toward it, since he kept it with him all his life. The plot of the play concerns illicit, though noble love. The heroine is strong and decisive, yet tender. Was this opera associated with a particular woman or ideal of a woman for Rachmaninoff? The question suggests itself—for it could provide a plausible reason for why the unfinished opera remained so special to Rachmaninoff.

Rachmaninoff's love of the theater and acquaintance with well-known theater actors/managers expressed itself in the only composition he was to realize in 1908, "Letter to K.S. Stanislavsky." It was composed on the occasion of the tenth anniversary of the Moscow Art Theatre in October of that year. The musical letter was in the form of a joyous greeting from afar, since Rachmaninoff was already in Dresden and could not attend the celebration. What makes this small composition stand out in Rachmaninoff's corpus is that he wrote both the music and libretto himself. It was written for voice and piano, and brought to life by Feodor Chaliapin who performed it in person for Stanislavsky at the event. Two items in the libretto are noteworthy: Rachmaninoff's reference to Maeterlinck's play "The Blue Bird," which Stanislavsky had successfully staged the previous month; and the wish for *mnogaia leta* for Stanislavsky—a prayerful wish exclaimed many times during the Russian Orthodox liturgical year: "God grant you many years." Rachmaninoff was sending Stanislavsky his heartfelt wishes, and at the same time reminding the Moscow music and theater community in a witty way of his existence.

Early in 1910, subsequent to his return to Russia from his American tour, Rachmaninoff provided an interview to the American music magazine *The Etude*, which was titled "Ten Important Attributes of Beautiful Pianoforte Playing," and described as "Especially secured for *The Etude* from an interview with S.V. Rachmaninoff, Supervisor General of the Imperial Conservatories of Russia." The article, published in English in March 1910, does not specify an interpreter or translator—but at this time in his life Rachmaninoff could not have provided such detailed comments in English himself, for his command of the language was minimal at best. It does, however, reveal what he as the supervisor of the Russian Tsar's government conservatories considered of primary importance pedagogically and musically in general. He stressed that, in approaching a new piece of music, students should acquire a deep understanding of its conception, its movements as a whole. He also underscored the helpfulness of genuine talent in those planning a career in music:

> Talent! Ah, that is the great thing in all musical work. If he [the student] has talent, he will see with the eyes of talent—that wonderful force which penetrates all artistic mysteries and reveals the truths as nothing else possibly can. Then he grasps, as if by intuition, the composer's intentions in writing the work, and, like the true interpreter, communicates these thoughts to his audience in their proper form.[13]

He underscored technical proficiency as essential but reminded readers that technique should not become mechanical and could not replace genuine musicality in interpreting a given work for performance.

Consistent with Rachmaninoff's understanding that a pianist must "deliver" the musical piece for a viewing audience, that a musician needed to develop a striking individuality that would be integral to and considerably enhance the performance of a composition, are his following thoughts:

> Of course, a successful performer must have a strong individuality, and all of his interpretations must bear the mark of this individuality, but at the same time he should seek variety constantly. A Chopin Ballade must have quite a different interpretation from a Scarlatti Capriccio. There is really very little in common between a Beethoven Sonata and a Liszt Rhapsody. . . . Each piece must stand apart as possessing an individual conception, and if the player fails to convey this impression to his audience, he is little better than some mechanical instrument. Josef Hofmann has the ability of investing each composition with an individual and characteristic charm that has always been very delightful to me.[14]

Rachmaninoff also alluded to his belief in a "culminating point" in the performance of each piece of music in the following words:

> The student must see, first of all, the main points of musical relationship in a composition. He must understand what it is that gives the work unity, cohesion, force, or grace. . . . In all good pianoforte playing there is a vital spark that seems to make each interpretation of a masterpiece—a living thing. It exists only for the moment, and cannot be explained. For instance, two pianists of equal technical ability may play the same composition. With one the playing is dull, lifeless and sapless, with the other there is something that is indescribably wonderful. His playing seems fairly to quiver with life. It commands interest and inspires the audience. What is this vital spark that brings life to mere notes? In one way it may be called the intense artistic interest of the player. It is that astonishing thing known as inspiration.[15]

Overall, Rachmaninoff maintained, the pianist must have inside himself a firm commitment to an artistic mission, to the creative process, and to rejecting anything but the highest standards in all forms of musical activity. Clearly these comments offer insights into Rachmaninoff's own cherished views on the vocation, even calling, of a musician composing and performing for the public.

Rachmaninoff's experiences abroad enabled him to appreciate the importance of European culture, both on its own merits and for its influence on the development of modern Russian culture. Whether in Europe or Russia, he kept abreast of intellectual currents especially in his native country. He read widely in Russian musical journals, the Russian press, Russian philosophy, and poetry in several languages. His patriotism involved a love for all things Russian; it never became nationalistic, but instead was expressed through the sum total of a well-traveled composer's carefully considered sensibilities and cultural experiences. Irina Brandt recollects about Ivanovka:

> Sergei Vasilievich [Rachmaninoff] wrote many letters, for all intents and purposes, every day. I was always struck by the fact, that not a single missive to him went unanswered. He always sorted the mail himself that was brought from the station after dinner. . . . The amount of mail he received was just enormous. For a long time he would sit in the gazebo, reading letters and looking through newspapers.[16]

He would receive many offers to perform in concerts, to record his compositions, and many letters from abroad. He also received letters from admirers and young composers who sent him their compositions and sought his advice about them.

Rachmaninoff admired early nineteenth-century Russian poets, setting many of his art songs to their poems. Thus his creative thinking was profoundly poetic. What did Rachmaninoff's admiration for poetry signify? Embedded in poetry are the complexity of philosophical speculation, the musicality of words arranged in rhythmic and melodic patterns, and the multifariousness of human emotions—features intrinsic to his creative works. Poetry remained a fundamental component of his artistic identity and a means for expressing his most sacred thoughts; poetry was second only to his main area of endeavor, music. Symbolist poet and religious philosopher Vladimir Soloviev elaborates the relationship of poetry to religion and philosophy in words that evoke Rachmaninoff's commitment to aesthetic expressiveness: "Perfect art in its definitive mission should embody the absolute ideal not only in imagination, but also in actual fact—should animate and transubstantiate our real life."[17] Rachmaninoff's own words from the interview in *The Etude*, that "In all good pianoforte playing there is a vital spark that seems to make each interpretation of a masterpiece—a living thing." This seems another way of understanding what Solovyov describes as the "definitive mission" of "perfect art"—to "animate and transubstantiate our real life."

In addition to his abiding connection with poetry, Rachmaninoff retained a serious interest in Russian religious philosophy throughout his life; while living in New York he regretted not being able to attend a series of lectures by Russian philosopher Georgy Petrovich Fedotov at the New York Public Library because he was away on a concert tour. (He was present only at a discussion of one of Fedotov's lectures.) This openness of his creative mind influenced the genres he selected for composition. It was both the mysterious, otherworldly origins of poetry, perhaps through the Greek Muses, and the understanding of the creative act as intellectually and culturally determined that characterized Rachmaninoff's view of art. In the words of philosopher Nikolai Berdyaev, whose ideas Rachmaninoff may have discussed among his colleagues and friends in the European emigration between the two world wars: "Creativity is a spiritual action, in which man forgets about himself, foregoes himself in the creative act, is absorbed by his subject. In creativity man tests out the extraordinary ascent of all his being."[18] For Rachmaninoff the creative act was a necessary expression of the self, and an overcoming of the temporal self in favor of the eternal self. The creative process of seeking a "divine idea . . . unconditional fullness of being" and "realizing this idea" meant for Rachmaninoff a lifelong search for perfection of artistic expression, both for the self-knowledge this process would bring and to communicate his most cherished musical ideas to others. The intensely personal nature of his music, along with the evidence that the dedicatees of major works were women enormously important to him, adds an unmistakable romantic content to Rachmaninoff's search for beauty and longing for the feminine ideal as embodied in a particular woman.

Four categories of Rachmaninoff's creative identity can help us to understand the richness of his aesthetic universe.[19] In these categories one finds the essence of Rachmaninoff's compositional process: (1) *Thematic: Love and Orthodox Kenosis*, (2) *Formal: Beauty in the Classical Sense*, (3) *Conceptual: Integral Approach to Art*, and (4) *Authorial: Meta-Position of Control*. Rachmaninoff's creative ethos evolved out of his love for the essential features of Russian culture, a lasting attachment to the Russian countryside, and a deep-seated loyalty to Russia as his homeland. These attitudes emerge to a greater or lesser degree in the various genres in which he crafted his music: his solo piano music, art songs, operas, symphonies, symphonic poems, vocal-symphonic music, chamber music, concertos, music for piano ensemble, and transcriptions of music by other composers.

Rachmaninoff held in his mind an aesthetic ideal, the impossibly high standard of unattainable perfection—and, of course, he could never reach it. In this light his self-criticism is often mistakenly thought to signify his lack of confidence and insecurity—but considering the evidence of Rachmaninoff's towering authority among his peers and his humbly proud awareness of his own musical accomplishments that emerges from his letters, this would be an incorrect explanation. In reality, his self-criticism was measured against the ideal of perfection. How did this tension between the ideal of perfection and reality of less-than-perfection translate itself in the course of Rachmaninoff's musical activities? The answer makes complete sense: Rachmaninoff's standards for himself were so exacting that he could concentrate on *only one aspect* of his tripartite musical identity (composing, conducting, piano performance) at a time. When he was not working, he would become restless; in Switzerland Rachmaninoff offered some reflections about Leo Tolstoy and creativity that he also applied to himself:

> Take Tolstoy: if he had a stomach pain, he talked about it all day long. But the trouble was not in the stomach at all; it was in the fact that he could not work that day. This is what made him suffer. There is not enough understanding of what a creative artist needs. This is why Tolstoy was so miserable. Yes, this is tragic." And in a low voice he added: "We are all like this."[20]

It is worth recalling that even during Sergei's honeymoon with Natalia, his music work was never far away: in Lucerne, Switzerland, they rented a piano for his composing needs, and in Bayreuth, Germany, they attended a number of important operas.

Poetry remained the means for conveying Rachmaninoff's feelings for his family and other persons of major importance to him, his religious tradition, and his belief in the future of Russia. He made several statements linking poetry with music. In an interview in English published in 1927 in *The Musical Observer* he notes, "Of all the arts I love poetry the best after music. Our Pushkin I find admirable. Shakespeare and Byron I read constantly in the Russian. I always have books of poetry around me. Poetry inspires music . . . They are like twin sisters."[21] Though culturally refined, these words sound stilted, in large part because for Rachmaninoff English was his fourth language and he did not feel comfortable expressing himself in it. In the same important interview he noted, "Love inspires as nothing else does . . . Everything of beauty helps . . . Real inspiration must come from within . . . nothing from outside can help if the divine spark of creative faculty is lacking within the artist."[22]

Rachmaninoff set eighty-four nineteenth- and early-twentieth-century Russian poems to music in his art songs in seven separate opus numbers between the years 1890 and 1916. His choice of poems for these songs was dictated by his personal experiences. For this reason, each of Rachmaninoff's songs provides a glimpse into his inner world at a particular moment of his life and yields important information about his affinities and beliefs. Each song contains a vast world of emotions and actions in miniature, creating a narrative that tells a story. Here as elsewhere, the music is linear, pulling listeners along by the notes the way in which a story or novel pulls readers along by the words. Rachmaninoff's embeddedness in his native culture connects his music especially with the ideas of the Slavophiles. One fine example of a poetry / music collaboration of his is with the Slavophile poet Aleksei Stepanovich Khomiakov (1804–1860). Considered Russia's first lay theologian, Khomiakov wrote masterful poems steeped in Russian Orthodoxy that especially appealed to Rachmaninoff. Robert Bird noted about Khomiakov that he "found in traditional Russian culture a sense of community . . . buttressed not by a sense of common profit or security, but by love."[23] Rachmaninoff believed in these values as well. The fact that he selected two of Khomiakov's poems to set to music indicates the thematic and emotional connections he felt with the poet-theologian's work. An examination of the two songs Rachmaninoff set to these poems provides insights into his aesthetics and compositional process.

In the first art song "To My Children" of 1906 (from Khomiakov's poem by the same name), Rachmaninoff offers music that is tender and reverential: the song treats the theme of a father mourning the deaths of his children. Its drama unfolds by contrast: the first stanza underscores that in the past the father would visit his children's bedroom in order to look upon them in great tenderness, give them his blessing with the sign of the cross, and pray for their peace and well-being. The oil lamp whose light has died out serves as a powerful metaphor for the children whose "light" has also died out. Khomiakov asks his children, now in heaven, to pray for the one who has prayed for them: the communities of souls, both living and dead, are engaged in ceaseless prayer for each other. Thus the cycle of prayer is complete; for Rachmaninoff, the choice of this poem was made for two reasons: it depicts a heartbreakingly sad moment that lends itself well to a musical framework, and it reflects Rachmaninoff's Orthodox beliefs. The song was indicated for "middle voice"; it was dedicated to Maria and Arkady Kerzin.

The second art song that uses one of Khomiakov's poems is "The Raising of Lazarus" (1912). Rachmaninoff emphasizes the dignity of the epiphanic moment of the raising by several means: the song is written for the lowest voice range, either bass or contralto (evoking the mystery and solemnity associated with the low end of the musical register); its tempo is one of the slowest—*grave*; and its brief, three-stanza construction presents its content in a concise form. Artistically the power of the episode increases when the reader is allowed the fullest range of his or her imagination. The song was dedicated to Rachmaninoff's musical collaborator and lifelong friend Chaliapin, who performed it in concert to Rachmaninoff's piano accompaniment. The song moves quickly from the high tragedy of Lazarus's death to the radiant light of his raising. It concludes with the praise of God; its drama underscores the Orthodox belief in a literal and complete resurrection of the physical body, as well as the soul.

The four categories of Rachmaninoff's aesthetics can be viewed in the light of the existing connections among the features of his life, the poetry that attracted him, and his compositional process:

THEMATIC: LOVE AND ORTHODOX KENOSIS

Rachmaninoff was nurtured in the Orthodox soil of spirituality that embraces the concept and practice of kenotic love, in which active love is offered as a willing sacrifice but also brings a profound fulfillment to the giver. Kenotic love leavens the personality and is understood both as an ascetic and a joyous act. George Ellis points out, "The master exemplar [of kenotic love] is the life of Christ, kenotic in its character from the temptations in the wilderness to his sacrificial death on the cross."[24]

The search for the aesthetic ideal in his creative works was bound up for Rachmaninoff with the search for spiritual betterment. N. V. Beketova explains, "The quality of confession in Rachmaninoff's poetics simultaneously belongs to the cultures of Romanticism and Orthodoxy. In these cultures confession is the 'text of a life,' the self-reckoning of the inner person, a breakthrough to eternal truth by the overcoming of the barriers of chronological and eternal time, being and consciousness . . ."[25] Rachmaninoff's aesthetic search was also inextricably bound up with the search for the "other," conceived as both the beloved human ideal and as the cherished native culture. This creative search remains a profoundly human process, a quest for harmony and perfect love. When one examines the body of work that Rachmaninoff created over the course of his life, one encounters, along with the evolution of personal style, a consistently developed and well-integrated artistic vision, a clear statement embracing the persons he loved, whose shining images he transformed and ennobled in his art, as well as the country he held sacred—Russia as idea, as traveling icon and as homeland.

FORMAL: BEAUTY IN THE CLASSICAL SENSE

The creative works of Rachmaninoff must be understood in the context of the sensibilities and content of Russian Orthodoxy, which in its thousand-year tradition has displayed similarities to the Platonic concept of beauty (grounded in principles of harmony, symmetry, and proportion) and has been nurtured by Greek patristics. These wellsprings of the aesthetic thought of Antiquity and Christian ascetic spirituality remain prominent in the Orthodox Church, and this fact can help us to better understand the essence of Rachmaninoff's worldview. The composer underscored in an essay titled "How Russian Students Study" that music should be founded on ancient principles of beauty in art: "Let us have the kind of new music that only the greatest genius of the world can create; let it be rich and original; but first and foremost, let it be based on ancient principles of genuine beauty, and not on what is false to art."[26] Rachmaninoff's affinity for Platonic aesthetics and Russian Orthodox sensibilities combine in his music to manifest a search for beauty, a longing for harmony and fulfillment, and the striving to realize a spiritual ideal of beauty. In addition, he was raised in a culture inherited from Greece and Byzantium that highly valued philosophical reflection and the belief in the power of the word (both in poetry and prose).

Rachmaninoff's creative life was animated by an aesthetic ideal that integrated the ideal/spiritual, the physical, and the intellectual: many accounts of his demeanor portray him as an individual who lived in the material world, but also inhabited an intense and vital world of his own that remained protected from the world around him. Abram Chasins writes, "Rachmaninoff's forbidding manner and gaunt face with the stern sorrows of the ages engraved upon it created the impression of a creature not of our time or kind, but rather one from some historical era of past glories which he alone seemed to remember."[27] His introverted, introspective mien most likely stemmed from the constant scrutiny to which he subjected his compositions, as well as from his discomfort in cultures so unlike the Russian ways that had formed his identity.

Rachmaninoff appreciated the legacy of the ancient world, being influenced by the West's cultural achievements; he recognized, however, that the West needed to integrate into its own identity the artistic and spiritual riches of Russia as a legitimate successor to the culture of Antiquity. The West inherited from classical Greece its philosophy, architecture, and pagan culture, while the Russian East received from Greece (through Byzantium) some primary elements of Orthodox Christianity, such as the Liturgy of St. John Chrysostom (an early Church Father who in 398 C.E. became Archbishop of Constantinople). Rachmaninoff's was the worldview of an enlightened Slavophile, one who appreciated the contributions that European civilization had made to world culture, but who understood as well that the time had arrived for Russia to also make its rich donation to that same cultural repository.

CONCEPTUAL: INTEGRAL APPROACH TO ART

The content of Rachmaninoff's life with all his convictions and emotions can be viewed as a well-integrated whole; his ethics and musical integrity bring to mind Vladimir Soloviev's religious philosophy of integral knowledge (*tselnoe znanie*). This philosophy, which engages the highest and most honorable aspects of an individual's identity, captures Rachmaninoff's approach to composing: creative work contains the sum total of the composer's identity. Rachmaninoff's creative activity synthesized his ethical principles, religious views, relationships with persons important to him, and musical erudition. For him not only did the ideas for his compositions appear in their totality, as was the case with his *Isle of the Dead* of 1909 (". . . they come: all voices at once. Not a bit here, a bit there. All. The whole grows"[28]), but his artistic conception of them was unified, with a sense of the whole that he never lost in the performance of a piece. Rachmaninoff made the same assertion that the first theme of his Piano Concerto No. 3 "simply 'wrote itself'" when replying to a request from musicologist Joseph Yasser about whether that theme was influenced in its melodic and structural elements, even subconsciously, by the Kievan-Pechersk Russian Orthodox chant performed at Vespers services, "Thy grave, O Savior, guarded by warriors" (which Rachmaninoff possibly heard when he was in Kiev in 1893). He mentioned in his reply to Yasser's letter that he "wanted to 'sing' the melody on the piano, as a singer would sing it and to find a suitable orchestral accompaniment, or rather one that would not muffle this singing."[29]

Concerning one of his performances of Chopin, Berlin critics wrote, "Only a great personality, a poet, can take a Nocturne in this slow tempo and produce breathless tension that never lags . . . rhythm, tempo, color, and form are forged together into a unity, and with what direct comprehension!"[30]

Robert Threlfall, an authority on Rachmaninoff's and Frederick Delius's music, saw Rachmaninoff perform *fourteen* times in London. In the early twentieth century Threlfall had the golden opportunity to witness in performance many of the luminaries of the piano world: in addition to the concerts of Rachmaninoff, he saw in concert Paderewski, Gieseking, Hofmann (twice), Horowitz, and Argerich (in the 1990s). Threlfall as an appreciative eyewitness maintained that Rachmaninoff had an unfair advantage over other pianists in that he had such a distinctive identity as a composer as well. He stated, "Rachmaninoff had a level of interpreting, understanding the music that just wasn't there, perhaps just wasn't possible for other pianists. His performances were unfailingly flawless; he *created* the works."[31] Threlfall saw Rachmaninoff in concert enough times to form an overall impression of what was consistent about his stage and performance manner. He described that Rachmaninoff would come onto the stage, walk over to the piano, bow to various parts of the auditorium, sit down, and start playing. He walked onto the stage with his left hand held close to his chest. While he was playing he kept his eyes on the keyboard. At the end of the concert he would hold both arms at his sides in a relaxed, "normal" way. And he always smiled at the end of his concerts, thereby dispelling the notion that he was gloomy and impassive as a performer.[32]

Rachmaninoff practiced an integral philosophy of the creative process, stating:

> Composing is as essential a part of my being as breathing or eating; . . . Music should, in the final analysis, be the expression of a composer's complex personality. A composer's music should express the country of his birth, his love affairs, his religion, the books which have influenced him, the pictures he loves. It should be the product of the sum total of a composer's experiences. Study the masterpieces of every great composer, and you will find every aspect of the composer's personality and background in his music. Time may change the technique of music, but it can never alter its mission . . .
> What I try to do, when writing down my music, is to make it say simply and directly *that which is in my heart when I am composing*. If there is love there, or bitterness, or sadness, or religion, these moods become a part of my music, and it becomes either beautiful or bitter or sad or religious.[33] [emphasis added]

AUTHORIAL—AUTHORIAL STANCE: META-POSITION OF CONTROL

Rachmaninoff's music has been referred to by Russian musicologists as an "ocean of passion," but scholars generally acknowledge the composer's Second Concerto as the turning point in his aesthetics. Grigory Ganzburg writes,

"What was new was that, in remaining an ocean of passion, [Rachmaninoff's music] concomitantly became the [drops of water] placed under the lens of a microscope."[34] After 1901, the year he completed the Second Concerto, Rachmaninoff attained a greater degree of intellectual control in the creation and performance of his works. Curiously, because of his transcendent pianism and careful crafting of his musical performances, sometimes Rachmaninoff was criticized for a seeming dispassionate style of performance. What the critics were noticing was actually this meta-authorial position of control: Rachmaninoff as performer remained in full control of each piece he was playing, weighing the import and color of each note and phrase, measuring as a linen-measurer the progression of the music left until the conclusion of the piece. His works and performance of them no longer manifested exclusively a Wordsworthian "spontaneous overflow of powerful feelings," as had been the case before 1901, but rather were characterized by "emotion recollected in tranquility," a stronger position of authorial control. Rachmaninoff maintained this level of control so that emotion and aesthetics could be brought more firmly into the service of beauty.

Feodor Chaliapin articulated the same meta-authorial position in his own approach to performance art, and this is not surprising since he and Rachmaninoff spent long periods of time together in which they would have discussed and evolved their theories of art. He describes his meta-position as the very difficult task of "splitting identity" (*razdvoenie*) on the stage:

> When I am singing, the embodied image in front of me is always being examined. It is before my eyes every second. I sing and listen, act, and observe. I am never on stage alone. On the stage are two Chaliapins. One performs the role, while the other controls it. "You cry too many tears, brother," says the corrector to the actor. "Remember that it is not you crying, but the character crying."
>
> Not for a moment do I part from my [dual] consciousness on the stage. Not for a second do I lose the capability and habit of controlling the harmony of the action.[35]

In the aforementioned four categories, we can discern the abiding features of Rachmaninoff's aesthetics, which are informed by various rich periods of world culture, both ancient and modern. But Rachmaninoff also evolved his musical style and developed his own voice in connection with the changing influences and national surroundings he experienced. Even in Russia in the early years of the twentieth century, when Rachmaninoff's pianism and compositions dominated Moscow, he continued to experiment musically. His Études-Tableaux of 1911 (Op. 33) and 1917 (Op. 39) represented sophisticated emotionally controlled compositions for their day.[36] His Second Sonata for Piano of 1913 (Op. 36) in its dense textures and intensity continued to expand the pianistic vocabulary beyond Lisztian techniques. And the song cycle of 1916 (Op. 38) that was the product of his rewarding collaboration with the poet Marietta Shaginian (1888–1982) has a distinctly Modernist feel. Two of the six songs of Opus 38, "Daisies" and "Rat-catcher," are drawn from Symbolist poets and provide evidence of Rachmaninoff's expanding appreciation of poetic and musical styles.

Rachmaninoff's Second Sonata for piano in B flat minor presents powerful evidence of his growth as a composer, one who also understood perfectly how to write for the piano. In December 1912 the Rachmaninoff family left Russia to spend some time in Europe for relaxation and solitude for composing: their itinerary included Berlin; points near Lake Lucerne, Switzerland; and Rome. In the latter city he was able to work intensively on the sonata, with the intent of returning to Russia for Pascha. Unexpectedly, while on the working vacation in Rome, Rachmaninoff's daughters became ill with typhoid fever and they left Italy to seek medical treatment for the girls in Berlin, after which they returned to Ivanovka. With the crisis of his daughters' illness, Rachmaninoff worked on the sonata in fits and starts between January and August 1913, completing it on September 13 of the same year at Ivanovka. The result was one of his most tightly integrated works musically and one distinguished by its intellectual, rather than emotional character. The sonata was dedicated to his fellow "bear cub" at Zverev's Matvei Pressman. Martyn writes:

> The Second Piano Sonata not only takes its general tone and dramatic plan from the Third Concerto but shares with it a number of structural features, including: three musically interrelated movements; a contrasting pair of themes in the outer movements and a single idea freely treated in the middle; a quiet close to the opening movement and a precipitate launch into the last, where a rhythmic first theme is contrasted with a Rachmaninoff "big tune" . . . , this is decked out in all its finery for its final appearance.[37]

Rachmaninoff premièred the Second Sonata in December 3, 1913, in Moscow. One reviewer of the performance, Boris Tiuneev, noted: "The sonata . . . is the composition of a mature and great talent . . . but you will find Rachmaninoff the lyricist in it in only a very small degree—rather the reverse: there is a certain inner reserve, severity and introspection. The composer speaks more of the intellect out of the intellect than of the heart out of the heart."[38]

Concerning Rachmaninoff's working method with a conductor and orchestra interpreting a freshly minted composition of his, he would evolve the composition in three phases. The first involved the actual creation of the given musical work, the writing down of his creative vision in a master score of all the necessary parts. The second was the testing of the work, when possible, in a limited context—in rehearsals or performances of the work to a smaller audience. Upon hearing such performances, Rachmaninoff would make additional corrections and changes to his composition. V. I. Antipov elaborated Rachmaninoff's creative method as follows: Rachmaninoff wanted to share what he had composed with others, and worked intensely, sometimes in a rush, to finish the given composition so that he could send it to his publisher Gutheil when it was ready. Antipov separated Rachmaninoff's method into three phases consistent with the aforementioned: (1) intensive—he wrote down the music that was stirring within him; (2) suggestive—played it on the piano, considered its effect, viewing it as an artist and performer; and (3) conclusive—he made corrections for the publisher.[39]

An interview in 1968 of the great conductor Leopold Stokowski, who had conducted Rachmaninoff's Piano Concerto No. 2 with the Philadelphia Orchestra in the 1920s, further elaborates the working method of Rachmaninoff with some personal details:

> When Rachmaninoff had finished a composition for orchestra, he did me the great honor of sending it to me. I would study it, and when I knew it thoroughly I would rehearse it with the orchestra. But then, as in the case of his four piano concertos or in the Variations on a Theme of Paganini, he would come to Philadelphia and we would rehearse the music. Then it always happened that he would be dissatisfied with the orchestration, and then he would begin to say why does not this sound clear, why is this too prominent or not prominent enough? And we would talk it over and we would make changes, but the trouble was that his music had already been printed. I mean the scores and the orchestral parts were already printed in New York. So, unfortunately, the persons who play that music today, they do not know the changes which he made at that time. Rachmaninoff was an extremely simple man, very melancholy. I used to meet him in Paris and we used to go into a certain cellar, deep underhouse [sic] where one was really in Russia, because everything was Russian down there and we used to drink certain kinds of drink from Russia, not vodka, but other simpler drinks [perhaps *kvass*, a fermented drink similar to mead] . . . He longed to go back to his native land and renew all those joys that he had known as a child.[40]

In the second decade of the twentieth century, Rachmaninoff's musical creativity was in full flower. He was composing intensively in many genres and was able to perform his works in collaboration with some of the finest musical talents of his generation, including Feodor Chaliapin, Antonina Nezhdanova, and Nina Koshetz. His relationship with Chaliapin represented an enduring, lifelong professional and personal bond. Sergei's esteem of Antonina Nezhdanova was extremely high; her sweet coloratura soprano voice is immortalized in his famous art song "Vocalise" (1915), which has been transcribed for many instruments as well as for orchestra. The relationship he formed with soprano Nina Koshetz began as a professional one when they were touring in southern Russia, but evolved into an intense personal relationship that spanned the last years of his life in Russia and trickled into his first years in America. In 1916 he dedicated the six songs of Opus. 38 to her—song-settings of poetry suggested and provided to him by Marietta Shaginian. The dedication of Opus 38 to Koshetz was deeply disappointing to Shaginian, since she had worked closely with Rachmaninoff to identify the six poems and develop the song-settings for them. Shaginian was very attached to Rachmaninoff emotionally—for her, it was an undeveloped love. In 1912 he had dedicated to her the song "The Muse" (Op. 34, No. 1), while she dedicated her first book of poetry *Orientalia* (1913) to him. They lost touch with each other after the Rachmaninoffs left Russia.

In addition to dedicating the Opus 38 songs to Nina Koshetz, instead of to Shaginian, who was far more deserving of that honor, Rachmaninoff gave Koshetz the sketches of two unpublished sacred songs that belonged to this same 1916–1917 period of the Opus 38 songs. The two songs are titled "Prayer" (*Molitva*) and "Glory to God" (All Things Wish to Sing [*Vse khochet pet*]). The religious nature of the songs surely indicated that the bond between Rachmaninoff and Koshetz, whatever had been its nature in 1916, would change to one of fondness and shared "higher" convictions.

Rachmaninoff's two cycles of Études-Tableaux, composed, respectively in 1911 and 1917, manifested the density, intellectual observation, and extraordinary tonal beauty for which Rachmaninoff became well-known. In their day, as distinguished pianist Sviatoslav Richter observed, these complex pieces represented the "cutting edge" of musical creativity in Russia:

> I did as I was told and played [Prokofiev's] Second Sonata in the second half of the programme, together with six Preludes by Rachmaninoff, a composer whom Prokofiev loathed, no doubt because he had been influenced by him. (It's enough to look at the cutting-edge Études-tableaux to see that Prokofiev's style stemmed, to a large extent, from Rachmaninov's. It was these works that he hated most of all.)[41]

Rachmaninoff composed the Études-Tableaux not only to expand the resources of pianistic language, continuing to build from the broadening of that language by Franz Liszt, but also to give an organized and dignified expression to images—tableaux—encapsulating his various emotions. The composer affirmed that, just as his words gave expression to his thoughts, his music recorded the contours of his emotional life. Thus his music must be understood not as abstract experimentation for the sake of innovation alone, but as constitutive of emotional responses to his life's experiences—the quintessential credo of Late Romantic music.

Rachmaninoff would adhere to his views on the nature and purpose of music to the end of his life: he would stay in step with modern innovations in all areas, including music, but would integrate into each new composition only those elements of various musical currents that he determined would enrich his music and not result in its straying from its mission. He gave an interview for the *New York Times* early in 1932, in which he restated his opinion on modern music:

> The poet Heine once said, "What life takes away, music restores." He would not be moved to say this if he could hear the music of today. For the most part it gives nothing. Music should bring relief. It should rehabilitate minds and souls, and modern music does not do this. If we are to have great music we must return to the fundamentals which made music of the past great. Music cannot be just color and rhythm; it must reveal the emotions of the heart.[42]

The Études-Tableaux were composed during an apocryphal period for Russia: the country was increasingly becoming destabilized because of Marxist-Bolshevik challenges to tsarist rule, World War I was devastating her cultural and industrial infrastructures, and the Revolution of 1917 was uprooting the traditional way of life Russia had known for many centuries. Rachmaninoff's undefined relationship with Nina Koshetz also complicated his personal life in significant ways. The emotional tension arising from this complex moment in Rachmaninoff's life accounts for the dramatic restlessness and resistance to resolution—the dialogue between two voices seeking harmony, but not finding it—that characterize both sets of the Études-Tableaux. It seems clear from a letter that he wrote to Koshetz on July 5, 1919, after he had been in America for over six months, that he wanted to sever contacts with her; he ended the letter with the words, "Be well and happy, which I wish you with *all my heart.*"[43]

This period, although filled with anxiety and uncertainty about the future, was also poignant, for many aspects of Rachmaninoff's difficult early years had finally fallen away and been replaced by greater stability and fulfillment. His family life provided tremendous satisfaction and pleasure: he was now owner of Ivanovka, a relatively contented husband, and doting father of two spirited daughters. But the tragic cataclysms Russia would experience during the years of World War I, 1914–1918, and violent overthrowal by the Bolsheviks of the monarchy (culminating in the assassination of the royal family of Nicholas II) would destroy the life he had built and lead him to consider whether to leave his beloved homeland. Fires set by peasants whose emotions were whipped up by local Communist activists in Uvarovo Region and throughout the south of Russia, along with the gruesome persecution of Russian Orthodox priests as part of the campaign to eradicate Russia's foundational faith tradition, alarmed him and his relatives. One account that has become part of the collective memory of the inhabitants of the Cossack village Nezamaevskoe in Krasnodar Region involves the storming of a church during the celebration of the Midnight Office and Liturgy of Pascha (Orthodox Easter) on May 4, 1918. A group of Red Army soldiers broke into the Nezamaevskoe Church of the Prophet of God Ilya: they tortured and killed the parish priest Fr. Ioann Prigorovsky in front of the faithful celebrating the sacred holiday.[44]

This was a typical occurrence; similar violence against specific social classes was carried out all over Russia for several years, targeting, among others, priests, intellectuals, artists, and members of the nobility (which would include Rachmaninoff and his relatives). Artificially engineered famines were also well-known: Soviet tanks would surround a peasant village that resisted being dismantled and transported to a commune, take the inhabitants' food supplies, and wait until all the people had starved.[45] The atmosphere was extremely tense, and as Rachmaninoff saw the violence creeping ever closer to Tambov and Ivanovka, he knew that he had to arrange somehow to leave Russia, until (as he assumed at the time) the Bolsheviks had been defeated. The Rachmaninoffs' departure proved not to be temporary: as late as the 1930s at their villa Senar in Switzerland he would still long for Russia.

NOTES

1. F.I. Chaliapin, *Maska i dusha: Moi sorok let na teatrakh* (Moscow: Moskovskii rabochii, 1989), 174, trans. VZN.

2. See the detailed article about this friendship by Natal'ia Vostokova and Tat'iana Gamazkova, "S.V. Rakhmaninov. Brasovo, Leto 1911," *Muzeinyi listok, Prilozhenie k Rossiiskoi muzykal'noi gazete* (November 2003), 40: 4.

3. Sergei Bertensson and Jay Leyda, *Sergei Rachmaninoff: A Lifetime in Music* (New York: New York UP, 1956; repr., Bloomington, IN: Indiana UP, 2001), 144.

4. This musical connection has also been noticed by Patrick Piggott, *Rachmaninov: Orchestral Music*, BBC Music Guides (Seattle, WA: University of Washington Press, 1974), 30; and Barrie Martyn, *Rachmaninoff: Composer, Pianist, Conductor* (Burlington, VT: Ashgate, 1990), 181–83.

5. Paraphrase of Martyn, 181.

6. Ken Meltzer, "Program Notes: Sergei Rachmaninoff, Symphony No. 2 in E Minor, Opus 27," 2020, https://fwsymphony.org/program-notes/rachmaninoff-sergei-symphony-no-2-in-e-minor-opus-27.

7. Piggott, 32–33.

8. Paraphrase of Martyn, 188.

9. Ibid., 188.

10. Ibid., 191.

11. Ibid., paraphrase of 191.

12. David Salazar, "A Look at Sergei Rachmaninov's Long-Forgotten Operas," Opera Wire (blog), April 1, 2017, https://operawire.com/a-look-at-sergei-rachmaninoffs-long-forgotten-operas/.

13. S.V. Rachmaninoff, "Ten Important Attributes of Beautiful Pianoforte Playing," *The Etude* (March 1910).

14. Ibid.

15. Ibid.

16. Irina Aleksandrovna Brandt, "Pis'mo 2," in *Ivanovka: Vremena. Sobytiia. Sud'by*, comp. by A.I. Ermakov and A.V. Zhogov (Moscow: Publications of the Irina Arkhipova Foundation, 2003), 78, trans. VZN.

17. V.S. Soloviev, *The Heart of Reality: Essays on Beauty, Love, and Ethics*, ed. and trans. Vladimir Wozniuk (Notre Dame, IN: University of Notre Dame Press, 2003), 80–81.

18. Nikolai Berdyaev, "Salvation and Creativity," trans. Fr. Stephen Janos, *Put'* 2 (January 1926): 26–46.

19. A discussion of these four categories of Rachmaninoff's creative identity, in an earlier version, appeared in Valeria Z. Nollan, "Rachmaninoff's Music and Khomiakov's Poetry," *Aleksei Khomiakov: Poet, Philosopher, Theologian*, ed. Vladimir Tsurikov, Readings in Russian Religious Culture 2 (Jordanville, NY: Variable Press, 2004): 174–95.

20. Bertensson and Leyda, 288.

21. Basanta Koomar Roy, "Rachmaninoff is Reminiscent," *The Musical Observer* 26 (May 1927), 16, accessed at https://www.pianostreet.com/smf/index.php?topic=17183.0.

22. Ibid.

23. Robert Bird, "General Introduction," in Boris Jakim and Robert Bird, eds. and trans., *On Spiritual Unity: A Slavophile Reader* (Hudson, NY: Lindisfarne Books, 1998), 14.

24. George Ellis, "Introduction," in *The Work of Love: Creation as Kenosis*, ed. John Polkinghorne (Grand Rapids, MI: William B. Eerdmans, 2001), xii.

25. N.V. Beketova, "Sergei Rakhmaninov: lichnost' kak simvol kul'turnogo tsykla," in *Tvorchestvo S.V. Rakhmaninova v kontekste mirovoi muzykal'noi kul'tury*, ed. M.A. Klimkova (Tambov: Izd.-vo Tamb. gos. tekh. un-ta, 2003), 10, trans. VZN.

26. S. Rakhmaninov, untitled and undated essay, in *S. Rakhmaninov: Literaturnoe nasledie*, ed. Z.A. Apetian (Moscow: Sovetskii kompozitor, 1978), 1: 91, trans. VZN.

27. Abram Chasins, Liner notes from *Rachmaninoff: The Four Piano Concertos*, RCA Red Seal LM-6123, no date.

28. Interview of Rachmaninoff concerning *The Isle of the Dead*, quoted in Bertensson and Leyda, 156. Complete information for the interview not given.

29. The case that Yasser makes for a subconscious influence of the Kievan-Pechersk chant influence on Rachmaninoff's Piano Concerto No. 3 in D minor is more than plausible. See Joseph Yasser, "The Opening Theme of Rachmaninoff's Third Piano Concerto and Its Liturgical Prototype," *The Musical Quarterly*, vol. LV, no. 3 (July 1969), 325. A representation of this ancient hymn can be heard as "The Soldiers

guarding Thy Tomb, O Saviour," Bulgarian chant, Kathisma hymn on Holy Saturday in a service in Jerusalem, May 1, 2021, https://www.bing.com/videos/search?q=Thy+grave+o+Savior+guarded+by+warriers+Orthodox&docid=608041599729948818&mid=D1377D3AC95E95E9C235D1377D3AC95E95E9C235&view=detail&FORM=VIRE. See also Note 25 of Chapter 9 of the present biography.

30. Review of Rachmaninoff's recital on November 9, 1928, *8 Uhr Abendblatt*, November 10, 1928, quoted in Bertensson and Leyda, 255, critic not credited.

31. Personal interview with Robert Threlfall, London, June 24, 2005. Emphasis Threlfall's. Threlfall also observed that Gieseking at his best was "glorious."

32. Ibid.

33. Bertensson and Leyda, 368–69.

34. G.I. Ganzburg, "Rakhmaninovskii krizis 1897–1901 godov: sushchnost' i posledstviia," *Tvorchestvo S.V. Rakhmaninova v kontekste mirovoi muzykal'noi kul'tury*, ed. M. A. Klimkova (Tambov: Izd.-vo Tamb. gos. tekh. un-ta, 2003), 15.

35. Chaliapin, 130, trans. VZN.

36. B. S. Nikitin personally viewed the dedicatory note of Rachmaninoff of the Études-Tableaux of Opus 39 (1917) to Nina Koshetz. The dedication was shown to Nikitin by Koshetz's daughter Marina Koshetz, who was an operatic soprano (date of Nikitin's interview of Marina Koshetz unknown). In catalogues of works of Sergei Rachmaninoff there is no dedication listed for Opus 39. It is likely that Rachmaninoff's wife Natalia requested that he remove the dedication to Koshetz of this opus number. Personal interview of B. S. Nikitin, Moscow, June 13, 2004.

37. Martyn, 248.

38. Boris Tiuneev, *Russkaia muzykal'naia gazeta* 48 (1913): 1104, quoted in Martyn, 249.

39. Personal interview with V. I. Antipov, Moscow, June 27, 2005.

40. Steve Cohen, "The Stokowski Story: Rachmaninoff," audio interview, WHYY-FM, Philadelphia, 1968, https://www.stokowski.org/sitebuilderfiles/stokowski_story_1968_rachmaninoff.mp3, accessed December 29, 2020.

41. Bruno Monsaingeon, *Sviatoslav Richter: Notebooks and Conversations*, trans. Stewart Spencer (Princeton, NJ: Princeton University Press, 2001), 43. V. I. Antipov theorized that Prokofiev also hated Rachmaninoff because of their differing social classes: Rachmaninoff was of the nobility, while Prokofiev himself came from a more modest social background. Personal interview, July 20, 2007.

42. Sergei Rachmaninoff, "Rachmaninoff Assails 'Heartless' Moderns; Music of Present Must Return to Fundamentals, He Says—'Color and Rhythm' Not Enough," *New York Times*, February 25, 1932.

43. Sergei Rachmaninoff, letter to Nina Koshetz, July 5, 1919, Section B1: Correspondence of Sergei Rachmaninoff, "A," Music Division, Library of Congress, trans. VZN, underlining original. Note: the original Russian uses the phrase "with all my soul" ("soul" is used in Russian in expressions in which Americans would use "heart").

44. Alina Iosifovna Beschetnova, *Sviatoi Ioann Prigorovskii* (Pavlovskaia: Poligrafika, 2018), paraphrase of 68–99.

45. Ibid.

Chapter 9

Rachmaninoff's Religiosity
(1873–1943)

Rachmaninoff did not attend church regularly, but he tried to be present as often as his schedule and circumstances permitted. His Russian Orthodox piety was well-known among his close friends in the Russian international community; he kept his religious faith to himself as much as possible. Among the many ways in which he expressed his religious convictions was the composition of sacred choral works in the Orthodox liturgical tradition, which evolved from ancient Greek and Byzantine Christian spiritual practices. This tradition draws from a religious-philosophical and intellectual body of writings; as a well-educated man, Rachmaninoff had knowledge of these foundations of Eastern Christianity. His intimate knowledge of the Russian Orthodox Church, its theology and *praxis*, and its various chants enabled him to write some of the most inspired sacred works in the Orthodox Christian tradition. To compose these unaccompanied choral masterpieces, Rachmaninoff researched the history of Russian Orthodox chant, for the purpose of ensuring that what he created would recognizably stay within this thousand-year tradition. The resultant sacred choral music he produced would represent one of his singularly spectacular achievements in the discipline of music. Those unfamiliar with the Orthodox Christian aesthetic tradition may assume that composers of Orthodox sacred music wish to express their own musical ideas in extending the traditional chants into new and uncharted directions. Rachmaninoff had a "subjective, personal approach . . . artistically it resulted in works which were remarkably innovative and fresh, wherein the eloquent poetry and profound message of the original hymnography found a forceful and, one might add, not inappropriate, musical expression."[1] While the composition of music in Orthodox Christianity offers many opportunities for individual creativity, it is in the Orthodox tradition *not* to go beyond accepted liturgical styles and forms. In this spirit Rachmaninoff composed his sacred choral works: he created them within the prescribed aesthetic-spiritual norms of Orthodoxy. He evolved the tradition, staying within it and not departing from it in significant ways. He took his place in a long line of Byzantine-Russian Orthodox artists who, century after century, in a dynamic process, produced "forms which were more stable, because through elaboration they were freed from everything superfluous and inconstant."[2]

In a consideration of Rachmaninoff's religiosity, the role and significance of the Russian bell-ringing practices deserve special mention. Rachmaninoff experienced nostalgia for the Russian culture in the Motherland that was lost to him, and the majestically clanging church bells of Orthodox services represented an enduring source of that sentiment. During the Twelve Great Feasts of the Orthodox calendar, as well as on important church holidays and even on Sundays as a component of the Divine Liturgy, the bells would ring memorably. The beauty of bell ringing was also expressed when bell concerts would take place. In Western churches bells are installed to swing from side to side, whereas in the Orthodox tradition church bells are stationary; they are arranged in the bell tower in order from smallest to largest, each possessing its own distinctive tone. Russian bells of a given bell tower are tuned to a common scale, and this creates a bright unity in their sound. Bell ringers are taught to hold ropes connected to several bells and move these ropes in certain ways to elicit the crisp metallic harmonies of the prescribed bell music patterns. For both the Orthodox faithful and visitors to Russian Orthodox churches the impression is unforgettable.

Many religious sensibilities are embedded in the clanging of Orthodox church bells; the presence of the bells even affects how worshipers interact with their churches. Bells call the faithful to services, mark significant milestones within the services, express the joy of the Divine Liturgy, and underscore the sorrow of a funeral. Orthodox bells in Eastern Christian theology evoke a response to God and the church, connecting the individual to the Divine in a personal way. Even though the sound is awe-inspiring and uplifting, the bells never stray from their fundamental purpose of calling the faithful to action and remembrance of God. These deeper meanings connect directly with the grandeur and appealing dissonance in Rachmaninoff's music. In Orthodox Christian practice there is no separation of the music from the service itself. The music *is* the service: the service is celebrated by means of the music, and the two aspects function together and inextricably from each other to create the liturgy. In contrast to the West, where the sermon occupies center stage and hymns are sung as interludes to the other parts of the services, in Orthodox churches the *a cappella* chanting of the choir (or chanters) forms a continuous call-and-response fabric with the priest and deacons, a responsorial hymnography that comprises the whole of the liturgy. For Rachmaninoff the meaning of Russian church bells lay even deeper:

the bells became emblematic of the church itself, of the Russian spiritual nature—and as such, the very idea of the bells represented for him the broader cultural roots of Russia. He reminisced:

> The sound of church bells dominated all the cities of Russia I used to know—Novgorod, Kiev, Moscow. They accompanied every Russian from childhood to the grave, and no composer could escape their influence.
>
> All my life I have taken pleasure in the differing moods and music of gladly chiming and mournfully tolling bells. This love for bells is inherent in every Russian.
>
> If I have been at all successful in making bells vibrate with human emotion in my works, it is largely due to the fact that most of my life was lived amid vibrations of the bells in Moscow.[3]

One of the most important influences on the young Sergei was his grandmother Sofia Aleksandrovna Butakova, at whose estate near Novgorod Sergei spent several summers as a child and adolescent. Sofia Aleksandrovna encouraged his interest in music, and provided him with material and moral support. Because his grandmother was also his godmother, according to Orthodox practice they were connected by familial ties and "by the Cross." It was thus Sofia Aleksandrovna's responsibility to attend to her godson's religious education, and, as all devout Orthodox *babushki* (elderly women), she took this charge seriously.[4]

Rachmaninoff's sister-in-law Sofia Satina writes in her memoir of Rachmaninoff that his grandmother Butakova's main characteristic was her piety (*nabozhnost*).[5] Satina elaborates:

> Grandmother loved to go to church, and he [the young Sergei] would take her to services; he began to listen more closely to the sacred chanting and bask in the music of it. An even deeper impression was made on him by the pealing of the church bells and liturgy in Novgorod, at the monasteries, and in the cathedrals to which he took his grandmother, when he lived with her in the summer just outside of Novgorod.[6]

Rachmaninoff would recall many times in his later years that his grandmother Butakova would take him to the ancient Cathedral of St. Sofia in the Novgorod Kremlin, and they would stand together through the long services, surrounded by the magnificent liturgical chanting, the aromatic incense, and the rhythmic, sparkling clanging of the Russian church bells:

> One of my fondest childhood recollections is associated with the four notes of the great bells in the St. Sofia Cathedral of Novgorod, which I often heard when my grandmother took me to town on church festival days.[7] The

bellringers were artists. The four notes were a theme that recurred again and again, four silvery weeping notes, veiled in an everchanging accompaniment woven around them.⁸

The ethos of Russian Orthodoxy would inform much of Rachmaninoff's music, not only his choral music and liturgical compositions but also many of his non-choral works. The influence of Orthodox services is felt in his compositions to the point that the brightly discordant church bells themselves become the main subject or form a leitmotif. Major examples of Rachmaninoff's use of the chordal and harmonic structures inherent in the sounds of Russian church bells occur in his Prelude in C# minor; Fantasia for two pianos [First Suite] (third movement, titled "Tears," and fourth movement, titled "Russian Pascha"); Piano Concerto No. 2 in C minor (first movement); and Piano Concerto No. 3 in E minor.

The period of Sergei's childhood, from the late 1870s until 1885 when he was sent to Moscow to live and study with Nikolay Zverev, provides enough evidence of the Russian Orthodox religiosity of Rachmaninoff's family that this faith tradition of Russia must be considered a foundational feature in any exploration of his life and music. His mother Liubov Rachmaninoff remained a devout follower of all church practices throughout her life, and, along with the piety, liveliness, and general inspiration that his grandmother Butakova gave him, her influence produced in Rachmaninoff a lifelong attachment to his Russian Orthodox roots. Sofia Satina, with whom he remained very close throughout his life, described his piety in a letter to Z. A. Apetian of November 30, 1965, that intended to correct Anna Trubnikova's [Sergei's cousin's] impression that Rachmaninoff did not go to confession, which is connected with the sacrament of communion in Orthodoxy:

> The affirmation made by Trubnikova that "Seryozha never went to confession" is completely inaccurate. Trubnikova reached this conclusion because of the fact that he refused to be coerced into going to confession. Sergei Vasilievich was extremely protective about keeping his inner world hidden. But several times before his wedding he asked me to accompany him to church; during these times he would make his confession and would insist that I tell no one at home that he goes to confession. Only I and our aging nanny Feona Dmitrievna (who would wake us early so that we could go to church) knew about this. His favorite church was the old Church of the Assumption on Mogiltsy near Vasilievsky and Mertvy Lanes.⁹

During the summers in the first decade of the twentieth century when Rachmaninoff and his family lived at Ivanovka there was regular interaction between the inhabitants of Ivanovka and the priests of the churches nearby. Irina Brandt writes,

[Sergei Vasilievich] along with his entire family went to church to attend the liturgy on all the holidays. Often he would also go to the cathedral alone. The priest would also come to Ivanovka, and he and Sergei would converse with each other for a long time, either in Sergei Vasilievich's study or in the gazebo in the park.[10]

A serious occurrence—the illness of both of Rachmaninoff's daughters—illustrates the reliance of their parents on their faith to sustain them and provide recovery for the daughters. In the spring of 1913, when the Rachmaninoffs were vacationing in Switzerland and Italy, their daughters Irina and Tatiana fell ill with typhoid fever. The family, living at that time in an apartment near the Piazza di Spagna in Rome, hurriedly left Italy for Germany to seek medical treatment from German doctors (whose care they trusted more than that of the Italians). In Berlin the daughters' condition stabilized enough for the family to return to Russia, to their estate Ivanovka. The peasant woman Ekaterina Ivanovna Shtyrlina, who worked for the Rachmaninoffs at Ivanovka, remembers the tense situation of the daughters' illness and recovery:

I remember that terrifying summer:

> None of the usual laughter could be heard on the estate. The head of the household [Rachmaninoff] turned positively dark and gloomy, almost every day driving to Viazov to the church, and requesting a *moleben* [prayer for a specific occasion]. Almost every day the priest would arrive at the estate from Viazov and would serve a *moleben* at Ivanovka . . . each evening [Natalia Aleksandrovna] would pray for her daughters' health . . . Later I heard from my mother that the [Rachmaninoffs] were giving additional lands to the inhabitants of the village of Ivanovka, in gratitude for the Lord's having sent good health to Tania and Irina. That summer Sergei Vasilievich looked all worn out—but he began to play for hours after the recovery of his daughters. . . . I saw the entire family standing for church services in Viazov. I saw how Sergei Vasilievich would personally, in his car, bring the priest from Viazov, and how the priest would chant the service right on the lawn in front of the house, and then would bless that wing and the entire house with holy water. We, the yard servants, were all at that service.[11]

These church-related activities of Rachmaninoff and his family, as well as his desire to have conversations on religious matters with the local priest at Ivanovka, present a picture of sustained participation in the cycle of church services that was normal for the milieu in which they organized their lives.

The aesthetic and physical features of Orthodox Christian worship connect with the direct intensity encountered in Rachmaninoff's music: An awareness of these features can enable Rachmaninoff's music to be understood on its own terms and as it relates to his cultural foundations. The exuberance and passion in his music stem from his spiritual nature, but it is the particular spiritual nature of an Orthodox Christian. In Orthodoxy the faithful move independently during the liturgy and use their physical selves to express their piety: They light candles, inhale the incense symbolizing prayers offered up to God, kneel and make prostrations to the floor, chant the prayers and hymns along with the chanters, taste the bread and wine of communion, and visually interact with the icons lining the walls and ceiling of the church. The ornate beauty of the church interiors is intended to be an external material representation of the Kingdom of God on Earth. All of the senses are engaged; the worship experience produces the effect of synesthesia, integrating all the senses almost simultaneously. In Orthodoxy the physical expression of piety is displayed in a way that signifies acceptance of both the spiritual and material natures of human existence. Rachmaninoff's understanding of the place of the physical was developed at the most formative stages of his life, in which parental guidance, social mores, and religious training were interwoven in his consciousness. This understanding could not but influence, indeed become a marked feature of his music as a whole.

During the last decades of the nineteenth century and pre-revolutionary period of the twentieth century Rachmaninoff found his impulse to write choral music (both sacred and secular) perfectly in step with the development of that genre in Russia:

> One of the prime factors that contributed to the development of the New Russian Choral School was the creative environment fostered by the Moscow Synodal Choir, as it evolved in the late 1880s from a mediocre church choir staffing the Kremlin Dormition Cathedral into a first-rate choral ensemble that embodied the highest artistic and professional standards. Intimately connected with the success of this remarkable choir and its parent Moscow Synodal School of church singing were a number of individuals who also played a significant part in Rachmaninoff's role as a composer of sacred choral works.[12]

Among these composers, pedagogues, conductors, musicologists, and performers were Petr Tchaikovsky, Nikolay Rimsky-Korsakov, Mily Balakirev, Vasily Orlov, Stepan Smolensky, Aleksandr Kastalsky, and Nikolay Danilin—all of whom were in some crucial way connected with supporting, promoting, or collaborating musically with Rachmaninoff in his activities in Moscow. He was inspired by these luminaries, who themselves were setting Orthodox prayer services to music. Boris Vladimirovich Asafiev—composer, music critic, and professor at the Leningrad Conservatory—observed, "Choral music, as a stylistically distinctive mode of composition, emerges first in Russian opera, but externally from opera experiences its fullest development in Kastalsky, Taneev, and Rachmaninoff."[13]

In 1896 Stepan Vasilievich Smolensky invited Rachmaninoff to become a member of the teaching staff of the Moscow Synodal School, but he did not accept the offer.[14] Rachmaninoff was never drawn to pedagogical activity: during those rare times when he was compelled out of financial circumstances to take on private tutoring, he typically became impatient if pupils would come to lessons unprepared or poorly prepared and would send them home early if he was dissatisfied with their progress. Whenever he was offered pedagogical work, he turned it down. Rather than devoting himself to the time-consuming and often exhausting activity of teaching, Rachmaninoff found himself turning to the composition of Orthodox sacred music in the Russian tradition. He maintained a close professional relationship with Smolensky, an authority on Russian church music, and dedicated his magisterial fifteen-part *All-Night Vigil* (1915) to the memory of this tireless champion for the ancient sacred genre.

All of his sacred choral works were premièred by the Synodal Choir of Moscow; during the period of his composition of sacred music, Rachmaninoff was fortunate to be able to work with the Synodal Choir's distinguished music director Aleksandr Dmitrievich Kastalsky. His first composition of sacred music was the sacred choral concerto *O Mother of God, Perpetually Praying*, for mixed choir (1893). Rachmaninoff's choice of the subject for this musical work would indicate a clear familiarity with the icons, prayers, and tradition of veneration of the Mother of God among both Orthodox and Catholic Christians. Not only is the religious subject of importance theologically, but the concept of perpetual prayer by Mary, Mother of God, also would be commonly understood and appreciated among the Russian Orthodox. Rachmaninoff completed the choral concerto only one year after he had graduated from the Moscow Conservatory, but, as Orthodox choral music specialist Vladimir Morosan notes, it

> foreshadows the hand of a master, not only in terms of treating thematic material, but also in terms of choral sonority. Quite simply, the twenty-year-old composer wrote a piece of choral music that was more complex, imbued with greater emotional power, and pushed the choral instrument to greater extremes of range and dynamic contrast than anything hitherto composed in the realm of Russian church music. . . . Present already are the inimitable spun-out, undulating melodies (later to become a Rachmaninoff trademark), which at times are wedded to the text and at other times take on an independent life of their own.[15]

Rachmaninoff used lines 3–6 of the first stanza of Aleksey Khomiakov's poem "Kremlevskaia Zautrenia na Paskhu" (1849) for the epigraph to the fourth and last movement of his Fantasia (Suite No. 1) for two pianos (Op. 5, 1893), which was dedicated to his mentor and idol Tchaikovsky. Referring to Orthodox Pascha (Easter), Rachmaninoff titled the movement "Radiant

Holiday" (in the original Russian: *Svetlyi prazdnik*). Images of a dignified happiness, the fulfillment of Pascha, and an active brotherly love pervade the poem, which is written in two stanzas.

Rachmaninoff's musical presentation of Russian Paschal bells being rung from a bell tower next to an Orthodox church must surely represent the most accurate rendering of a bell concert by Russian stationary bells in music history. The majesty of the Paschal morning, with its ending of the strict Great Fast of Lent and its affirmation of the Resurrection, is made almost palpable in the massive low chords and innovative modulations that characterize this movement. The Orthodox piety of Rachmaninoff finds its fullest expression in the composer's appropriation of lines from the philosopher-theologian's Paschal poem.

This first sacred-music masterpiece of Rachmaninoff's (*O Mother of God, Perpetually Praying*) and the religion-related sections of his Fantasia (Suite No. 1) for two pianos were followed by *Panteley the Healer* (choral work, 1900); "Before the Icon" Op. 21, No. 10 (art song, 1902); "To My Children" Op. 26, No. 7 (art song, 1906); "Christ is Risen" Op. 26, No. 6 (art song, 1906); *Liturgy of St. John Chrysostom* Op. 31 (choral work, 1910); "The Raising of Lazarus" Op. 34, No. 6 (art song, 1912); "From the Gospel of John" [Ch. XV, verse 13] Without Opus (art song, 1914); and *All-Night Vigil* Op. 37 (choral work, 1915).

The spread of these dates of composition reveals a sustained period of Rachmaninoff's immersion in church history, music notation, and style of liturgical chant in Eastern Christianity. Because of Rachmaninoff's background as an Orthodox Christian, he had experienced on many levels the most commonly celebrated service of this faith tradition, the Divine Liturgy of St. John Chrysostom. Resultantly, the setting of the Liturgy—belonging to the genre of Orthodox Divine Liturgy settings—to his own composed music represented a special, even exciting project. In the context of the material presented in this chapter and previous ones about Rachmaninoff's spirituality and education, one must dismiss assessments such as that of Geoffrey Norris: "As is apparent from the circumstances of his marriage, Rachmaninoff was no churchman, and it was a considerable undertaking for him to set the liturgy, with little or no knowledge of ecclesiastical matters."[16] A difficult undertaking, yes, due to the complexity and ancient roots of the Liturgy—St. John Chrysostom, who "revised the prayers and rubrics of the Divine Liturgy, or celebration of the Holy Eucharist," was elevated to Archbishop of Constantinople in the late fourth century CE[17]—but not due to Rachmaninoff's lack of knowledge of the Russian Orthodox Church and details of its liturgical practices. On at least one occasion he made reference to the Orthodox prayer book he kept with him: while composing the *Liturgy of St. John Chrysostom*, he explained, "The third antiphon I shall . . . set, according to my prayer book."[18]

Rachmaninoff completed his *Liturgy of St. John Chrysostom* on July 30, 1910; on the last page he wrote, "Konets i slava Bogu" (The end and glory be to God). The next day he wrote to Morozov: "I have finished the Liturgy. . . . Long ago I thought about the Liturgy, and long ago I strove towards it. I set about it somehow unexpectedly and was at once carried away by it. And then I finished it very soon. I haven't composed anything for a long while . . . with such pleasure."[19] The choral work was first performed on November 25 of that same year in Moscow by the Choir of the Synodal School under the baton of the eminent Nikolay Danilin. The performance was a resounding success, and it would remain special to Rachmaninoff for one additional reason: it brought him into contact for the first time with the young child soloist Sergei Zharov (known subsequently as Serge Jaroff) whose career path as the brilliant organizer and conductor of the Don Cossack Choir would in many ways parallel Rachmaninoff's own. Rachmaninoff recalled, in reminiscences prepared for a journalist:

> The Choir sang beautifully. For one number of the Liturgy, "We sing Thy praise, O Lord," the whole Choir supplies a humming accompaniment for the solo of a boy soprano. At that performance the voice rang out in such crystalline, ethereal beauty against the rich, deep harmonies of the choral background, that I experienced a moment of sheer delight. After the performance I asked to see the boy soloist. A shy, blushing lad was presented to me, and I patted him on the shoulder and thanked him for his exquisite singing. Years later, after a Berlin concert of the Don Cossacks, its very able conductor, Sergei Jaroff, was introduced to me and he said at once that he had already met me. I have a good memory for faces, but I could not recall him. "Where was it we met?" I asked, and he told me that he was the boy who had sung the soprano solo in the *Liturgy*.[20]

Along with the Kuban and Don Cossack hosts, Sergei Zharov was forced to evacuate Russia on November 13–16, 1920, from Crimea during the Russian Civil War in the massive yet extraordinary organizational feat of Petr Nikolaevich Wrangel, commanding general of the anti-Bolshevik forces in Southern Russia. On board 126 ships in exceedingly difficult conditions the refugees were taken to Turkey and later to Yugoslavia.

After the Don Cossack Choir had been organized in emigration under the devoted leadership of Zharov, the ensemble began what would be a storied performing career of Russian Orthodox liturgical music, art songs, and Russian soldiers' songs. Rachmaninoff met with Zharov several times in Europe (presumably in the late 1920s and 1930s), serving as a mentor to him. Rachmaninoff gave Zharov many suggestions on how to improve the sound of the choir, and also advised him on effective ways of conducting. The result was that Zharov's famed and subdued style of conducting—through facial expressions and small gestures—evoked Rachmaninoff's own style. Feodor Chaliapin also worked professionally with Zharov's choir; in one anecdote, "At the palace of an Indian royal, Jaroff met with the famous Russian bass Feodor Chaliapin who said to him, 'It will be better for us to get a drink in a small bar . . . I'm getting tired of all these hotels and palaces.'"[21]

All of these aforementioned influences on Rachmaninoff—his childhood and youth, music study, and his connections with superb practitioners of the art of music—enabled him to produce his *magnum opus*, the *All-Night Vigil* (op. 37). It remains a supremely respected choral masterpiece in national and international arenas.[22] The choral work was premièred on March 10, 1915, by the Synodal Choir under the direction of N. M. Danilin in the auditorium of the Charitable Works Foundation of Moscow. Aleksandr Kastalsky wrote about the *All-Night Vigil*:

> The new composition of S.V. Rachmaninoff the *All-Night Vigil* indisputably represents a major contribution to our sacred-music literature, while the prospect of the première of its performance is a consummate musical event among the extraordinary programs of the concerts of the Great Fast [Lent] of the present season. When compared with the *Divine Liturgy*, its author in his

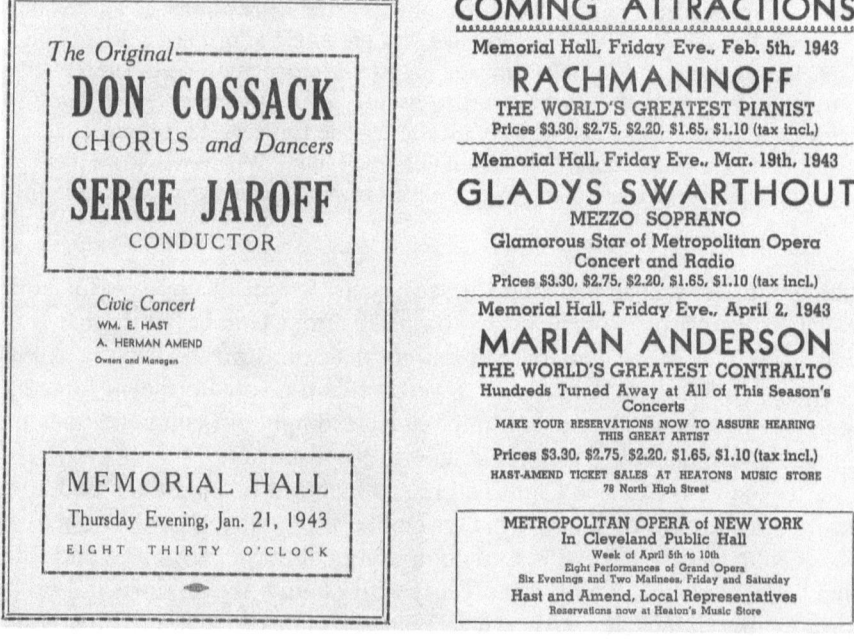

Figure 9.1 Memorial Hall, Columbus, Ohio, Program of Serge Jaroff and the Don Cossack Chorus, with Announcement of Rachmaninoff's Recital There Two Weeks Later. Author's collection.

new composition makes a major step forward in moving away from the "part-singing" style of structuring church melodies. Instead, he takes them directly from the [Byzantine / Slavonic] canon of Common Usage (*Обиход*). But one must hear for oneself the splendor into which the simple, guileless melodies are transformed in the hands of a major musical artist. Everything is contained in this statement.... Whether or not Rachmaninoff comes close to capturing the style [of the *Vigil*], of course, will be debated.... Especially praiseworthy in the composer is his loving and respectful attitude towards our ancient melodies. And this [attitude] guarantees a positive future for our sacred music.[23]

The *All-Night Vigil* was composed in fifteen parts as an *a cappella* choral composition. Bertensson and Leyda clarify that in the accepted practice of the Orthodox Church, specific parts of the Vigil service must follow the traditional chant patterns, but six of the individual parts allow for a broader interpretation that would enable the composer to create new and unique melodies.[24] Concerning the required traditional chants, Rachmaninoff used the melismatic *Znamennyi* chant for movements 8, 9, 12, 13, and 14; he used the recitational Greek / Byzantine type of chant for movements 2 and 15; and he used the Kievan chant for movements 4 and 5. Thus he fulfilled these obligations in order to stay within church tradition. The remaining six movements—1, 3, 6, 7, 10, and 11—could be characterized by Joseph Yasser's concept of the "conscious counterfeit" of the musical chant of the *Obikhod* [The Book of Common Chant], keeping in mind the overall unity of the music within the expectations of the church. Yasser and Rachmaninoff enjoyed a warm and friendly relationship in the 1930s and had discussed in some detail the musical possibilities of subconscious versus conscious counterfeit of a deeply seated phrase or melody.[25] In the case of the *All-Night Vigil*, Rachmaninoff's extended and regular connections with Russian Orthodox services could make a convincing case for the "conscious counterfeit." Morosan points out, "Rachmaninoff's 'counterfeits' are so skillfully created that a person not intimately familiar with the actual chant repertoire would have a difficult time distinguishing them from the genuine melodies."[26] An amusing and culturally revealing anecdote concerning Rachmaninoff's most loved movement of the *All-Night Vigil* ("Lord, now lettest Thou Thy servant depart in peace," No. 7) relates to his playing of the entire choral work—a momentous occasion—for Kastalsky and Danilin. Rachmaninoff described:

> Towards the end [of movement No. 7] there is a passage sung by the basses—a scale descending to the lowest B-flat in a very slow pianissimo. After I played this passage Danilin shook his head, saying, "Now where on earth are we to find such basses? They are as rare as asparagus at Christmas!" Nevertheless, he did find them. I knew the voices of my countrymen, and I well knew what demands I could make upon Russian basses![27]

In addition to its clear origins in Byzantine / Slavonic Orthodox sacred melodic traditions, for Rachmaninoff the sustained prayers of the *All-Night Vigil* issued a call of sorts for mercy and help from God. The horrors of World War I were being unleashed upon the Russian land, and Russia's own political instability was palpable in all corners of the country. There was much to fear and much to inspire a deeper search for resolution to these monumental problems. As Rachmaninoff acknowledged about his creative springs, they were an external expression of his thoughts, hopes, dreams, and fears. And the *All-Night Vigil* was no exception. His own family as well as many of his friends and colleagues would be drastically affected by the turbulence of this period, even culminating for many in the decision to emigrate from Russia for safer locations. The tragic and unnatural waning of the genre of sacred choral music in Russia, along with Rachmaninoff as a major exponent of it, is captured by Vladimir Morosan:

> Sergei Rachmaninoff's emergence as a composer coincided with the renaissance of Russian sacred choral music in the late nineteenth and early twentieth centuries. After a period of decline in the mid-nineteenth century, during which serious composers did not compose for the Church—by and large the result of severe bureaucratic control by Imperial Chapel censors—sacred choral music once again came to the attention of leading musicians in Russia. . . . What resulted was an enormous outpouring of compositional activity, which began in the 1880s, gained strength in the 1890s, and continued until it was abruptly cut off by the Bolshevik Revolution of 1917.[28]

Not only did the composition of religious music stop, but the Moscow Synodal School and its superb Synodal Choir were no longer allowed to function. One can safely conclude, "It is perhaps not coincidental that after 1917, when the Moscow Synodal School was closed and the Synodal Choir disbanded, Rachmaninoff wrote no more sacred choral works."[29]

This statement represents in a nutshell the tragedy Rachmaninoff faced in exile in Europe and the United States: the loss of the immediate, daily environment that nurtured and sustained his native culture. Outside of these continuous influences of everything Russian on him, not to mention the musical roots that had influenced him at every stage of his development, he would find in foreign lands and cultures that he was unable to continue his composing in certain genres, such as sacred choral works and art songs. Because the latter ideally required native-Russian-speaking vocalists, the prospects for Rachmaninoff to collaborate with professionals on his level were slim indeed.

During this period Rachmaninoff also set poems expressing Orthodox sensibilities to music in several art songs, including "Before the Icon" (1899), "Christ is Risen" (1906), "To My Children" (1906), and "The Raising of Lazarus" (1912). In informal settings with musical colleagues and friends he enjoyed singing in his bass voice, and these experiences provided for him an additional entry to the potential of vocal production. Because of his attentiveness to the qualities of the human voice and singing, many passages in his compositions are considered by scholars to be undeveloped vocal or choral music; the instrumental and vocal parts are sensitively intertwined with each other. Since Rachmaninoff composed music to poems that were already written, the sensibility of the final product is highly metaphorical. In his songsettings the mood of the music closely matches the theme of the words, so that both convey the same overall meaning.

A special case needs to be made here for inclusion of two of Rachmaninoff's relevant compositions in a discussion of his sacred compositions: the symphonic poem *Isle of the Dead* (Op. 29, 1908) and the choral symphony *The Bells* (Op. 35, 1913). Seemingly secular works, the two pieces of music were inspired by non-musical art forms (respectively, painting and literature), but also connect powerfully with Rachmaninoff's spiritual life. Because of the multi-layered meaning of these two works for him, he chose large-scale musical formats for their expression. The theological understanding in Orthodox Christianity maintains that connection with God is attained most surely through lengthy periods of prayer and contemplation, and thus for Rachmaninoff the need to enable *Isle of the Dead* and *The Bells* to reveal their spiritual resonance logically was conveyed through longer forms of musical expression.

Isle of the Dead was composed while the Rachmaninoffs were in Dresden in 1908. Sergei had seen a black and white reproduction of a painting on that subject by Swiss symbolist artist Arnold Böcklin in Paris the year before, and he carried the stark image in his memory for the months until the composition was completed. His work on the symphonic poem took place between January and March 1909; its manuscript is dated April 17, 1909. On April 18 of that year Rachmaninoff conducted its première in Moscow. He made additional revisions to it before it was finally published in June 1909. A cursory interpretation of the painting would indicate the Greek mythological origins of Charon transporting by boat a soul of one deceased across the River Styx (or Acheron). Böcklin completed several renditions of the painting at his studio in Florence, Italy, which was located not far from the English Cemetery. Both the mythological and biographical sources clearly connect with the themes of life, death, and immortality—and it was this theme that Rachmaninoff strove to convey musically in his symphonic poem. The work's relatively unusual time signature of 5/8 approximates the motion of rowing a boat across a still body of water.

Rachmaninoff also included in *Isle of the Dead* variations on the ancient Latin sequence *Dies irae* (day of wrath), which is used in the Roman Catholic Requiem Mass; it is in this symphonic poem that his use of the Latin sequence is most central and pronounced. The *Dies irae* musical cell evokes the terrifying association with the mystery of the end of life on earth for someone who, as Rachmaninoff, had a marked fear of death. Many people who interacted with Rachmaninoff witnessed his aversion to talking about death. One well-known instance, which relates to the summer of 1915, was described by poet Marietta Shaginian:

> He was obsessed with the fear of death. I remember he asked my mother to tell his fortune with cards—was he to live much longer? A story by Artzibashev, about death, had made a terrible impression on him—"It's impossible to live while one knows one must die after all. How can you bear the thought of dying?" While saying this, he had unconsciously begun to eat from a plate of roasted salted pistachio nuts that we always had ready for him. He ... looked at [the plate], realized the incongruity, and broke into laughter.[30]

About the painting itself, Rachmaninoff remarked famously when he later viewed the original in color that it would not have inspired him as had the black and white (presumably starker) painting.

The connection between products of creative inspiration and the fear of death is one that lies deep within the creating consciousness; it is summed up dramatically in the reflections on art by Russian filmmaker Andrei Tarkovsky:

> Art is born and takes hold wherever there is a timeless and insatiable longing for the spiritual, for the ideal. ... The artist is always a servant, and is perpetually trying to pay for the gift that has been given to him as if by a miracle. ... Artistic creation demands of the artist that he "perish utterly", in the full, tragic sense of those words.
>
> The aim of art is to prepare a person for death, to plough and harrow his soul, rendering it capable of turning to good.[31]

If not at a conscious level of his thinking about the purpose of his life and need to create music, Rachmaninoff in his actions, decisions made about how he would interact with the profession of musician, and understanding of how he was placed in life and in some sort of absolute eternity—or death—moved through his life with an intensity, conviction, and apprehension of the coming of death. This signified for him not only the end of his human life on earth, but the cessation of his "creating identity"—and thus, the performance and composition of his works as staving off a death that was unavoidable.

The choral symphony *The Bells* was composed in 1913 (Op. 35) and is based on a poem by Edgar Allan Poe that was translated by the poet Konstantin Balmont. Along with his opera *Monna Vanna* and the *All-Night Vigil*, *The Bells* remained one of his favorite personal compositions.

Rachmaninoff himself linked the concept of *The Bells* with his experiences of hearing the church bells pealing in Novgorod and Moscow. This time his source was a literary work in translation, which was suggested to him while he was vacationing in Rome. An anonymous letter arrived together with a copy of the Russian translation of Poe's work—the identity of the correspondent was later revealed to be that of a student from the Moscow Conservatory, Maria Danilova. Danilova's suggestion was sound and appealed to Rachmaninoff. Rachmaninoff directed the work's première in St. Petersburg; it was dedicated to conductor Willem Mengelberg and the Dutch Royal Concertgebouw Orchestra. The choral symphony is in four movements, corresponding to the four parts of Poe's poem and also the four major stages of a person's life:

1. "The Silver Sleigh Bells" in A flat major
    This opening movement represents the exuberance, boundless optimism, and carefree enjoyment of the life of young people.
2. "The Mellow Wedding Bells" in D major
    The second movement portrays the transition in a person's life from the carefreeness of youth to the sublime happiness connected with marriage and entry to adulthood.
3. "The Loud Alarm Bells" in F minor
    The bells in this third movement are characterized as a "wailing alarm," indicating a terrifying emergency and alluding to the fragility of life.
4. "The Mournful Iron Bells" in C sharp minor
    These bells toll for a person's death, mourning and "groaning," serving as a reminder of death in general, but also remembering the fullness of a human life.

Geoffrey Norris writes concerning the finale: "Here, Rachmaninoff's chromatic word-painting on the word 'stonet' (moaning) in the last line is a masterstroke, the chorus building to a climax of terror before the music subsides and the Soul finds peace in death, in the soft, serene D flat of the conclusion."[32] The magisterial composition utilizes a full orchestra and large choir (often several choirs combined); the four movements take the listener on an unmediated emotional journey in vocal and instrumental form.

After Rachmaninoff had left Russia and settled in New York, he regularly supported the church his family had joined, St. Nicholas Cathedral at 15 East 97th Street. This church parish was closely connected with Russia: Tsar Nicholas II had donated a large sum of money for its construction in 1900–1901, and a student of Kastalsky, Ivan Gorokhov, became the director of its choir—a first-rate choral organization modeled on the Moscow Synodal Choir. Rachmaninoff on occasion advised the choir in its performances of sacred music; through this church his connections with Russia, Kastalsky, and the Synodal Choir were continued. For Rachmaninoff the Russian Orthodox Church in emigration represented even more than his national faith tradition: the church became the repository for all the essential features of his native country and culture for which he yearned so powerfully.

Concerning Rachmaninoff's composition of sacred works, biographer Max Harrison's attempts to figure out why he wrote such music exemplify the struggles of those unfamiliar with Rachmaninoff's Russian identity and Orthodox Christian piety. Two quotations disclose Harrison's attempts to place Rachmaninoff's sacred works logically within the rest of his artistic corpus:

> One's impression from the general tenor of [Rachmaninoff's] life is that *he was an easygoing agnostic, rather like Turgenef.* Yet this view is hard, perhaps, to sustain in the face of his two great religious works, the Liturgy of St. John Chrysostom, which he now wrote, and the All-Night Vigil of a few years later [1915]. After all, Milos Velimirovic refers to them as "the highest artistic achievements in the realm of Russian church music."[33] (emphasis added)
>
> His producing *so fervent a score* as the Liturgy of St. John Chrysostom is still a *matter for some surprise* although it needs to be remembered that at the start of the twentieth century there was a revival of interest in religion among Russian intellectuals . . . *Rachmaninoff was not an intellectual* and would have been reserved about such volte-face, yet it may have had its effect.[34] (emphasis added)

It is surprising that Harrison felt so surprised. Aside from the myriad forms of evidence of Rachmaninoff's religiosity, we have his own statements about his faith, which cannot be construed any other way. In an interview, when asked where his genius and talent for music had originated, Rachmaninoff answered, "I owe to God the gifts given me, to God alone. Without him, I am nothing."[35]

Harrison's pronouncement that Rachmaninoff was an "easygoing agnostic" does not represent Rachmaninoff's religious orientation. Nothing in Rachmaninoff's character was easygoing at any time during his life (a reading of his letters in the original Russian will dispel this notion), and there exists no evidence suggesting that he was an agnostic. The statement, "The point seems to be that Rachmaninoff loved the music, that it was the singing, not the religion, that affected him,"[36] manifests a faulty understanding of the Russian religious mind in general and of Rachmaninoff's experiences with Orthodoxy in particular. In historically Orthodox countries the practice of giving concerts in church buildings does not exist, unless the building is no longer used for church services. It is against Orthodox church doctrine for music to be performed separately from the liturgical experience—for that would take the sacred chant outside the context of the liturgy and be disrespectful of the church interior as representing the mystical presence of God. If an Orthodox parishioner refers to the chanting, however beautiful it may be, it is beautiful *precisely because* it is prayerful and participates in the words that are believed to ascend along with the incense to heaven.

As one prayer book for Holy Friday Matins puts it:

> The Twelve Gospel readings, however, are only a part of the Service. Another large part is composed of liturgical hymnography. This hymnography (the antiphons, verses and kanons sung during the Service) sets the gospel readings within the consciousness of the entire Church, with all of her history and people. The Gospel texts narrate the events. The hymnography gives the *response of the Church*, the community of true Christian believers from all ages, to these events. The hymnography clarifies and gives deeper meaning as well as the proper sense of significance, to the narrations which the Gospel relates with such epic simplicity.[37] (emphasis original)

Another common misconception held by those with limited knowledge of Eastern Christianity involves the concept of attending church in order to enjoy the service as an artistic experience—for, indeed the Orthodox liturgical drama, with its dignified ritual and intense aesthetic features—is beautiful. However, enjoyment of the service for its visual beauty would be foreign to Russian religious theology and *praxis*. The term "artistic experience" does not capture how the Russian faithful understand the long services of Orthodoxy, in which they stand the entire time and prostrate themselves on the floor at prescribed times. Rather, the Orthodox faithful conceptualize their religious sensibilities in other ways: the service is participatory, requiring ascetic feats and struggles (fasting before communion, standing, etc.); this sensibility is incompatible with watching a religious service and being comfortably detached enough to "enjoy" it. In the context of the categories of religious services, the Orthodox liturgy constitutes a type of "liturgical drama," but this is understood only within the mystical context of the faith tradition's dogmatic theology.

Orthodox Christianity represents a way of life: the features of the faith wrap themselves around the believer from cradle to grave. Orthodox Christians typically set up some sort of icon corner in their place of residence. This corner may contain icons of the Trinity and of Orthodox saints, a hanging oil lamp, prayer books, holy water, and dried palm branches. The Rachmaninoff family's icons, for example, included one of St. Panteley the Healer. As half of the Orthodox theology of word and image, icons are much loved and respected by the faithful. If one is Orthodox, one venerates icons and has them visible and apparent in one's daily life.

Because of the deeply embedded monastic tradition in Orthodoxy, with the asceticism of its desert dwellers and practice of silent prayer, the attendance of church services is understood as an extension of prayer rituals and blessings carried out in the daily life of the faithful. Attending church as often as possible is the expectation in Orthodoxy, but the Orthodox faithful would not necessarily conclude that if someone does not attend church regularly, that person is not religious. Even those with little time for prayer will routinely make the sign of the cross over themselves when passing by the icon corner. Rachmaninoff would tenderly make the sign of the cross over his daughters, saying "Christ be with you," even when they were adults, and he did this whenever they left his house—even if only for the night.[38] One example occurs in a letter from his Swiss villa Senar to his cousin/sister-in-law Sofia Aleksandrovna; in closing, Rachmaninoff writes, "Good-bye, dear Sonia, may Christ be with you. I send you a big kiss!"[39]

The question of whether or not Rachmaninoff was an intellectual needs to be considered carefully. If one defines an intellectual as someone who is well educated in a broad way, participates in the currents of high culture and the life of the mind by reading books associated with the best of the culture of the day, attending those places where art is performed and exhibited, maintaining a flexible and creative outlook on life, and participating in contexts in which one's thoughts are tested and challenged, then Rachmaninoff was an intellectual. His attendance of a discussion of at least one of Georgy Fedotov's lectures in Russian religious philosophy at the New York Public Library on 145th St. has been documented.[40] He read the great works of Russian prose and poetry, knew four languages reasonably well, followed world political and social developments, and stayed abreast of trends in his own profession. His reticence about discussing aesthetic and intellectual matters outside his immediate circle of friends stemmed both from his introverted nature and his seeming awkwardness about living in a foreign country. He was a private man and protected that privacy with all the resources at his disposal; it should not be surprising, then, that he would also keep his spiritual and intellectual life to himself and his closest friends in the Russian community.

The connection between the intellect and Orthodox piety expresses itself in particular in the intellectual depth of the theological writings of the Church Fathers of the fourth century CE, even as the scholasticism of Western Christianity is foreign to the mysticism and "tender emotion" typical of Orthodoxy. The high philosophico-theological level of Orthodoxy stems from the richness of the writings of such first-millennium Church Fathers as St. John Chrysostom, St. Gregory of Nazianzus, and St. Basil, which are studied by the priests and used in their sermons. Orthodoxy does not try to explain the mind of God, for example, but leaves for the Divine understandings that the human mind cannot grasp. The intellectual side of human experience is set aside in favor of spirituality that comes from the heart and physical senses, but at the same time in the Divine Liturgy the priest intones the words that it is a "rational" offering to God (rather than, for example, an ecstatic or charismatic one). Rachmaninoff's sacred music is linked with Russian literature and religious philosophy precisely through its mystical-spiritual power:

> The quality of confession in Rachmaninoff's poetics simultaneously belongs to the cultures of Romanticism and Orthodoxy. In these cultures the confession is the "text of a life," the self-reckoning of the inner person, a breakthrough to eternal truth by the overcoming of the barriers of chronological and eternal time, being and consciousness.[41]

The composition of sacred music, which would engage theological canons of life, death, and immortality, would keep at the forefront of the composer's mind the belief system governing his own life. Whether consciously perceived or not, the very process of composing sacred music for his own faith tradition would for Rachmaninoff involve his participation in a kind of confession and absolution—a creative act of goodness and offering to God.

After *O Mother of God, Perpetually Praying*, the second sacred work Rachmaninoff composed provides a telling case in point of how the fullness of his Orthodox religiosity is often missed by critics in the West. His *a cappella* work for mixed chorus *Panteley-Utselitel* (Panteley the Healer) was set to Alexei Tolstoy's poem by the same name. Harrison describes the content of the work as follows:

> This was Panteley the Healer, a setting for unaccompanied SATB of an 1866 poem . . . about a rustic healer who knows the secrets of all the beneficial and poisonous plants and herbs. . . . The writing is smoothly accomplished, the tone of the music somewhat serious, faintly religious. . . . Yet aside from such agreeable trifles as these.[42]

Barrie Martyn similarly misses the Orthodox Christian context of Rachmaninoff's composition, describing the subject of the work as "a kind of rustic deity who practices herbal medicine. As he walks around the field, greeted by the flowers, he shakes his knobbly stick at the poisonous herbs and collects the wholesome ones, which he uses for his healing work."[43]

The surface content of Tolstoy's poem represents only a limited metaphor of what both Tolstoy and Rachmaninoff understood within Orthodox sacred tradition: Panteley is considered a miracle-working saint. The Orthodox faithful appeal to his intercession with God when they are ill or when they have lost an important object. St. Panteley, or Panteleimon, was a late-third- / early-fourth-century physician who healed the sick in the name of Christ. He was a martyr during the persecution of Christians in Rome in 305 CE and thus is formally known as Great martyr St. Panteley. He is one of the most important saints venerated regularly by the Orthodox faithful, many of whom keep an icon of him in their residences. Very likely icons of St. Panteley were kept for veneration at Rachmaninoff's grandmother Butakova's estate and at the Satin estate Ivanovka, but it is beyond dispute that icons of this beloved saint would be inscribed on the walls of the churches and monasteries Rachmaninoff had visited as a young man. Thus a sustained acquaintance of Rachmaninoff with St. Panteley would indicate that the meaning of this composition for him was surely greater than being an "agreeable trifle." In times of illness or approaching death the faithful in their prayers to St. Panteley ask him to pray to God for the well-being of the person who is ill or dying. Sergei and Natalia kept such an icon with them wherever they lived; the icon of St. Panteley hung in the bedroom of their Elm Street house in Hollywood. The fact that Rachmaninoff and his wife kept this icon near them—and that it was very likely the last Orthodox icon he saw in the hours before his death—would underscore that his writing of the sacred chorus about St. Panteley even at only age twenty-eight contained music that was more than "somewhat serious" or "faintly religious." At the end of his life as Rachmaninoff lay dying of cancer, as his devoted nurse Olga Georgievna Mordovskaia recorded, when he was brought home from the hospital, "on March 2 [1943], lying in his bed, he attentively looked around his bedroom, rested his gaze on the ancient family icon of St. Panteley, and said, 'How good it is that I'm at home.'"[44]

In 1916 at Ivanovka immediately following the death of Sergei's father, Irina Brandt recalls the interaction between Sergei and Fr. Nikolay, priest of the Viazov Church. When Sergei arrived from the Caucasus where he had been on a concert tour, Varvara Arkadievna Satina (his mother-in-law) went to the train station eight miles away to meet him; from the station they went directly to Viazov. There Sergei talked with Fr. Nikolay, very likely receiving some grief counseling from the priest and also working out preliminary details for how his father's burial should be handled—for Vasily Arkadievich had committed suicide.[45]

Because Rachmaninoff as a child and young adult was steeped in the ascetic spirituality and poetic sensibilities of Russian Orthodoxy, he developed typical Orthodox personality traits: his wife and close friends described him as being humble (though not self-effacing), forgiving, charitable, and non-judgmental. While he was a complex human being, he manifested in his life a consistency of these qualities that was observable to others in his circle of acquaintances. Though not exclusive to Orthodoxy, these traits are foregrounded by the faith's Church Fathers and revered saints, such as St. Seraphim of Sarov (1754–1833). One anecdote concerning Rachmaninoff's tact and non-judgmental deportment was set in Beverly Hills at his last home on Elm Street. He was listening with Boris Chaliapin, Feodor's son, to Shostakovich's Symphony No. 7 in C major (the "Leningrad Symphony") for the first time on the radio on July 19, 1942. Chaliapin asked him what he thought of the symphony. Rachmaninoff instantly disliked it, but instead of being critical simply replied, "Let's go and have some tea."[46] Chaliapin did not pose the question a second time.

In her published reminiscences Natalia Rachmaninoff provides some more nuanced details about the aforementioned personality traits:

> I can say about Sergei Vasilievich's character that he was noble-hearted, kind, exceptionally honest, and direct in his assessments of others. He was very strict with respect to other people, but his demands of himself were the same as of others. Sergei Vasilievich was not afraid of stating the most severe truth to others right to their faces, which often astonished and embarrassed me.... I don't think he ever forgot if a person insulted him, although he never spoke of the insult afterwards.[47]

Rachmaninoff was in tune with the spirituality, traditions, and practice of Orthodoxy, both in its theology and on the parish level. In his professional life, in the context not only of what he did for a living but more importantly of who he was, Rachmaninoff became an inheritor of liturgical musical traditions and a contributor to the vitality of those traditions. His role in the evolution of sacred music in Russia is considered one of the most brilliant and influential in the history of this major genre:

> The composers who took part in this singular flowering of choral composition, in the midst of a musical culture dominated by instrumental genres, comprise what has been termed the "New Russian Choral School." Rachmaninoff's compositions [in] this movement encompassed the period temporally: his first sacred choral work ... was composed and first performed in 1893, while his last work in the genre ... was composed and first performed in 1915. [Although Rachmaninoff did not write a large number of sacred works] ... his contributions are among the crowning achievements of the epoch: in terms of scope, musical complexity, and expressive power they overwhelmingly surpass most works written by Rachmaninoff's contemporaries.[48]

And those contemporaries included the most celebrated composers of the era—Tchaikovsky, Rimsky-Korsakov, Balakirev, Liadov, Taneev, Grechaninov, Kalinnikov, Cherepnin, and many others.

According to Orthodox theology and ecclesiology, the faithful are reminded of the presence of God through what they can access through their senses: what they can see, feel, hear, taste, and even smell. They are reminded that God uses physical, material things to convey and set his seal on spiritual, unseen realities. God does not need this reminder, but the faithful do: they need the material reality in order to remind them of the unseen reality of God. "God appeals to our senses in bestowing His Sanctification and redemption on the world. His unseen grace works through and by means of what is seen by [human beings] of flesh and blood."[49] "God truly sets His seal upon physical creation and upon the dual spiritual/physical nature of [the human being]. Matter is not evil, not despicable. It is good . . . It is created" and sanctified "by God in love and for the outpouring of His own glory."[50] Rachmaninoff came of age and matured in the environment of these kinds of theological statements.

Rachmaninoff's documented ties with Russian Orthodox musical groups in Russia until he was forced to leave the country in 1917, and his financial support for the Russian Orthodox Church in the United States in the 1920s and 1930s, affirm his commitment to the faith tradition of his countrymen. In Manhattan (New York) he supported first the St. Nicholas Cathedral, and subsequently the Church of Christ the Savior (which became a major center for the Russian emigration of that period).

Metropolitan Platon (Rozhdestvensky), in a letter of 1926 thanking Rachmaninoff for his financial assistance, stated, "your sacred music tells us what the Church means to you and what you mean to the Church . . . I will always help you and pray for you."[51] In 1932 Rachmaninoff responded to a request from Archimandrite Vitaly (Maksimenko) to help a Russian community of Uniates convert to Russian Orthodoxy in Czechoslovakia; the composer sent $400 (a large sum in this post-Depression era) for this cause. He helped Orthodox church communities in Dresden and Berlin, and in Paris his regular financial support was crucial for the establishment of the distinguished St. Sergius Orthodox Theological Institute. This institute's faculty was comprised of the most outstanding Russian religious-philosophical thinkers of the twentieth century, and their books (now translated into English) make a stunning contribution to modern religious thought and intellectual life.[52] The institute has counted among its faculty such remarkable philosophers and theologians as Sergey Bulgakov, Paul Evdokimov, Georges Florovsky, John Meyendorff, and Aleksandr Schmemann.

Among the qualities associated with Rachmaninoff's religious piety, perhaps the most notable and most remarkable was his ability to forgive his enemies. During World War I, he refused to vilify the Germans who were attacking his homeland. He forgave prominent musicians, such as Aleksandr Glazunov, who almost ruined his career in its early stages. He lost members of his family, his house and belongings, his friends, his country, his language, his religion, his culture, his artistic roots—everything—and yet he was able to forgive those who took these things from him.[53] His is almost the story of Job, and yet he maintained an attitude of devotion in the midst of grief: He continued to love Russia and everything Russian deeply, distinguishing what was Bolshevik and Soviet from what was authentically Russian. Throughout his life he was inspired by beauty, as well as finding solace in the aesthetic principles of Russian Orthodoxy. He expressed his emotions and convictions through his sacred compositions, which remain among his most personal works. To the present time his contributions to the repertoire of choral sacred music in Russia continue to be highly esteemed by conductors and musicians in the international musical arena.

In an act of forgiveness and an effort to unify the Russian emigration in support of the war effort, Rachmaninoff donated the entire proceeds from his concert of November 1, 1941, directly to the Soviet General Consul V. A. Fediushin. By this time for Rachmaninoff his patriotic feelings for his native country eclipsed any political considerations. Rachmaninoff asked Fediushin for something in return—for some of his music scores and especially the master score of the *All-Night Vigil* to be returned to him. The Soviet Union fulfilled his request.[54]

During the years 2004–2007 there was talk in Russian musical circles of proposing Rachmaninoff as a candidate for canonization in the Russian Orthodox Church. The proposal was entertained on the strength alone of his having composed the *All-Night Vigil*, considered by many to be the pinnacle of the thousand-year tradition of Russian Orthodox liturgical music.[55] Every year since the 1920s, to mark the anniversary of Rachmaninoff's birth, at least one church in Moscow courageously has performed the *All-Night Vigil*.[56] Rachmaninoff wanted to have his beloved fifth movement of it, "Lord, now lettest thou thy servant depart in peace," sung at his funeral, but in 1943 in the United States it was not possible to honor his wish. Taken from Luke 2:29–32, the movement's words are as follows: "Lord, now lettest thou thy servant depart in peace, according to thy word: / For mine eyes have seen thy salvation, / Which thou hast prepared before the face of all people; / A light to lighten the Gentiles, and the glory of thy people Israel." These verses are sung toward the end of every Vespers service in Russian Orthodoxy, depicting the radiant emotions of St. Simeon when he first held the Christ Child—Simeon was granted the understanding of Christ's future life and resurrection. For Rachmaninoff the themes of repentance, a peaceful death, salvation, and devotion to God would have encapsulated the main elements of Orthodox Christianity that he held in his mind both as a composer and human being.

NOTES

1. Vladimir Morosan, ed., *Sergei Rachmaninoff: The Complete Choral Works*, Bilingual edition (Madison, CT: Musica Russica, 1994), Series IX, 1–2: xlviii.

2. Krista M. West, *The Garments of Salvation: Orthodox Christian Liturgical Vesture* (Yonkers, NY: St. Vladimir's Seminary Press, 2013), 25–26.

3. Sergei Bertensson and Jay Leyda, *Sergei Rachmaninoff: A Lifetime in Music* (New York: New York UP, 1956; repr., Bloomington, IN: Indiana UP, 2001), 184.

4. S.A. Satina, "Zapiska o S.V. Rakhmaninove," in *Vospominaniia o Rakhmaninove*, ed. Z.A. Apetian, 5th ed. (Moscow: Muzyka, 1988), I: 16.

5. Ibid.

6. Ibid., 18, trans. VZN.

7. Rachmaninoff's reference to "church festival days" has to do with the twelve major feast days of Orthodoxy.

8. In June 1996 the author of this book had the opportunity to stand below the large bell tower beside the St. Sofia Cathedral in Novgorod and witness a dazzling bell-ringing performance after a wedding that had taken place in the medieval cathedral.

9. S.A. Satina, in Apetian, I: 499, trans. VZN.

10. A.I. Ermakov and A.V. Zhogov, comp., *Ivanovka: Vremena. Sobytiya. Sud'by* (Moscow: Irina Arkhipova Foundation, 2003), 75, trans. VZN.

11. Ibid., 148, trans. VZN.

12. Morosan, xlvii.

13. S.I. Savenko, *Sergei Ivanovich Taneev* (Moscow: Muzyka, 1984), 156, trans. VZN.

14. Ibid., l.

15. Ibid., xlix.

16. Geoffrey Norris, *Rachmaninoff* (New York: Oxford University Press, 2001), 148.

17. "John Chrysostom," https://orthodoxwiki.org/John_Chrysostom, accessed July 21, 2021.

18. Morosan, liii.

19. Bertensson and Leyda, 168, edited by VZN.

20. Ibid., 171, 387, 393. The reminiscences of Rachmaninoff were part of a project in 1931 of an American journalist who planned a biography of Rachmaninoff that did not materialize.

21. George Gerich, "Sergei Jaroff and the Don Cossack Choir," December 1, 2015, https://orthochristian.com/88292.html. In the late 1930s Jaroff [Zharov] moved to New York City, settling on 72nd St., which would not be far from where the Rachmaninoffs lived.

22. A note about the type of service celebrated in Rachmaninoff's composition: All too often this choral work is translated as "Vespers." This is incorrect, for the Orthodox Vespers service is not the same as the Vigil service. The Vespers, a shorter service lasting about one hour, is contained in the All-Night Vigil service, which is celebrated more in monasteries than in churches (in the latter the Vigil is often celebrated before or on major feast days). The Vigil service also contains the Divine Liturgy; as a result, this larger service can last for as long as three hours. It is the latter, longer service that is the source for Rachmaninoff's composition.

23. A.D. Kastal'sky, "*Vsenoshchnoe bdenie* S.V. Rakhmaninova," in S.G. Zvereva, ed., *Aleksandr Kastal'sky. Stat'i. Materialy. Vospominaniia. Perepiska* (Moscow: Znak, 2006), 108, trans. VZN.

24. Bertensson and Leyda, paraphrase of 190–91.

25. See the excerpt from Rachmaninoff's letter to Yasser of April 30, 1935, in I.S. Yasser, untitled, in *Pamiati Rakhmaninova*, ed. Sophie Satin [S.A. Satina] (New York: Grenich Printing Corp., 1946), 172–73. An example of an "subconscious counterfeit" in Rachmaninoff's music is the opening musical phrase of his Piano Concerto No. 3, which is strikingly similar to the Kathisma hymn sung on Holy Saturday in the Kievan chant style. The parallel musical example 110a provided by Barrie Martyn in his *Rachmaninoff: Composer, Pianist, Conductor* (Burlington, VT: Ashgate Publishing Co., 2000), 211, is absolutely convincing to the present biographer.

26. Morosan, lxi.

27. Bertensson and Leyda, 191.

28. Morosan, xlvii.

29. Ibid.

30. Bertensson and Leyda, 198–99.

31. Andrey Tarkovsky, *Sculpting in Time* (Austin, TX: University of Texas Press, 1987), 38–39, 43.

32. Norris, 155.

33. Max Harrison, *Rachmaninoff: Life, Works, Recordings* (New York: Continuum, 2005), 163.

34. Ibid., 163–65.

35. n.a., "Ludo Patris," Brussels weekly, May 12, 1933, n.p., quoted in Bertensson and Leyda, 297.

36. Harrison, 164.

37. Very Reverend Paul Lazor, "Introduction" to *Holy Friday Matins* (Yonkers, NY: St. Vladimir's Seminary Press, 1980), 7.

38. Personal interview, Alexandre Rachmaninoff, Senar, Weggis, Switzerland, July 16, 2004.

39. S. Rakhmaninov, Letter of August 8, 1931, in *S. Rakhmaninov. Literaturnoe nasledie. Vospominaniia. Stat'i. Interv'iu. Pis'ma*, ed. Z.A. Apetian (Moscow: Sovetskii kompozitor, 1978), 2: 312, trans. VZN.

40. Rachmaninoff felt a kinship with Fedotov's philosophical thought. The lectures given by the philosopher were organized by the Society of Friends of Russian Culture; Rachmaninoff attended a discussion of at least one of them in December 1942. See Boris Nikitin, *Sergei Rachmaninov. Feodor Chaliapin* (Moscow: OTiSS, 1998), 132–33.

41. N.V. Beketova, "Sergei Rakhmaninov: lichnost' kak simvol kul'turnogo tsykla," in *Tvorchestvo S.V. Rakhmaninova v kontekste mirovoi muzykal'noi kul'tury*, ed. M.A. Klimkova (Tambov: Izd.-vo Tamb. gos. tekh. un-ta, 2003), 10, trans. VZN.

42. Harrison, 88.

43. Barrie Martyn, *Rachmaninoff: Composer, Pianist, Conductor* (Burlington, VT: Ashgate, 1990), 121.

44. Liudmila Kovaleva-Ogorodnova, *Sergei Rakhmaninov* (Sankt-Peterburg: Vita Nova, 2015), II: 165, trans. VZN.

45. Ermakov and Zhogov, trans. and paraphrase of 86.

46. Solomon Volkov, *Shostakovich and Stalin: The Extraordinary Relationship between the Great Composer and the Brutal Dictator* (New York: Alfred A. Knopf, 2004), 181.

47. N.A. Rakhmaninova, "S.V. Rakhmaninov," *Vospominaniia o Rakhmaninove*, ed. Z.A. Apetian, 5th ed. (Moscow: Muzyka, 1988), II: 317, trans. VZN.

48. Morosan, xlvii.

49. "Theophany: The Sacramentality of Matter," in *Go Forth* 17, no. 3 (January 21, 2007), Publication of the Orthodox Church in America.

50. Ibid.

51. S.G. Zvereva, "Blagotvoritel'naya deyatel'nost' Sergeya Rakhmaninova v otnosheniy Russkoi Pravoslavnoi Tserkvi," in *Rakhmaninov—Natsional'naya pamyat' Rossii*, ed. I.N. Vanovskaia (Tambov: Tamb. gos. muz.-ped. in-t im. S.V. Rakhmaninova, 2008), 25, trans. VZN.

52. See Matthew Lee Miller, *The American YMCA and Russian Culture* (New York: Lexington Books, 2013), 201–19.

53. I am grateful to V. I. Antipov for this observation. Personal interview, Moscow, July 3, 2003.

54. Zvereva, in Vanovskaia, 32.

55. I am grateful to V. I. Antipov for this observation. Personal interview, Moscow, July 3, 2003.

56. B. S. Nikitin, personal interview, Moscow, June 13, 2004. The church has not been identified, but Nikitin noted that it was located on Ordynka Street. Moscow has two streets by that name: Bol'shaia Ordynka and Malaia Ordynka.

Chapter 10

Transitions
(1914–1923)

" . . . the sun became black as sackcloth . . . and the moon became as blood"

—Revelation 6:12 (KJV)[1]

During the years of 1914–1918, the Rachmaninoffs experienced tremendous instability and personal tragedy. Russia was involved in the military drama of World War I, which would prove to be a catastrophe, while the country's political system was crumbling before Rachmaninoff's eyes. At a time of musical success and almost total domination of the music scene in Russia (Scriabin had died of an illness in 1915, while Prokofiev and Stravinsky were in Europe), Rachmaninoff was also keenly aware of the new government's hostility toward everything his music and social class represented. In the midst of this chaos, Rachmaninoff's father died suddenly. The circumstances surrounding his death are unclear, but Irina Brandt provides some clues:

> I arrived at Ivanovka in 1916 late . . . while still at the train station, I learned about the death and funeral of Vasily Arkadievich from the coachman Yakov. There were rumors that, after he came to Ivanovka to visit his sister and son, he either fell ill or got drunk, refused to be seen by a doctor. . . . The servants whispered that Vasily Arkadievich had committed suicide, and that for this reason Fr. Nikolay—the priest of the Viazov Church—refused to perform the funeral service . . . People said that Sergei Vasilievich spent a long time talking with the priest. The next day Sergei Vasilievich drove to Viazov alone and stood through both the Matins and the Vespers services.
>
> This kind of secrecy and haste led me to conclude that Vasily Arkadievich had committed suicide. I felt genuinely sorry for this talented, kind, but completely useless and irresponsible person. . . . The next year Varvara Arkadievna

herself, on the one-year anniversary of his death, confirmed the fact of his suicide.²

The political turmoil in Russia and general instability in the world because of World War I made it difficult for Rachmaninoff even to create space in his life for mourning his father. He also sensed that he would lose Ivanovka, the home he had worked so hard to keep and into which he had invested his hard-earned money. It was the only stable home he had ever known. It was as dear to him as an icon that had been blessed, with each pathway among the birches and pines well-trodden. He would be giving up sounds of the cows lowing in the distance, and a silence so pure as to be interrupted only by the occasional clip-clop of a horse's hooves as a horse and wagon would draw twilight across the horizon. Frogs would croak for their mates in the ponds on the estate, and people could see their mirror image in the clear pond water. The scent of cherry blossoms would hang in the air, not far from the lilac bushes and lilies-of-the-valley near the estate's main entrance. The peasants who worked there would keep a samovar hot for tea and sweet rolls available all day at Rachmaninoff's favorite gazebo by the pond. Rachmaninoff would long for Ivanovka all his life, as an ascetic longs for the desert. In a section of his reminiscences written when he was already living in America he revealed in detail:

> In every Russian person there exists a longing for the earth, greater than in any other nation. In other nationalities, for example, the Americans, I don't notice it at all. It seems that here [in the U.S.] such a longing is absent.
> When I speak about a longing for the earth, don't assume that in this feeling I have in mind the love for [material] acquisition, i.e., that feeling best of all expressed in the famous story by Leo Tolstoy about the horse "Linen-Measurer." The horse relates that people possess the need to call as many things as possible "mine." No, in the thoughts of the Russian people about the earth there is some kind of striving for peacefulness, for quiet, for the contemplation of nature in which they live; and in part, the striving for seclusion, for aloneness. I think that each Russian person has something in common with a hermit.
> I began to speak about this longing for the earth because I possess it as well. The Russian people lived in this manner: peasants did not ever abandon their plot of land. If they were separated from their land, they traveled to new locations [plots of land] in search of happiness. People of greater means would spend half a year on their land, specifically summertime, which was associated with more intensive work cultivating the soil. The second half of the year they would live in the cities . . . I always strove to go to Ivanovka either for a vacation and complete peacefulness, or, to the contrary, for sedentary work, to which the surrounding tranquility is conducive. (How wise it is, that in your country [the U.S.] many universities and colleges are constructed away from cities.)

Shall I describe this estate [of Ivanovka] to you? It did not possess the type of natural beauty that is associated with mountains, cliffs, or seas. This estate was in the steppes, and the steppe is also a sea, without end and limitless, where in place of water there was nothing but fields of wheat, oats, etc., from horizon to horizon. People often praise the sea air, but if you only knew how much better is the air of the steppes with its aroma of the earth and everything growing in it—and there is no seasickness. . . . During the last years I spent there I very much enjoyed coordinating the agricultural work on the estate. This enthusiasm of mine was not shared by my family, whose members feared that agricultural interests would take me away from musical activity. But I industriously worked during the winters, "made money" by giving concerts, and in the summers I invested most of that money into the land, making improvements in its management, livestock, and equipment. . . . In August [1914] the war began. I don't want to talk about that time.[3]

Rachmaninoff made the memorable statement, "I have said that to that place, Ivanovka, I always aspired to return. With my hand on my heart, I must say that even to this day I am striving to return there."[4] He had indeed invested enormous financial and physical resources in maintaining the estate of Ivanovka. It had been mortgaged several times by the Satin family, and by the beginning of World War I he owned it outright. The various activities and upkeep necessary to keep this enterprise functioning smoothly were shared by all those, peasants and aristocrats, who lived on the estate or in the village nearby. Rachmaninoff took great pleasure in the work: ploughing, gathering hay, assessing the condition of the stables and horses, discussing various tools and machines that were being improved in function, and taking children of the estate and the nearby village on rides along the dirt roads in his new car. The estate's routines were determined mainly by cyclical, rather than linear calendar time; they were well known, providing a sense of certainty and security. Photographs taken by enthusiast photographer Varvara Arkadievna show her daughter Natalia and friends with farm tools in their hands after gathering hay, her daughter Sofia interacting with kindness with the dogs on the estate (she patiently tended to their medical needs the best she could), and various members of the estate community carrying out the many daily tasks necessary to maintain order according to the cycles of the seasons—whether in education, translation from foreign languages, labor for the estate (cooking, cleaning, washing), or errands to Tambov.

A great deal of Bolshevik propaganda misrepresented, because their version served specific political ends, the generally successful and intertwined relationship between these two social groups of Russia.[5] However, with the upheavals of World War I and instability in the national government, a growing discontent among some of the peasants at Ivanovka adversely affected what had been a well-established way of life. Despite his love for Ivanovka—the estate, way of life, and land—Rachmaninoff was concerned enough about political developments both in Russia and internationally to think seriously about selling this ancestral home. Irina Brandt worked at Ivanovka in the summer of 1916—she had not been there for two years—and recalled:

> When I arrived at Ivanovka the next summer I was struck by how run-down it was. Traces of fires had been patched up. In the *fligel* [house next to the main house] part of the windows had been covered up with bricks. The *fligel* itself had been painted in a terrifying shade of yellowish-brown. The main house's two-story veranda, which looked out onto the fountain, had been broken apart. I remember that traces of fires were on many of the outbuildings. Everything looked sad and depressing. . . . At Ivanovka the guards started keeping many dogs. These aggressive dogs were kept in kennels during the day, but at night were let out on chains to run around virtually the entire estate. They barked angrily. And at night, especially when it rained, it was just horrific.
> Sergei Vasilievich quarrelled for a long time about something with Natalia Aleksandrovna, Sofia Aleksandrovna, and Varvara Arkadievna. Some men came to see him, and people said that they came from Moscow. Rumors were circulating that Sergei Vasilievich came up with the idea to sell Ivanovka, but his relatives were opposed to it, and he couldn't at all convince them to do it.
> Summer 1916 at Ivanovka was very nerve-wracking. Everyone quarrelled with everyone else, people were constantly frowning. In the course of all the years of my working at Ivanovka, I don't recall any other time like that.[6]

Only the most dire and heart-wrenching circumstances could have prompted Rachmaninoff to consider taking the step of selling Ivanovka.

Despite the unstable environment at Ivanovka and in Russia in general, Rachmaninoff found the strength of will and inspiration to compose his second set of Études-Tableaux (Op. 39). He worked on these nine pieces in the fall of 1916 after his troubling stay at Ivanovka, and in February 1917. He first performed eight of them in Petrograd on November 29, 1916; two of them, No. 5 (Appassionato, E flat minor) and No. 9 (Allegro moderato, Tempo di marcia, D major) bear a completion date in February 1917. Barrie Martyn rightly observes that these pieces reflect a "dark introspection" on Rachmaninoff's part—his father had died that summer, and he was worried to the point of panicking about the outcome of the war and the political events in Russia. Martyn writes:

> Eight of the nine pieces are in the minor key, and the majority of them feature *Dies irae* in one form or another. Although there is no proof whatever this was due to the death of Rachmaninoff's father, the obsessive recurrence of the chant

throughout the set is likely to have come from something more than the usual mystical fascination it had for the composer.⁷

He wanted to dedicate this piano cycle to Nina Koshetz, but because of talk of their being more than professionally involved, decided not to take that step. This was Rachmaninoff's second foray into this personally created genre: he had composed a set of six Études-Tableaux (Op. 33) in 1911 (three additional Études for this set were omitted from publication at the time by the composer). What these supposed pictorial representations in music underscored, and not for the first time, was Rachmaninoff's compositional and pianistic connection with Chopin's twenty-four piano études and with the tradition of writing music with underlying poetic narratives established by Chopin's ballades and Liszt's Transcendental études.⁸

The major cataclysm of the Bolshevik Revolution of 1917 hung in the air. The Russian nobility felt its traditional way of life disappearing, evaporating with each passing day—and it was clear that the new political system would cause a great deal of trouble for the aristocracy as the ruling class. The Rachmaninoffs and Satins did indeed lose Ivanovka, as part of a massive social restructuring by the revolutionaries. One of the earliest laws set into motion by the Bolsheviks was the land decree of October 26, 1917:

> [the decree] abolished all private ownership without compensation, and called on village and *volost* (rural district) land committees to redistribute the land thus secured to the peasants on an egalitarian basis. The decree was couched in the words of a Peasant Congress of June 1917. It reflected the Socialist Revolutionary programme and gave the peasants what most of them wanted at the time, while making no mention of the ultimate Bolshevik aim of nationalization of the land.⁹

Thus the Bolsheviks intended to betray everyone in all class categories. But this eventual nationalization of land was as yet unknown to the peasants. Believing they were empowered and finding themselves in an atmosphere of lawlessness and fluidity, peasants in Tambov Region (in which Tambov and Ivanovka were located) roamed the countryside armed with weapons, threatening the landowners and their families and often setting their estates on fire. Not only the nobility and their estates, but Russian Orthodox churches as well—religion as a whole—were being demolished and even dynamited in the cities.¹⁰

Initially attracted by the promises of the Socialist Revolutionaries and Bolsheviks that a few basic national programs would improve their lives, the peasants came to trust only those of their own social class. In the black-earth region of southern Russia (which included Tambov) support for the Communists in general was not strong; thus the looting and accompanying violence were aimed against the new government as well as expressing frustration at the suffering that all classes of Russia had endured at least since the start of World War I in 1914.

Peasants' revolts against their landowner employers, however, by no means represented a unified movement; in 1920–1921 the Tambov Rebellion was a major peasant revolt against the Bolshevik regime in response to grain requisitioning for the cities without compensating the peasants. Shortages of food supplies, and the Bolsheviks' treatment of the peasants, had the effect of turning peasants and city dwellers against each other. The peasants heard the sensationalist propaganda from the new government that the "bourgeoisie" in the cities would not buy their food, while the city dwellers were falsely told by the new government that peasants in the countryside were refusing to provide them with food. Many railroad lines were blocked, further disrupting the movement of food and other necessities.

During the same month in which the Rachmaninoffs were to leave Russia, December 1917, the following political attitude toward undesirable classes was promulgated by Vladimir Lenin:

> Already in December 1917 Lenin had called for "a purge of the Russian land from all vermin," by which he meant the "idle rich," "priests," "bureaucrats," and "slovenly and hysterical intellectuals." And on 31 August 1918 *Pravda* exhorted:
> "The towns must be cleansed of this bourgeois putrefaction. . . . All who are dangerous to the cause of the revolution must be exterminated."[11]

The "intellectuals" referred to a broad category that included writers, philosophers, artists, and musicians, who overnight became undesirables and "enemies of the people." In the following year the so-called Red Terror would sharpen the persecution of all but two classes: "It became unnecessary for an actual crime to be proven against any person of non-worker or non-peasant origin. His very existence could be held to imply that he was at war against the Soviet system, and therefore with the people as a whole."[12]

All features of Imperial Russia were to be eradicated by any means necessary. However, religious belief in a divine power was replaced by a fanatical belief in the "wisdom" of the Communist Party and its leaders. As philosopher Nicolas Berdiaev, who himself was forcibly exiled on the "philosophers' ship" in 1922, explained:

> The Communist State is quite different from the ordinary lay, secularized State. It is a sacred, "theocratic" State, which takes over the functions that belong to the church. It forms men's souls, gives them an obligatory creed, demands their whole soul, exacts from them not only "what is Caesar's" but even "what is

God's." It is most important to grasp this pseudo-theocratic nature of the Communist State. Its whole structure is determined by it.[13]

Because the Bolsheviks aimed to overthrow the tsar of Imperial Russia, it was Russia herself and the foundational features of Russian culture that they were determined to destroy utterly and completely. These included Russian Orthodoxy, the monarchy and nobility, intellectuals who were broadly educated, and artists who did not create works that expressed the ideology of the Soviet state—even though during these years (1917–1930) it was not clear to anyone exactly what were the characteristics of ideologically acceptable creative works.

Even music, which would seem to manifest a universal language with meanings accessible to all humankind, became a target for the Bolsheviks. All genres of musical expression had to be twisted into specific forms that unambiguously served the state. In classical music history, composers such as Beethoven created incomparable masterpieces (the Symphony #9 in D minor, Op. 125) that have been analyzed for their intrinsic greatness but also can be viewed through a nationalist lens. As Martin Stokes notes:

> Music is intensely involved in the propagation of dominant classifications, and has been a tool in the hands of new states . . . of those classes [in this case, of those subscribing to a rigid ideology] which have the highest stake in these new social formations. This control is principally enacted through state control or influence over universities, conservatories, and archives, and is disseminated through its media systems.
>
> Musical styles can be made emblematic of national identities in complex and often contradictory ways.[14]

It was this association with Russia's imperial heritage that the Bolsheviks wished to disrupt, and hence music, just as philosophy, literature, film, and painting, had to be "made" according to specific formulas that would be codified in the early 1930s under Stalin. Art for art's sake, to express a person's individual hopes, dreams, emotions, and convictions—the creative process by which Rachmaninoff conceived and composed his music—would be virtually forbidden and punishable by the 1930s. Filmmaker Andrei Tarkovsky describes:

> By means of art man takes over reality through a subjective experience. . . . An artistic discovery occurs each time as a new and unique image of the world, a hieroglyphic of absolute truth. It appears as a revelation, as a momentary, passionate wish to grasp intuitively and at a stroke all the laws of this world.
>
> Art is born and takes hold wherever there is a timeless and insatiable longing for the spiritual, for the ideal: that longing which draws people to art . . . true affirmation of the self can only be expressed in sacrifice.
>
> Art acts above all on the soul, shaping its spiritual structure.[15]

The absolute, infinite, spiritualized, and deeply personal approach to art that nourished Sergei Rachmaninoff's creative inner world—and that of an entire generation of Russian writers, musicians, and artists—was rejected, despised, ridiculed, and eventually made criminal under the new Bolshevik regime.

The experiences and arrest of Rachmaninoff's cousin Aleksandr Siloti, who had become a brilliant transcriber of classical music and trend-setting impresario in St. Petersburg, made a profound impression on him. In May 1917 Siloti had been appointed to the position of director of the prestigious Mariinsky Theater in St. Petersburg. The formerly magnificent city was in shambles, because the revolutionaries had destroyed the heating, electrical, and water systems. People's wages were also cancelled, and all the performance halls were nationalized—which meant that directors such as Siloti would lose their artistic control over concert programs, employees, and other aspects of concert program operations. In early December, only weeks before Rachmaninoff and his family would leave Russia forever, Siloti refused to turn over the keys to the Imperial Box of the Mariinsky Theater to the Bolshevik government, stating that he would give them only to a "legal" government. This statement brought about his arrest the following day. His son Levko was also arrested on vague charges, threatened with death, and then released. One can imagine how these events, faced by his cousin's family, affected Rachmaninoff.[16] The following description of the Siloti family's living quarters further illustrates the Bolsheviks' humiliation of the aristocracy:

> As a living place for his wife and five children he was given the kitchen of his own house and a small adjacent room. The rest of the house was occupied by young men of the new regime where they led a life of debauchery. In order to survive, Siloti and his family had to do the most impossible and degrading things. The only valuable they managed to hide was a necklace.[17]

After being arrested by the Cheka (secret police) and accused of being a "saboteur" against the new government, Siloti was thrown into prison for a brief time, then released and kept under house arrest. The Rachmaninoffs heard nothing from or about him for several years. Siloti availed himself of the first legal opportunity to leave the country, and emigrated first to Finland and Germany, and finally made his way to New York in December 1921. He performed in concerts in America, impressing his peers and audiences with his pianistic brilliance. Several years later, in 1926, he was offered a position at the prestigious Juilliard School, where he taught until 1942.

Rachmaninoff himself had to take his turn at guarding at night the premises of the Moscow apartment building on Strastnoi Boulevard in which he and his family were living that year, which had been transformed into a communal residence. He also was irritated at having to attend meetings with the other residents of the building, meetings infused with political rhetoric. The Rachmaninoffs were living at this residence on October 25, 1917 (New Style November 7, 1917), the fateful date when the Bolsheviks seized power in Russia—with the horrifying image of the storming of the Winter Palace in St. Petersburg that was promulgated worldwide and later made the subject of Sergei Eisenstein's film *October* (*Ten Days That Shook the World*, 1927). The palpable changes in how the landowning nobility was treated and perceived were radical; because of the swift transformation and even destruction of the various civic institutions of Russia on which Rachmaninoff had depended, he realized that he and his family were facing dangerous times, with an unpredictable outcome. He worried that it would be only a matter of time before the new regime would arrest his family or force him into an ideology that would constrain his freedom to compose music that was genuine and meaningful.

These were some of the major factors that led Rachmaninoff to decide that he had to leave Russia. He hoped it would be for only a short time. The violent Communist government had targeted his social class for annihilation and seduced peasants into believing they now owned all the land. Regardless of how they aligned themselves politically, as supporting or opposing the new government, the peasants began to rise up and threaten Ivanovka—eventually it was "looted and reduced to dereliction."[18] The son of one of the grooms who worked for the Rachmaninoffs and Satins at Ivanovka recalled:

> In the fall [of 1917] the landlord arrived [at Ivanovka]; the estate was almost completely torn apart. He arrived with Sofia Aleksandrovna. They gathered together some papers and put them into trunks, took some books, some kind of pictures, and then Yakov drove them, not to Rzhaks [train station], but to Tambov. When he returned, Yakov led the three best horses into his own farmyard; the peasants in only a few more days dragged away everything that remained. Davyd Kupriakov set up a flea market of their things right in the wing of the main house.
>
> When the Antonov [peasant] gangs were in the area, almost every day they would bring someone to Ivanovka and kill him there; they would throw the bodies down a large well behind the stable.[19]

The patriarchal way of life that Rachmaninoff valued and that nourished his creative springs was being systematically destroyed. Churches were ransacked, priceless icons were desecrated, and the church hierarchy was interrogated and intimidated. The bells Rachmaninoff loved were silenced, and they were torn away from their supports and hurled several stories to the ground. Orthodox believers often witnessed this desecration of their faith, standing in a shocked silence or weeping quietly in fear.

A militant atheism declaring itself the sole source of veneration and legitimizing any means at all in order to achieve its communistic ends replaced the ancient form of Christianity that taught humility, active love, and asceticism for the purpose of growing closer to God. Human life lost its absolute value, each individual instead becoming expendable as a cog in the machinery of the state. Rachmaninoff and his family could not have known this at the time, but their (in effect) escape from Russia saved them from the horrors of the Civil War and ensuing famines of the early 1920s. They would hear from afar about the suffering of their friends and those relatives who remained behind.

During these difficult months and years Rachmaninoff continued his music activities: he conducted the Bolshoi Theater Orchestra in a major concert of his own music on January 7, 1917—a real triumph for him (the program consisted of *The Crag*, *The Isle of the Dead*, and *The Bells*). He did not know it, but this would be his last time conducting an orchestra in Russia. He generously organized a series of memorial/charity concerts for Scriabin's family after the composer-pianist's untimely death of septicemia, and he gave several charity concerts in Moscow in support of the Russian Army during the war years. In one of them on the date when the February 1917 Revolution started in St. Petersburg he broke a record of endurance and pianism by performing *three* piano concertos: Tchaikovsky's Piano Concerto No. 1, and his own Piano Concertos Nos. 2 and 3. Despite the turbulence all around him, which included regular gunfire near his apartment building, he worked on a revision of his Piano Concerto No. 1 in F# minor. He traveled to Ivanovka in April 1917, discovering that members of the Socialist Revolutionary Party had taken over the property and were using it as a headquarters for their regional operations. The entire way of life Rachmaninoff had known, and monarchist system of government to which he was accustomed, was being undermined.

Rachmaninoff's views on the monarchy as a system of government are not entirely clear, but if one recalls that he was an adolescent in 1881 when the generally popular tsar-reformer Aleksandr II was assassinated (with the ensuing social anxiety and ultra-conservative measures of his son Aleksandr III), it is not hard to conjecture that he strongly opposed radical social change. Because of the vicissitudes experienced by both him and his close friend Chaliapin, the two friends held the same negative views about the Bolsheviks. Rachmaninoff even stated by comparison with how violently and unilaterally the Bolsheviks made decisions about destroying the traditional sociopolitical system, that under Tsar Nicholas II life was much more democratic. His own comment to Marietta Shaginian that he hated any kind of extremism would also confirm that he would have preferred Russia's traditional monarchy or an evolving constitutional monarchy to the violent upending of everything he held dear. He and others hoped that the radical turn of events was only temporary and that the Bolsheviks would not be able to hold power for long.

But in 1917 the writing was on the wall. Rachmaninoff conferred with Aleksandr Siloti about the possibility of leaving Russia, confiding his intentions only to his family and closest friends. How could an exit visa be arranged at such a chaotic and dangerous time? Salvation came through connections and a well-timed invitation from Sweden for a tour of ten recitals in several Scandinavian countries: Rachmaninoff accepted the offer immediately. It was more than serendipitous, because he and his family were among the last families to receive a visa to leave Russia—which took place on December 23, 1917. Rachmaninoff left from Moscow for St. Petersburg (renamed "Petrograd" since the beginning of World War I) by himself to obtain the documents for departure for his family in advance. The only person who saw him off at the train station in Moscow was Sofia Satina, his sister-in-law; it must have been a terrible moment, for they surely wondered if they would ever see each other again. When the final arrangements had been made and Rachmaninoff's family had joined him, they departed from Russia at the Petrograd train station. Chaliapin sent them some caviar and bread he had baked himself, along with a note to say goodbye. This thoughtful gesture from his longtime friend and musical collaborator touched Rachmaninoff deeply. One can imagine the sadness, bitterness, and genuine fear that the Rachmaninoffs experienced during their final moments of departing from Russia. Rachmaninoff's longtime friend from Dresden, the well-educated amateur musician Nikolay von Struve, was to travel with them to Finland and finally to Sweden.

Rachmaninoff was so concerned about being detained on the Russian border that he followed all the customs directions to the letter, which meant that he and his family took a minimum of their belongings with them in their departure from their homeland. The contents of their Moscow apartment would be looked after by Maria Ivanova. Sergei and Natalia took with them only a small amount of money (the maximally allowed sum of five hundred rubles per person), their personal belongings, some of his notebooks with drafts of compositions-in-progress, and the scores of only two large-scale works: the first act of Rachmaninoff's unfinished opera *Monna Vanna* (based on the play by Maurice Maeterlinck) and Rimsky-Korsakov's opera *The Golden Cockerel*. It is noteworthy that the plot of Maeterlinck's play, on which the opera is based, resolves with a rare happy ending. Surely at some level of his thinking Rachmaninoff was longing for the happy ending in his own existential circumstances. Instead, the reality that awaited him in Copenhagen was a demanding period of intensive practice in a foreign country in the midst of personal anxiety for his extended family and friends still in Russia.

The recital tour on which Rachmaninoff was embarking very likely saved his and his family's lives, or, at the very least, spared them the struggles for survival encountered by their artist and musician friends who chose to remain in Russia or did not have a way to leave at that time. Even if the Rachmaninoffs' lives were spared by the Bolsheviks, the dramatic changes they would have had to endure to their way of life, along with the necessary re-education for artists who would be forced to produce their artworks as propaganda in service to the newly and violently forming Soviet state, and loss of their estate and financial resources—all these features of a militant communism would have destroyed the Rachmaninoffs in spirit. Among those who stayed behind were Chaliapin (who as a peasant was not in any immediate danger, but who left Russia permanently in 1922 on a European tour), writer Marietta Shaginian, and opera singer Antonina Nezhdanova.

Rachmaninoff's tour was planned for six months, from February to July of 1918. In a state of anxiety the Rachmaninoffs left Petrograd for Helsinki, traveling through southern Finland on an open sledge that exposed them to the harsh winter winds and snow. In Helsinki they transferred to a ship that carried them to Stockholm, and traveled from there to Denmark: in January 1918 they decided to settle in Copenhagen, in order for Rachmaninoff to prepare for his coming performances. If one imagines the circumstances, one can also grasp in the mind's eye the complete disorientation the Rachmaninoff family experienced during the Christmas and New Year's holidays (celebrated by the Russian Orthodox on the Julian calendar, on which December 25 is marked on January 7 of the Gregorian calendar). Christ's Nativity and a brand new year normally would hold the promise of joyous festivities with family and friends, but for the Rachmaninoffs the year ushered in a lonely period of displacement and wondering if they would ever return to their homeland. They missed attending a radiantly joyous service of the liturgical year (second only to Pascha, the Feast of Feasts)—the Nativity of Christ. Along with the loss of the New Year's church service, the absence of these two liturgies in their lives would have weakened them spiritually and only increased their anxiety about their own immediate future and the future of their ravaged homeland Russia. However, Rachmaninoff fulfilled all the obligations of his recital tour.

In July 1918, Rachmaninoff's grueling Scandinavian tour was concluded. He had performed a series of twelve concerts in Denmark, Sweden, and Norway, with the proceeds from them enabling him to improve his family's financial affairs. He had a complex decision to make: Should he take the chance of returning to Russia or remain abroad and develop himself professionally there? That year as well his brother-in-law Vladimir, his niece Sofia's father, was arrested and imprisoned in Moscow—for no other reason than being a member of the nobility.[20] (Sofia's mother managed to bribe a guard and secure her husband's release.) Rachmaninoff needed time to recover from the shock of leaving behind all the features of the country and culture that were familiar to him and reorient himself in Europe. But Europe was ravaged and exhausted by the years of World War I; as a result, both Russia and Europe seemed unstable. The political situation in Russia was worsening, rather than improving. Rachmaninoff worried about earning enough to support his wife and two daughters. Composing was out of the question, for he needed peace, stability, continuity, and most of all, inspiration for the creative springs to flow. And the earnings from composition would not necessarily be stable and regular. He would have to radically transform his musical identity, and, moreover, in a different artistic context from the one in which he had been trained. Although his studies, both as a student and as a professional, included a knowledge of Western classical music, his piano recitals and concerts had focused mainly on the Russia tradition and mainly his own music. He set himself the difficult task of rebranding himself as a virtuoso pianist who would ideally tour as a recitalist and perform with major world orchestras. His composing work would have to take a back seat, at least for the foreseeable future. This was a demand that he logically had to place on himself—to suppress his stirrings for composition, in order to concentrate exclusively on building a formidable technique and committing to memory a large number of Western classical works. The fact that he was able to accomplish such an enormous task without falling into utter despair provides concrete evidence of his steely resolve and perseverance—for if he were to fail in this undertaking, his own and his family's financial well-being would be compromised, if not destroyed. Moreover, he would have to continue to prepare new repertoire in the Western classical canon virtually every year.[21]

Rachmaninoff spent the months between July and November of 1918 preparing a rewarding and marketable piano program that he could perform to audiences in the United States. His new repertoire included works by Western classical composers, such as Bach, Beethoven, Mozart, Chopin, Debussy, Grieg, Liszt, Mendelssohn, Scarlatti, Schubert, and Schumann, among others. His considerable efforts were fruitful. He would add to this repertoire each year, building an impressive selection of well-known masterpieces from the Western classical canon for his newly minted concert career. Those who observed and knew him during the period of his European and American years would comment many times on how hard he worked. No doubt because of his unstable childhood and young adulthood, his determination to be successful was fueled by the desire to protect his two daughters from a similar fate.

The situation was critical, and so was Rachmaninoff's consideration: he took calculated risks that were in line with his principles. In Europe when he was virtually penniless and jobless with a wife and two daughters to support, he turned down three prestigious job offers in America: On two occasions he was offered the conductorship of the Boston Symphony Orchestra, and he was offered that same position in the Cincinnati Symphony Orchestra. Natalia Rachmaninoff's devotion and mettle were tested during this time, for she was extremely worried about how her family would survive, and yet her husband had turned down three outstanding conducting offers with major American symphony orchestras. Even if her trust in his judgment was complete, after the family's recent departure—even escape—from a country in chaos, her emotions would have been strained to their limit. After all, they were no longer in Russia with extensive family connections; they were in foreign lands left to their own instincts for survival. During these first years away from the Soviet Union, before the restrictions for travel were tightened, the Rachmaninoffs' former house manager Marina was able to travel to Europe to bring him some of his manuscripts. She found the Rachmaninoff family very different from how she remembered them: she noted that they were all thin and very distracted and that Rachmaninoff worked a great deal.[22]

Rachmaninoff was concerned about supporting his family, for he had known plenty of instability and even scarce means in his childhood and young adulthood. But his musician's experience cautioned him against accepting a prominent position for which he might be unprepared. The three conducting positions would involve exhaustive study of Western music scores that were not as familiar to him as the Russian ones, and he would have little time for composing or further improving his piano performance techniques. In addition, he was experienced enough to know that a position as music director of a major symphony orchestra would also involve negotiating politics and intrigues behind the scenes—moreover, all this in a new country and language. His reasoning was sound, and his wife, as a professionally trained pianist who also knew the music world, understood his logic and supported his decisions.

Rachmaninoff was a discerning and practical man, but he also had a higher vision for his musical gifts. Based on the enthusiastic reception of his recitals in Europe, he made an educated guess that both financial security and personal satisfaction for him would lie in concertizing as pianist and occasional conductor. After careful reflection and discussions with a perspicacious wife, Rachmaninoff began to make concrete plans for a concert performance career. Before he left Europe, the wealthy émigré Russian banker Boris Abramovich Kamenka "heard of the risk that Rachmaninoff was taking—to live in the United States for a while before being able to work there—he advanced him enough to cover a considerable delay in employment, an assistance that the composer always recalled with deep gratitude."[23] In addition, just after the Rachmaninoffs boarded the Norwegian steamer that would take them to America, a courier located them and handed Sergei Rachmaninoff a box filled with cash (presumably another expression of Kamenka's generosity).[24] He sailed to America with his family from Oslo, Norway, on the ship the *Bergensfjord* in the dangerous waters of the Atlantic Ocean on November 1, 1918, ten days before the end of World War I. The atmosphere on the ship during the crossing was tense and subdued; to avoid detection by the enemy, the ship's windows had to be blacked out at night.

The *Bergensfjord* arrived on the shores of New York on November 11, Armistice Day—the celebrations of which were somewhat bewildering to the tired but relieved travelers. Once in the United States, Rachmaninoff's friends and colleagues, such as Josef Hofmann and Fritz Kreisler, helped him to become oriented in the ways of the musical world in this new country and culture. Kreisler in particular would become one of Rachmaninoff's closest friends and musical collaborators in the United States. The family initially settled in uptown Manhattan near the church they would attend, the St. Nicholas Cathedral on 15 East 97th St. between Fifth and Madison Avenues. Tsar Nicholas II had donated 7,500 rubles for the church building, which was consecrated in 1901. St. Nicholas Cathedral provided a necessary spiritual succor, but also connected the Rachmaninoffs with other Russian émigrés—all of whom were profoundly disoriented, yet struggling to make sense of the ways of a new country, culture, and language. They were a well-educated group with a strong sense of propriety and traditional values.

The Rachmaninoffs quickly became integrated into this lively Russian community endeavoring with considerable energy and hard work to make its way in the United States. Perhaps more importantly, the international and American music communities were well aware of Rachmaninoff's towering musical stature and prestige—it was in their interest to help him get settled in America so that he could continue to contribute his performances and compositions to the music world, which would make money for everyone involved. During his first concert tour of the United States between November 1909 and January 1910 his abilities as a musician and appeal to American audiences were noted by the music community, and in November 1918 (only twelve years since that tour) there still existed a fresh memory of the earlier tour. Since news of the Rachmaninoffs' arrival had traveled quickly in New York, they were pleasantly overwhelmed by well-wishers and persons associated with the American music scene. Offers for concerts, endorsements, booking agents, player piano companies producing piano rolls, and recording companies poured in. This massive, enthusiastic welcome of Rachmaninoff to one of America's most culturally sophisticated metropolises vindicated his decision to leave Europe for a career in the New World. Bertensson and Leyda describe Rachmaninoff's impact on the music world in America:

For musicians the arrival of Rachmaninoff was news more immediately joyful than the armistice. . . . In New York at that time were Hofmann, Kreisler, Zimbalist, Elman, Ysaye, and Prokofiev, who had also just arrived from Russia . . . Everyone had something to offer the newcomer. Some offered him money, some recommended their favorite concert bureaus, others tutored him in what to say and how to behave in doing business with Americans. Prokofiev paid his tribute by including works by Rachmaninoff in his first New York recital.[25]

Because Rachmaninoff's knowledge of English was only rudimentary, it was vital for him to assemble a staff that would enable him to organize his professional activities. He decided to enter into a contract with the concert bureau of Charles Ellis, who had made a positive impression on him in negotiations with the Boston Symphony. Rachmaninoff made an excellent choice in Ellis, who is considered America's first professional orchestra manager. He was experienced, efficient, and very personable. He was Rachmaninoff's manager between 1918 and 1923; when he retired, management of Rachmaninoff's concerts would pass to Charles Foley. Foley had been Ellis's representative who traveled with Rachmaninoff to ensure that the details of his concert locations—transportation, hotel stays, local venue staff, management of stage details—were in place and running smoothly. Because Foley was promoted to be the head of the concert bureau at Ellis's retirement in 1923, and in this new capacity could no longer be away from his responsibilities for long and complicated concert tours, Charles Spalding became the new representative of the bureau who would accompany Rachmaninoff. While Rachmaninoff grew very fond of Spalding, it was Foley who would be trusted with the most important management details of his music activities until 1937. Foley would also manage many of Rachmaninoff's business affairs, eventually becoming an intimate friend of the Rachmaninoff family; interestingly, in the 1920s and 1930s he was also the manager of violinist and close friend of Rachmaninoff's Fritz Kresler. Charles Foley, Inc. became Rachmaninoff's music publisher and adviser to the Rachmaninoff family after Sergei's death. It is likely that he and Irina Rachmaninoff Wolkonsky were involved as more than just friends.[26]

In addition to setting up a contractual agreement with a concert bureau, Rachmaninoff gave his name in endorsement of the Steinway piano and developed a lifelong warm friendship with the Steinway family in the process. His entry into the American music world during the period of 1918–1925 was also auspicious since it coincided with major advances made in the film and recording industries: Rachmaninoff signed a recording contract with the Edison Company. Perhaps most of all he needed a secretary to help him determine and coordinate his responses to all this good fortune.

Dagmar Rybner, a Danish-American musician who had exchanged letters with Rachmaninoff while he was still in Russia, sent the Rachmaninoffs at their hotel a gracious note of welcome and offered her help. The next day Natalia Rachmaninoff invited her to their hotel. Rybner recalled:

> Needless to say, I dropped all my plans for the day (and many to follow) and rushed to the hotel, grabbing a bunch of roses along the way. I was greeted by Mme. Rachmaninoff, though there was no sign of him, but after a little while the curtains of the adjoining room moved slightly, and out of the corner of my eye—I saw him peering at me. Soon, very timidly, he came in, with his equally shy younger daughter Tatiana . . . He pointed to his piano covered with letters, telegrams, and messages and asked me to help him with "all that." From then on I took charge, unraveling the tangle of mail and telephone calls, and later attending to the mass of problems that he was unable to cope with, partly from not knowing the English language, as well as being unaccustomed to American ways.[27]

Rybner remained Rachmaninoff's secretary for many years, becoming a trusted friend to the family as well. Her father Martin Cornelius Rybner was at that time head of Columbia University's Department of Music, a composer, and concert pianist and violinist. Not surprisingly, Prof. Rybner was an influential member of New York's musical societies: Among other responsibilities that he held, he was a Governor of the prestigious Bohemian Club and highly supportive of Rachmaninoff's nomination for membership.

The Bohemian Club was established formally in New York in May 1908, with the goals of promoting "good fellowship, camaraderie, and the encouragement of the art of music and its practitioners," and at a later point of providing aid for the "social welfare of needy musicians."[28] Its incorporation in the State of New York utilized a more formal language for the Club's goals— "to promote social intercourse among its members, to further the cause of music and the interests of musicians." The Club became a nexus for many of the most prominent musicians in the international concert arena; soon after it was founded its first guest of honor at the Hotel Astor in January 1909 was Gustaf Mahler. Anne McLean describes:

> The Bohemians gave the widest rein to the planning of social activities: from informal Smokers to some of the most elaborate and sumptuous banquets ever presented in New York; from hilarious cabarets to serious chamber and operatic concerts, Mozart's *Der Schauspieldirektor*, for example. Their music-making from the outset also encouraged contemporary music and works that stood outside normal concert fare.[29]

Sergei Rachmaninoff was accepted as a member of the Club in 1919 and would remain in it until his death in 1943.

On December 8, 1918, Rachmaninoff played his first recital, which took place in Symphony Hall in Boston with the Boston Symphony. He performed pieces that he worked extremely hard to prepare in Europe as part of his newly expanded repertoire in the months after he left Russia. The following day's review of the recital written by H. T. Parker for the *Transcript* not only set the tone for Rachmaninoff's reception by American audiences but also surely must have been reassuring for Rachmaninoff—for even with the warm welcome he had received upon arrival in New York, the stakes were high for him to initiate and maintain a successful concertizing career in the United States:

> No more impressive figure has crossed the stage of Symphony Hall these many years than Mr. Rakhmaninov when he came first to the piano yesterday afternoon. . . . Plainly the past had worn him, yet had not left him in the present wearied. Obviously Mr. Rakhmaninov lives much within himself, wears no surface moods and emotions, cultivates no manner for audiences, shuts himself from the world except so far as his music and his playing may reveal him. Therein speaks the man who, having found his means of self-expression, first makes himself unobtrusive master of them; who by this mastery discloses more amply, more exactly the treasures of a penetrating, reflective, many-sided mind, of a grave yet ardent imagination . . . a man in whom all things run deep and strong, devotions and ideals, passions and affections, sensations and achievement.
>
> Once embarked upon performance . . . he neither regards nor disregards his listeners; he merely bids them hear. With hands, with body he has not a trick of physical or technical display. There he sits, wholly absorbed in his task, entirely concentrated upon it, summoning, marshaling into it all that his faculties may give . . . The piece ends; with grave courtesy Mr. Rakhmaninov acknowledges the applause with which the audience yesterday heaped him: seeks neither to emphasize not to prolong it; returns as quietly, as briefly, to the next item in the programme of the day. . . . With grave good will he fulfills every obligation to his hearers—and vanishes.[30]

Although there were and would continue to be critics in the United States and Europe who disdained Rachmaninoff's style of performance and his late-Romantic compositional idiom—seemingly out of step with atonal and Modernist artistic experiments—he continued to evolve his own musical ideas and his popularity with audiences remained high and consistent.

On January 5, 1919, Sergei and Natalia Rachmaninoff were honored by approximately 500 guests associated with the New York musical world at the Bohemian Club's glittering evening in the Ballroom of the Biltmore Hotel. This event was considered so exclusive, with a large gathering being anticipated, that Sigmund Herzog, chairman of the Special Entertainment Committee, suggested that "each member be limited to two tickets at $3.00 each." Proceeds from the banquet came to the large sum of $1,106.[31] Since Sergei and Natalia did not speak English well at this time, they no doubt experienced both delight at being the guests of honor and confusion about much that was said by the speakers of the evening. However, what was clear was that they were welcome in one of the most important centers of musical entertainment in the world and that they could finally regain some peace of mind—and financial security—in a country whose government was not in the throes of a revolution.

The die was cast: Rachmaninoff's new life had begun. He committed himself to becoming successful in a new country, entering this little-known geographical sphere of professional activity with his characteristic careful planning and thorough musical preparation. He would maintain a high-powered schedule circulating in the rarefied atmosphere of classical music's international luminaries until only a few weeks before his death in 1943.

NOTES

1. Scripture quotation from The Authorized (King James) Version. Rights in the Authorized Version in the United Kingdom are vested in the Crown. Reproduced by permission of the Crown's patentee, Cambridge University Press.

2. A.I. Ermakov and A.V. Zhogov, comp., *Ivanovka: Vremena. Sobytiya. Sud'by* (Moscow: Izdatel'stvo Fonda Iriny Arkhipovoi, 2003), 86, trans. VZN.

3. Ibid., 6–7, trans. VZN.

4. Ibid., 6, trans. VZN.

5. Soviet Russian writer Vladimir Soloukhin, with whom I worked in Moscow over the course of ten years, described in detail in one of his major literary projects the successful and relatively prosperous way of life of the peasants. Born in 1924 in a peasant family of ten children, Soloukhin knew this way of life from personal experience and much observation. On the work ethic of both peasants and aristocrats, see Vladimir Soloukhin, *A Time to Gather Stones*, trans. Valerie Z Nollan (Evanston, IL: Northwestern University Press, 1993), 79–161. The writers of the Village Prose literary school set as a major goal to record peasant life and overturn the prevailing stereotypes about it.

6. Irina Brandt, "Pis'mo 2," in Ermakov and Zhogov, 77, trans. VZN.

7. For a detailed analysis on each of the individual Études-Tableaux of Op. 39, see Barrie Martyn, *Rachmaninoff: Composer, Pianist, Conductor* (Burlington, VT: Ashgate, 2000), 269–77.

8. Program Notes of piano recital, Brian Ray, Rhodes College, September 22, 2014.

9. Geoffrey Hosking, *The First Socialist Society* (Cambridge, MA: Harvard University Press, 1985), 58.

10. In autumn 1985 on a walking tour of Moscow with Vladimir Soloukhin, the author of this book listened to him describing some of the over 500 churches that were destroyed in Moscow alone in the years immediately after 1917.

11. Hosking, 70.

12. Ibid.

13. Nicolas Berdyaev, *The Russian Revolution* (Ann Arbor, MI: University of Michigan Press, 1961; first published by Sheed and Ward, 1931), 84.

14. Martin Stokes, "Introduction," in Martin Stokes, ed., *Ethnicity, Identity and Music* (Oxford, UK: Berg Publishers, 1994), 10, 13.

15. Andrey Tarkovsky, *Sculpting in Time* (Austin, TX: University of Texas Press, 1987), 37, 38, 41.

16. See Charles F. Barber, *Lost in the Stars: The Forgotten Musical Life of Alexander Siloti* (Lanham, MD: Scarecrow Press, 2002), 171–74.

17. José Maria Corrédor, *Conversations with Casals* (New York: Hutchinson, 1956), 211, quoted in Barber, 169.

18. Annalena McAfee, "Symphony for a True Survivor," *Evening Standard*, March 25, 1993.

19. S.A. Fedorov, "Rasskazyvaet Sergei Anan'evich Fedorov," in Ermakov and Zhogov, 152, trans. VZN. The Antonov uprisings supported some positions of the Socialist Revolutionaries, but eventually mounted their thousands of peasant forces against the Bolsheviks.

20. Ibid., trans. VZN.

21. See Martyn, 387–95, for a listing of the works Rachmaninoff added to his concertizing repertoire each season between 1918 and 1943.

22. Ermakov and Zhogov, paraphrase of 76.

23. Bertensson and Leyda, 213.

24. Ibid.

25. Ibid., 214.

26. Personal interview, Alexandre Rachmaninoff, Senar, Weggis, Switzerland, May 4, 2005.

27. Ibid.

28. Anne McLean, "Rachmaninoff: The Bohemian," *Studies in Music from the University of Western Ontario* 15 (1995): 95–96.

29. Ibid., 96.

30. Bertenssen and Leyda, 215–16.

31. McLean, 97, 99, quote and paraphrase.

Chapter 11

The Legendary Virtuoso Pianist
(1912–1943)

Perhaps the greatest pianist of his generation, Rachmaninoff will remain one of the finest pianists of all time. Similar to the mystical tales that circulated about Paganini during that virtuoso violinist's life, the superlative accounts of those who saw Rachmaninoff in concert exude astonishment and disbelief that such dazzling pianism could be possible. His playing and deep understanding of music seemed otherworldly, not something a mere mortal could achieve. Moreover, he was able to integrate all the elements of a superlative musical performance into a harmonious and seamless whole. From his student years at the Moscow Conservatory, when his playing was so superior to that of the other students' efforts that he typically did not participate in competitions—for he would always win—to his concertizing tours that left audiences mesmerized by his musicality and impeccable technique, Rachmaninoff's stature as a virtuoso pianist would only keep growing. His reputation as the artist par excellence was earned during what was surely the golden age of extraordinary pianists. This was the age of such luminaries as Ignacy Jan Paderewski, Josef and Rosina Lhévinne, Josef Hofmann, Wanda Landowska, Arthur Rubinstein, Walter Gieseking, Vladimir Horowitz, Sviatoslav Richter, and Emil Gilels. A witty anecdote involving Arthur Rubinstein provides an insight into how Rachmaninoff's contemporaries viewed his stature among musicians: "Arthur Rubinstein [was] asked by an American reporter who he thought was the greatest living pianist. Rubinstein replied 'Horowitz.' The reporter, pushing his luck, said 'Not Rachmaninoff?' Rubinstein retorted, 'You asked me about pianists. Rachmaninoff is a god.'"[1]

As for Rachmaninoff himself, he especially admired the pianism of Josef Hofmann, Walter Gieseking, and Vladimir Horowitz. Among his pianist-contemporaries he acknowledged only Hofmann as perhaps better than himself, or at least as an equal in terms of individualizing each performed piece and creatively projecting an inspiration and total involvement with the music he performed. He deeply admired Gieseking's expressiveness and fluidity at the keyboard. Horowitz as a younger exponent of the same national pedagogical tradition who lionized Rachmaninoff was a gifted pianist with whom Rachmaninoff could privately play two-piano reductions and share news of their lost homeland of Russia. The only qualification Rachmaninoff noted about Horowitz was, in the midst of his many outstanding features as a pianist, a lack of musicality in his interpretations of music. Rachmaninoff would no doubt have admired the accomplishments and dedication to performing his works of Ruth Laredo (1937–2005), who reflected:

> Rachmaninoff makes the piano into an orchestra. There is so much going on at every moment. He never just lets the melody speak for itself. It's very beautiful but it makes it so difficult, pianistically and mentally. I take Rachmaninoff's music much more seriously than I ever did before because I never realized what kind of work was involved in playing it. If you compare him with Brahms and Schumann, he seems so elegant, so much more ornate.[2]

Laredo is referring to the ways in which Rachmaninoff's expansion of the language of piano of the late nineteenth century produced the combination of melody, ornamentation, and elegant style distinctly associated with his music.

Rachmaninoff as a dazzling pianist and musician in general stood on the shoulders of the prominent tradition of Romantic virtuoso pianists, exemplified most famously by Liszt and conveyed to Russia and Rachmaninoff through Alexander Siloti, one of Liszt's last students who was Rachmaninoff's older cousin and teacher at the Moscow Conservatory. Benning Dexter, who studied piano with Aleksandr Siloti at Juilliard during the years 1934–1939 and saw Rachmaninoff in concert very likely more than once, summarized:

> [Rachmaninoff's] memorable characteristics included consistent clarity and a projection of structure, line, and unity. In the best sense he played like a composer. Melodies were highly profiled along with a clear delineation of bass line. Many bass tones were . . . placed in beautiful balance with the voices above. There was extraordinary rhythmic excitement, a sense of forward motion in the usually brisk tempos he chose. Withal, there was a remarkable freedom, warmth, and a wonderful sense of timing. The latter was related to rhythm, and to exactly graded ritards. He was a romantic pianist of commanding authority, conviction, and sincerity. Because he performed in large halls, the dynamic levels were generally high. He was a big player and was never covered by an orchestra.[3]

Rachmaninoff was educated and made his way as a musician in the thick of the Romantic era, remaining a major exponent of that style and ethos of music well into the Late-Romantic era of the twentieth century. The mystique of the technically and lyrically endowed virtuoso pianist was by then well entrenched in Russia and also transplanted to American soil—in large part because of the reputations and superb musical abilities of Russian and European pianists who were forced to emigrate from their native lands to the United States and thereby raised the level of American classical musicianship. Jim Samson described the late nineteenth- and early twentieth-century Romantic virtuoso as a creative artist who "stood for freedom, for the Faustian man, for the individual in search of self-realization—free, isolated, striving, desiring. Heroically overcoming his instrument, he was a powerful symbol of transcendence."[4] As an enormously successful composer-conductor-pianist in Tsarist Russia, Rachmaninoff determined that he could best make his way in Europe and the United States as a performance-oriented musician, utilizing the short summer breaks for composition and rest.

As a Paganini of the piano, Rachmaninoff in the controlled power, expressiveness, melodic sweep, and personal charisma of his recitals would give rise in thoughtful audience-goers to the question: Were his prodigious abilities at the piano a gift from God or bargain made with the Devil? His compositions and pianistic abilities could support either of these contentions: the surpassing beauty of his Symphony No. 2 in E minor and wistful, tender lyricism of the second movement of Piano Concerto No. 2 in C minor would suggest inspiration from God, whereas among his Moments Musicaux the E minor Moment (performed according to *presto* dynamics) suggests something diabolical, and the devilish playfulness of the *Rhapsody on a Theme of Paganini* more than implies a fateful pact with the Devil.

Rachmaninoff's expansive style of playing followed in the tradition derived from Liszt through his cousin and teacher Alexander Siloti, one of Liszt's last pupils. He came of age and was taught at the Moscow Conservatory by some of the most gifted musicians in the world at the time, collectively forming the Russian School of Piano—still acknowledged as the most outstanding of its kind in the world.[5] Rachmaninoff was made to be a pianist: his large hands, absolute pitch, phenomenal memory, and natural musicality all contributed to his staggering performance of a wide range of musical pieces. Moreover, his 6'4" height gave him an advantageous view of the entire keyboard and engaged his body in powerful and creative interpretations of music whose themes and melodic/harmonic lines he gathered up into a distinctive sound unparalleled in his generation. About his playing, Y. Nikolsky concluded:

> No one could extract from the keyboard a sound like Rachmaninov's sound, which was very flexible, beautiful, and expressive. . . . One can compare every

piece of music he played with a building erected by a great architect where colossal walls, well-proportioned columns and all the details, including molded ceilings, door handles, and the design of the parquet—everything was perceived as a harmonious whole. It was always a composition.[6]

The fact that he was a composer as well as a pianist gave him the advantage of analyzing and grasping a given work through the lens of a co-creator who himself had traversed the pathways of the creative process and hence understood the many layers of meaning of the work he was performing. He understood how the parts and the whole fit together.

Rachmaninoff's practice regimen during the concert season involved between three and four hours of daily work at the piano. He played scales to achieve a beautiful *legato*, and carried out piano exercises to ensure that each finger remained strong and flexible. His wife Natalia recalled that his technique was staggeringly precise, especially his playing of octaves.[7] He observed about his discipline at the piano:

> The greatest art is that which is done unconsciously. Of course, there must be years of grinding labor to produce any great end or reach any high goal. One does not soar to the heights of art like an angel. The work, the climb is there. But the difference is that the great artist usually forgets that he is working, so completely does his love and enthusiasm for what he is doing camouflage drudgery.[8]

New York Times music critic Harold Schonberg goes even further in comparing pianistic technique of the present to that of the past era that included Rachmaninoff:

> The best romantic pianists—and this point cannot be overemphasized—were *not* self-indulgent. Their playing, by and large, had few of the eccentricities, textual changes or misreadings, insane virtuosity or abuses in taste so commonly believed to be an integral part of romanticism. They were musical aristocrats whose apparently free playing was under strict rhythmic and emotional control. They also had techniques better than anything to be heard today. A rash-sounding statement; but listen to the Lhevinne recording of the *Blue Danube*, the Moiseiwitsch of Liszt's *La Leggierezza*, the Hofmann of Liszt's *Venezia e Napoli*, the Rachmaninoff of Schumann's *Carnaval*, and the listener is faced with an order of technique that has largely vanished from the earth.[9]

One can perhaps qualify Schonberg's categorical assessment and name pianists such as Vladimir Leyetchkiss (one of the last students of the great Heinrich Neuhaus) and Nikolai Lugansky, a direct descendant of Rachmaninoff's technically precise and emotionally controlled pianistic style, who continued the authentic Romantic tradition that eschews self-indulgence and eccentricities. But there are not many of them.

Though not demonstrative on stage in performance, Rachmaninoff captured all the voicings, conveyed the concept and structure of what he was playing, and never lost sight of the whole. He remained in control of each piece, performing without sentimentality and at as rapid a speed as the piece could justify—in order to convey the melodic lines and essence of that whole. Rachmaninoff's authorial control unfolded through his duality of interaction with each piece of music while on stage: the process of *creating* the given musical work in performance, and the meta-observation *controlling* that process.[10] This meta-level of control would propel the architectural lines of that piece to a "culminating point" that needed to be reached and expressed manifestly in order for the playing to be successful. This precise, even severe attention to the "point" he developed from Feodor Chaliapin and the latter's theories of stage performance. Here we have an example of a major concept that is equally applicable and critical in (at least) two genres of art. It is the architecture of two linear modes of expression, of how the movement forward develops in (depending on whether it is music or acting) its tonality, pitch, dynamics, staging, acting style, and overall effect as perceived by an audience. Both Rachmaninoff and Chaliapin understood their art forms so profoundly that they recognized that the climax of a musical or theater performance provided the highest level of understanding of the meaning of the work itself. Audience members fully committed to hearing/seeing the given piece performed would experience sheer delight, while for the performer, expressing the culminating point would bring him / her closer to the ideal of the piece in question.

Chaliapin surely also influenced Rachmaninoff's sense of stage presence of the performer, in the way the composer-pianist conceptualized the entirety of an audience's experiencing of a performance—it was a visual as well as aural event, theater as well as music, the reception of which to no small degree was determined by the personality and manner of the performer:

> the personality of a great musician has a great deal to do with it. If personality does not count, then why not listen to the phonograph or the radio? Why go to concerts at all? Take one concrete example. Mr. Kreisler [Fritz Kreisler, the celebrated violinist and close friend of Rachmaninov] has a tremendous personality. He comes on the stage, he plays and he conquers. Now suppose at one of his concerts he played from behind a curtain. Do you think the audience would enthuse as much as is usually the custom? The personality of the musician influences the audience, consciously or unconsciously, in the appreciation of music. In the enjoyment of music human hearts play a more important part than human brains.[11]

This is what is so often referred to in the twenty-first century as the indescribable sensual appeal of "live music," which is almost universally considered superior to recorded music.

Poetess Marietta Shaginian, who had advanced musical training and collaborated with Rachmaninoff on the cycle of art songs of Op. 34 (1912), noted:

> Rachmaninoff was a major composer, but as a pianist he was magnificent—and our epoch does not have a virtuoso greater or more impressive than he in the art of piano performance. His playing was absolute, demonic. When seated at the piano, he could convince a person of anything at all; an example of this is his powerful and categorical impact on a listener when playing his E minor *Moment Musical,* unparalleled in the entire musical literature.[12]

Such was the seduction of Rachmaninoff: he brought confidence, power, and an indescribable quality absolutely his own to his playing. In general terms these features of his identity served him admirably in his musical life, but on one major occasion a generous act on his part elicited more criticism than praise for his noble intent. When his compatriot composer-pianist Alexander Scriabin died unexpectedly of septicemia in 1915 in Moscow, Rachmaninoff declared that he would devote an entire season of performances to Scriabin's works in order to help his friend's widow—whose finances would otherwise have been in dire straits. However, instead of commending Rachmaninoff for his generosity, critics did not appreciate Rachmaninoff's interpretation of Scriabin's compositions—stating that Rachmaninoff imposed his own more dramatic style of pianism on music by Scriabin that was conceived as lighter, more mystical, and more ethereal.

Shaginian described what Rachmaninoff sacrificed of himself wherever he happened to be performing: "whenever he sat down at the piano, he had to construct, create each piece, convey it absolutely, burn himself out in it, and after the performance be as a squeezed lemon, pale and perspiring, spent to the point of exhaustion."[13]

Chaliapin, who had known and performed with Rachmaninoff for several decades, characterized him as a musician thus:

> A marvelous pianist, Rachmaninoff at the same time was one of the few extraordinary conductors whom I met during my life. With Rachmaninoff on the conductor's podium, a singer could be completely at ease. The spirit of the musical work would be realized by him with a delicate perfection, while if a *ritardando* or pause were needed, it would be executed absolutely precisely.... When Rachmaninoff sat at the piano as accompanist, one would have to say, "It's not I who sing, but *we* who sing." As a composer Rachmaninoff is the embodiment of simplicity, clarity, and sincerity. He sits in his armchair but will

move neither to the left nor to the right in order to please spectators. When he needs to scratch his right ear, he does this with his right hand, but not the left extending across his entire back. Because of this stance some "innovators" did not approve of him.

Rachmaninoff's appearance was dry, gloomy, even severe. But this man possessed such childlike kindness, and was such a lover of laughter. When I would go to visit him, I always prepared an anecdote or story—because I loved to make my old friend laugh.[14]

In Rachmaninoff's lifetime repertoire the most prominent place was reserved for his own solo piano works, but he also performed a large number of major works by Beethoven (whom he especially esteemed), Chopin, Tchaikovsky, and Liszt. He could memorize the most challenging and dense pieces of music within a few days and perform them as if he had studied them for months. His was a composer's insight, in which careful study and creative dynamics were born of a deeper knowledge of the original composer's intent. Sometimes in performance he altered a composer's indicated dynamics dramatically and with such persuasion that critics and audiences were convinced this was how the given piece should sound. Rachmaninoff's recording of Chopin's famous B flat minor Sonata represents a well-known case of his uncanonical reading of that piece. W. J. Henderson, a highly respected American critic, wrote in 1930 concerning Rachmaninoff's live performance of this sonata:

> The logic of the thing was impervious; the plan was invulnerable; the proclamation was imperial. There was nothing left for us but to thank our lucky stars that we had lived when Rachmaninoff did and heard him, out of the divine might of his genius, re-create a masterpiece. It was a day of genius understanding genius. One does not often get the opportunity to be present when such forces are at work. But one thing must not be forgotten: there was no iconoclast engaged; Chopin was still Chopin.[15]

A similar endorsement of Rachmaninoff's audacious, yet convincing study and rendering of the Chopin's B flat minor Sonata was penned by Jan Holcman in 1958:

> The greatest conflict [in the musical world] centers around his extremely intensive reading of the Chopin Sonata. . . . Though Rachmaninoff's crescendoes here are also "terrific" and the pedalling generous, even at the feverish velocity he chooses he does not blur and manages somehow in the midst of the nightmare to impart a kind of wild-organ sound to the piano. . . . Why should this stunning, imaginative version of Chopin's most mysterious piece be less acceptable than any other? Is it because it is less dull? . . . For me, personally, Rachmaninoff

wins the contest . . . his performance is unmatched for its continuity and unrelenting tension.[16]

He gave special attention to the color of the sound and heightened attentiveness to the tonal quality of his playing—these were features associated with musicians of the celebrated Russian School of Piano. He noted in an interview in 1934, "I am well aware that my playing varies from day to day. . . . In a way this is unsatisfactory for me, but, artistically, it is perhaps a better thing never to be certain what one will do than to attain an unvarying level of performance that may easily develop into mere mechanical routine."[17] Rachmaninoff's performance style thus was fresh, direct, passionate, and artistically controlled. He worked to maintain expressive beauty and technical precision in his concerts, incorporating a larger number of major works than necessary into each year's concert repertoire, in part so that he could make last-minute changes in his concert programs—to preserve the spontaneity and excitement of his programs.[18]

The concepts of the "quality of the sound" and "color of the sound" are understood among Russian musicians and musicologists as the delicate, highly nuanced renderings of pitch on a finely tuned instrument. The artistic training and musicality of the performer bring out the various shades of sound in his or her playing of the instrument. The attentiveness to these features of sound by conservatory pedagogues runs throughout a student's musical training, and is present in critical assessments of professional musicians' performances. Natalia Rachmaninoff was attuned to her husband's extraordinary pianistic expressiveness, both as a devout listener and as a Silver-Medal-awardee from the Moscow Conservatory in her own right. Nikolay Medtner, much of whose professional pianistic life paralleled Rachmaninoff's own, described Rachmaninoff's sound in lofty aesthetic terms: "This unbroken contact of his entire being with art itself can be sensed each time his touch produces sound. This sound, in score or keyboard, is never neutral, impersonal, empty. It is as distinct from other sounds as a bell is different from street noises; it is the result of incomparable intensity, flame, and the saturation of beauty."[19] Harold Schonberg recalled Rachmaninoff's "incredible bronze sound; I can't remember hearing anything like it. It was a sound capable of all kinds of nuance. After all, he was one of the two greatest pianists of my time [Hofmann was the other]."[20]

Not only are music and poetry related in their musicality, but this relationship becomes even closer and more pronounced in languages such as Russian, which are highly inflected and thus intrinsically poetic. Well-known Soviet Russian classical pianist Lazar Berman points out about the culture of sound: "Each word by Pushkin is a word of gold and every *sound* should be golden to true musicians, both in its quality and as it relates to the composition as a whole. Everything must be completely clear and listened to with ease—the way we easily read Pushkin, knowing of course that these elements cannot be called 'easy.'"[21] The overall musical culture and respect for the arts (especially literature) in the traditional way of life on Russian country estates provided the firm foundation for world-class composer-musicians such as Rachmaninoff.

In Europe in 1918 Rachmaninoff as a fully formed forty-five-year-old musician faced a daunting task: to redirect his efforts from a more balanced career that included composing, conducting, and piano performance to a career concentrating almost exclusively on giving concerts.[22] Determining that this would be the most reliable way to support his family outside his native country, he embarked on a career of numerous recitals, maintaining an intense schedule that by each season's end would leave his hands aching and his physical health in a state of exhaustion. From the 1918–1919 concert season until his last season in 1942–1943 he would follow the pattern of giving recitals and concerts in the United States in the fall, continuing the performance schedule in Europe in the winter and early spring, and in late spring and summer relocate to a villa in Europe for rest, spa treatments for his hands and general health, and excursions to various places on the Continent to join relatives and meet with friends (usually from the music, literature, and arts communities). Rachmaninoff was in good health on the whole, but he suffered from chronic headaches and some nerve pain in his face. As a heavy smoker, he would in the summers make efforts to curtail his smoking and adopt a routine of physical exercise by hiking in the environs of the given villa, boating in a nearby lake, and playing tennis. Thus in the summer of 1919 the Rachmaninoffs rented a house in Palo Alto near Menlo Park in the San Francisco Bay Area. They would not be far from other Russians who were in California, and they could enjoy the almost ideal climate. In the summer of 1920 they rested and recuperated in the village (not town) of Goshen, New York—a picturesque location of farmland and rolling hills. By the summer of 1921 their financial situation would be stable enough for them to stay in Dresden, the home city of Natalia's relatives.

Rachmaninoff expended enormous effort to retrain himself and become thoroughly familiar with a new culture very foreign to him. His efforts to assimilate were successful, up to a certain point: he and his family, now living in New York at 505 West End Avenue, retained their Russian identity and practices as faithfully as possible. Raised during an era in which social class and status were the primary determinants for advancement, Rachmaninoff was struck by the degree to which in the United States money governed all decision-making. The fierce competition for performances and promotion that he noticed in the American music world prompted him to write to his close friend, the pianist-composer Nikolai Medtner (who was living in

Germany at that time), not to come to America. Medtner was much more uncompromising and impractical in his approaches to his career than Rachmaninoff, who, while also seeking the highest standard in his composing and performing career, could evaluate the artistic terrain before him and make practical choices. Rachmaninoff rightly felt that Medtner would have a difficult time finding suitable work in music in the United States; for this reason, he supported his close friend and colleague by sending him monthly stipends while the latter was in Germany.

Writing from New York, Rachmaninoff gave the same sound advice to longtime musical colleague Nikolai Avierino on November 1, 1920:

> My dear friend Nikolay Konstantinovich,
> I received your letter. Today I'm sending you 1500 drachmas. Forgive me that it's so little! I can't afford to send any more.
> You write and ask about America!? May God preserve you from coming here. Here for every musical position there are ten applicants. And you won't even receive a visa according to the new rules that appeared several weeks ago, all of them because of the unprecedented influx of foreigners. Go to Paris, London, wherever you want in Europe, but forget about the "Princess of Dollars"!
> I send you my best wishes and a friendly greeting.
> S.R.[23]

Despite Rachmaninoff's well-intentioned advice, Avierino was able to move from Europe to New York during the following year of 1921.

When Rachmaninoff was forced to leave Russia in 1917 he was at the top of his field: he had Moscow, and indeed Europe, at his feet, composing and performing one masterpiece after another in the major capitals. In the United States he had to recreate himself in a culture completely alien to what he had known in his homeland. He felt displaced in geographical and cultural space, but also suffered accusations of being out of step with the musical times. One can imagine how difficult it was for him to interact in this culture in English or become a part of a musical milieu that was foreign to him: from the innovations of jazz (which Rachmaninoff admired and viewed seriously) to atonal experimental music (which he disdained) he had to insert himself into a landscape far different from what he had known in Russia and Europe. His tonal compositions were dismissed as being out of date in an increasingly atonal period that remained in vogue for much of the twentieth century, although the perceived chasm between Rachmaninoff as Late-Romantic composer and the Modernists was not as wide as is often portrayed. For example, Scriabin at his most Romantic very closely resembles Rachmaninoff at his most Modernist.[24] He composed almost nothing new between 1918 and 1926: he was working on his Piano Concerto No. 4 in G minor during this time, but produced little else.

The disorientation of exile and nostalgia for Russia weighed heavily upon him. Rachmaninoff felt like a "ghost wandering in a world grown alien."[25] He continued,

> I have made intense effort to feel the musical manner of today, but it will not come to me. . . . The new kind of music seems to come, not from the heart, but from the head. Its composers think rather than feel. They have not the capacity to make their works "exult," as Hans von Bülow called it. They meditate, protest, analyze, reason, calculate, and brood—but they do not exult.[26]

Rachmaninoff valued Beethoven's ninth symphony as one of music history's supreme creations; this piece had the quality of "exulting" that he felt was lacking in modern and atonal music. He was able to remain open-minded about the "new" music, however: despite the fact that he and Igor Stravinsky had drastically different styles of composing, Rachmaninoff was deeply moved by the end of Stravinsky's ballet *The Firebird*. Rachmaninoff's alienation from the changing musical times in the United States was exacerbated by his being outside his native culture and not fluent in English. Even though he developed some degree of fluency in the language, it was of utmost importance for him to preserve his native language of Russian. He understood without analyzing it that the ties between language and culture enable one to retain the worldview of the native land, its history, its collective memory, and its origins in the experiences of the ancestors. These ties enabled him to retain his Russianness, which served as an anchor for his authentic identity in a foreign land.

Rachmaninoff would not compromise his standards or understanding of what constituted genuine music. In this regard, he knew who he was and would not change his identity to suit others' musical proclivities. Natalia Rachmaninoff remarked, "It's strange, that no other musical performer was pressured to play 'modern' music as intensely as was Rachmaninoff. However, he did not extend his performance repertoire any further in that direction than the works of Debussy, Ravel, and Poulenc."[27] Interestingly, his reserve in the face of everyday American cultural circumstances was transformed when he was on stage: his playing especially of his own compositions was intense and outgoing, with the enormous dynamic sweep so characteristic of Russian music. His wife affirmed that performing on stage brought him immense pleasure:

> The public inspired him; he experienced the works he performed as if he had composed them himself. . . . In playing them, he became inspired and then himself inspired his listeners. In his performance most of all I valued the overall

conception, that musical impulse, the crescendos and peaks of sounds that he achieved. The sonority of his chords was of orchestral dimensions, and for this reason, in performing the piano concertos with an orchestra, the confluence of these sonorities was complete.

Figure 11.1   Rachmaninoff on the Cover of *Musical America*, December 25, 1932. Author's collection.

Among the numerous musical works that I heard in his interpretation, I believe that best of all he played his own piano concertos, Piano Concerto #1 of Beethoven, and the piano concerto of Schumann. Among his solo pieces I can cite the sonatas of Beethoven (the Appassionata, op. 31 No. 2, and op. 10 in D major), the C minor variations and both sonatas of Chopin, "Carnaval" of Schumann, "Funérailles" and Sonnet 104 of Petrarch by Liszt, the Andantino with Variations of Schubert-Tausig, the Italian concerto of Bach, etc.[28]

B. S. Nikitin concludes concerning Rachmaninoff's attitude toward performing on stage:

No matter what people said about his required concert activity, he loved to play for the public, probably not less than composing music. In America, notwithstanding his extreme fatigue from travels to various cities and giving concerts, he began to love performing on stage even more. "I'm a stage performer," he admitted in 1929, "that is, I love the stage and in contrast to many artists I don't grow tired of the stage, but rather become stronger and at just a single sound of the piano I feel capable of [creating] new inventions and discoveries even for myself."[29]

Throughout his life Rachmaninoff would ponder which of his artistic identities mattered the most to him. As far as his brilliance as composer, conductor, and pianist was concerned, his creative work in all three areas of musicianship received the highest praise from his musical colleagues and critics. But for himself, the time required to achieve the standards he set for himself in either composing or virtuoso piano performance, along with the resultant need to choose on which area he would concentrate his efforts, led to the tension in his mind concerning what could not be resolved. He would concentrate on only one activity at a time—either composition or performance—and sometimes conducting, which he enjoyed but perhaps saw as a necessity for the interpreting of his own compositions for an audience. Composition or performance? He gained deep satisfaction from them both:

I don't know which brings me the greater pleasure: to compose music or to perform it. If I have worked a great deal on a musical phrase and . . . know that it is crafted well, then I experience a feeling of the deepest satisfaction. When I play in concert and I have a successful day . . . , then I think that this is indeed the greatest happiness . . .[30]

A major difficulty encountered by Rachmaninoff during his international touring lay in the acoustics of the various concert halls in which he performed. His wife noted how frustrated he would become if a specific stage had heavy velvet curtains hanging from it—for they would absorb sound and he could not hear himself playing. In the massive Royal Albert Hall of

London, for example, the acoustics during the 1920s had the major problem of an echo, which meant that a performer would hear the notes that he or she played twice as they circled around the cavernous space. Rachmaninoff performed there in the 1930s, but the problem evidently was corrected before he played, because upon testing the piano on the stage he was reassured that the acoustics for such a huge space were as they should be.[31]

The complex situation Rachmaninoff and his family faced in Europe and the United States can aptly be called an "agony of exile." There were not many Russians in the music or arts world living in the United States at that time, and those who could be found were located on the two coasts—mainly in New York and California. Rachmaninoff was constantly on the move, concertizing in the United States and sometimes Canada during the months of the performance season and spending the summer months in Europe. Because of his busy touring schedule from October through April of each year, he had little time for developing any large-scale compositions. His compositional output consisted of only an arrangement of three Russian folk songs for voice and piano. His wife Natalia coordinated the household and their two daughters' activities, providing a stable environment in which her husband could accomplish his work and their family could maintain its routines. She also attended to the myriad details involved in her husband's concert tours and the peripatetic nature of the family's moves between the United States and Europe. Rachmaninoff maintained contacts with relatives and friends in Soviet Russia as regularly as was possible, in the context of the strained political situation and intense whirlwind of music activities into which fate had thrust him. Henry Z. Steinway (1915–2008), with whose piano-building family Rachmaninoff developed a lifelong and warm association, recalled that he always felt sorry for Rachmaninoff, because the latter seemed compelled to give so many recitals. Steinway attended many of Rachmaninoff's recitals, as well as performances of his contemporaries; his own preference for pianistic interpretation was split between Rachmaninoff and Josef Hofmann.[32]

Bradley Bambarger sums up Rachmaninoff's powerful influence on the musical world of his day:

> In his book *The Great Pianists*, critic Harold Schonberg depicted Rachmaninoff as one of the purest, most complete pianists who ever lived. He was a towering virtuoso—with vast hands and a near-photographic memory—who blended modernist rigor with Romantic poetry. "At any Rachmaninoff concert, one noted the sharp rhythmic thrusts (these were his trademark), the virility and the sense of sonority the man had," Schonberg wrote. "And, above all, a musical elegance in which phrases were shaped with exquisite finish. When he played a Liszt transcription of a Schubert song, one immediately realized how unimaginative and unmusical most singers were." Rachmaninoff left many records of his playing—piano rolls, acoustic discs, electrical recordings. He recorded hit

versions of his four piano concertos with the Philadelphia Orchestra (under Leopold Stokowski and Eugene Ormandy), along with conducting the orchestra himself in his Third Symphony, great tone poem *Isle of the Dead* and popular *Vocalise*.[33]

Bambarger's assessment, that Rachmaninoff as a virtuoso pianist "blended modernist rigor with Romantic poetry," is problematized by Vladimir Chinaev in the 1993 article "Stil modern i pianism Rakhmaninova." While not invalidating in any way Rachmaninoff's genius as a virtuoso, Chinaev advances the theory that Rachmaninoff in his pianistic interpretations was actually in step with Modernist characteristics by *parodying* the Romantic style of performance. Specifically, Chinaev cites examples of Rachmaninoff's recorded performances of many shorter pieces (Liszt's Hungarian Rhapsody No. 2, the Menuet of Paderewski, Scherzo No. 3 of Chopin, his own "Polichinelle" Op. 3 No. 4, his transcription of Kreisler's waltz "Liebesfreud," etc.) as well as his famous (or infamous?) reading of Chopin's Sonata No. 2 in B flat minor Op. 35. Chinaev posits that Rachmaninoff's performances of music of the Romantic era include irony as well as parody of that era, but also apply a classically purist and "ornamental" style to his playing that is completely in step with Modernist understandings of art. Rachmaninoff, according to this theory, architecturally "deconstructs" a Romantic piece in performance through various musical devices, interprets it anew, and then "reconstructs" it in a Modernist vein.

Chinaev's description of this process can apply directly to Rachmaninoff's noncanonical recorded performance of the Chopin Sonata No. 2:

> One of the principles of Rachmaninoff's architecture—the effect of [his] returns to those agogic [accents occurring by increasing the time value of a note], rhythmic, and dynamic "incorrections" that at first are perceived merely as an improvisational performative caprice, as a fashionable and witty prank. The "incorrect (from the point of view of standard practice) words" that seemingly destroy the smooth "rhythm," return again and again, and the "liberties" and "flaws" of Rachmaninoff's performance turn out to be imaginary. In repeating themselves, as in the system of mutually reflecting mirrors, Rachmaninoff's hyperbolas of rubato, diminuendo, and accelerando take on a significance wholly not of destructive "improvisations," but rather of constructive constants. Out of the broken apart, intensified, arrhythmic rhythms [that Rachmaninoff employs] arise newly poetic rhythms [in the musical work in question].[34]

Chinaev's hypotheses on Rachmaninoff's pianism represent an iconoclastic and provocative, yet fascinating *reception* of Rachmaninoff performance techniques—but in terms of Rachmaninoff's own *intention*, judging by his own statements on creating and performing music, his composing and performing credos were linked with the aesthetics of Antiquity, rich possibilities of Romanticism in creative work, and also the features of Modernism (lush ornamentation of the melody, straightforward and intellectual delivery of a musical work in performance, and experimentation with form) that did not radically break with the tradition of Romanticism. It is simply going too far to suggest that Rachmaninoff viewed the musical traditions in which he was raised with irony or in his performances parodied them. It is, however, the case that Rachmaninoff in his aristocratic, integral, and completely serious approach to his own art—both composing and performative—attempted to ennoble each piece he played, regardless of its genre, style, or quality. An especially insightful point that Chinaev makes is that Rachmaninoff's aestheticism in composition and performance, as Nabokov's in his literary works, serves as a mask to hide an existential pain and dreariness, accretions that formed almost imperceptibly.[35]

In the 1920s in America and throughout his life Rachmaninoff remained fascinated by various advances in the recording of music, as well as by the development of various other practical machines (such as the lowly vacuum cleaner). He recorded on the piano rolls of the American Piano Company (Ampico), and subjected himself (as he would very likely put it) to recording in sound booths for RCA Records. Concert pianist and author Charles Rosen describes:

> Before tape, a record lasted at most 4 ½ minutes. It is not that difficult with music that one knows well to play 4 ½ minutes with perfect accuracy. Rachmaninov was said to walk into a recording studio and refuse to warm up; he would start recording immediately upon taking off his gloves. Then he would play a work as many as sixteen times. Even with all this effort, there are still occasional wrong notes in his recordings (I remember notably a passage in the Scherzo of Chopin's Sonata in B flat Minor), but his great performances would not be much improved by removing these blemishes.[36]

Rachmaninoff did not warm up publicly before rehearsals with orchestras or, in the above case, before a recording session out of a sense of professionalism (not to impose on another musician's or technician's time) and propriety (warming up on the piano was to be completed at home before the given event).

Rosen notes the disadvantages of recording in a sound booth over performing a piece before an audience: "In a concert, an effect that does not quite come off matters very little if the whole performance has vitality. In a recording, however, a slight slip of memory, a wrong note grazed are an irritant. They are an obstacle to the attempt to forget our own concerns and let the music take over our consciousness."[37] A caveat to this statement would be Rachmaninoff's exasperation if in a concert he missed conveying "the point"—the properly prepared culminating point—of a piece of music.

His desire for absolute perfection in the execution of a piece of music was impossibly high. He reflected: "The artist tries, and tries again to achieve the impossible. Sometimes he is lucky and gets a little nearer to his goal. But all of the time he is forced way out someplace, way out where no one can comfort him, nothing can help him."[38]

Rachmaninoff's varying perceptions of his performances (both live and on recordings) aside, valuable perspective can be gained in Alex Ross's remarks:

> A recent assessment of his place as a pianist in his lifetime is one by Alex Ross, who wrote, in a New Yorker review of recordings of the "hundred greatest" pianists of the 20th century, "The most immediately impressive volumes are those in which a player's personality swamps every piece on the program. The lord of them all is probably Rachmaninoff. Of the Slavic pianists who fill the twentieth-century pantheon, Horowitz may have produced more electricity and Paderewski more tears, but Rachmaninoff is the one who pins you in your chair with the force of his mind."[39]

The aspiration for perfection was not Rachmaninoff's alone; it is associated with many superb creative artists in the various genres who are unable and unwilling to trade the radiant ideals of what they might achieve for a lesser result. Rimm considers both Medtner and Rachmaninoff to share "an almost pathological perfectionism in their public performances . . . Despite his fantastic successes, Rachmaninoff simply could not tolerate anything less than perfection."[40] His musical associates admired him for his legendary preparedness for musical events, but he himself suffered deeply if his performances did not live up to his expectations. And yet, sometimes they did. As Feodor Chaliapin typically performed, but at the same time was analyzing his performance every step of the way, Rachmaninoff as a performer also, while creating the given piece on stage, was also intellectually keeping the musical lines, melodies, overall structure, and dynamics firmly in mind and in control. He could not have loved performing on stage and each time confronting the challenge of hearing himself, both in his fingers and in his mind, create anew each piece he programmed in his recitals if he did not feel satisfied with the quality of his performances. The creative, artistic act for him at the piano in concert was fulfilled again and again. In this highest artistic challenge lay the consummate pleasure he would experience when performing before a live audience. Despite the occasional doubts in himself stemming from an innate modesty, Rachmaninoff understood well his position, authority, and accomplishments in the international musical landscape.

NOTES

1. The Revd Norman Bird, "Letters: The Misappliance of Science," *The Guardian*, November 18, 2001, https://www.theguardian.com/news/2001/nov/18/letters.theobserver.

2. "Ruth Laredo, 1937–2005: Renowned Performer of Rachmaninoff and Scriabin," *Clavier* (July/August 2005), 27.

3. Benning Dexter, "Rachmaninoff in the Flesh: Two Eyewitness Accounts," in Newsletter of the Rachmaninoff Society, 2004. Dexter became a professor of music at the University of Michigan in 1949, serving as chair of the Piano Division at the University of Michigan between 1961 and 1973.

4. Jim Samson, *Virtuosity and the Musical Work: The Transcendental Studies of Liszt* (Cambridge, MA: Cambridge University Press, 2003), 75–76.

5. See Valeria Z. Nollan, "piano performance, Russian/Soviet (Russkaia fortepiannaia shkola)" in *The Encyclopedia of Contemporary Russian Culture*, edited by Karen Evans-Romaine, Helena Goscilo, and Tatiana Smorodinskaya (London: Routledge Ltd., 2007), 463–64.

6. Y. Nikolsky, Liner Notes, *Rachmaninoff Plays and Conducts*, CD, Vista Vera-00039 (2003).

7. N.A. Rakhmaninova, "S.V. Rakhmaninov," in *Vospominaniia o Rakhmaninove*, ed. Z.A. Apetian, 5th ed. (Moscow: Muzyka, 1988), II: 311.

8. Sergei Rachmaninoff, "How Russian students work," *Etude* (May 1928), 298, quoted in Robert Rimm, *The Composer-Pianists: Hamelin and The Eight* (Portland: Amadeus Press, 1985), 138.

9. Harold C. Schonberg, *The Great Pianists: From Mozart to the Present* (New York: Simon and Schuster, 1987), 143.

10. G.I. Ganzburg, "Rakhmaninovskii krizis 1897–1901 godov: sushchnost' i posledstviia," *Tvorchestvo S.V. Rakhmaninova v kontekste mirovoi musykal'noi kul'tury*, ed. M.A. Klimkova (Tambov: Izd. Tambovskogo gosudarstvennogo tekhnicheskogo universiteta, 2003), 15.

11. Basanta Koomar Roy, "Rachmaninoff is Reminiscent," *Musical Observer* 26 (May 1927), 16, accessed at https://www.pianostreet.com/smf/index.php?topic=17183.0.

12. Marietta Shaginian, "Vospominaniia o S.V. Rakhmaninove," in *Vospominaniia o Rakhmaninove*, ed. Z.A. Apetian, 5th ed. (Moscow: Muzyka, 1988), II: 155–56.

13. Ibid., 157.

14. F. I. Chaliapin, *Maska i dusha: Moi sorok let na teatrakh* (Moscow: Moskovskii rabochii, 1989), 151–52, trans. VZN.

15. Bradley Bambarger, "Sergei Rachmaninoff," https://www.steinway.com/artists/sergei-rachmaninoff, accessed August 11, 2021. The quote is taken from Harold C. Schonberg, *The Great Pianists: From Mozart to the Present* (New York: Simon & Schuster, 1987), 398.

16. Jan Holcman, "Hidden Treasures of Rachmaninoff," in *Saturday Review* 41 (August 30, 1958), n.p.

17. Interview by Norman Cameron in *The Monthly Musical Record*, March–April 1932, quoted in Sergei Bertensson and Jay Leyda, *Sergei Rachmaninoff: A Lifetime*

in Music (New York: New York UP, 1956; repr., Bloomington, IN: Indiana UP, 2001), 301.

18. Ibid.

19. John L. Holmes, *Composers on Composers* (Westport, CT: Greenwood Press, 1990), 115; reprinted in Rimm, 143.

20. Rimm, 143. Schonberg was interviewed by Rimm in New York, March 1999.

21. Rimm, 90. Berman was interviewed by Rimm and Anzhela Reno in Italy, October 1997.

22. For a complete list of Rachmaninoff's conducting and piano repertoires, see Barrie Martyn, *Rachmaninoff: Composer, Pianist, Conductor* (Burlington, VT, 1990), 526–62.

23. S. Rakhmaninov, Letter, in *S. Rakhmaninov. Literaturnoe nasledie. Vospominaniia. Stat'i. Interv'iu. Pis'ma*, ed. Z.A. Apetian (Moscow: Sovetskii kompozitor, 1978), 2: 110.

24. For comparison's sake, one can listen to Scriabin's Prelude in E flat minor (Op. 11, No. 14) and any of Rachmaninoff's Etudes-Tableaux or the six songs of his of Op. 38.

25. Leonard Liebling, "Variations," *The Musical Courier* 127 (April 5, 1943): 17.

26. Ibid.

27. Rakhmaninova, "S.V. Rakhmaninov," in *Vospominaniia o Rakhmaninove*, II: 311–12, trans. VZN.

28. Ibid., 311, trans. VZN.

29. Boris Nikitin, *Sergei Rakhmaninov. Feodor Chaliapin* (Moscow: OTiSS, 1998), 143, trans. VZN.

30. Sergei Rakhmaninov, untitled interview for *The New York World-Telegram* on October 15 or 16, published on October 17, 1940, quoted in Liudmila Kovaleva-Ogorodnova (Sankt Peterburg: Vita Nova, 2015), I: 128, 130, trans. VZN.

31. Author's archival work in Royal Albert Hall, London, May 27, 2014.

32. Personal interview, Steinway Hall, New York, January 9, 2006.

33. Bambarger, https://www.steinway.com/artists/sergei-rachmaninoff, accessed August 11, 2021.

34. Vladimir Chinaev, "Stil' modern i pianism Rakhmaninova," *Muzykal'naia akademiia* 2 (1993): 202, trans. VZN.

35. Ibid., 203, trans. VZN

36. Charles Rosen, *Piano Notes: The World of the Pianist* (New York: The Free Press, 2002), 144.

37. Ibid., 143–44.

38. Abram Chasins, *Speaking of Pianists*, 2nd ed. (New York: Alfred A. Knopf, 1967), 41, quoted in Rimm, 150.

39. Alex Ross, "The Chosen," *The New Yorker* (March 29, 1999), 113, quoted in Richard D. Sylvester, *Rachmaninoff's Complete Songs* (Bloomington, IN: Indiana University Press, 2014), xiv.

40. Rimm, 151.

Chapter 12

Rachmaninoff as Humanitarian
(1914–1943)

"For I was hungered, and ye gave me meat:
I was thirsty, and ye gave me drink"

—Matthew 25:35 (KJV)[1]

In addition to his multifarious activities as a musician of international stature, Rachmaninoff was a humanitarian. Alexander Ivanovich Ermakov, director of the Ivanovka Museum-Estate, calculated that over the course of his lifetime Rachmaninoff gave away at least a quarter of his earnings to charitable causes.[2] Although some of his humanitarian activities are mentioned elsewhere in this book, the present chapter examines their meaning within the Russian Orthodox context of active love, forgiveness, and self-sacrifice. Rachmaninoff had experienced difficulties of many kinds during his childhood and adolescence, and these tribulations, along with his moral values and empathy for others, motivated his broad-ranging humanitarian work during his lifetime. His niece Sophia Vladimirovna Satina recalled about her uncle:

> He always was polite and never raised his voice. He enjoyed a good story or a joke, but never made nasty remarks about fellow musicians or colleagues. He kept silent about the amount of money which he donated to friends in need or a good cause. Some people remarked after his death, that he was stingy, but his well-earned money was never squandered in shady deals or gambling.[3]

Rachmaninoff helped many people in need, those who were relatives or strangers, ordinary or famous. His help would often come in the form of financial gifts to various individuals, which he called "loans," even though he knew they could not be repaid. His entire manner of giving was humane, unobtrusive, and in the spirit of preserving the dignity of the recipient. An especially touching anecdote involves a peasant family's loss of their cow that died unexpectedly. The family in question lived in the village of Ivanovka and was employed for work on the estate of the same name. Anna Pavlovna Artemova, a daughter in the family, was a young girl at the time of the events. She narrates:

> When Father was conscripted to fight in the German war [World War I] it became so difficult for us to live. And then in summer of 1916 our cow died. She returned from the herd, Grandmother brought her some slops, but she didn't drink them. Grandmother kept coaxing her to eat and drink, but she was silent. Then she lay down on the grass and died. Grandmother began to cry, and we cried as well. Thus we were left without our milk-giver.
>
> We were incredibly surprised when about two days later, after coming home [from work], we saw a dappled cow by the cowshed, and beside her sitting on a stump was Grandmother who was weeping from joy and repeating:
>
> "May the Lord grant him and his children good health."
>
> It turned out that Grandmother had been crying at the estate [of Ivanovka] and telling the women of our distress, and Sergei Vasilievich overheard it. And so with the groom Yakov they brought us a cow from the landowner's barn. Grandmother was afraid that the landlord would be angry, but Sergei Vasilievich reassured her about this. At this point Grandmother fell to his feet in a full prostration and began to thank him, but he became annoyed at her for such a gesture.
>
> Later Grandmother went to the church at Viazov and said prayers for the health of Sergei Vasilievich.[4]

In another account of Rachmaninoff's compassion and respect for the peasants employed at Ivanovka, when he learned that a woman who was an especially talented baker was ill, he visited her at her house. Her granddaughter relates:

> All the Satins and Rachmaninoffs loved my grandmother. Once Sergei Vasilievich came to our house with a tall, rather thin man with a beard. But our grandmother was sick and was lying by the stove. Squinting, Sergei Vasilievich entered our cabin.
>
> "What's going on, my dear one, that you feel so unwell? And we've missed your bread so much. My friend here also wants to try some of your bread. Please be so kind as to get better soon!"
>
> They brought Grandmother some different medicines, and candy that she gave to us kids. When Grandmother baked bread, she chased everyone away. She would add certain herbs to the dough. The round loaves of bread turned out aromatic and tasty.[5]

These are acts carried out only by persons who think of the well-being of others, are not self-centered, and arrive at a plan for action to improve the living conditions of those others.

Rachmaninoff performed benefit concerts for the Russian army at the start of World War I, and during the first years of World War II when he was in America he performed charity concerts for the Red Army and to send medical supplies for civilians in the Soviet Union. His expressions of empathy for others extended to sending material aid to another continent to soldiers he would never meet. It seemed that everyone was appealing to Rachmaninoff for help: the sick, the elderly and infirm, students needing money for their education, and Russian social organizations with the mission of helping the aged, orphans, and handicapped. Rachmaninoff's money supported the Red Cross, artistic and scientific unions, libraries, conservatories, and a Russian Orthodox foundation for assistance to its clergy.[6] After he and his family had settled in New York in November 1918 and had joined the parish of St. Nicholas Russian Orthodox Cathedral, he not only made regular donations to the church but also provided coal for heating its interior.

For many years Rachmaninoff had suffered from pain in his right temple, with the nerve occasionally swelling to the point of being noticeable. This pain was apparently brought on when he was doing close work with his eyes in composing music, at which times he had to write down music notations in a small, very precise handwriting. The pain plagued him more and more, but strikingly it subsided when he was on the concert stage. He consulted various doctors in Russia and America, but not a single one could diagnose the problem accurately. One speculated that it could be neuralgia, another said it could be an infection in the jaw or teeth. The pain became so severe that he even contemplated giving up composing. As a result of the pain and uncertainty, after his concert season of 1920–1921 was finished, he agreed to have an operation in New York in the spring. During the surgery the doctors removed fourteen of Rachmaninoff's healthy teeth in an attempt to eradicate what might be the source of his pain, but the operation failed. Rachmaninoff wrote to Dagmar Barclay, "After numerous visits of the dentist an abscess developed on my upper lip. Evidently the plaster wrapping they used [on my face] was not sterilized properly. Half of my face has become swollen and is covered with bandages."[7] During this time in Soviet Russia the Satins were granted approval by the government to apply for emigration. They obtained the necessary documents to fill out, but while this matter was in progress they heard a rumor that their relative Rachmaninoff had died in the hospital. This caused all sorts of confusion, because their emigration had been approved and they were preparing to move to Germany. In the meantime, Rachmaninoff was gradually recovering in a pleasant residence at Locust Point, New Jersey.

By 1922 Rachmaninoff and his family had successfully set up their lives in America, and after over four years they anticipated with joy a reunion with their relatives in Dresden. This was made possible with Rachmaninoff's financial help: in effect, he paid all their expenses of traveling and getting settled in another part of the world. These family members included Sofia Aleksandrovna, his sister-in-law, who found work at the Higher Technical Institute in Dresden and subsequently at the Carnegie Research Laboratories in Cold Springs Harbor, New York. The family of Vladimir Aleksandrovich Satin, brother of Sofia and Natalia, settled in Dresden. Their parents Aleksandr Aleksandrovich and Varvara Arkadievna also chose to remain in Dresden. In the summer of this year Sergei and Natalia had a heartwarming reunion with the Satins in Dresden. Rachmaninoff rented a villa for his family there, and also visited a doctor daily for electrical treatments for his head and hands. At the end of this summer they returned to the United States to stay once again at the house in Locust Point. Here they could rest by the waters of the Navesink River and Claypit Creek, with boating, long walks, and enjoying a slower-paced life—in anticipation of the busyness of the coming concert season.

With both the burgeoning success of his career as a virtuoso pianist and the devastation experienced by his relatives and friends in his beloved Russia, Rachmaninoff also had to accept a resignation from his first secretary in America Dagmar Rybner, who planned to be married to a Mr. Barclay. From Dresden he wrote to her in the late summer of 1922, "Do not forget to show much love and attention to your parents. If you have to part, it will be very hard for them, as I can well understand, being myself a father. All pessimists, faced by two possibilities—one joyous and the other sorrowful—always prefer the latter."[8] Rachmaninoff, however, would find good fortune in his next secretary as well, Evgeny Somov, whom he had met in Moscow through the Satins. As with Dagmar Rybner, Rachmaninoff would become very attached to Somov and his letters to Somov would be especially soul-searching and introspective.

Rachmaninoff continued supporting his large extended family after they had settled in Dresden, including providing the funds for them to buy a house. An account of his support in 1923 comes from his niece Sofia Vladimirovna Satina: "Uncle must have helped us to buy a large plot of land in a suburb of Dresden called Striesen. Here a small house was built without any luxuries like central heating. But it was our own and, though it was not spacious, everybody had a room . . . we were happy, and now we were 'landowners' again."[9] That summer of 1923 the Rachmaninoffs would not stay in Europe, but instead would stay once again at the Locust Point residence.

As for Liubov Petrovna, Rachmaninoff's mother, it is not known for certain whether he asked her to relocate with his family to America. However, it is well known that his mother wished to remain in Russia and that her son made sure on a regular basis that she had enough food and money for all her needs and more. He sent money to his mother in Novgorod, as well to relatives, friends (such as Maria Ivanova), and the family members of women who were important to him (such as Anna Lodyzhenskaia). A short letter that Rachmaninoff wrote to his mother several years later (he corresponded with her regularly) on February 1, 1928, expresses the tenderness the son felt toward his mother:

> My dear Mama,
> Right now I've stopped for only one day in New York, where I received your letter. I want to tell you that I'll take care of all the requests that you detailed in your letter, while I have enough strength [to attend to them]. So please don't worry about that! With my whole heart I wish you good health and more good health. I send you big hugs and kisses. Please excuse me for not writing more. I don't have very much time.
> Your S.R.[10]

It may be that Rachmaninoff's wife Natalia did not approve of having her mother-in-law relocate to possibly living with her family, since Liubov Petrovna had vigorously opposed her marriage to her son (on religious and familial grounds). In a word, Rachmaninoff's wife and mother had a cordial relationship with each other at best, and a tense one at worst.[11] It goes without saying, that to the end of her life—she died on September 19, 1929—Liubov Rachmaninoff missed her son terribly. A letter Rachmaninoff received from one of her friends after her death described that she was deeply saddened that she could not see her son before she died.[12]

Rachmaninoff also provided financial assistance to Russian families and creative artists in Europe. He did not forget his friends in Russia who were suffering under the yoke of the Soviet Union under Lenin and Stalin. Not only did he worry about these people, but he took steps to ease their straightened material circumstances; quite often he would not even know if his help had reached its destination. This kind of assistance to others without expectation of recompense represented only the beginning of many acts of kindness and financial help on the part of Rachmaninoff. In one account:

The Moscow main post office and bank became so accustomed to receiving the numerous packages and money transfers from Rachmaninoff, that they started complaining: Someone named Rachmaninoff keeps sending packages and money. His friend Nikita Semenovich Morozov, having received his regular money transfer [from Rachmaninoff] at the bank, was told by the cashier, "Half of Moscow is receiving things from Rachmaninoff."[13] A certain E. Malysheva described Rachmaninoff's discrete manner of sending aid to others: "All of his acts of assistance were carried out quietly, and virtually no one knows what enormous sums of money he spent in supporting youths in need, helping a variety of people in all ways possible, and sending many things to Russia."[14]

In Soviet Russia, conditions for survival were worsening, with famines and diseases affecting people of all professions and socioeconomic classes. Rachmaninoff was able to renew contact with friends and colleagues who had been virtually lost to him because of the whirlwind of events sweeping through Russia. He began to receive more and more letters, and the descriptions in them were terrifying:

> A letter from G.P. Lunts-Orlova came from England . . . on March 21, 1922.
> "Deeply Esteemed Sergei Vasilievich. I am taking the liberty of forwarding to you the letters of my friend[s], from which one can imagine to oneself the unbelievably difficult living conditions of our Russian musicians and pedagogues. All of them are in need of food, clothing, printed music, and music staff paper."
> In a letter from Mikhail Slonov from Moscow, March 21, 1922: "We are all struggling to keep from dying of hunger, cold, and infectious diseases. . . . And many people, the majority of them prominent and familiar to you as well, have died. All people . . . right now are in an extremely difficult situation and wait for death as a savior from their undeserved suffering."[15]

On his birthday of April 2, 1922 [according to the Gregorian calendar for the twentieth century] Rachmaninoff performed his second and third concertos in a benefit concert, which brought in the especially large proceeds of $7,500. The entire amount was sent to Russia, which was suffering from the chaos and famines of the Civil War: the money was designated for professors, teachers, scholars, actors, writers, composers, and artists—all those whom the Bolsheviks considered of little use in the proposed new government. B. S. Nikitin summarizes:

> According to Rachmaninoff's instructions, parcels of food products were sent to the university [Moscow State University], the Conservatory, the Bolshoi Theatre and Malyi Theatre, and other cultural and scientific organizations of Moscow, Petrograd, Kharkov, Kiev, Kazan, Nizhnyi Novgorod, Odessa, and Saratov. K.S. Stanislavsky wrote to Rachmaninoff, "You are doing a really good deed, since the actors are in truth starving, but they keep working . . . I thank you again both from myself, my wife, and children, and from those actors who will be able to eat thanks to your provisions. We consider ourselves in your debt."[16]

Another letter from the same period of the early 1920s was written by T. L. Shchepkina-Kupernik:

> I never thought, highly-respected Sergei Vasilievich, when I was sitting in the White Ekaterininsky Hall [Tsarskoe selo] and glorying in your music, that the day would come when in the place of spiritual joy I would receive from you "my daily bread." I was touched more than I can say, that you remembered about

me, an unrelated and unknown person. I have many "friends" in the country in which you live—but none of them did this for me. I want to believe, want to hope, that sometime in my life there will still be a miracle . . . and your "bread will be transformed into roses," which I will give to you, my favorite composer-poet. I thank you again.[17]

Russian music critic Natalia Ostrom described about Rachmaninoff, "As if justifying the meaning of his ancestors' nickname [Rachmanin came to mean 'hospitable' and 'generous'], he was very generous in helping those in need . . . his secretary kept in the address book thousands of names of people whom he did not even know, and many of them later said that Rachmaninoff had saved their lives."[18]

For Rachmaninoff, Russian patriotism and humanitarian work were often intertwined. In the United States during the 1920s and 1930s he continued his charity work, appearing often at the Soviet Embassy in Washington and contacting other designated organizations to request ways for helping Russia. In a letter of April 18, 1922, to Frank C. Page of the American Relief Administration on 42 Broadway in New York, which was sending various kinds of assistance to Russia, Rachmaninoff appended two lists for recipients of relief. List 1 included 31 individuals and 2 associations, requesting that 35 drafts of $10 each be prepared. List 2 provided 23 individual addresses for food drafts, to be sent on the 25th day of May, June, and July of 1922. The monetary amount for the entire relief request came to $1,040, and Rachmaninoff enclosed a check in full.[19]

He continued to send money to Europe for many years to help Russian composers and writers who could not find employment, such as Nikolai Medtner, Ivan Bunin, and Igor Severianin. In 1939 he financed the departure from Europe to the United States of the entire family of Vladimir Nabokov.[20] During the years of World War II (up to his death in March 1943), Rachmaninoff through the International Red Cross sent many parcels to the Soviet Union to help people in desperate need of food and other supplies. He was committed to helping Russia in its times of apocalypse, continuing to support his lost homeland until the end of his life. As a contribution to the future victory, he singlehandedly financed a military tank for the Allied cause.

Which personal qualities and existential reasons motivated Rachmaninoff to demonstrate such extraordinary generosity toward others, to empathize with them and not forget their suffering? Two clues can give us entry to his motives: he manifested the virtue of active love foregrounded in his Russian Orthodox upbringing, and he had endured extreme hardship, both emotional and financial, in his childhood and young adulthood. As a consequence, Rachmaninoff retained a compassion toward those in need that was noticed by everyone who came into contact with him. A related characteristic of his is the sincere gratitude he always felt when someone would go out of his/her way to do a kind deed for him or his family. Rachmaninoff never forgot when someone, without being asked, would help him when he was in need. The factors that enabled him to offer assistance to others included his famous name, wealth acquired by hard work and discipline, reputation for fairness and honorable intentions, and persistence in the face of obstacles. Often one reads explanations of the dearth of new compositions on Rachmaninoff's part during the decade after his departure from Russia, but observers seldom draw the connection between the disaster of the 1920s in Russia and the efforts he expended (even with a staff to help with the logistics) to render help when it was desperately needed.

The quality of compassion was experienced by him not only in principle—it was a feeling that he translated into action. Rachmaninoff spent considerable amounts of time sympathizing with the fates of others, but also used his status in the international music world and his financial resources to alleviate the suffering of these "others." Representative anecdotes of his humanitarian acts can establish the international scope of his charity. They also can lead to conclusions for why Rachmaninoff maintained such a vast network of humanitarian efforts throughout his life, both in Russia and in emigration in Western Europe and the United States. His work ethic was legendary—he worked because he could not refrain from working, for he had to give voice to the creative springs within himself—but, equally importantly, he labored because he was supporting many people who depended on him for their livelihood and even survival.

Rachmaninoff saved the Sikorsky Aircraft Corporation from financial collapse by donating money to the company's efforts to build a cargo plane and helicopter. In the fall of 1923 he paid a surprise visit to the Sikorsky Aero Engineering Corporation on Long Island of New York. Russian engineer-inventor Igor Sikorsky and his loyal employees were working on a twin-engine, fourteen-passenger transport plane on a chicken farm, because they could not afford a suitable hangar for their work. Arriving at the farm in a Packard limousine, Rachmaninoff stepped out and walked around the plane in silence. He and Sikorsky entered into a long conversation. The result was that on the spot he loaned Igor Sikorsky $5,000 (equivalent to approximately $100,000 in twenty-first-century terms) to keep the struggling aircraft company from closing. The composer wanted to help this hardworking Russian engineer-inventor and told him that he believed in him and the planes his company was producing. Very moved, Sikorsky promised to pay him back. Soon afterward he invited Rachmaninoff to be the company's first vice president, and the composer accepted this gesture of appreciation. His name provided much prestige for the fledgling company, helping it to develop on a more solid footing. A close friendship between Rachmaninoff and Sikorsky was formed. In 1929 Sikorsky was able to pay Rachmaninoff back—with interest. Sikorsky's son Sergei adds that this gesture on Rachmaninoff's part was not made for investment purposes, but rather because the composer wanted to help a hardworking Russian who was in need.[21] A marvelous poetic outcome to Rachmaninoff's aid to the Sikorsky company was its first real profit of $500 from its airplane's transportation of two grand pianos from New York to Washington, D.C.

In 1925 Rachmaninoff financed the TAIR publishing house in Paris (1925–1935), in order to give his daughters a meaningful activity and to provide penniless Russian émigré composers and writers with an avenue for publishing their work [TAIR was an acronym of the first two letters of his daughters' names]. He was especially concerned that Irina not fall into a depression, since her husband Petr had died in August of that year, and he viewed the publishing house as a way to help her through the period of mourning. TAIR was vitally important for Russian creative artists as well, for their usual sources of publishing—in Soviet Russia—were closed to them. TAIR published many of Rachmaninoff's works and piano transcriptions during the years of its operations. Rachmaninoff loaned his close friend Ivan Bunin a large sum of money in the 1930s when the latter had a "stateless" residence in France. Bunin had won the Nobel Prize in literature in 1933, and had, in a similar act or generosity, used up the prize money by dividing it among Russian émigré intellectuals in desperate need. Consequently, he himself was left without a means of support. He appealed to Rachmaninoff in a moving letter full of dignity, assuring Rachmaninoff that he would repay the money. But they both knew this would be impossible. Rachmaninoff played his role in this sensitive exchange, advancing Bunin the money without any questions.

In the late 1920s as well Rachmaninoff maintained a correspondence with Bishop Antonin (Pokrovsky), who was assigned to Alaska to minister to the needs of the Russian Orthodox and Aleuts in that state. The composer sent Bishop Antonin a sum of money in a letter that illustrated his delicacy in offering financial assistance to others. Rachmaninoff wrote, "I am sending you the promised check for your church. But if your personal circumstances are difficult, I would be very happy if you spent the money for your own needs. And I will add that I was extraordinarily moved by your giving me your blessing before I embarked on my trip."[22]

Rachmaninoff's money helped to support the struggling Russian Orthodox Church in Europe and the United States during the years when the Russian emigration was trying to establish a church for its spiritual needs; his financial support rescued and sustained an untold number of Russian Orthodox church communities in the 1920s and 1930s. On January 3, 1929, Rachmaninoff sent His Eminence Evlogii, Metropolitan of the Russian Orthodox Churches of Western Europe a check for 2,500 francs (for the Russian

Orthodox Church and Russian émigrés in Europe); in the letter Rachmaninoff refers to a previous letter that he had written to the Metropolitan on December 26, 1928, indicating some level of acquaintance between the two men.[23] His prestige in the world of the arts and belief in the need for a Russian church to minister to the faithful in the Russian diaspora contributed in a significant way to strengthening and unifying the Russian Orthodox community in exile from the Motherland. The disastrous political situation in Russia prompted him to seek out ways to be in contact with his homeland by the assistance he was able to provide to individuals and organizations. In the Russian cultural context Rachmaninoff as a young adult had encountered powerful examples of brotherly love in the great classics of nineteenth-century Russian literature, particularly the novels of Dostoevsky and Tolstoy.

In fall 1929 a catastrophe befell Rachmaninoff's close friend and fellow composer-pianist Nikolai Karlovich Medtner after completing a series of recitals and lectures in Swarthmore and Haverford, Pennsylvania. The musical events met with tremendous success, but Medtner received the larger portion of his payment in a check for $2,500 that was falsified. When his wife Anna Mikhailovna arranged to deposit the check into a French bank, she learned that there were no funds backing the check and that it was a fake. Anna Mikhailovna would not rest until she contacted their dear friend Sergei Rachmaninoff to find a way to resolve the matter. Rachmaninoff legally "bought" the amount of the check and was issued the legal right to intervene in the situation, in order to attempt to identify the criminal who had created the fake. He corresponded with the lawyer entrusted with the case, paid the lawyer's fees, and remained in contact with Alexander Greiner, head of the Concerts and Artists division of Steinway & Sons, in order to advocate for the Medtners. Nikolai Medtner described this as a "terrifying time,"[24] for his family's ability to take care of their material needs was seriously compromised.

Medtner's personality in emigration turned out to be categorical and uncompromising concerning his music and the question of making a living from musical activities: he resisted the need to perform the works of other composers and was caught in the tide, as was Rachmaninoff to perhaps a lesser degree, of modernist music. He was less pragmatic and perhaps had a different kind of strength of will to survive than did Rachmaninoff. However, the Medtners' financial situation was never completely secure. He and his wife were able to leave Soviet Russia the same fall of 1921 as Aleksandr Siloti. Unable to establish himself in Germany, Medtner entered into a correspondence with Rachmaninoff that would result in the latter's sending him monthly stipends for several years in the 1920s. The Medtners in exile lived first in Germany, then in France, and finally settled in London.

Rachmaninoff's aid in the 1920s and 1930s involved not only money but also the use of his famous name for supporting American anti-Bolshevik organizations. In a letter of January 27, 1931, to Ralph M. Easley of the National Civic Federation (NCF) in the Metropolitan Tower, New York, Rachmaninoff praised the work of the NCF and hoped for cooperation between American patriotic organizations and the Russian National Antibolshevik Organization. In the letter Rachmaninoff referred to waging a war against "enemies of civilization and culture," clearly having in mind the Bolsheviks. He referenced possibilities for cooperation between American and Russian anticommunists. Rachmaninoff also cited in this letter the National League of Americans of Russian Origin, whose president Prof. Ivan Ostromyslensky was a good friend of his. He acted with dignity, but with great determination and concern for the destructive acts the Bolsheviks could still perpetrate in Russia.[25] Rachmaninoff maintained his involvement in local and international organizations who could help his compatriots in Russia, but he acted with caution as well—for the 1930s were the years of Stalin's clampdown on all the arts and tightening of his political surveillance of those in the Soviet Union. That Rachmaninoff acted with considerable courage goes without saying.

In a more lighthearted vein from his West End Avenue house in New York Rachmaninoff wrote to violinist Nikolai Konstantinovich Avierino on November 11, 1933:

Good-hearted Nikolai Konstantinovich,
    In answer to your letter . . . I want to tell you that I'll be at your place to dine with your friends, among whom in advance I warmly greet the monarchists and reproach the socialists.
    Addio, mio caro!
    S. Rachmaninoff[26]

Nikolai Avierino was a longtime musical associate of Rachmaninoff; before he left the Soviet Union he had been a professor at the Rostov Musical Conservatory of the Imperial Musical Society in Russia. He played many seasons in the Moscow Philharmonic Orchestra under the baton of Sergei Rachmaninoff. Their friendly association dated even further into the past: Rachmaninoff and Avierino had studied together at the Moscow Conservatory. On occasion Rachmaninoff, at Avierino's request, would send him money to help with his expenses.

During his years in Europe and America Rachmaninoff maintained regular contacts with the Soviet Embassy in Washington, D.C. (which he always referred to as the "Russian Embassy"). Instead of harboring feelings of resentment toward the government that had taken away his home and entire way of life, Rachmaninoff sought to help Russians in any way possible. His actions during this time were informed by his basic humanity, clear grasp of geography and politics as experienced personally, and general agreement with the philosophical ideas of his contemporary, the well-known Russian thinker Georgy Petrovich Fedotov (1886–1951). The latter wrote, "People think that they live by means of their love for Russia, but in actuality they live through their hatred of the Bolsheviks. But hatred of evil, even of the most justified, does not give birth to goodness. Most often the negation of evil gives rise to a new evil."[27] B. S. Nikitin rightly observes that this attitude reflects the Christian principle: "My beloved, do not take revenge! But overcome evil with goodness."[28] That Rachmaninoff found these religio-philosophical ideas congenial is supported by his humanitarian acts over the course of his life and even by his choice of the epigraph of his Symphony No. 1 in D minor: "Vengeance is Mine; Thus saith the Lord."[29] The evidence of Rachmaninoff's life and actions demonstrated that, even in times of bitterness toward the Bolsheviks for the catastrophe they brought about in his life, his Orthodox faith and evenness of temper mitigated against giving in to thoughts of evil. It may be that he did not formulate his thoughts this way, but he must have believed that faith and good works have the potential to overcome evil—one of the core philosophical positions of Fedotov.

Fedotov possessed a legitimacy in the Russian emigration, not only for his distinction as a religious philosopher and philologist, but because he himself had lived for several years in the Soviet Union and had witnessed firsthand the brutality of the Bolsheviks. In addition, his philosophical project converged with the particular conceptualization in Russian Orthodoxy of the Kingdom of God, namely that it is possible on earth. According to this belief, the Kingdom of God exists not only in the heavens but on earth as well; and not only in the church but in all people as having an absolute value and in all places. Matter is sanctified because it is a reflection of and is connected with heaven. Individuals must strive to dedicate their works to God; the dedication to the divine begins in its highest form in the human soul.[30] In his philosophy Fedotov was a worthy successor of the philosophical novelist and great thinker Fyodor Dostoevsky, and to some extent of the more liberal Russian religious philosopher Vladimir Soloviev.

While Rachmaninoff was not called on to give assistance to Georgy Fedotov, he did receive a request for help from another important Russian philosopher, Ivan Aleksandrovich Ilyin. Ilyin was a highly erudite philosopher of law and religion, who published works on Russian civilization, anti-Bolshevism, inner freedom, and various topics of philosophy East and West. In the 1920s, when Ilyin was in emigration in Berlin, he did not miss an opportunity to see Rachmaninoff in concert there. He deeply admired Rachmaninoff's music: the day after Rachmaninoff's concert in that city on December 5, 1929, Ilyin wrote to him:

Dear Sergei Vasilievich!

I returned home yesterday [after the concert] stirred to the depths of my soul. I wanted to write to you immediately, but I didn't know how to gather my strength for it. What sounds! What power! . . . This music is in truth superhuman. There were moments [during the concert] when I even felt terrified, as if I were on very high snowy mountains. . . . Will I ever succeed in finding the words to write about your music?

Your Ilyin[31]

Ivan Ilyin may not have succeeded in finding words to write about Rachmaninoff's music, but he did succeed in writing a four-part book titled *The Foundations of Art* [*Osnovy khudozhestva*, 1937], and he dedicated Part 1 "What is Art" [*Chto takoe iskusstvo?*] to Rachmaninoff.

Rachmaninoff rendered several different kinds of invaluable assistance to Ilyin. During the years 1927–1930 Rachmaninoff helped Ilyin financially in Germany, also providing monetary help to Ilyin's Russian-language journal *The Russian Bell* [*Русский колокол*], which was published those same years.[32] With the rise of Nazism in Germany Ilyin believed between the years 1934 and 1938 that he was being surveilled by the Nazis in the hopes of securing his support for a coming invasion of Ukrainian Russia. His only option lay in leaving Germany for Switzerland, where colleagues were waiting to help him settle into the academic community there. However, he could not obtain a visa to travel to Switzerland without a fee of 4,000 francs. He did not possess this sum of money, appealing to Rachmaninoff for assistance. Rachmaninoff quickly transferred the money, enabling Ilyin to emigrate to Switzerland; Ilyin thanked Rachmaninoff in a letter dated August 30, 1938, considering that his life had been saved by Rachmaninoff's financial intercession. Rachmaninoff helped Ilyin a second time when the latter was already in Switzerland by contacting the Swiss government with a character recommendation of Ilyin. This assistance enabled Ilyin and his wife to receive a residence permit for the country in 1939, which would also give him the right to work and earn a living.[33] On January 10, 1939, Rachmaninoff sent a letter to Ilyin: "Highly-esteemed Ivan Aleksandrovich, I received your letter of December 28 [1938] and am genuinely happy that your matter has been satisfactorily settled. I send Natalia Nikolaevna [Ilyin's wife] and you our sincere congratulations and best wishes for the New Year."[34]

Through the Embassy and the International Red Cross Rachmaninoff sent: parcels of food to Russians and Ukrainians—widows, orphans, and penniless musicians and artists—during Stalin's Terror-Famine of 1933; relief supplies to the Red Army in Russia; and parcels of food and medicine to Russian prisoners of war (POW) in Germany during World War II. Because Stalin did not officially acknowledge that there existed any Soviet prisoners in Germany, the Red Cross found it extremely difficult to minister to them, and as a result the prisoners were in appalling condition.³⁵ Moreover, Hitler treated the Russian prisoners far worse than he treated the French and British prisoners—for the Russian POWs were targeted for extermination, whereas the French and British POWs were being held as a matter of the protocols of war, with reasonably adequate rations of food. The Rachmaninoff archive at the Library of Congress is filled with heart-wrenching letters of gratitude from Ukrainians and Russians describing how their families would have died without the food relief and medicine they received from Rachmaninoff.

During the years of World War II Rachmaninoff's attention was anxiously focused on the needs of Soviet Russia far away: in 1942 he undertook to play several benefit recitals for the Soviet Red Army. That summer he was in California. Nikolay Mandrovsky, his private secretary from 1939 to 1943, forwarded to him some letters of criticism from New York from the organizers of these recitals and others in the music world. Rachmaninoff's response was direct and annoyed: "Of course I'll play again for Russia. To help Russia now is to help America. But everybody helps the latter and not many are helping Russia. I am still a Russian and therefore it's natural for me to go on advocating for her [Russia]."³⁶ He was indescribably distraught at the torments suffered by the people on the Eastern Front: "The mere thought of the hundreds of thousands of Russian people meeting their death, and of the barbarous destruction of priceless ancient Russian monuments made him shudder."³⁷ To keep his spirits as optimistic as feasible, Rachmaninoff asked members of his family to summarize to him, three times a day, the latest news of the war. He could not bear to hear the details.

An intriguing question arises with respect to Rachmaninoff's regular searches in Tambov in the late 1930s and early 1940s, quietly through his representatives in Soviet Russia. During those years, in part because of the Stalinist Terror and in part because of the displacement of millions of Russians throughout Russia and around the world, virtually every Russian language newspaper contained the section "In Search of" (*Розыск*). The Russian émigré newspaper based in New York, the *New Russian Word* (*Новое русское слово*), contained such a section. Thus Rachmaninoff's representatives in Tambov searched on a regular basis for persons important to him. But who could these individuals have been? His entire immediate family and all their relatives were either in Europe or America.

In Tambov, there exists a longstanding mystery concerning a former rector of the Institute of Music Pedagogy, Sergei Mikhailovich Glagolev, photographs of whom show a striking resemblance to Sergei Rachmaninoff. He was born on October 8, 1909 in the village of Chernianoe not far from Tambov. Glagolev's mother Anna Vasilievna was a resident of Tambov who never disclosed the father of her son Sergei, and a photograph of her husband

Mikhail Georgievich shows him to have an appearance radically unlike their son Sergei's. The legend circulates widely in this city that Rachmaninoff was the father of this child.[38] It is also striking and noteworthy that Glagolev was unusually tall and thin (as Rachmaninoff), and that he possessed extraordinary musical abilities.[39] In 2003 the accomplished Russian pianist Victor Merzhanov came to Tambov to perform, and in a conversation during a break in his recital stated, as if it were a well-known fact, "Glagolev was the son of Rachmaninoff."[40]

Sergei Glagolev died on January 24, 1977. Aleksandr Sergeevich Bazikov, former rector of the Tambov Institute of Music Pedagogy Named for Rachmaninoff, assumed his post in 1985. At that time there were people alive who remembered Rachmaninoff and the more recently deceased Glagolev; Bazikov as rector was able to speak with them at length. He characterized their impressions as perhaps being exaggerated, but true in their essence. What he heard from various individuals was consistent and quite different from the iconic image of Rachmaninoff as a gloomy and introverted man. Rachmaninoff was described to Bazikov as full of life, passionate, and very active in the social life of Tambov. The individuals who spoke with Bazikov indicated that Rachmaninoff without a doubt had short-term affairs with several women in Tambov.[41] It was not clear whether these encounters took place before or after he was married. Even if we factor in some exaggeration, the conclusions arise that Rachmaninoff was not the ascetic some believed him to be, and that he may not have been absolutely faithful to his wife. The existence of a child left behind in Tambov for whom Rachmaninoff felt some responsibility, and very likely a powerful familial bond, would explain his concerted efforts to locate someone halfway around the world to see if that person needed any material assistance.

What emerges as especially noteworthy is that one learns of Rachmaninoff's generosity and philanthropic activities from other sources, rather than from him himself. Boris Nikitin writes:

> No matter how often we return to this subject [of his humanitarian work], what is the most striking is the complete silence on the matter of Rachmaninoff himself. One never, at any point, heard from him that he had helped someone, that he had done something for someone. We learned about almost all of his humanitarian activities only after his death in various documents and letters. On one occasion the American pianist Newell Oler observed in an interview with especially insightful emotion: "He [Rachmaninoff] never had in himself anything flashy. His generosity was not illuminated in the newspapers. But he is one of the blessed, most generous people on the earth. I am certain that very few people know how much money he donated to the American Red Cross in Russia."[42]

Figure 12.1 Sergei Mikhailovich Glagolev, 1960s, Tambov, Russia. Permission of Tambov State Institute of Music Pedagogy Named for Rachmaninoff.

Only when one has undergone a specific experience can one fully understand others who are in the same circumstances. Rachmaninoff well understood the benefits not only of financial intervention but also of using his influence to rescue a Russian actor-director whose livelihood fell apart during the war in 1942–1943. This was Mikhail Chekhov, nephew of the famous playwright and short story writer Anton Chekhov, whom Rachmaninoff had met several times and whose stories he loved. Rachmaninoff held Chekhov in high esteem both personally and as one of the most gifted students of Stanislavsky's in Russia. Chekhov had studied method acting with Stanislavsky in the Moscow Art Theater (which the latter had taken from Feodor Chaliapin's acting philosophy) and moved to Berlin in 1928. He made his way to England, where he opened an acting studio in the 1930s. He found the means to transfer the studio from England to Ridgefield, Connecticut and then opened a branch in Manhattan in 1941. His acting studio developed financial difficulties early in 1943. Harlow Robinson explains: "The financial subsidies that had supported the acting school were coming to an end, and the draft was taking away most of the talented members of the company. It was at this moment that Rachmaninoff, who had only a few months to live, and Gregory Ratoff came to Chekhov's rescue."[43]

Even with his own preoccupations with his family's circumstances and a demanding composing and performing schedule, Rachmaninoff vowed to help Chekhov in significant ways. From his Beverly Hills home base, he made arrangements for the financing to transfer Chekhov's acting school to Hollywood, where he would be assured of many prominent students. Chekhov recalled:

> The war forced me to close my theater school and my new theater that had just been established . . . Sergei Rachmaninoff, having found out about this (and not saying a word to me), began to concern himself about my future fate. At this time he was in Hollywood. Out of his boundless kindness Sergei Vasilievich didn't spare either his labors or time to attain his goal and didn't cease his efforts until my arrival in Hollywood had been financially secured. He turned to Ratoff (a director who made films on Russian life), and Ratoff did everything in his power to fulfill Rachmaninoff's wish. And several times, when he was already ill, Sergei Vasilievich inquired about my situation. I kept waiting for the day when I could thank him personally for the irreplaceable help he had rendered to me, but he was fading quickly, and I did not succeed in seeing him . . . I thanked him mentally as I was kissing his cold, beautiful hand at the *Panikhida* [prayer service for the dead] in the Holy Virgin Mary Russian Orthodox Cathedral in Los Angeles.[44]

Rachmaninoff's intervention in Chekhov's fate came at a time when the latter's career could have ended; as a result of Rachmaninoff's help (and Chekhov's brilliance as an innovator in theater and film), Chekhov developed a sterling reputation especially as a pedagogue. Among his famous students were Marilyn Monroe, Yul Brynner, Ingrid Bergman, Gary Cooper, Gene Kelly, Patricia Neal, Gregory Peck, Anthony Quinn, and many other film stars.[45]

The particulars of Rachmaninoff's life explain his considerable capacity for responding to others in need. In this regard it is an accepted truism that suffering deepens a person's character and ability to empathize with others. Rachmaninoff in later years would reflect, not without some bitterness, on the personal hardship he had experienced:

> I had my full share of sorrows, sufferings, and privations. Though born in a wealthy family I soon discovered that I had to support and educate myself. Something went wrong with our family fortunes. So trouble began. As a boy I made good progress in music, and began giving lessons in piano when I was only sixteen years old. It was necessary for me to earn money by this means in order to continue my musical education . . . I am proud to say that I am a self-made musician. So after much trial and tribulation, when appreciation came I was happy.[46]

His Russian Orthodox moral virtues also guided his decisions to help others. He possessed a genuine attentiveness to others' sufferings and showed empathy for others precisely because of the hardships of his own life. He was able to balance his work ethic, clear desire to live and provide for his family at a high level of material wealth, and consciousness of the suffering of others. All of these sensibilities coexisted in his psyche in a sustained way made possible because his own daily needs were not directed toward luxury: he was happiest when composing at home or performing on the concert stage, enjoying time with his children and grandchildren, tending the flowers and trees in his garden, and reading Russian literature.

Rachmaninoff's daughter Irina Wolkonsky reflected on his manner with others in these extraordinarily complex and difficult times; she noted that as her father grew older he became more and more closed to outsiders:

> My father could be sociable only in the circle of his close friends, but even with them his sociability had strictly delineated boundaries, which he almost never crossed. These boundaries were noticeable in everything that had to do with his emotions and his inner feelings. He rarely expressed them in words. He was generally sparing in words. Evidently, this was why he didn't like to give interviews and did everything possible to avoid them.[47]

In this regard, it is also possible that guilt was a motivating factor for Rachmaninoff: he enjoyed tremendous wealth and international success at a time when other extremely talented Russian musicians and intellectuals were starving. He knew he would find it difficult, in the fourth language in which he felt least comfortable, to describe or express what for him was best accessed through his music. For him to speak about the pain of not being able to return to or even visit his homeland would have been devastating, beyond what he could bear. On at least one occasion, a dinner with the Horowitz family in Beverly Hills, he did express the guilt he felt at living in luxury when other Russians were struggling.[48] But instead of allowing this guilt to crush him, he transformed it into music and active love toward others that took the form of wide-ranging activism and humanitarian work.

NOTES

1. Scripture quotation from The Authorized (King James) Version. Rights in the Authorized Version in the United Kingdom are vested in the Crown. Reproduced by permission of the Crown's patentee, Cambridge University Press.

2. Personal interview, Ivanovka, July 23, 2003.

3. Sophia Satin, *A 20th Century Life: The Memoirs of Sophia Satin* (London: Rachmaninoff Society, 1997), 37–38.

4. Anna Pavlovna Artemova, "Rasskazyvaet Anna Pavlovna Artemova," in A.I. Ermakov and A.V. Zhogov, compilers, *Ivanovka. Vremena. Sobytiya. Sudby* (Moscow: Publisher of the Foundation of Irina Arkhipova, 2003), 158, trans. VZN.

5. Ibid., 157, trans. VZN.

6. See S.G. Zvereva, "Blagotvoritel'naia deiatel'nost' Sergeia Rakhmaninova v otnoshenii Russkoi Pravoslavnoi Tserkvi," in *Rakhmaninov—Natsional'naia pamiat' Rossii*, ed. I.N. Vanovskaia (Tambov: Iulis, 2008), 23–25.

7. Letter of Rachmaninoff to Morozov of April 4, 1923, in *S. Rakhmaninov. Literaturnoe nasledie . . .* , ed. Z.A Apetian (Moscow: Sovetskii kompozitor, 1980), 2: 143, trans. VZN.

8. Sergei Bertensson and Jay Leyda, *Sergei Rachmaninoff: A Lifetime in Music* (New York: New York UP, 1956; repr., Bloomington, IN: Indiana UP, 2001), 226.

9. Satin, *A 20th Century Life: The Memoirs of Sophia Satin*, 22–23.

10. Z.A. Apetian, ed., *S.V. Rakhmaninov. Pis'ma* (Moscow: Gos. muz. izd., 1955), 520–21, trans. VZN.

11. Boris Nikitin, *Sergei Rakhmaninov. Feodor Chaliapin* (Moscow: OTiSS, 1998), 144–45, trans. VZN.

12. Ibid., 145, trans. VZN.

13. Ibid., 144, trans. VZN.

14. E. Malisheva, in Sophie Satin [S.A. Satina], compiler, *Pamiati Rakhmaninova* (NY: Grenich Printing Corp., 1946), 62–63, trans. VZN.

15. Kovaleva-Ogorodnova, I: 335, trans. VZN.

16. Nikitin, 135, trans. VZN.

17. Ibid., trans. VZN.

18. Natalia Ostrom, Untitled liner notes in *Rachmaninov Plays and Conducts*, Vista Vera VVCD-00023 (1999), vol. 2: 6, Compact Disc, 7.

19. Sergei Rachmaninoff, letter to Frank C. Page, April 18, 1922, Section B1: Correspondence of Sergei Rachmaninoff, "A," Music Division, Library of Congress.

20. Stacy Schiff writes, "In the spring [of 1938] the composer Sergei Rachmaninoff responded to a dire SOS [from Vladimir Nabokov] with a generous twenty-five hundred francs, repayable whenever fortune permitted." Stacy Schiff, *Véra (Mrs. Vladimir Nabokov)* (NY: Random House, 1999), 94.

21. See Vadim Prokhorov, "Oldies and Oddities: Sikorsky's Piano Man," *Air&Space/Smithsonian*, November 2002, https://www.smithsonianmag.com/air-space-magazine/oldies-amp-oddities-sikorskys-piano-man-36005729/.

22. S.V. Rakhmaninov, Letter of March 20, 1927, in *S. Rakhmaninov. Literaturnoe nasledie . . .*, ed. Apetian (Moscow: Sovetskii kompozitor, 1980), 2: 206, quoted in Zvereva, 29–30.

23. Sergei Rachmaninoff, letter to Metropolitan Evlogii, January 3, 1929, Section B1: Correspondence of Sergei Rachmaninoff, "A," Music Division, Library of Congress.

24. Z.A. Apetian, ed., *N.K. Medtner. Vospominaniia. Stat'i. Materialy* (Moscow: Sovetskii kompozitor, 1981), paraphrase of 147.

25. Sergei Rachmaninoff, letter to Ralph M. Easley, January 27, 1931, Section B1: Correspondence of Sergei Rachmaninoff, "A," Music Division, Library of Congress.

26. Sergei Rachmaninoff, letter to Nikolai Avierino, November 11, 1933, Section B1: Correspondence of Sergei Rachmaninoff, "A," Music Division, Library of Congress.

27. Nikitin, 132–33, trans. VZN.
28. Ibid., 133, trans VZN.
29. Ibid., trans VZN.
30. Ibid., paraphrase of 133. See also Georgy Fedotov, *The Russian Religious Mind* (New York: Harper, 1960).
31. Kovaleva-Ogarodnova, I: 33, trans. VZN.
32. Viktor Klenov, *I.A. Ilyin: Pro et Contra. Lichnost i tvorchestvo Ivana Ilyina v vospominaniiakh, dokumentakh, i otsenkakh russkikh myslitelei i issledovatelei*, Russkii put' Series (St. Petersburg: Izd. russkogo Khristiianskogo gumanitarnogo instituta, 2004), excerpt in Klenov, "Russkii put Ivana Ilyina" (2013), https://proza.ru/2013/02/23/1286.
33. Ibid.
34. Z.A. Apetian, *S. Rakhmaninov. Literaturnoe nasledie* . . . (Moscow: Sovetskii kompozitor, 1978), 3: 141.
35. Eyewitness account of Eugenia Andreevna Caseria, who was forcibly taken from Ukraine to Germany in September 1941; in the region of Hamburg she sometimes secretly transferred food to the Russian prisoners. She recalled, "They were so terribly hungry. . . ." Personal interview, December 7, 2003.
36. Bertensson and Leyda, 376, translation edited by VZN.
37. Ibid., 373.
38. Personal interview with A. S. Bazikov, Tambov, Russia, July 7, 2003.
39. I viewed these photographs in the Museum of the Tambov Institute of Music Pedagogy Named for Rachmaninoff, July 8, 2003.
40. Personal interview with A. S. Bazikov, Tambov, Russia, July 7, 2003.
41. Personal interview with A. S. Bazikov, Tambov, July 8, 2003. Bazikov is currently a professor and chair of the Department of Folk Instruments of the Peoples of Russia at the Gnessin Academy of Music in Moscow.
42. Nikitin, 138, trans. VZN.
43. Harlow Robinson, *Russians in Hollywood, Hollywood's Russians* (Lebanon, NH: Northeastern University Press, 2007), 137.
44. M.A. Chekhov, untitled recollections, in *Vospominaniia o Rakhmaninove*, ed. Z.A. Apetian, 5th ed. (Moscow: Muzyka, 1988), II: 291, trans. VZN.
45. See Robinson, 138–39.
46. Basanta Koomar Roy, "Rachmaninoff is Reminiscent," *Musical Observer* 26 (May 1927), 16, accessed at https://www.pianostreet.com/smf/index.php?topic=17183.0.
47. Nikitin, 205–206, trans. VZN.
48. Robinson, 129–30.

Chapter 13

Paradise Regained
The Villa Senar (1920–1939)

After spending over a decade in the intense routine of concertizing in the United States during the fall and winter, and regaining his creative strength in Europe in the late spring and summer, Rachmaninoff felt secure enough financially to begin searching for a more permanent residence in Europe. Upon settling in the United States, the Rachmaninoffs had to adjust to yet another culture and improve their proficiency in English. Sergei was never comfortable with his English (humorously calling his command of the language "vile"), while Natalia developed a passable fluency in the language. They were deeply concerned about the political turbulence taking place in Russia and the suffering of her people. They had lost everything and had to rebuild their lives, both emotionally and financially.

The 1920s turned out to be difficult years in all ways. Their oldest daughter Irina developed a serious relationship with Prince Petr Wolkonsky, who came from a distinguished Russian family. Rachmaninoff's niece Sofia Vladimirovna Satina (the Rachmaninoffs' niece) relates the events that took place in Dresden, where her family was living and where the Rachmaninoffs were frequent visitors:

> Our next door neighbor was Count Obolensky and his family . . . The Obolensky daughter and son came almost every evening to be with us and the Rachmaninovs. Amongst them was a young man, a lodger who was studying art and wanted to be a painter. His name was Prince Petrick [Petr] Volkonsky. He was a very kind young man, very good looking as far as I remember, no comparison with some of the members of the Don-Cossack choir who came to visit us, too, and who were to my mind less aristocratic.
>
> As a nine-year-old child I was not aware that a courtship had started in our garden. Petrick and Irina were walking in the orchard every evening after dinner, and there he must have proposed to her. Everybody seemed to be happy

and excited about the event. The wedding took place [in 1924] in our lovely church in Dresden.[1]

Soon after the marriage Irina became pregnant, but in August 1925 tragedy struck: Petr committed suicide, for reasons the family kept private. But the reason trickled out: Petr was a homosexual, and his attempts to live a heterosexual life proved impossible. A credible immediate reason for the suicide was that Petr had struggled with his sexual orientation, tried to hide it from Irina, and shot himself when he found out that Irina knew of it.[2] Sophia Satina recalled:

> Arriving home, sad news [sic] was awaiting us. Petrick Volkonsky had died in a clinic in Paris. His daughter, Sophinka, was born after his death. Poor Irina became a widow not quite a year after their wedding. Much later I understood that Petrick had committed suicide being *in a confused state of mind*. But the older members of the family [presumably Sergei and Natasha Rachmaninoff] kept quiet. It was like a conspiracy not to let the outside world know the full truth.[3]

This conspiracy of silence, as it were, existed because of the adults' wish to guard the privacy of their family, to protect their daughter Irina in her grief, and also to avoid public disgrace—since the presence of a homosexual member in the family could be a major embarrassment. The Rachmaninoffs were devastated, because they loved their son-in-law very much and understandably worried about Irina's happiness. In a letter to Vladimir Wilshaw from Paris on April 19, 1926, Rachmaninoff expressed frustration about the hectic nature of his schedule, but also tenderness for his family and their loving treatment of him. He wrote, ". . . evidently somewhere in my life I did one good deed, for which God sends me this joy. I . . . had a son-in-law who was as good and whose treatment of me was like that of my children. But he did not survive."[4]

It is not clear whether the Rachmaninoffs knew about Petr's sexual orientation before his and Irina's marriage, but probably they did not. This would not have been a detail Petr would have shared with his future in-laws, and it is not certain that he shared it with his future wife. In Rachmaninoff's extended family it seems unclear what specifically prompted Petr to end his life. Sophia Satina related the following: "Petya Volkonsky committed suicide under some delusion that he was the martyred Christ."[5] If this latter account is accurate, it would point to some kind of mental illness, rather than the dilemma over a sexual orientation incompatible with heterosexual marriage. The Rachmaninoffs were concerned that the shock of Petr's death could adversely affect Irina's pregnancy, but their worries proved unfounded: on September 1, 1925, their first grandchild, Irina's daughter Sophia, was born healthy. It was at this time, with his career enjoying marked success but his family's misfortunes troubling him, that Rachmaninoff realized the development of the publishing house TAIR (the acronym of the first two letters of his daughters' first names). One year before these events, in 1924, he had published under the name "TAIR" the transcription of his song "Daisies" (Op. 38, No. 3), so clearly he had the idea for such a publishing house before his son-in-law's death.[6] One intent of this smart project was to occupy his emotionally distraught daughters—Tatiana, too, was affected by Petr's death—in meaningful and profitable ways (although it turned out that they had no interest in the project), and to provide a dignified means of livelihood for exiled Russian writers and artists who had no other way to promulgate their creative works. Rachmaninoff's very capable partners in the TAIR project were Gavriil Paychadze, Julius Conius, and Charles Foley.[7]

Both Rachmaninoff's own compositions and various book-length works by other individuals were published by TAIR. He published several of his transcriptions, the score and two-piano reduction of his Fourth Concerto, the score and piano reduction of *Three Russian Songs*, and the *Variations on a Theme of Corelli*. Among the book-length works that appeared under the imprint of TAIR are the following: *S. I. Taneev. Reflections on Creative Work and Recollections on Life*, by Leonid Sabaneev; *The Muse and Fashion*, by Nikolay Medtner; The Light of Reason, by Ivan Shmelev; *The Favorite Legends of Moscow. Three Hearts* and *Whirlwind Russia* by Aleksey Remizov; and *My Journey in Song*, by Nadezhda Plevitskaia.[8] This partial list of book-length works demonstrates Rachmaninoff's efforts to promote the name of his beloved teacher Taneev, assist his close friend and colleague Medtner financially through a book publication, promote the works of writers Shmelev and Remizov, and promote the singer Plevitskaia.

In the late 1920s, Sergei and Natalia had profitably sold their New York house at 505 West End Avenue; from 1929 to 1931, they had spent the summers at an estate named "Le Pavillon" in Clairefontaine-en-Yvelines, in the heart of France. During their last summer at Clairefontaine in 1931 Rachmaninoff composed the last of his solo piano works, the *Variations on a Theme of Corelli* (Op. 42). Dedicated to Fritz Kreisler, the set of twenty variations was first performed in Montreal on October 12 of that year. Anne McLean makes a convincing case for the influence of Kreisler as a violinist on Rachmaninoff's *Corelli Variations* and the *Rhapsody on a Theme of Paganini*:

> during the 1920s and 1930s . . . Rachmaninoff collaborated with [Kreisler] in recitals and recordings which gave him an insight into Kreisler's repertoire, technique, and style.

[Kreisler's repertoire] certainly included Corelli's Sonata for violin and continuo, op. 5, no. 12 (*La Folia*), which he played in a New York recital as early as 16 February 1908, and Paganini's twenty-fourth Caprice, which he also played in New York but on 13 December 1914. Was it the Kreisler connection that prompted Rachmaninoff to take up the *La Folia* tune in his new set of piano variations?[9]

McLean then introduces the question of the similarity between the *Folia* and *Dies irae* themes—the latter of which represents a persistent theme used by Rachmaninoff in many of his compositions. The melodic content of the two themes is almost the same, with the "matching pitches [providing] their own 'signature.'" The four notes traditionally representing the basic *Dies irae* melodic cell (F, E, F, D), with the "D" as a falling third, are commonly recognizable. McLean continues,

> Some composers need only quote the first four notes (which include the falling third) to establish the theme's identity. Rachmaninoff himself, in the Intermezzo of the *Variations on a Theme of Corelli*, the unnumbered variation between numbers XIII and XIV, alludes to this four-note melodic cell from the *Dies Irae* chant in the bass line.[10]

It is entirely plausible that the influence on Rachmaninoff of Kreisler and other prominent violinists such as Jascha Heifetz and Albert Spalding prompted him to compose music with string-influenced figurations. McLean points out, "Several variations, as well as the central Intermezzo and Coda, illustrate such string influences, for example, slurred bowing (Var. II), spiccato (Var. II), string crossing (Var. VII) and open 4ths and 5ths (Vars. XVI and XVII)."[11] However, in creating music with string figurations in mind, Rachmaninoff was able to make the necessary adjustments to translate the language of violin to a proper piano idiom. The richness of the *Corelli Variations* also lies in its rhythmic connections with American jazz, a movement in music that seriously interested Rachmaninoff. Thus many musical influences converged in the early 1930s to produce the *Corelli Variations* and the *Rhapsody on a Theme of Paganini*.

The *Variations on a Theme of Corelli* received mixed reviews, but the musicologist Joseph Yasser praised the work, even as he pointed out to Rachmaninoff that he had mistakenly given credit to Corelli for a theme that had been used at an earlier point by other composers of the seventeenth century.[12] Rachmaninoff graciously acknowledged the error, inviting Yasser to meet with him—not so much to discuss the error in crediting but to request Yasser's help to provide him with the full text of the medieval chant *Dies irae*. Even though the summers provided some respite from his concert tours, his need to compose, to write down in musical notation what was inside him, could not be suppressed.

Rachmaninoff also had the overwhelming desire to purchase land on which he could build a house for both composing and gardening when he was released from the contracts of concertizing. He especially wanted to find a parcel of land that could accommodate a large house for himself and his family for relaxation during the summer months and privacy for his composing work. His search ended in August 1930 with the purchase of land high on a cliff overlooking Lake Lucerne at 6 Zinnenstrasse in Weggis-Hertenstein, Switzerland. The jagged Swiss Alps rise in the distance, with Mt. Pilatus clearly visible from the Rachmaninoffs' land. Across the road from the site of Rachmaninoff's proposed estate is the Bildungshaus Stella Matutina (at 7 Zinnenstrasse), a Roman Catholic convent whose stately architecture and peaceful grounds must have conferred a sense of permanence and spirituality onto the wider region. The Bildungshaus is a pale peach building with white trim, which makes a cheerful impression on visitors when viewed from the gravel road. It stands at a higher elevation than Senar; one can walk uphill to the Bildungshaus to see beyond the high wooden fence of the villa and catch a glimpse of the main house of Senar. The community of Weggis-Hertenstein is known for its cherries and roses: a rose festival takes place there in June, which underscores the local appreciation for cultivating beautiful flowers—something Rachmaninoff in his fondness for gardening would have appreciated. The relatively temperate climate enables holly bushes, wild strawberries, magnolias, paper-bark birches, and pine trees to flourish; the air is humid enough to produce moss on the stones outside Senar. The soil in general is stony, which Rachmaninoff would not have appreciated, for this would require the soil in the property to be enriched and cleared of the larger stones before planting of the trees and flowers that he envisioned could commence.

The process of acquiring the land on which Senar was constructed is described by Ettore F. Volontieri, manager of the Serge Rachmaninoff Foundation:

> Rachmaninoff came to Switzerland and particularly to the Lake of Four Cantons, or Lake of Lucerne, for his honeymoon with his wife Natalia. He was up to the Rigi Hohflue, which is a beautiful mountain, from which you can see all the lake of Zurich and its amazing landscape. They both loved the place. There are several letters of Rachmaninoff saying how beautiful this place was. Then, we all know that 1929 marked the worst crisis for the American economy and then the World economy. By 1929 Rachmaninoff, thanks to his American activities, mainly piano concert performances and all the recordings, was able to amass a certain fortune. It was a bad time for people to have money, because the stock exchange was in a terrible shape due to the crisis. So I have a feeling that

Rachmaninoff was keen to invest his money so as not to lose it. Rachmaninoff had a great friend, Oskar von Riesemann, who lived in Lucerne. Suddenly, we see it from the archives of Villa Senar, the correspondence started between Rachmaninoff and Oskar about a beautiful piece of land becoming available for sale on the lake of Four Cantons [Lake Lucerne]. It belonged to a German businessman, who had a small spice factory and a Swiss chalet on the site. The site of 20 000 square meters was right on the lake in a beautiful location. . . . Rachmaninoff immediately jumped on the idea and bought this piece of land. Later Rachmaninoff asked a German architect to develop an extension for the chalet. However, the suggested projects were not appealing, and Rachmaninoff made a clear decision to build a completely new house, hiring two Lucerne architects, Krebs and Möri.[13]

The location of the house was in Weggis (part of the postal division of Hertenstein), not far from picturesque shore of Lake Lucerne, with the Alps surrounding the irregular borders of the lake. Not only was there ample room on the land for a main house, guest house, garage, and gardens, but the parcel also included the steep wall of a cliff with a rough descent to an old boathouse on the lake. The natural setting for the estate has been compared to the painting by Arnold Böcklin that inspired Rachmaninoff's orchestral tone poem *Isle of the Dead* (1909). Each summer Rachmaninoff would be able to retreat from his busy schedule of concertizing and various

Figure 13.1 Villa Senar, Weggis, Switzerland. Photo by © Pius Amrein / Luzerner Zeitung.

professional demands, and this retreat would take him as far away as possible from city life to a pastoral setting of idyllic beauty and tranquility. Only his closest friends would at these times have access to this inner sanctum of Senar.

Two houses stood on this large plot of land. The Rachmaninoffs decided to demolish the larger, three-story house that stood on the property, preferring instead to build a new house to their own specifications. First, the smaller two-story guest house, called the Gärtnerhaus, was completely remodeled. The Rachmaninoffs would live there, while the main house—planned in a modernist Bauhaus architectural style—was completed. It turned out that they lived in this smaller structure for two years while the larger main house was constructed from the ground up. Natalia teased Sergei that he was trying to recreate Ivanovka, and there was undoubtedly some truth to her words. Despite Rachmaninoff's reputation of being somehow "mired" in the nineteenth century, the architectural style of the house, its décor, and the Rachmaninoffs' collection of original art contemporary to the period, all attest to Sergei's desire to be firmly in step with the changing times.

Part of the cliff of the property had to be dynamited in order for a suitable foundation to be prepared for the main house, because there was a huge boulder that occupied the place where the foundation needed to be laid. Rachmaninoff enthusiastically participated in the planning of the house and gardens, planting some of the bushes and pine trees with his own hands and supervising the design of a rose garden. Volontieri clarifies:

> Rachmaninoff was able to create this place absolutely how he wanted. We can say that Senar was one of his compositions—there is so much of his personal taste, his presence. He made every single decision on how the house should be built and even which plants were to be planted in the garden. At Villa Senar we have a detailed archive of all the documents related to the construction of the house and one can see the personal contribution of Rachmaninoff in many ways.[14]

The house and landscaping projects were completed by 1933.[15] The Rachmaninoffs named their villa SENAR (an acronym for their first names, SErgei and NAtalia, and the 'R' of the family name). In a letter of April 19, 1932 to Dagmar Rybner Barclay, Rachmaninoff, who playfully began calling himself Wilhelm Tell of Senar, wrote: "Over here we earn our daily bread with hard labor—from morning till night we dig, plow, plant flowers, bushes, and trees—we blow up rocks and build roads—we go to bed with the hens and rise with the roosters. How hard the life is of a Swiss Bürger!"[16] In interactions with close friends Rachmaninoff was loquacious, witty, and self-consciously amused at himself and his activities. In the first years of

Figure 13.2   View of Villa Senar Complex, Weggis, Switzerland. Author's photo.

the twenty-first century there were still pine trees on the estate that Rachmaninoff's grandson could identify as having been personally planted by his grandfather.[17]

In July 1932, the Rachmaninoffs invited their friends Alfred and Katherine Swan (with whom they had become acquainted in the summer of 1928 in France) to visit them at Senar. Highly educated and active in the world of American music, the Swans were dear friends of the Rachmaninoffs. They were kind and compassionate people who were concerned about the fate of Russians in the aftermath of the Bolshevik Revolution. Sergei playfully called them "gusi-lebedi" (geese-swans) from the well-known children's folktale of that name. After the Swans had arrived and gotten settled in their quarters, over amiable dinner conversation Rachmaninoff complained about how much work and time it was taking to make the villa habitable, and how drastically the construction and establishment of his picturesque summer domicile interfered with his creative work. The role of a musical artist's wife prompted the following reflections on Sergei's part:

> A creator is a very limited person. Always he revolves around his own axis. There is nothing for him but his own creative work. I agree that the wife has to forget herself, her own personality. She must take upon herself all the physical care and material worries. The only thing she should tell her husband is that he is a genius. Rubinstein was right when he said that a creator needed only three

things—"praise, praise, and praise." The most frequent mistake of the wives is that they take the creator for a human being, an ordinary man.[18]

Sergei offered these reflections not out of a sense of superiority or self-importance, but rather with a touch of sadness concerning the existential condition of the creating artist. It was also true, however, that instead of living aloof from the world, he led a full life with lively interests in his family, international news, gardening, and art.

In April 1934, the main house of Senar and plans for the gardens were finished; the Rachmaninoffs were able to finally move into their permanent (for the summers) living quarters. Sergei's happiness was made complete by the delivery of a gift from the Steinway family, who had shared in and contributed to the fortunes made by his concerts and endorsements of their legendary piano, and who maintained the warmth of a genuine personal friendship with the Rachmaninoffs. Nikitin describes:

> On the morning of April 12 Sergei Vasilievich came down to his studio. The piano stood there, still covered with protective paper [Steinway pianos are sometimes delivered gorgeously wrapped in red and black satin]. . . . Only a pianist can know the happiness of touching the keys of such a grand piano. Sergei Vasilievich could not wait to extract from this gigantic instrument at the least a few chords, but Natalia Aleksandrovna was asleep upstairs, and he didn't want to disturb her sleep.
>
> And yet: "I carefully lifted the lid and softly played 'God Save the Tsar'"—Sergei Vasilievich wrote in a letter to A.V. Greiner, the representative of the Steinway Company. How marvelous this was: the first thought that came to mind at the new grand piano was for the lost Motherland! In published editions of the Soviet "Literary Heritage" of Rachmaninoff's letters, at each of his mentions of the words "God save the Tsar" these words were edited out, as was much else considered inappropriate for those times.[19]

The period of 1932–1939 represents one of the happiest periods of Rachmaninoff's life: his contentment and creative output during these years issued from the beneficial influence of Senar. Both his personal and musical identities were affected in positive ways. The dramatic natural location of Senar suggested asceticism and astonishing beauty, qualities connected with Rachmaninoff's identity and musical aesthetics. In addition to providing Rachmaninoff with a retreat for his spirit in the summers, Senar became a nexus for the gatherings of some of the most distinguished creative artists of that era. The families of Vladimir Horowitz and Nathan Milstein, who lived not far away on Lake Lucerne, were frequent guests, with Rachmaninoff, Horowitz, and Milstein often playing through musical scores together in Rachmaninoff's enormous studio. The studio held Rachmaninoff's library in a set of bookcases with glass doors lining the back wall, opposite to where his Steinway grand piano stood.[20] Feodor Chaliapin's visits were always a highlight for Rachmaninoff, since they understood each other so well and Chaliapin had the uncanny ability to make Rachmaninoff laugh boisterously at his jokes and turns of phrase.

A dark note inserted itself into this otherwise serene period for Rachmaninoff when Chaliapin, who was living in Paris, became ill with terminal leukemia during the year 1937. He had become a legendary actor-singer in his own time, and yet, as Rachmaninoff, he continued to long for Russia until the end of his life. The well-known journalist Andrei Sedykh recalled Chaliapin as lamenting, "Tell me, why do I have to sing in Bordeaux, or in Munich, and not at home, in Saratov?"[21] On April 10, 1938, two days before he died, Rachmaninoff came to visit him. In a letter to Sofia Aleksandrovna of April 20, 1938, Rachmaninoff described his last days of seeing Chaliapin, noting that in Chaliapin's final weeks he had visited him twice every day. He wrote:

> I saw him [Chaliapin] for the last time on April 10. As I used to do in the past, I succeeded in entertaining him a little; and he, just when I was getting ready to leave, began to relate that after his recovery he wanted to write another book for actors, the subject of which would be the art of the stage. Of course, he spoke very, very slowly. He was breathing heavily. His heart was hardly beating. I waited for him to finish and said, as I was standing up, that I, too, have plans: that as soon as I finish my concerts I as well will write a book, the subject of which will be Chaliapin. He smiled at me and patted my hand. At this moment we parted. Forever. The next day, April 11, I came to see him in the evening. He had been given a shot of morphine, was not conscious because of the narcotic, and thus I didn't see him.[22]

The next morning Rachmaninoff and Natalia Aleksandrovna set out for the drive to Switzerland to Senar. They arrived at 5:30 in the evening; they learned later that fifteen minutes before their arrival Chaliapin had died. Rachmaninoff did not attend the funeral, for he could not bear the thought of seeing his longtime friend in a coffin. He sent a large cross made of white flowers, with the inscription, "To my friend."

Activities at Senar were multifarious, and life continued in its usual rhythms. There were visits to Senar by Nobel-prize-winning writer Ivan Bunin, with strolls around the gardens and clambering carefully down the rough-hewn stone steps to the boathouse for a motorboat ride on the lake. Rachmaninoff had known Bunin since 1901, when the two of them circulated among the intellectuals, literati, and musicians in Russia. The Rachmaninoffs' daughters also enjoyed visits to Senar: Tatiana was an especially strong swimmer and would often be found in the water, rather than on it in a boat. Sergei's life was stable, peaceful, and fulfilling during this decade.

Some sources from Rachmaninoff's extended family attributed his happiness of this period in large part to the proximity of Elena Dahl, the mysterious woman whose fuller identity has to be verified and described. Alexandre Rachmaninoff recounted that Rachmaninoff had brought her to Weggis and she had settled in a house across Lake Lucerne. Natalia Rachmaninoff asked Sergei not to bring Elena to Senar; he respected her wishes on this point.[23] Sophia Vladimirovna Satina also affirmed the existence of other women in Rachmaninoff's life. Her husband Harold Tillek recounted: "I mention it because Sonia's remarks give real substance to it . . . She did not speak lightly to me about her uncle."[24] For Rachmaninoff only the marriage of his younger daughter Tatiana caused some consternation: she became engaged to Boris Conius, son of the violinist Julius Conius (1869–1942), but Rachmaninoff disliked the son so much that he did not attend their wedding on May 8, 1932. The Rachmaninoff and Conius families had known each other since Sergei's and Julius's musical training days at the Moscow Conservatory, but even this longstanding friendship did not persuade him to overcome his negative feelings toward his new son-in-law. He considered Boris's tastes unrefined and was concerned about his treatment of Tatiana. Their marriage lasted, but was not an easy union; they decided to make their home in Paris, where Boris had business interests. Alexandre Rachmaninoff did not speak much about his father, but admitted with distaste that Conius had no real profession and pursued a lifestyle that could be considered cheap and banal. Sophia Satina, who had a close relationship with her cousin Tatiana, recalls in words written down by her husband:

> Sonia [nickname for Sophia] thought that Tanya's husband Boris Conius was a slight and superficial man. He had lots of "good ideas" for starting enterprises (to be financed at Tanya's expense). One time it would be the making of a film. Then it would be the importing of tea to be distributed to selected clients. In the latter case Tanya was recruited to run around in a little van to distribute the tea to the various households. Sonia felt bitterly that Rachmaninoff's daughter should never have been asked to do such work . . . Sonia also said that Boris would tell "funny stories" at the dining table and laugh heartily at them. Tatiana would suffer quietly.[25]

Rachmaninoff's musical activities were extensive during this period. The spectacular beauty of the site of Senar, with snow-capped mountains and a royal-blue lake that could be seen through the large windows of his studio, could not but inspire the broad, sweeping musical thoughts he wrote down. Influenced by his family happiness and contentment with the ongoing gardening project of Senar, Rachmaninoff would compose some of his most important works during the 1930s. He adored his granddaughter Sophia and noticed in her a talent for poetry and song, which he felt she had inherited from her mother Irina. In 1933 he set some of Sophia's poetry to music.[26] That same year the Rachmaninoffs welcomed into their growing extended family Boris and Tatiana's newborn son Alexandre.

Rachmaninoff's concert season of 1933–1934 was finished with the last performance taking place in London early in March; a letter he sent to his secretary Somov reveals the transformational effect that an audience exerted on him before a performance: "The London concert went very well: plenty of people—nearly filled! and I played successfully. As for the welcome, it would seem that nowhere am I received with such pomp as here. Before the concert I didn't feel so well and came out on the platform rather 'sourly.' But the welcome touched me so that I decided to play well."[27]

Sergei and Natalia traveled to Paris where they spent several days and then set out for their final destination for the spring and summer, Weggis, Switzerland. Rachmaninoff wrote to Somov to share with him the joy of arriving at his beloved home:

> We drove through the gate of Senar just after seven that evening. It was already dark. But anyway, I went alone to inspect places around the big house, though I didn't go inside. Even in the darkness the impression was quite imposing. Then I went through the garden to examine all the trees. Everything is still rather bare, but there are tiny buds on some trees. This means we've come at my very favorite time—every day I'll be able to watch the trees and flowers opening.[28]

In the summer of 1934, with the main house of Senar being completed, Rachmaninoff composed one of his most memorable pieces, *Rhapsody on a Theme of Paganini*, a symphonie concertante. He worked on it between April and August of that year. The piece is a tour de force, consisting of an introduction (in which the theme of the last of Niccoló Paganini's *Caprices* for violin is established) and twenty-four variations on the theme. Along with Rachmaninoff's *Chopin Variations* (1903) and the *Corelli Variations* (1931), the *Rhapsody on a Theme of Paganini* completed the compositions by Rachmaninoff in the theme-and-variations form. The fascination of this process, of quoting a theme by another composer and composing a set of variations on it in different styles and tempos, kept the creative springs flowing for Rachmaninoff in a dynamic period of his life—filled with concert touring and the personal fulfillment of renovating a staggeringly beautiful piece of land for a longed-for haven from the vicissitudes of the world.

This composition is almost unique in the reception of Rachmaninoff's works—it was acclaimed by *both* critics and audiences. Robert Threlfall noted, "The *Rhapsody* is a complete repertoire in and of itself."[29] The piece is witty and playful, expressing various moods and musical textures and manifesting the composer's self-confidence and authorial control. In terms of artistic creativity, it reveals Rachmaninoff's fascination both with the concept of the virtuoso and with the legend of Paganini, whose extraordinary violin technique prompted his contemporaries to wonder if he had sold his soul to the devil—for aesthetic perfection and the love of a woman. As with the legend of Paganini, through this music Rachmaninoff's identity would endure. . . . Rachmaninoff programmed the *Rhapsody* immediately for the coming concert season: his first performance of it was in Baltimore on November 7, 1934, with the Philadelphia Orchestra, conducted by Leopold Stokowski. The *Rhapsody's* success was instantaneous, which delighted Rachmaninoff to no end—even as he was a little nervous about the composition being received with wild acclamation by absolutely everyone. During his American concert tour of 1935 an admiring critic exclaimed about his performance of the *Rhapsody*: "[Rachmaninoff] is the same crafty sorcerer, the gaunt, wise ogre in evening dress who shambles to the piano to draw from it the blazing fires of eloquence and the slow flame of poetry."[30] The *Rhapsody* led to an enjoyable collaboration between him and Russian choreographer-dancer Mikhail Fokin, who successfully used the music of the *Rhapsody* for his ballet titled *Paganini* (1939). Music from the *Rhapsody*, especially the lyrical Eighteenth Variation, has been adapted for use in numerous Hollywood films (examples include *The Story of Three Loves*, 1953, and *Somewhere in Time*, 1980). Threlfall opined about the Eighteenth Variation, "If ever there was a case of genius in our own time, that's it."[31]

Conductor Eugene Ormandy, who enjoyed a warm and fruitful professional collaboration with Rachmaninoff in the 1930s and until the latter's death, recounts his impressions of Rachmaninoff and first experience with him when Ormandy was musical director of the Minneapolis Symphony Orchestra. His recollections were recorded (on paper and cassette tape) in an interview with Morris Henken in 1973:

Morris Henken: You worked professionally with him [Rachmaninoff] on many occasions. Can you describe his physical appearance?

Eugene Ormandy: He was frightening. When I first looked at him and I first talked to him, I was afraid of him, because he was so much taller than almost anybody I knew at that time, that it took a long time before I realized that he was a very warm person, although he never appeared to be.

MH: Can you recall any instances when he was especially understanding and considerate, or, for that matter, when he was not?

EO: I was a very young conductor then, just started in Minneapolis, and one of my first soloists was—the legendary Mr. Rachmaninoff. He was playing his new . . . *Paganini Variations* [November 1935] . . . So I wrote to him, would he receive me and maybe we can discuss tempi, interpretation, etc. . . .

When I returned to Minneapolis, I rehearsed that work so hard . . . Every detail was worked out. Among other things, there's a variation . . . I've forgotten which one, sixteen or seventeen, where he plays all by himself. It's a rather fast variation. And I told the orchestra, "I won't conduct through the variation, but four measures before they enter, I start conducting."

At the performance, when we got to that particular variation I meant, he got lost almost immediately, and he began to play all over the place in different keys. Now, if he had remained in the same key, I would probably follow that, more or less as he was playing, but he was playing something entirely different . . . he was playing something else, but I should have come in. I looked, gave him a "scared to death" look, and he looked at me while playing, he says, "Play!"

So I forgot the four bars I promised the orchestra. I came right in, and we played. Of course everything went fine to the end, excepting that I had decided that I made a terrible mistake by leaving radio; I should have remained in radio where I had a fairly good reputation. Symphony is not my profession, and if things like this happen, this man is liable to do anything by the time the concert is over. So I was scared to death. When he finished, I was perspiring.

Everything went fine from then on, and when he got up, I didn't know what he was going to do. He got up . . . and walks over to me, shook hands with me. He says, "I am sorry. . . ."

So he pulled me into his dressing room. Every time he took a bow, he pulled me along, six and a half feet, with five and a half feet, like a little boy, and he was just so grateful to me.[32]

After the concert Rachmaninoff confided to Ormandy that he had just returned from London, where he had heard his friend and music colleague Benno Moiseiwitsch perform his *Paganini Variations*. Moiseiwitsch reached the point of the variation in question—and got lost. Rachmaninoff reacted in almost a superstitious way by fearing that he, too, would get lost upon approaching that same variation the next time he performed the work. And with the young Ormandy conducting, he did.[33] From this rather inauspicious, though colorful beginning, Ormandy and Rachmaninoff were to concertize together for many years, building a storied relationship of deep mutual respect and admiration. Ormandy would remain with the Minneapolis Symphony until 1936; in 1938 he became the maestro of the Philadelphia Orchestra, an organization that Rachmaninoff would elevate even over the first-rated Berlin Philharmonic.

In addition to his home-building, landscaping, and musical activities of the years 1932–1939, Rachmaninoff had the pleasure of seeing his major works, such as *The Bells* and the Third Symphony, performed in England and America in the concerts, respectively, of renowned conductors Sir Henry Wood and Leopold Stokowski. While he was still on the continent finalizing the score of the Third Symphony for its premiére in America, Rachmaninoff had the opportunity to attend a performance of *The Bells* at the Sheffield Festival on October 21, 1936. He had just previously performed his *Rhapsody on a Theme of Paganini* with the London Symphony Orchestra, and was looking forward to the program at Sheffield where he would perform his Second Concerto and hear *The Bells* under the baton of Sir Henry Wood. The Sheffield Festival Committee had corresponded with Rachmaninoff while he was still living in Russia as far back as 1913, but the various cataclysms of wars and social dislocations had kept delaying the inclusion of this massive choral work in one of the Festivals. During this process Rachmaninoff had made some cuts to the score that, while painful to him as a composer, were considered to improve the reading and performance of the work. Sir Henry Wood described concerning Rachmaninoff's edits in *The Bells* in the program notes for the Sheffield of 1936:

> The voice parts of this [third] movement were entirely rewritten for the Sheffield Festival last October 1936, and published separately, as the composer told me he found the choral writing too complicated, that it did not make the effect he intended. Certainly at Liverpool in 1921, I had the utmost difficulty in getting the chorus to keep up the speed and maintain any clarity, amongst the great mass of chromatic passages, and certainly vocal power was out of the question, and I feel the composer did very wisely in re-writing this section of the work. As it now stands, the chorus writing is splendidly distinctive, full of color, and easily "gets over" the brilliant orchestral texture.[34]

Sir Henry Wood was obviously relieved that Rachmaninoff had made the necessary changes in the third movement of *The Bells*—for when all the instruments (vocal and instrumental) in this choral symphony are performing simultaneously, the effect is overwhelming, and if the dynamics and acoustics of the concert hall are not properly calibrated, the choir can indeed be drowned out by the orchestra.

Wood further relates a humorous anecdote about Rachmaninoff and *The Bells* during the preparations for the Sheffield Festival: "An amusing incident occurred when the composer first played through his work to me, remarking that the piano arrangement in the published vocal score by A. Goldenweiser, was much too difficult for him to tackle, but he would do his best with it. Certainly it is the most difficult vocal score that I have ever seen."[35]

During the summers of 1935–1936, Rachmaninoff completed another major work at Senar, his Symphony No. 3 in A Minor, often referred to as his "Russian symphony" because of its embedded motifs of Russian folksongs and harmonies that were discernible mainly to Russian ears. This third symphony was for his grandson Alexandre the personal favorite of all three of Rachmaninoff's creations in this large-scale genre.[36] In its three movements and less dense textures this symphony, containing passages both stern and haunting in their nostalgic feel, also manifested a greater economy of musical expression. Robert Walker explains:

> The proliferation of the first two symphonies, for example, is replaced by a comparatively sparer style . . . which curiously enhances the emotional power of the work. The first movement, deeply tragic, is not morbid, but depicts a collapse so awesome in its inexorable tread that Mahler is often recalled. But unlike Mahler, Rachmaninoff's vision has the fateful objectivity of a Greek tragedy, finally overcome in the powerful finale.[37]

The quality of a "greater economy of utterance" (in Walker's words) pointed to Rachmaninoff's continuing to evolve his musical style in a more contemporary, modernist direction. The symphony successfully gestures to past classical forms, including as a motif the Latin sequence of the *Dies irae*.

Critical reception of Rachmaninoff's Symphony No. 3 was more on the negative side, and Western audiences (not recognizing the Russian musical contexts of the work) were also not appreciative. This is despite the masterful use of melodies, the impeccable orchestration, and well-organized structure of the whole—all of which Rachmaninoff as an experienced composer knew perfectly well. The less than positive reception of the symphony was disappointing and even bewildering to him. This had to do in large part with the unfamiliarity of American audiences and critics with the embedded Russian themes and motifs in the symphony—a feature that was recognized and appreciated in later years by Russian audiences. Thus this symphony became the "Russian" symphony of Rachmaninoff. Even though Rachmaninoff affirmed throughout his life that he "wrote down" only music stirring inside himself, and that his music was not nationalistic, in this symphony composed several years after he had passed the seventh decade of his life, ". . . here he heard his nation. This was a richly detailed dramatization of his feelings about Russia, his memories, love, and friendships there, his loss—an articulation in music of thoughts otherwise unspoken."[38] Rachmaninoff maintained confidence in the work, however, and his affirmation of the symphony was reinforced at its premiére by the Philadelphia Orchestra and its conductor Stokowski on November 6, 1936. Edwin Schloss of the *Philadelphia Record* wrote, "The new Rachmaninoff symphony was a disappointment at least to one member of yesterday's audience. Written in three movements, there are echoes in the music of the composer's earlier lyric spaciousness of style. But sterility seems largely written in the pages of the new score."[39] Schloss clearly was not cognizant of the Russian musical leitmotifs in the symphony, nor did he give Rachmaninoff credit for evolving a less ornate texture in this work.

A representative positive review of the same performance of the third symphony was published by Samuel L. Laciar in the *Public Ledger*:

> The symphony . . . is a most excellent work in musical conception, composition and orchestration. Emotionally, it is full of that defiant melancholy which is one of the outstanding characteristics of the composer. Mr. Rachmaninoff,

as always, has been conservative in his harmonizations, and he has given us another example in this work that it is not necessary to write dissonant music in order to get the originality which is the greatest—and usually the single—demand of the ultra-moderns. This symphony is thoroughly understandable musically at a single hearing, although several will be required before all the complexities of the technical side of the composition will be entirely clear, especially the contrapuntal writing of the final movement. Its single drawback seemed to be insufficient contrast in tonality and mood.[40]

Rachmaninoff would have appreciated the above review as not only complimentary and fair-minded, but he would also have noted (with some hidden delight) the not-so-veiled verbal jab at the "ultra-moderns" for their elevation of "dissonant music" as the definer of what is "original" in composition. The critic Laciar seemed to defend Rachmaninoff's symphony as being original, but without having to be atonal or dissonant in order to achieve that originality.

In 1939 Rachmaninoff himself conducted a performance of his Symphony No. 3 with this orchestra, which was recorded; in general he was cautious with the reproduction of live music, but he considered the Philadelphia Orchestra the best in the world and for this reason allowed the recording project to go forward. Taken together, both the *Rhapsody on a Theme of Paganini* and Symphony No. 3 represent Rachmaninoff's sophistication and maturity as a composer, enabling him to retain his own musical identity but also confidently incorporate into his pieces the musical impressions and influences of the world around him.

As the decade progressed it became increasingly clear to him and other Russians living in Europe that Hitler's military build-up posed a serious threat to their security on that continent. Once again Rachmaninoff would have to flee the gathering storm clouds. The summer of 1939 was tense, although the Rachmaninoffs tried to enjoy their family gatherings and the natural beauty of the setting at Senar as much as possible. In June Rachmaninoff made the decision to purchase a modest villa for his daughter Tatiana, for the family conversations had turned to the very real likelihood of leaving Europe for America perhaps sooner than they had planned. Irina and her daughter Sophia would join them in the United States as soon as possible, but Tatiana decided to remain in France—a decision difficult for her parents to accept. It was entirely understandable that with a war in the air in Europe every fiber of their being militated against being separated from their daughter by a vast ocean. Sergei did not like, trust, or respect his son-in-law, and this only intensified his conviction that he had to ensure Tatiana's material well-being as much as possible. The villa was located outside of Paris in the village of Chaudejoute, where she would be living alone with her son (her husband would continue to work in Paris). Rachmaninoff calculated that this second residence would give Tatiana a place to retreat to, if she felt she would be safer there than in Paris.

He played his last concert in Europe in Lucerne on August 11, 1939, conducted by Ernest Ansermet, in what was very likely a distressed and tense frame of mind. He kept his commitment to the artistic venue—but left Senar five days later for Paris and subsequently on the 23rd to travel to New York on the *Aquitania*. Sophia Satina reflected, "It must have been a bitter feeling for Uncle, when the family left Senar in 1939 rather hastily, as the war was imminent. This refuge in Switzerland was something which he created and had put his love and effort into building. And now again he had to leave something behind which was almost a replacement for Ivanovka."[41]

The Rachmaninoffs left Europe only nine days before Hitler invaded Poland on September 1, 1939. It has not been clarified how much Sergei and Natalia Rachmaninoff knew about Tatiana's fate during these years, because for those living in the United States during the war, news about relatives in Europe was scarce. The material circumstances Tatiana endured during the German occupation turned out to be quite difficult. Her son Alexandre would recall many years later that he had a younger brother who died soon after birth (possibly of starvation), but he and his mother survived.[42] Sergei would never see his daughter Tatiana or grandson Alexandre again, and he did not live to see the end of the war. He was never to learn the victorious outcome of the terrible invasion and destruction of his homeland.

NOTES

1. Sophia Satin, *A 20th Century Life: The Memoirs of Sophia Satin* (London: The Rachmaninoff Society, 1997), 23.

2. Personal Interview with A. A. Naumov, Moscow, July 8, 2004. Naumov referred to the archive of preeminent Rachmaninoff scholar Z. A. Apetian as the source for this information. No further information is currently available.

3. Satin, 25, emphasis added.

4. Sergei Bertensson and Jay Leyda, *Sergei Rachmaninoff: A Lifetime in Music* (New York: New York UP, 1956; repr., Bloomington, IN: Indiana UP, 2001), 245.

5. Sophia Satina, "Conversations with Sophia Vladimirovna Satina about Her Uncle Sergei Vasilievich Rachmaninoff," unpublished memoir edited by Harold Tillek and given by him to the author, London, June 24, 2005.

6. Liudmila Kovaleva-Ogorodnova, *Sergei Rakhmaninov* (Sankt-Peterburg: Vita Nova, 2015), I: paraphrase 366, trans. VZN.

7. Ibid.

8. Ibid.

9. Anne McLean, "Rachmaninoff: The Bohemian," *Studies in Music from the University of Western Ontario* 15 (1995): 103.

10. Ibid., 104.

11. Ibid.

12. Paraphrase of Bertensson and Leyda, 277–78.

13. Yulia Savikovskaya, "Villa Senar: A Magical Place Supported by Rachmaninoff Foundation," interview with Ettore F. Volontieri, posted on May 28, 2021, https://www.russianartandculture.com/villa-senar-a-magical-place-supported-by-rachmaninoff-foundation/.

14. Ibid.

15. N.A. Rakhmaninova, "S.V. Rakhmaninov," in *Vospominaniia o Rakhmaninove*, ed. Z.A. Apetian, 5th ed. (Moscow: Muzyka, 1988), II: 321–22.

16. Bertensson and Leyda, 286.

17. Personal interview, Alexandre Rachmaninoff, Senar, Weggis, Switzerland, June 23, 2004.

18. Ibid., 287–88.

19. Boris Nikitin, *Sergei Rakhmaninov. Feodor Chaliapin* (Moscow: OTiSS, 1998), 234.

20. The author of this biography played the Steinway piano in Rachmaninoff's studio for several hours during three visits to Senar for the purpose of meeting with Alexandre Rachmaninoff.

21. Andrei Sedykh, "Далекие, близкие" [Those far away and near], *Новое русское слово*, New York (1979), 131, quoted in Victor Borovsky, *Chaliapin: A Critical Biography* (New York: Alfred A. Knopf, 1988), 532. Sedykh became editor-in-chief of this major Russian émigré newspaper in 1973.

22. S. Rakhmaninov, Letter, in *S. Rakhmaninov. Literaturnoe nasledie. Pis'ma*, ed. Z.A. Apetian (Moscow: Sovetskii kompozitor, 1980) 3: 125, trans. VZN; see also Borovsky, 532–35.

23. Personal interview with Alexandre Rachmaninoff, Weggis, Switzerland, June 23, 2004.

24. Personal interview with Harold Tillek, London, June 24, 2005.

25. "Conversations with Sophia Vladimirovna Satina about Her Uncle Sergei Vasilievich Rachmaninoff." Sophia Vladimirovna's cousin Tatiana helped her [no doubt with Rachmaninoff's financial assistance] to locate her missing brother: "News that her younger brother, who had disappeared during the war, had been found in a camp in Siberia, brought her back to Europe [from Canada, where she had been living]. With her cousin and close friend Tatiana Rachmaninov, the composer's daughter, she fought to get her brother released." Annalena McAfee, "Symphony for a True Survivor," *Evening Standard*, March 25, 1993.

26. This song cycle was discovered in October 2004.

27. Bertensson and Leyda, 301.

28. Ibid., 302.

29. Personal interview, Robert Threlfall, London, June 24, 2005.

30. John K. Sherman, Review, *Minneapolis Star*, 1935, quoted in Bertensson and Leyda, 315–16.

31. Personal interview, Robert Threlfall, London, June 24, 2005.

32. Eugene Ormandy, Interview with Morris Henken, Philadelphia, PA (1973), Annenberg Rare Book & Manuscript Library, University of Pennsylvania. WorldCat record id: 155901926.

33. Ibid., paraphrase of the conclusion of this anecdote told by Eugene Ormandy.
34. Sir Henry Wood, Program Notes, quoted in Bertensson and Leyda, 322.
35. Ibid., 322–23.
36. Personal interview, Alexandre Rachmaninoff, Senar, Weggis, Switzerland, June 23, 2004.
37. Robert Walker, *Rachmaninoff: His Life and Times*, 2nd ed. (Neptune City, NJ: Paganiniana Publications, Inc., 1981), 119.
38. Bertensson and Leyda, quote and paraphrase, 325.
39. Edwin Schloss, Review, *Philadelphia Record*, November 7, 1936, n.p.
40. Samuel L. Laciar, Review, *Public Ledger*, November 7, 1936, n.p.
41. Sophia Satin, *A 20th Century Life*, 39.
42. Alexandre Rachmaninoff told the author of this book that he had a brother who died shortly after birth. Personal interview with Alexandre Rachmaninoff, Senar, September 3, 2004. He also told V. I. Antipov about the death of his brother.

Chapter 14

The Last Bow
Rachmaninoff and America (1920–1943)

Americans are drawn to Russian music, perhaps without realizing that a rich admixture of influences defines this national music tradition: Byzantine and Russian Orthodox liturgical chant, Russian folk music, and European classical music. Rachmaninoff's compositions contain this interweaving of influences, and whether because of them or for purely aesthetic reasons, his music has always been popular with American audiences. Critics would engage in various polemics about the style (too traditional, not modernist enough), themes, and other features of his compositions, but audience reception of his music was consistently positive. The English composer-pianist Kaikhosru Shapurji Sorabji profoundly admired the music of Rachmaninoff, expressing his appreciation in various articles and letters. His assessment of Rachmaninoff's colossal talent in the context of twentieth-century critical reviews is articulated thus:

> During the mid-twentieth century, Rachmaninov was the subject of harsh critical opinion that generally saw his music as syropy, showy, and saccharine, though it remained highly popular with audiences. Rachmaninov's great melodies and obvious romanticism have at times masked the inspired craft, the finely spun counterpoint, and the structural cohesion indicative of the greatest composers. His stature continues into the twenty-first century, with many of his orchestral works and concertos being heard by sellout crowds.[1]

Rachmaninoff's Concerto No. 2 for Piano and Orchestra in C minor was in the twentieth century and remains in the twenty-first one of the most popular concertos programmed by American orchestras, because of its compelling melodies and impressively balanced orchestration. Despite the occasional critical disapproval of his music, not on its own terms, but because it was (according to the critics) out of step with modernism and atonal music, Rachmaninoff's "25 American tours were a chain of unbroken public successes, and a 1939 poll voted Rachmaninoff the third most popular living composer, after Sibelius and Richard Strauss."[2]

These tours, which in themselves involved travel to many places and culminated in summer vacations in Europe, brought Rachmaninoff into contact with some of his era's most distinguished and fascinating musicians and intellectuals. In a real sense Rachmaninoff's receptions and dinners in New York, some of them very likely taking place after a Bohemian Club event, became gatherings for the world musical elite. With Rachmaninoff's entry to America and its culture, he and this country entered into a marvelous symbiotic relationship: he united Russia and America perhaps more than any other exponent of Russian culture of that era, while America provided for him a way of life filled with dignity and professional acclaim.

It is a known fact that knowledge of a foreign culture's particulars results in the breaking down of stereotypes of that culture in the population receiving and experiencing the monuments of the "other." It follows, then, that the stereotypes of Russia and Russians were dispelled or at least challenged in Americans when Russian émigrés performed their music in America and attempted to assimilate themselves into American ways. Feodor Chaliapin was a conqueror in Italian opera, astounding the highly discerning Italian audiences in Milan with his majestic, expressive voice and also breaking down their stereotypes of a "boorish Russian bear" being able to live up to their standards and perhaps even surpass them. Musicologist Igor Yuzefovich observed, "the multi-ethnic nature of the musical folklore in Russia and the United States combined with the presence of a large number of Russian musicians in America 'fostered the affinity that Americans felt toward Russian culture.'"[3] Americans' acquaintance with the Russian musical world was rooted in the nineteenth-century tour in America of Russian virtuoso Anton Rubinstein in 1872, which consisted of an astonishing 215 recitals in 239 days. This major event, according to Anne Swartz, "brought the modern [and especially Russian] piano repertoire to small towns and regions where there would have been little opportunity for concerts of classical music."[4] Even for those familiar with the Western classical canon, Rubinstein's performance style, dynamics, and colossal piano technique would have introduced a different cultural idiom to the American public. There were dramatic differences between Western and Russian classical musics, as elaborated by Truman Bullard, who identified the "audible characteristics of Russian musical style" as foregrounding a "deeply emotional quality," an unmediated directness of connection with the listener, unpredictability, fluidity of style and form (rather than standing squarely on the shoulders of a centuries-long European tradition), a vivid "narrative and pictorial character," philosophical inspiration, and indirect expressive elements of humor and satire.[5] These features produced a totality far different from the qualities to which American and Western audiences were accustomed.

Another connection with American musical culture is found in Rachmaninoff's melodic and harmonic structures, where one discerns echoes of jazz, that authentic African-American music whose intimacy and complexity attract listeners of all socioeconomic classes. Andrew Huth notes concerning Rachmaninoff's works of the American and European periods (1920–1943): "These later works develop and deepen the unchanging features of his musical style, but also contain new and even somewhat surprising elements—a more acerbic harmonic sense, sharper contours, distinct hints of a jazz influence."[6] Huth was referring to the Piano Concerto No. 4 (1926), *Variations on a Theme of Corelli* (1931), *Rhapsody on a Theme of Paganini* (1934), the Symphony No. 3 (1936), and *Symphonic Dances* (1940). These major (and except for the solo piano Corelli Variations) large-scale compositions completed between 1926 and 1940, when viewed along with Rachmaninoff's heavy concert schedule, represent a sustained outpouring of creative work that in the ways outlined above can be examined as a group.

Contrary to stereotypes about Rachmaninoff's music, when one delves deeper one encounters an enormous breadth of expression and consummate compositional technique, along with the wit and emotion characteristic of American jazz. The similarity between some of Rachmaninoff's compositions and jazz is apparent in his cross rhythms and predilection for a *rubato* that still manages to capture the beat. Contemporaries of Rachmaninoff noted that when he was at home in New York he would improvise jazz in a marvelous way at the piano. Rachmaninoff kept up with developments in jazz in New York and California; his patronage of the musical performances of Paul Whiteman (who called himself "the king of jazz") and his orchestra in the 1920s is a matter of record. Among other events that he supported by being an audience member, Rachmaninoff attended Whiteman's famous Aeolian Hall concert of February 12, 1924.[7] On December 7, 1924, Rachmaninoff gave a recital in Providence, Rhodes Island; after the recital he stayed (perhaps one or two days longer) to hear Whiteman and his orchestra, who were performing in that same city. After the performance Rachmaninoff expressed his gratitude, perhaps to be conveyed to Whiteman himself:

> Mr. Rachmaninoff said: "My compliments to Mr. Whiteman! He has the finest orchestra of its size I have ever heard. I have long been an admirer of his work, and each month I send to my daughter in Europe the records made by this remarkable organization.
>
> "The charm and interest of this orchestra for the musician is that it is undoubtedly new. That is to say, it expands and develops its material in a

characteristic and novel fashion which to me is absolutely fascinating. This may certainly be called authentic American music, for it can be heard nowhere else that I know of.

"My friend Medtner calls Mr. Whiteman the best storyteller he knows in music; storytelling is exactly what Mr. Whiteman's short pieces are. Excellent pointed anecdotes, crisply told, with all the human breeziness and snap that are so characteristic of the American people.

"And the arrangements of these pieces are a marvel to me. 'By the Waters of the Minnetonka,' for instance, is a beautiful theme developed in an ingenious manner that could not be excelled."[8]

Whiteman famously developed a jazz arrangement of Rachmaninoff's Prelude in C sharp minor, and when the latter heard it performed one evening, he stated wryly that he liked it better that way. Duke Ellington's jazz orchestra also often performed an arrangement of this prelude at the Cotton Club in Harlem during the years 1927–1932.

New York during the 1920s and 1930s was teeming not only with extraordinary classical musicians, but it also saw the rise of some of the most distinguished jazz pianists and band leaders to make their mark in that music genre. Rachmaninoff, Vladimir Horowitz, Artur Rubinstein, and Arturo Toscanini were among the many classical musicians dazzled by the masterful pianism and improvisations of Art Tatum. The serious interest that Rachmaninoff maintained in jazz became well-known enough in New York's music community that stride pianist "Fats" Waller was sometimes called "the Rachmaninoff of jazz." Both Rachmaninoff and Waller would become artists who signed with RCA Victor to market and preserve their music in recordings. In Hollywood in 1943, the year of Rachmaninoff's death, it is noteworthy that the connection between Russian émigré musicians and jazz was reinforced by Vernon Duke's (original Russian name Vladimir Dukelsky) composing of the music for the first all-black film-musical *Cabin in the Sky*.[9]

Several of Rachmaninoff's art songs could easily be incorporated into a recital of blues songs. Examples include "In My Soul," "Harvest of Sorrow," "Rat-Catcher," and "Daisies." Indeed, the convergence of classical and jazz styles in Rachmaninoff is perhaps most noticeable in the Opus 38 cycle of songs resulting from his creative collaboration with the poet Marietta Shaginian. The songs' haunting beauty, dense texture, and direct emotion move American listeners, but there may be another, more intriguing factor that draws American audiences to the Russian song. This factor concerns the similar origins of the Russian song and American jazz, especially in the latter's "blues" strain. It is well known that the Russian art song evolved from the German *Lied* of the late eighteenth and early nineteenth centuries. Significantly, the *Lied* in its Berlin tradition is connected with two qualities: it was *sangbar* (melodic) and *volkstümlich* (connected with the style of popular, or folk, singing).[10] These roots of *Lieder* in the musical style of the common people are similar to the origins of Russian art songs in the folk songs of peasants. Moreover, the role of the peasant lead singer (*zapevala*), who invites those working in the fields to join him in singing, closely resembles the call-and-response style of singing of African-American slaves—a style that, along with its tendency toward the minor scales, evolved into the blues of jazz. Rachmaninoff heard peasant singing for many years in the Russian steppes at Ivanovka. He was intensely attracted to the melodies of this singing—and later, in exile in America, he was fascinated by jazz, remarking that the future of American music lay in this new and intriguing musical idiom.

Rachmaninoff composed most often in the minor keys, and it may be that the tonal qualities evoked by these keys were what attracted him to the blues of jazz. A look at the basic Blues Scale will establish its minor sonorities. The scale is a variation of the Minor Pentatonic: C E^b F G B^b C. The Pentatonic scales are a class by themselves and do not need seven degrees, as in the diatonic scales. Thus the Blues Scale developed into the following (for example, in the key of C): C E^b F F# G B^b or 1 b3 4 #4 5 b7. The "blue" or "bended" note is the E^b. It is this degree of the scale that African-American slaves were "bending" down from the major sonority; the "bending" was the "expressive dissonance" that flowed out of their tragic, though not defeated, experiences in the culture that enslaved them.[11] Russian peasant singing also consisted of characteristically minor-key melodies and harmonies of surpassing beauty. The sources for the emotions the peasants expressed were not that different from those of the African-American slaves. Again, Rachmaninoff intuitively sensed the commonality and responded to it in his own compositions, including his art songs. Because the songs contained both poetic lyrics and an accompaniment often of equal value, the feelings expressed were doubly conveyed through the words and the music. When Americans hear Rachmaninoff's art songs, they may recognize in the dignity, suffering, and complex beauty of these songs the earmarks of a major multicultural genre of their own musical tradition.

Rachmaninoff's musical activities stretched across the American continent from New York to California, and even into Alaska. In New York, where he resided, he maintained ties with the cultural elite and helped the Russian Orthodox Church in emigration to establish itself, sometimes financially and sometimes providing advice on performance of his sacred music. In California he met often with Russian émigrés in the entertainment world, and excerpts from his music found their way into both Hollywood films and cartoons throughout the twentieth century. Among the numerous examples are *Grand Hotel* (1932), *A Day at the Races* (1937), *Brief Encounter* (1945), *The Seven-Year Itch* (1955), *Somewhere in Time* (1980), and *Shine* (1996). Rachmaninoff once wittily remarked to Walt Disney, after seeing one of the latter's completed cartoons, that the performance in it of "Maestro Mouse" (Mickey Mouse) of his Prelude in C sharp minor ranked among the best. Walt Disney had heard of Rachmaninoff even before he met him, and wanted to include Rachmaninoff's Piano Concerto No. 2 in his animated musical film *Fantasia* (1940)—which featured captivating silhouettes of conductor Leopold Stokowski.[12] However, for reasons that remain unknown, the Piano Concerto No. 2 was not selected for the film—despite the fact that the producers and directors at the Disney studio were clearly drawn to Russian sounds: they used in *Fantasia* music by Stravinsky, Shostakovish, and Mussorgsky.

An admirer of the films of Charlie Chaplin, Rachmaninoff had the opportunity to interact with him in private settings. Chaplin recorded a revealing conversation at a dinner attended by himself, Rachmaninoff, Horowitz, Toscanini, and conductor-cellist John Barbirolli:

> That evening I [Chaplin] said that art was an additional emotion applied to skillful technique. Someone brought the topic round to religion and I confessed I was not a believer. Rachmaninoff quickly interposed: "But how can you have art without religion?" I was stumped for a moment. "I don't think we are talking about the same thing," I said. "My concept of religion is a belief in a dogma—that art is a feeling more than a belief." "So is religion," he answered. After that I shut up.[13]

Rachmaninoff's choice of New York for a residence and base for his music activities enabled him to keep close touch with international cultural events, such as the 1922 tour of artists of the Moscow Art Theatre. Because of his background in Mamontov's private opera and strong interest in theater (solidified no doubt by his intensive collaboration with Feodor Chaliapin, the "singing actor"), Rachmaninoff admired and tried even from outside of Russia to keep up with news of the Art Theatre. When the Theatre came to New York, Sergei and Natalia Rachmaninoff attended as many performances as possible and hosted late-night receptions for the entire company at their home at 33 Riverside Drive. Sergei Bertensson, who was manager of the troupe during this tour, recalls:

> We came on nights after the performance, and what memorable nights they were! There were lively theatrical and musical recollections, discussions of the day's events, stories told by our host, his cousin Alexander Siloti, the choreographer Michael Fokine, Stanislavsky, Knipper-Chekhova, Kachalov, and Moskvin . . . Catching every word and watching every movement of Moskvin's expressive features, Rachmaninoff's face, usually so pensive and concentrated, would be transformed . . . he surrendered himself to the happiest and most carefree laughter, throwing back his head, and brushing away tears of joy with the back of his hand.[14]

Before the troupe of the Moscow Art Theatre returned to Europe, they visited Rachmaninoff at the Locust Point house in New Jersey that served as a kind of *dacha* for his family:

> After dinner everyone performed in [Rachmaninoff's] honor, with Chaliapin, who had come along, as star: he gave imitations of a breathless accordeon, the drunken accordeon player hauled to the police station, a lady adjusting her veil before a mirror, an old woman praying in church. At two in the morning, when the guests seemed about to go, Chaliapin barred their exit: "Where are you going? I only stopped for breath—Sergei Vasilyevich and I will really show you something!" With Rachmaninoff at the piano Chaliapin sang on and on—peasant songs, bits of opera, gypsy songs, and finally, at Rachmaninoff's request, "Dark Eyes" [*Ochi chernye*]. One of the guests, Ivan Ostromyslensky, recalled the occasion:
> On that hot July night at Rachmaninoff's house the small drawing room was divided in two, for the stage and the audience, the first row on the floor in Turkish style. With Sergei Vasilyevich at the piano Chaliapin pranked and charmed us all night.... Our party broke up only at 5 a.m.
> Next day at lunch I saw Rachmaninoff again ... "Tell me, Ivan Ivanovich, what made the greatest impression on you last night?" Without waiting for my answer, he went on, "I'm sure it was 'Dark Eyes'—I don't doubt it. How he sighed, that villain, how he sobbed 'you have ruined me!'—I couldn't sleep, for thinking, 'How God endowed you beyond other men!' ... Oh, that sigh!"[15]

Rachmaninoff was fascinated by the advances in piano manufacturing and by the advent of each method of sound reproduction, using his prestige in the music world to promote (in different ways) the Mason and Hamlin piano, and the Steinway piano. He completed some gramophone recordings and also made rolls for the reproducing piano (Ampico piano rolls) of a number of his own works in the 1920s. In 1919 Rachmaninoff made some recordings for the phonograph with Edison Records, which requested that he use the Lauter grand piano that they kept in their New York studios.[16] These important reproductions of Rachmaninoff's playing impressed not only the composer-pianist himself, but, more than any other medium, preserved for posterity the distinctive and delicate features of his pianism.

Max Harrison describes some results of Rachmaninoff's playing, as reproduced by the various recording methods of the 1920s:

> [Rachmaninoff] went to their [Ampico] New York studio and—as the sole exception to his use of the Steinway—recorded with their 6'6" Mason and Hamlin grand for just ten years (March 1919 to February 1929), cutting some 35 rolls, 29 of them in parallel with his gramophone recordings. Rachmaninoff's playing is always highly characteristic but, although instantly recognizable on the rolls, he is even more vividly himself on gramophone records, even those

Figure 14.1 Ampico Piano Roll of Rachmaninoff Performing His Prelude in C Sharp Minor. Author's collection.

from early acoustic sessions. The music recorded on rolls—and this applies equally to other great pianists—often sounds fractionally coarser than on the gramophone, whatever the latter's acoustic limitations.[17]

In 1920 he entered into contract with the Victor Talking Machine Company (later renamed RCA Victor), recording not only his own music but that of other composers, and once in a while collaborating with other musical artists (such as Fritz Kreisler). He continued his recording activities with RCA Victor until 1942.

One of the major diplomatic achievements of Charles Foley, manager of both Rachmaninoff and Fritz Kreisler, was to secure their recording with RCA Victor in 1928 of three violin sonatas with piano accompaniment. Recording of the three musical pieces was completed: Beethoven's G major sonata, Grieg's C minor Sonata, and the Schubert *Duo*. Foley described how the project materialized:

> The idea of collaborating for the sonatas was born in my house in New York City during a talk about music—what else?—between these two great men, and my house was the place selected for the rehearsal for reasons you might call "social protocol." Rather than have the rehearsals in Mr. Rachmaninoff's house one day and Mr. Kreisler's the next day, we decided on neutral ground. The two

Figure 14.2   Victrola Talking Machine Ad Featuring Rachmaninoff, April 1921. Author's collection.

friends—they had become close friends by this time—were assembled at my house, and the only listener to their rehearsals was a manservant I had, a Korean, who admired both but was not very much interested in occidental music. He made coffee for them, which they gratefully and copiously consumed. There they felt free to discard their coats and waist-coats, discuss and sometimes argue about tempi, shadings, etc., and as you might say—let their long hair down.[18]

The amount of work was huge: each of the six discs was recorded five times, or a total of thirty discs. From the thirty the musicians selected the best six and destroyed the remaining ones. During this process the differences in temperament between Rachmaninoff and Kreisler created some arguments about the quality of the results, as opera singer and actress Geraldine Farrar recalled:

Kreisler would come out of the studio in high glee, still aglow with the beautiful music, which he had helped to create. Rachmaninoff, on the other hand, emerged with his sad face, worried about this or that phrase which he thought had not quite come out as it should. He would continue to brood over the situation for days and finally decide that another recording ought to be made. His friend Fritz, however, thought only of the beauties of their ensemble effort and artfully dodge the issue of doing the whole thing over again. As Rachmaninoff put it to Miss Farrar in his slow deliberate way: "Fritz—he is like a flea; one just can't put a finger on him."[19]

By 1926 Rachmaninoff was able to say that he liked America immensely and had gotten into its rhythms of life.[20] While he would pine for Russia to the end of his life, at least he had grown comfortable in the United States and could experience the normal rhythms of living again. Concerts in America provided Rachmaninoff with a lucrative means of earning a living, which not only meant a secure future for his family but a source of funds for his humanitarian activities as well. He was one of the highest-paid pianists and musical celebrities of his time. While he felt overall that Americans devoted too much of their time to going after the dollar (at the expense of enjoying leisure time with friends and family), he appreciated how expertly business typically was conducted. In 1930, upon returning to New York after being on tour in New England and Canada, he noticed that he had several free days in his touring schedule that could not be used for relaxation or composition—they would be wasted days. On this occasion he asked Charles Foley to arrange for concerts not far from New York, so that he could easily travel to the given locations and return home on the same day after performing his recital. Foley set up concerts for him in Englewood, New Jersey and Mount Vernon, New York. Rachmaninoff was delighted to be able to use these days productively, earn some money, and have his morning coffee and evening tea at home.[21]

Rachmaninoff's concert schedule was packed, and he performed usually to sold-out houses. He would remain at the height of his career until his last concert only a few weeks before his death. His reputation and popularity reached Washington, D.C.: During the presidency of Calvin Coolidge of 1923–1929, through the invitations of First Lady Grace Coolidge (who was a gracious hostess) Rachmaninoff performed in the White House on three separate occasions by the summer of 1927. The dates of those performances are March 10, 1924; January 16, 1925; and March 30, 1927. In a letter to Nikita Morozov started on the day before the January 1925 recital (and finished on January 19), Rachmaninoff refers to playing "for the President at the White House" almost as a matter of course, after which his whirlwind schedule of touring would commence.[22] His concert schedule in America and Europe was so busy and so packed with high-profile engagements that a performance at the White House fit right in as one of many prestigious appearances.

Rachmaninoff had successfully executed seven demanding years of concertizing (1919–1925) and was financially in a good enough position to take time off in 1926. He needed the time for rest, but also desired to once again write down his musical thoughts. He sold his house on Riverside Drive at a profit, liquidated his affairs in the United States, and moved to Europe for a period of rest and composition. The year of 1926 saw the resurgence of Rachmaninoff's creative inspiration in the form of two noteworthy compositions, the Concerto No. 4 in G minor for piano and orchestra (Op. 40), and the *Three Russian Songs* for chorus and orchestra (Op. 41). These were among the few musical works he produced in the 1920s, but their melodic and stylistic craftsmanship affirmed to Rachmaninoff's colleagues and audiences that his compositional springs were still flowing. Conceived and completed between January and August of 1926, the Concerto No. 4 was dedicated to Nikolay Medtner. However, fragments of the concerto had been tested several years earlier: After Medtner emigrated from Soviet Russia in 1921, he met Rachmaninoff in Florence several times in April 1924 and possibly there the latter had played those fragments for him. Rachmaninoff began working on the piece two years later in earnest in New York, taking it with him on his family's spring and summer peregrinations of 1926—to Paris, Weisser Hirsch (outside of Dresden), and Cannes where they rented a Rothschild villa (that turned out to be quite expensive). Upon completing the composition and later receiving the copied piano score in Dresden, he was initially appalled at what he thought was its excessive length—110 pages. In correspondence with the dedicatee Medtner, Rachmaninoff expressed the concern, but received a magnanimous, complimentary, and yet soberly worded reply from Medtner on September 13, 1926, reassuring him about the length:

> I cannot agree with you, either in the particular fear that your new concerto is too long, or in general on your attitude to length. Actually, your concerto amazed me by the fewness of its pages, considering its importance. . . . Is it

possible that music in general is so unpleasant that the less of it the better? Naturally there are limitations to the lengths of musical works, just as there are dimensions for canvases. But within these human limitations, it is *not the length* of musical compositions that creates an impression of boredom, but it is rather the *boredom* that creates the impression of length.[23] [emphasis original]

Rachmaninoff had also shown the new concerto to Josef Hofmann, and the latter, similarly to Medtner, was extremely complimentary of this large-scale work. The concerto was to have a tortuous reception journey, most likely because critics and audiences were expecting a composition that resembled the Second and Third Concertos, instead of one that was architecturally more streamlined and less emotionally direct than the previous concertos. What was missing from the Fourth Concerto's three movements was in a real sense not Rachmaninoff's fault; rather, its tragedy lay in the critics and audiences not recognizing and not being sympathetic to Rachmaninoff's evolution of his style to a more sparse, modernist mode.

Even composer-musicians who esteemed Rachmaninoff very highly were troubled by the Fourth Concerto; Kaikhosru Sorabji wrote, "After the splendour and richness [of its predecessor] the Fourth Concerto is a stark, rather bare and gaunt work, that comes in style and treatment rather within the domain of the *sinfonia concertante* than the concerto in the proper sense."[24] Martyn notes, "the theme of the concerto's second movement seems to be in almost deliberate antithesis to the great sweeping melodies of earlier years, and the second subjects of the outer movements are both short-breathed and incapable of the kind of apotheosis so attractive in the Second and Third Concertos."[25] It is worth considering that if the Fourth Concerto had been conceived by a composer other than Rachmaninoff—one from whom the musical world and audiences would expect works of a more modernist and avant-garde bent, rather than from a Rachmaninoff whose style was in the Late Romantic vein but who was developing his idiom in very original and inspired ways—then the immediate reception by critics and audiences alike may have been much more appreciative.[26]

The Fourth Concerto was premièred in 1927 along with the *Three Russian Songs* on March 18–19 in Philadelphia under Stokowski's baton, and on March 22 in New York. Critical reception of it was overwhelmingly negative; an example is the review of Pitts Sanborn in the *Telegram*:

> The concerto in question is an interminable, loosely knit hodgepodge of this and that, all the way from Liszt to Puccini, from Chopin to Tchaikovsky. Even Mendelssohn enjoys a passing compliment. The orchestral scoring has the richness of a nougat and the piano part glitters with innumerable stock tricks and figurations. As music it is now weepily sentimental, now of an elfin prettiness, now swelling toward bombast in a fluent orotundity.

It is neither futuristic music nor music of the future. Its past was a present in Continental capitals half a century ago ... Mme. Cécile Chaminade might safely have perpetrated it on her third glass of vodka.[27]

With reviews largely skewering, trivializing, and dismissive of the Fourth Concerto, Rachmaninoff kept the commitments for performance of it that he had made with the Philadelphia Orchestra, but then withdrew the concerto from concert programming. He revised it some years later.

Both the composition and reception histories of the *Three Russian Songs* were diametrically opposed to the fate of the Fourth Concerto. The *Songs* were dedicated to Stokowski, who wrote to the composer:

> The more I try to penetrate the inner essence of your new [fourth] concerto and the Russian Songs, the more I love this music. For me these are two of your most wonderful works, and I am very proud that I am taking part in their performance and that the Russian Songs are dedicated to me, for there is so much of the beautiful ancient poetic spirit of Russia in them that I so greatly admire.[28]

Maestro Stokowski was preparing the première of the Songs at the Academy of Music in Philadelphia on December 18–19, 1966.

A letter to Leopold Stokowski of February 18, 1966, signed by a representative of Charles Foley, Inc. (Foley had been Rachmaninoff's manager during his lifetime, became a publisher of his music, and remained a close friend of Irina Rachmaninoff Wolkonsky) described the background for the *Three Russian Songs* (sometimes listed as *Три русские песни* or *Trois Chansons Russes*):

> Dear Mr. Stokowski:
> It has taken me longer than I thought to obtain information about the *Trois Chansons Russes*, which I promised you, as Mr. Rachmaninoff's daughter is not too well. I am sorry for the delay.
> I am happy now to relate what [Irina Rachmaninoff Wolkonsky] has told me:
> That her father composed the work in 1926. It was played for the first time in Russia in 1934 [at the Bolshoi Theatre], Golovanov conducting, in a "rather strange program" consisting of Scriabin's *Prometheus*, and *Poème de L'Extase*; *Songs on Hebrew Themes* of Moussorgsky, and the *Trois Chansons Russes*.
> Mr. Rachmaninoff, always sensitive to texts and the "sound of words," first saw the text of the first song in a folk song collection, and was touched by the plight of the drake and the wild duck; the orchestration and choral setting resulted.
> Chaliapin sang the second song to him—unaccompanied; later recorded it in Germany and gave one of the first copies to Rachmaninoff. Chaliapin recorded it again in the 20's with the Victor Co. here.

Rachmaninoff first heard the third song sung by Plevitskaya, a peasant who became famous in Russia for the singing of folk songs only. She gave successful concerts all over Russia, and sang also in Paris and New York. Rachmaninoff wrote a piano accompaniment to this third song, of which she made a record (which was never released [during Rachmaninoff's lifetime]).

Professor Wilshaw of the Moscow Conservatory referring to Trois Chansons Russes wrote: "Only a man who loves his country can write such songs, and only a man who is at heart a Russian—and such a man is Rachmaninoff."[29]

Concerning the third of the *Russian Songs*, a memorable event for Rachmaninoff was the concert tour in the United States of the accomplished Russian singer Nadezhda Plevitskaia in 1926. Plevitskaia specialized in gypsy and peasant songs, possessing both a keen musicality and "Russianness" in her singing that Rachmaninoff admired. Her informal performance in New York of the authentic gypsy song "You, My Cerise, My Rouge" produced a wistful nostalgia in Rachmaninoff, but also influenced the third of his *Three Russian Songs* for chorus and orchestra. Rachmaninoff convinced RCA Victor to record a performance of this song by Plevitskaia with him as accompanist.

Rachmaninoff used all his inner resources and emotional resilience to survive the critical blows he received concerning the Fourth Concerto. It is not difficult to imagine that, with such devastating responses to his concerto—and having this negative feedback aimed in his direction, questioning his music's relevance or even his competence as a composer, in a country foreign to his own culture—Rachmaninoff determined that his best chances at earning a living resided in his performances as a preeminent pianist. The superlative latter identity of his few could challenge in any convincing way. Martyn summarizes: "The 1926 sabbatical had meant the expenditure of a great amount of time and effort, not to mention a financial sacrifice, unrewarded by commensurate artistic success, and over the next four years Rachmaninoff's only work on composition was the brief piano transcription of Rimsky-Korsakov's *Flight of the Bumblebee*, completed early in 1929."[30]

Despite the temporary setback represented by the Fourth Concerto, Rachmaninoff was firmly settled into his concertizing activities in the 1920s and 1930s; his popularity with audiences was not on the wane. When relaxing with his family and close friends, he could be lighthearted. He loved to watch comedian Jack Benny, loved to laugh in general, and valued the ability of others, such as his dear friend Chaliapin, to make him laugh. He enjoyed the thrills and unusual attractions of the circus. He also enjoyed owning and driving expensive cars, such as his Cadillac (1919) and Packard (1938). Mikhail Chekhov related:

> Sometimes the soul remembers a departed great man in simple, unpretentious images: a word, glance, short encounter, moment of silence, smile. The soul

loves such moments. They don't diminish the greatness of the departed, but on the contrary—make his image come alive and be as close [to one] as in the past.

I remember that one time my modest car, covered with dust, found itself alongside [Rachmaninoff's] magnificent Packard, glittering in the sunlight. I began to feel a little awkward. He very likely noticed this, came up to me, and for a long time examined my "basic car" (not paying attention to the Packard).

Then he said convincingly, "You have a really good car."

And he said it in such a way that I actually believed that my car wasn't so bad at all.[31]

A highlight and source of genuine satisfaction for Rachmaninoff, a public summing up of his achievement in music, was the "Rachmaninoff Cycle" initiated and performed by the Philadelphia Orchestra under the baton of Eugene Ormandy in the fall of 1939. This was a series of concerts of solely Rachmaninoff's music, involving him as pianist and conductor, which took place at Carnegie Hall in New York and also the Academy of Music in Philadelphia. The concerts were intended to celebrate the thirtieth anniversary of the first concerts he had given in America. The New York program for the first concerts would be as follows:

November 26, 1939 Eugene Ormandy, Conducting
Symphony No. 2 in E minor, Opus 27
Concerto No. 1 in F sharp minor, for Piano and Orchestra, Opus 1
Sergei Rachmaninoff, Soloist
Intermission
Rhapsodie on a Theme of Paganini, Opus 43
Sergei Rachmaninoff, Soloist

December 3, 1939 Eugene Ormandy, Conducting
Concerto No. 2 in C minor, for Piano and Orchestra, Opus 18
Sergei Rachmaninoff, Soloist
Intermission
The Isle of the Dead, Opus 29
Concerto No. 3 in D minor, for Piano and Orchestra, Opus 30
Sergei Rachmaninoff, Soloist

December 10, 1939 Sergei Rachmaninoff, Conducting
Symphony No. 3 in A minor, Opus 44
Intermission
The Bells, for Soprano, Tenor, and Baritone Solos, Chorus of Mixed Voices
    and Orchestras; Susanne Fisher, soprano; Jan Peerce, tenor; Mack Harrell,
    baritone;

The Westminster Choir, with John F. Williamson assisting[32]

The November 26 concert was a resounding success that lifted Rachmaninoff's spirits and touched him—audience members rose from their seats in his honor, indicating their abiding affection and support for the composer-pianist and his music.[33] The *Historical Society of Pennsylvania* noted about the event:

> Conceived and directed by Ormandy in consultation with the composer, these concerts featured the 66-year-old Rachmaninoff in various roles as pianist, conductor, and special guest. The *Cycle* was billed as "one of the outstanding musical events of all time" and was a great success, critically and commercially. Following the *Cycle*, Rachmaninoff performed with the Philadelphia Orchestra five more times in the early 1940s, until his death in March 1943.[34]

Rachmaninoff and Ormandy had forged a relationship of respect and trust based on a sustained understanding of Rachmaninoff's music and an orchestra that was considered one of the finest in the world. Rachmaninoff not only performed his major works with this orchestra but also recorded a number of his compositions with it on RCA Victor Records: his First, Third, and Fourth piano concertos were recorded with Ormandy conducting; his Second concerto and the *Rhapsody on a Theme of Paganini* were recorded with Stokowski conducting. At a time when Rachmaninoff was at the peak of his career and fulfilled in his social and philanthropic activities, the cloud of Hitler's military activities in Europe was hanging over him. Because of his annual touring and stays in Europe for rest and renewal, as well as his personal knowledge of Russia—demoted to being the largest geographical unit of the Soviet Union—for him the cities and countries affected by Hitler's military build-up and political ambitions represented a concrete, personal reality. The Russians and Europeans in the Rachmaninoffs' circle of friends shared this understanding of these parts of the world, but for the Americans who had never been abroad the activities of Hitler seemed less concerning and more of an abstract. Rachmaninoff would find this divide difficult to bridge at times, but when possible would explain where this or that city in Russia or Europe was located and why it was important.

In summer 1940 the Rachmaninoffs rented the seventeen-acre Honeyman estate on Long Island, a secluded property with a beach, pier for boating, and a beautiful pastoral landscape. With the looming war always on his mind, Rachmaninoff found it difficult to concentrate on composing, and the distractions of long walks, boat rides, and relaxation from concertizing were fleeting for him. He plunged into work on a new large-scale composition, an orchestral suite in three movements, which he eventually titled *Symphonic Dances*. In

September of that year he invited Eugene Ormandy to the estate to review the work with him—they worked for many hours, as Ormandy humorously recollected, without eating. The *Symphonic Dances* reflect Rachmaninoff's evolving, more modernist style, with some passages reminiscent of Prokofiev's dissonant harmonies and Stravinsky's primitive rhythmic drive; the whole was expressive of the composer's intense emotions concerning the darkening political atmosphere in Europe and Hitler's growing threats to Russia. The piece is distinctive in its use in the first movement of an alto saxophone as a solo instrument, a nod to American jazz that extended the saxophone repertoire further into the classical realm. In the second movement, in waltz tempo, the melody's eeriness and figurations spotlighting individual instruments combine to create an unresolved atmosphere evoking witches dancing on the Sabbath. The third movement presents a struggle between the forces of Death (represented by the *Dies irae* motif) and of Christ's Resurrection (indicated by a quotation from the ninth movement of Rachmaninoff's *All-Night Vigil*). The Resurrection emerges victorious, but only after the music portrays its intense struggle with evil and death.

Evil became monstrously palpable for Rachmaninoff on June 22, 1941, when Hitler invaded the Soviet Union. Declaring all Russians "Untermenschen" (subhumans) and targeting Russia as "Lebensraum" (room for living), Hitler treated Russians and the Russian land with special savagery. Rachmaninoff worried about the fate of the millions of Russians being slaughtered in the war or left in conditions of starvation, the battles involving the Red Army, and the plight of his daughter Tatiana and her family in France. He continued to perform, however, playing a revised version of his Fourth Concerto in October 1941, and in July of the following year performing at the Hollywood Bowl. He regularly played benefit concerts for the Red Army, donated money for medical supplies for his native country's armed forces through the Soviet Embassy in Washington (which he always called the Russian Embassy), and arranged to have parcels of food sent to Moscow to feed the city's people in their time of great need. During this difficult period Rachmaninoff donated the proceeds of his concerts to the cause of the Red Army whenever possible.

On November 16, 1941, after a recital in Boston he returned to New York for several days, and on one of them—November 19—he arranged to have the following amounts of money transferred to the Soviet diplomat Viktor Fediushin: $3,920 from a concert of November 1, $25 from Aleksandr Siloti, $30 from Sofia Satina, and $25 from Albert Gallatin. In a letter that Fediushin sent to Rachmaninoff on November 27, 1941, he confirmed that, according to Rachmaninoff's wishes, the donated money was used to purchase medical equipment (specifically X-Ray machines) for hospitals in the Soviet Union.[35]

Anticipating his retirement from concert tours, attracted by California's warm climate, and valuing the Russian émigré community in the Hollywood area, Rachmaninoff early in 1942 rented a house on Tower Road that was private, located in a scenic and hilly neighborhood of Los Angeles, and large enough to accommodate two grand pianos. Not far away were the Horowitz and Stravinsky families, with whom he could reminisce about the past and share musical experiences. The two grand pianos provided him and Vladimir Horowitz with many enjoyable hours of playing through their favorite repertoire. An endearing anecdote involves Rachmaninoff's taking of a large jar of honey personally to Stravinsky.

Several months later the Rachmaninoffs purchased a house at 610 North Elm Drive in Beverly Hills. In an area available only to the wealthy, the Rachmaninoffs' house was one of the more modest—a two-story structure of stone with wood trim. The downstairs had a large, pleasant vestibule at the entryway with a ceiling about 22 ½ feet high. Overall in the house the ceilings were not especially high. The rooms were considered ample, but not large, yet Sergei and Natalia were very satisfied with the layout. Sergei immediately started to plan his garden in the relatively small backyard. They hosted evenings of music and conversation attended by many Russian émigrés who made their living in the arts in Hollywood, such as the successful and talented actor Akim Tamiroff and his wife Tamara, the actor-director Mikhail Chekhov, former manager of the Moscow Art Theatre and author Sergei Bertensson, pianist Vladimir Horowitz and his wife Wanda, and composer Igor Stravinsky—and many others. The Tamiroffs became very close friends of the Rachmaninoffs. As with Ivanovka and Senar, the Rachmaninoff home became a nexus of cultural and intellectual life—but this time, it attracted Russians nostalgic for their homeland. A particular source of pleasure for Rachmaninoff was his close association with Feodor Chaliapin, Jr., who had become a talented actor in the United States and who in many ways evoked his father—that warmhearted, expansive operatic genius who had shared so many triumphs and tragedies with him. Because Rachmaninoff was already internationally famous and wealthy before he moved to California, he was able to carve out his own identity and professional operations in Hollywood, thereby avoiding the superficiality, artifice, and extreme commercialism rampant in that milieu. While he interacted with the multinational film and music elite there, he never genuinely became a part of that culture, preferring instead to stay within the artistic community of Russian émigrés.

Rachmaninoff was deeply moved by a telegram that he received on June 27, 1942, from a group of Soviet soldiers:

> We send you . . . our very best wishes, many more years of life, health, and strength for your lofty service to art for the benefit of our beloved homeland.

Please accept along with these wishes our gratitude for your help of the combatants of our heroic Red Army, who with their whole bodies are defending the homeland and the interests of all future generations of humankind from the fascist barbarians.[36]

A revealing anecdote related by Mikhail Chekhov may relate to these days in Rachmaninoff's life: On one occasion Rachmaninoff was at a gathering at the Somovs' (presumably with Chekhov present), and they were listening to a recording of Soviet songs (possibly soldiers' songs among them). Chekhov recalled: "For a long time Rachmaninoff maintained his composure, but finally burst out crying."[37]

In January 1943 Rachmaninoff made a private visit to the General Consulate of the USSR in New York in order to make a formal request to return to Soviet Russia permanently. He had kept in touch with the Soviet embassy from the time that he arrived in the United States in 1918. He made this petition in 1943 to a young Andrei Gromyko, who that year had become the Soviet Ambassador to the United States. (Gromyko would subsequently rise in his career to become the Soviet Permanent Representative to the United Nations, Foreign Minister of the Soviet Union, and Chairman of the Presidium of the Supreme Soviet of the USSR; he was a major figure in articulating Soviet foreign policy decisions.) In his memoir titled *Pamiatnoe* (Memorable Times), Gromyko describes his meeting with Rachmaninoff, an encounter that provides some evidence that the composer-pianist was already ill with the cancer that would take his life and suggests that he knew he did not have much longer left to live:

> I met with this man only once. During the war Rachmaninoff applied to the General Consulate of the USSR in New York with the request to allow him to return to his homeland. He came to us in order to discuss with the Soviet representatives the details connected with this decision. It so happened that his visit to the Soviet office in New York coincided with my arrival to this city from Washington.
>
> When I entered the building of the consulate, Sergei Vasilievich Rachmaninoff was already preparing to leave. We met in one of the receiving rooms. I recognized him immediately—his image in portraits was sufficiently well-known even while he was still alive.
>
> "I am glad that you have decided to return to your homeland," I said to him. "You are a prominent composer, and our populace of course will enthusiastically approve of your decision."
>
> "Please try to conclude the decision as quickly as possible," he requested.
>
> "Sergei Vasilievich, I will do everything within the scope of my responsibilities to fulfill your request," I promised.
>
> Rachmaninoff observed, "With real admiration I am following the unparalleled heroic feats of the Red Army and Soviet people in the battle against Hitler's Germany."

Then he added: "Americans bow before the power and spirit of the Soviet people, and I personally have witnessed this many times."

I thanked him for his warmhearted words concerning our common homeland, the Soviet Union. I also thanked him for the fact that he performed in many concerts whose proceeds were donated for the purchase of medical supplies for the wounded soldiers of the Red Army.

And I said the following to him: "My wife has told me all about your concerts. She has attended them and has seen the enthusiasm with which the public has received you as a performer and composer...."

I noticed that the composer looked unwell. His face was pale, his figure was painfully thin. I did not want to ask him about his health or even to touch upon this subject, moreover, since one could anticipate the answer. He, too, did not say anything about it.

The man who accompanied Rachmaninoff to his apartment, the Secretary of the Consulate Pavel Ivanovich Fedosimov, described how the composer, after settling himself into the car, himself raised the question of his health.

"Here are my hands," he said, displaying them, "they can still press the piano keys, but soon they will be lifeless."

As Sergei Vasilievich uttered these words his lips were trembling. Fedosimov tried to comfort him....

Unfortunately, it was not possible to quickly make a decision regarding the question of the departure of the distinguished composer from the US to the USSR. The year was 1943. Our entire country was fighting a brutal war against the enemy. That same year Sergei Vasilievich died. Russian culture suffered a terrible loss. The preeminent composer and musician remains our national treasure. He was also a patriot. Seriously ill, Sergei Vasilievich Rachmaninoff, notwithstanding all the hardships of wartime, decided to return to the place from which he had departed in December 1917, to return to his homeland.[38]

It is entirely plausible that Rachmaninoff, upon experiencing significant pain, consulted a doctor secretly in January 1943 (or even some weeks earlier) without telling his family. The doctor took the necessary medical tests and confirmed the diagnosis of cancer. Sergei thus may well have known that he had only a few months left to live and wanted to go home to die in Russia. Most certainly he would have also applied for permission for his wife to go with him, but she may not have known about the meeting at the General Consulate of the USSR. Very likely Rachmaninoff, worried about his health and the citizenship status of his family, agreed to become an American citizen with his wife Natalia at this time. He did not especially desire this citizenship, since he was waiting to hear about a possible return to Russia, but he realized that it would beneficially affect the future of his family. Specifically, it would protect United States inheritance rights for his wife and daughters after his death. He and Natalia officially became American citizens in a New York ceremony on February 1, 1943.[39]

Rachmaninoff did not live to see the victory of the Allies at the end of the war, but he did follow the enormous drama of the Battle of Stalingrad (July 17, 1942—February 2, 1943), widely regarded as the turning point of the war in the Red Army's favor. This gave him genuine hope for the defeat of Hitler. His older daughter Irina and Irina's daughter Sophia had moved to the United States with her parents in September 1939 because of the rising winds of war in Europe. Rachmaninoff described his family's circumstances at this time in a letter to Arthur Hirst:

> My elder daughter and my granddaughter had great difficulty in reaching New York. If it weren't for the efforts of [Charles] Foley it is doubtful whether they would have succeeded at all. They came and brought four dogs with them, which is a little too much for wartime.
>
> I am sad and worried about Tatiana. Before leaving Europe, I bought her a little estate within forty miles of Paris, where she is living all alone, if you don't count her little boy [Alexandre]. . . . It is only possible to bear up under such conditions with as strong a character as Tatiana's. In the last two months she managed to obtain a French passport and a driver's license. This last fact worries me no less than the war. I never felt that she had any talent for driving.[40]

It was mixed, though not altogether bad news that Tatiana's husband had been mobilized into the French forces and thus was stationed away from her—but he was not sent into active combat. The Rachmaninoffs endured considerable suffering, as did the Stravinskys and other émigré families whose children were stranded in Europe because of the war. It was difficult to obtain news about Tatiana and her young son Alexandre.

What would become Rachmaninoff's final concert tour, the 50th season of his performance tours, started in Detroit, Michigan, on October 12, 1942, and ended prematurely on February 17, 1943, in Knoxville, Tennessee. He had performed in this city previously in 1925 at the Lyric Theatre (the former Staub's Opera House) on Gay Street and Cumberland, and his familiarity with this relatively small, yet cultured city may have influenced him to perform there again eighteen years later. Three thousand people purchased tickets to the recital at a price of $2.75 for premium seats and $1.10 for seating farther from the stage.

The tour began with reviews that were promising: the general consensus was one of admiration for Rachmaninoff's vigor and strength as a pianist. On November 7, 1942, in a recital at Carnegie Hall, which saw a sold-out auditorium with many added seats on the stage, Rachmaninoff played a large program with many encores. A review by Olin Downes in the *New York Herald Tribune* on November 8 praised his virtuosity to the skies:

> The essentials of Mr. Rachmaninoff's pianistic art have remained unaltered. His technique is astounding now, as it was thirty years ago. If anything, Mr. Rachmaninoff performs everything faster. His mastery of the mechanics of the instrument is still to be marveled at, not only because of the accuracy attained even in the most vertiginous tempi, but for the entrancing sounds he obtains, from whispered pianissimo to a pithy, never pounded fortissimo.[41]

In January 1943 he began noticing symptoms of fatigue, excessive loss of weight (he had always been slender), pain in his left side, and a persistent cough. He alternated between being alarmed at his symptoms and dismissing them as signs of nervous strain, exhaustion, or simply "old age." On his concert tour, the two cities of Louisville, Kentucky, and Knoxville, Tennessee, were scheduled for February. His old friends Leo and Olga Conius arranged to meet him and Natalia in Louisville; they had traveled there from Cincinnati where they lived. Olga Nikolaevna Conius wrote:

> Not having seen Sergei Vasilievich for over a year, we were struck by the change in him. It was evident that the man was seriously ill. We acknowledged, or rather, sensed an approaching catastrophe. Natalia Aleksandrovna was in a very alarmed state. Sergei Vasilievich was unbelievably sad. Often we would find him sitting at the piano . . . at one point he even asked us: "Tell me something cheerful."[42]

In addition to noticing the painful changes taking place in his physical self, Rachmaninoff missed his daughter Tatiana (who was still in France) very much and longed to return to Russia.

By the time of his recital in February at what was then the University of Tennessee's Alumni Memorial Auditorium (now the James R. Cox Auditorium[43]) in the Alumni Memorial Building, he felt seriously ill, although he managed to play an impressive program without the audience's noticing that anything was wrong: it included his own works, and also those of Bach, Chopin, Liszt, Schumann, and Wagner. The Chopin piece, Piano Sonata No. 2 in B flat minor, turned out to be a premonition: its third movement was the beautiful, yet chilling *March funèbre*. Rachmaninoff stayed at the prominent Andrew Johnson Hotel at 912 S. Gay Street. After the recital "Russian composer-pianist Sergei Rachmaninoff, suffering from undiagnosed cancer, spent a painful night at the hotel after what would be remembered as the final performance of his career."[44] He played his last concerts in extreme pain, got through them through sheer strength of will, and very likely knew that they were his last concerts.

After the Knoxville recital Rachmaninoff's condition worsened day by day to the point that he had to cancel concerts scheduled in Florida and Texas.

A tortuously slow train journey from Texas to California lasting three days ended with his being transferred directly from his arrival at the train station to the Good Samaritan Hospital in Los Angeles. He insisted on being treated only by a Russian physician, Dr. Aleksandr Golitsyn, who was trained at Moscow State University and was a prince by rank of Russian nobility. The diagnosis was dreadful: Rachmaninoff was suffering from cancer of the lungs and liver that was metastasizing rapidly into all parts of his body. His bones and muscles were already affected. Morphine injections were prescribed for his pain; because he had in his lifetime been neither an abuser of alcohol nor of drugs, he required only a minimal dose to ease his pain. He was discharged from the hospital and transferred to his home; in his bedroom the icon of St. Panteley brought him spiritual comfort.[45]

According to Alexandre Rachmaninoff, during these last difficult days of Rachmaninoff's life his wife Natalia, summoning her own dignity and love for her husband, contacted Elena Dahl and arranged for her to see, before he died, the man she loved but was not able to marry. Nothing more is currently known about this possible meeting.[46] Other longtime friends of Rachmaninoff came to visit him; Boris Feodorovich Chaliapin, son of Rachmaninoff's dearest friend Feodor Ivanovich Chaliapin, had also become very close to the Rachmaninoffs and visited Sergei Rachmaninoff every day during his illness. He had become a professional artist; his paintings were exhibited internationally, and he was retained by *Time* magazine as a cover illustrator for several decades. It was he who was given permission to clip Rachmaninoff's hair in the close-cut style the latter preferred.

Rachmaninoff's family chose to have the diagnosis withheld from him, but very likely he knew that his illness was fatal. Dr. Golitsyn recalled:

> At first [withholding the diagnosis] from him seemed successful, especially since Sergei Vasilievich, as the majority of all artists, had no conception about medicine, about the structure and functions of the body—these things simply held no interest for him and for this reason he was satisfied with the vague and implausible explanations that were necessary to give him for the various symptoms of the disease.
>
> In suffering from such a difficult illness, Sergei Vasilievich was always friendly and kind, often joked, was overjoyed at the visit of those few close friends who were permitted to see him during the intervals when his pain had subsided. But very quickly these bright and cheerful intervals became rarer and shorter; it was necessary to increase the doses of the narcotics, although they were still very small. . . . With each day his weakness increased, and along with this his mood became more gloomy; the complaints he expressed were accompanied by a sense of hopelessness; it is possible, that he felt the approach of death.[47]

Rachmaninoff may have played along with this questionable withholding of the diagnosis, out of delicacy allowing everyone to think that he did not know. Natalia Rachmaninoff described: "Sergei Vasilievich could be so secretive, that even to this day I am tormented by the question of whether or not he knew that he was dying. I cannot forget how unbearable the thought was that I should wish him a quick death—I, who loved him so much."[48]

In her memoir Natalia Rachmaninoff described that on March 26 Dr. Golitsyn advised her to contact their priest so that Sergei could take communion. At 11:00 a.m. on Saturday, March 27 Archpriest Grigory (Prozoroff) of Holy Virgin Mary Russian Orthodox Cathedral in Los Angeles administered the last rites to his famous parishioner. Later that same day Rachmaninoff fell into a coma, from which he did not regain consciousness. As midnight approached that evening, his cousin Sofia Aleksandrovna Satina suggested to Natalia Aleksandrovna and the Rachmaninoffs' daughter Irina that they lie down and get some rest. They left the room.

Sofia Aleksandrovna thus remained alone with him, a relative and dearest friend, perhaps one she wanted to marry but in this matter had deferred to her worthy sister Natalia. Sergei Rachmaninoff's breathing was even and untroubled. At approximately 12:45 a.m. Sofia heard a change in his breathing and rushed to his bedside. His eyes were open; he took several labored breaths and then died. She sat quietly, after a few minutes hearing the clock strike 1 a.m. "She knew she should rouse Natalia Aleksandrovna and Irina, but she couldn't move from where she was sitting. For about half an hour she looked at her departed friend, not wishing to acknowledge his death. Sergei Vasilievich's face was noticeably calm and peaceful."[49] It may have brought Sofia Aleksandrovna some consolation that she was able to spend some precious time in a sacred solitude with the man whose life and career she had followed so lovingly—in his final moments. Sergei Rachmaninoff's death was recorded as occurring on March 28, 1943. According to Russian Orthodox custom, his body was taken to this same cathedral (Holy Virgin Mary Russian Orthodox Cathedral) for prayers for the dead. That evening Boris Chaliapin went to the church and made a sketch of Rachmaninoff's face, the last image recorded of the composer-pianist whose life had been so remarkable.

Even in death Rachmaninoff was fated to move restlessly from place to place. His wife arranged to have his body transported back to the East Coast, where he would be buried. His remains were taken first to Woodlawn Cemetery in the Bronx, where many famous personages are buried. Natalia Rachmaninoff's preferred burial site was the Novo-Diveevo Russian Orthodox Convent Cemetery in Spring Valley, New York; however, rumors of a construction project that threatened to affect the territory of the convent dissuaded her from this location. Rachmaninoff's body was then transferred from Woodlawn to Kensico Cemetery in Valhalla, where it lay in the Kensico

Figure 14.3 Holy Virgin Mary Cathedral, Los Angeles, California. From church archives, used by permission.

Community Mausoleum in a vault for ten days (perhaps to allow time for relatives and friends to travel to the location of the funeral).

During the interval of dates between Rachmaninoff's death and funeral, it goes without saying that news of his passing spread to the four corners of the world. His death in many ways marked the departure of Late Romanticism's greatest exponent. It also brought about the end of an era in the Russian artistic émigré community, the so-called First Wave of Russian Emigration ("emigration," of course, was a misnomer—for many of them had fled . . .). And no musical figure possessed the charisma, financial means, hospitality, and operational staff that could replace what Sergei Rachmaninoff had provided for this talented group of displaced people. The reaction of pianist Benno Moiseiwitsch to the death of his close friend and colleague expressed the void that could not be filled:

> For years Moiseiwitsch gave annual Rachmaninov concerts in London, one of which was scheduled in late March 1943. Just before the concert, which was to feature the Second Concerto . . . Moiseiwitsch read that the composer . . . had died:
>
> Stunned and sorrowed, I felt that I could not possibly go ahead with the afternoon's concert and pleaded with the management to find a replacement. No other pianist could be found on such short notice, so at noon, I finally decided

not to let the orchestra and public down—but with three stipulations: I would go through with the concert on condition that there would be no rehearsal beforehand; that I should not be obliged to dress; and that there would be no applause as I walked on stage or when I finished. Promptly at 2:30, still in traveling clothes, I played the Second Rachmaninov Piano Concerto. Then, as 2500 people stood in silence, I played the Funeral March from Chopin's Sonata in B-flat Minor, walked off the stage without a word to anyone, and went directly home.[50]

Rachmaninoff was to be buried on June 1, 1943. On the same day as his burial, the American Society of Composers, Authors, and Publishers (ASCAP), of which Rachmaninoff had been a member, planned a Memorial Concert for him at Carnegie Hall in the evening. They programmed only music by Rachmaninoff. Rachmaninoff's close friend and music collaborator Fritz Kreisler "asked if he might assume the concertmaster's desk for the last work on the New York Philharmonic Orchestra's programme so that he could stand with all the other musicians in the playing of Sergey Rachmaninoff's own instrumental version of the beloved *Vocalise*."[51]

At the burial service earlier in the day on June 1, 1943, Metropolitan Theophilus (Pashkovsky) of San Francisco presided, and the choir of Platov Cossacks chanted the traditional hymn "Вечная память" [Memory Eternal]. Natalia Rachmaninoff was so moved by the choir's singing of this hymn that it stayed in her mind for weeks after the funeral. The funeral was attended by many people—musicians, friends, Russian and American admirers of Rachmaninoff's musical art, and even representatives of Soviet Russia who traveled from Washington, D.C. Charles Foley offered a great deal of help during these last days; in particular, he assisted with the logistics of guests arriving from out of town for the funeral.[52] Among the many flowers and wreaths that arrived to honor Rachmaninoff's memory were entire bushes of azaleas sent by the Steinway family from New York. Rachmaninoff's coffin was lined with zinc and sealed, as his wife explained, so that in the future his remains could be transferred to Russia.[53] Until that time, a tall marble Orthodox cross stands guard over his grave. The chosen gravesite was extremely successful, even poetic: Rachmaninoff's grave rests on a hill overlooking a lyrical grassy valley. One can envision his spirit extending its arms, ready to conduct an invisible orchestra.

It is touching that one of the first female interpreters of Rachmaninoff's music in America, the brilliant pianist Ruth Laredo, selected a gravesite within a stone's throw of his. She was laid to rest near her idol on May 27, 2005.[54] Preeminent pianist and pedagogue Rudolf Serkin, who was Laredo's teacher at the Curtis Institute in Philadelphia, was unable to dissuade her from pursuing her abiding aspiration to master and perform Rachmaninoff's music. "And in the end, she won her master's blessing . . . Indeed, Laredo became arguably the most devoted exponent of Rachmaninoff's music in the second half of the 20th century."[55]

Figure 14.4 Gravesite of Sergei and Natalia Rachmaninoff, and Daughter Irina (Rachmaninoff) Wolkonsky, Kensico Cemetery, Valhalla, New York. Author's photo.

After Sergei Rachmaninoff's death Lena Donnelly, an employee of Kensico Cemetery who was a young woman in her thirties at the time, remembered well Natalia Rachmaninoff's many visits to her husband's grave and retained a distinct impression of her.[56] Natalia had moved from California back to the East Coast and was living in Manhattan. She would come to the cemetery sometimes with her daughter Irina, but more often she came alone. Donnelly described her as "direct" and as someone who "did not put on airs." She recalled that Natalia was of average height, about 5'5". She further characterized Mrs. Rachmaninoff's demeanor as one of modesty and intelligence. She was soft-spoken, dignified, and spoke English well enough to be understood. She had brown eyes, wore her gray hair pulled back, did not wear make-up, and dressed simply. The expression on her face was invariably one of sorrow and pain. When asked if Natalia was pretty, Donnelly wavered and did not know how to respond. Her interlocutor helped by suggesting that Natalia perhaps was a "handsome woman."[57] Donnelly agreed.

In Rachmaninoff's will he left $688,176 to his wife Natalia, and at an earlier point before his death he had given each of his daughters $100,000—as he put it, "for independence."[58]

Natalia Rachmaninoff died on January 17, 1951, surviving her husband by only eight years; her funeral took place two days later on January 19 at Kensico Cemetery. Tatiana, who had suffered a great deal outside of Paris during

World War II and had inherited Senar after her father's death, died in 1961 at Senar. Her son Alexandre, who had spent much time at Senar and carried out activities to promote his grandfather's music, died in 2012.[59] Irina, who never remarried after the suicide of her husband, died in 1969 in the United States. Her daughter Sophia Wolkonsky (born in 1925) lived a relatively short time, predeceasing her mother by one year in 1968. The Rachmaninoff scholar B. S. Nikitin suggested that the family genes of the Rachmaninoffs, due to his marriage to a first cousin, were not strong.[60] Rachmaninoff would have been heartbroken that this cherished granddaughter, the apple of his eye, died so young. Natalia and Irina are buried beside Rachmaninoff at his gravesite. Irina's body was cremated, perhaps by her own directive. Sofia Aleksandrovna Satina died in 1975 at the age of ninety-five and is buried at the Novo-Diveevo Russian Orthodox Convent in Spring Valley just outside New York City. She outlived all of the relatives of her immediate family with whom she shared a living memory of Ivanovka and Russia.

Rachmaninoff's gravesite is visited by many admirers from around the world, and is considered one of the major sites of interest of Kensico Cemetery. On March 27, 1993, the Tolstoy Foundation (of which Rachmaninoff was a founder in 1939) and the Russian Orthodox Church Outside of Russia organized a gravesite memorial service to commemorate the fifty-year anniversary of the composer-pianist's death, with eulogies offered in both Russian and English. It was attended by his grandson Alexandre Rachmaninoff and a large group of Russian-Americans, for whom the service affirmed the achievements of one of their own. An ongoing consideration by Rachmaninoff's international admirers and the Russian government involves whether to return his and his family's remains to Russia. If the decision were to have been his, there is no doubt that he would have chosen to be buried in his homeland. However, his surviving heirs and Americans devoted to his music argue that his remains should stay in Valhalla. Alexandre Rachmaninoff insisted that Rachmaninoff was not nostalgic for Russia, but in this comment the grandson clearly transferred his own dislike for Soviet Russia onto the opinions of his deceased grandfather—whom he knew only until he was six years old. But the question of the transfer of the Rachmaninoff family remains for permanent burial hangs in the air.

In 2003 the Russian sculptor Viktor Bokarov cast a memorial plaster statue of Rachmaninoff and donated it to the City of Knoxville, requesting that it be bronzed and situated in a suitable public location. It was properly bronzed and named "Rachmaninoff: The Last Concert." The large statue was unveiled in Knoxville on September 14, 2005. It is located in the World's Fair Park at Cumberland Avenue and 11th Street in a clearing surrounded by graceful bushes and flowers. Rachmaninoff is depicted standing in a concert tuxedo and inclined humbly to acknowledge applause, his left hand resting on the

Figure 14.5 Statue of Rachmaninoff "The Last Bow," Knoxville, Tennessee. Author's photo.

score of Chopin's Piano Sonata No. 2 in B flat minor (which he had played at that concert). The statue is not far from the auditorium at the University of Tennessee, where he had taken his last bow.

NOTES

1. Robert Rimm, *The Composer-Pianists: Hamelin and The Eight* (Portland, OR: Amadeus Press, 2002), 140.
2. Voytek Matushevski, "Rachmaninoff's Last Tour," in *Clavier* (March 1993), 20.
3. Nicholas Wheeler, "Meeting Report: The Russian Influence on American Music" (Washington, D.C.: Kennan Institute, 2003), vol. XX, no. 11.
4. Ibid.
5. Truman Bullard, "An Introduction to Russian Music," in *Russia and Western Civilization: Cultural and Historical Encounters*, ed. Russell Bova (New York: Routledge, 2003), 210–38.
6. Andrew Huth, "Sergei Rachmaninov: man of steel and gold" in *Rachmaninov: Orchestral Works*, St. Petersburg Philharmonic Orchestra, conductor Mariss Jansons, 6 CD set (France: EMI, 2002), 14.
7. Sergei Bertensson and Jay Leyda, *Sergei Rachmaninoff: A Lifetime in Music* (New York: New York UP, 1956; repr., Bloomington, IN: Indiana UP, 2001), paraphrase of 235.
8. Bertensson and Leyda, 237. The type of communication of this comment (spoken or written) is not clear from the account given.
9. See Harlow Robinson, *Russians in Hollywood, Hollywood's Russians* (Lebanon, NH: Northeastern University Press, 2007), 134–35.
10. Don Michael Randall, ed., *The Harvard Dictionary of Music*, 4th ed. (Cambridge, MA: The Belknap Press of Harvard University Press, 2003), 462–66.
11. I thank jazz pianist Alex Nollan for his insights into the Blues Scale.
12. Robinson, 130.
13. Charlie Chaplin, *My Autobiography* (New York: Simon & Schuster, 1964), 395–97.
14. Sergei Bertensson, quoted in Bertensson and Leyda, 230.
15. Bertensson and Leyda, 232–33, a vivid recollection of Bertensson, who was present at the party.
16. "Lauter," Antique Piano Shop, https://antiquepianoshop.com/online-museum/lauter/, accessed on October 1, 2021.
17. Max Harrison, *Rachmaninoff: Life, Works, Recordings* (New York: Continuum, 2005), 223.
18. Charles Foley, Untitled liner notes, RCA reissue of the Grieg and Schubert Sonata recordings, 1959, LVT 1009 (RB 16154), quoted in Barrie Martyn, *Rachmaninoff: Composer, Pianist, Conductor* (Burlington, VT: Ashgate, 1990), 442.
19. Louis P. Lochner, *Fritz Kreisler* (London: Rockliff Publishing Corp. Ltd., 1951), 265–66, quoted in Martyn, 442–43. Rachmaninoff had performed his Second Concerto in a concert at the Metropolitan Opera conducted by Stokowski, which included Geraldine Farrar, on April 8, 1919.
20. Liudmila Kovaleva-Ogorodnova, *Sergei Rakhmaninov* (Sankt-Peterburg: Vita Nova, 2015), paraphrase of II: 34 and trans. VZN.
21. Bertensson and Leyda, paraphrase of 264.

22. Ibid., paraphrase of 237–38.
23. Nikolay Medtner, excerpt from letter, quoted in Bertensson and Leyda, 246.
24. Kaikhosru Sorabji, *Around Music* (London: Unicorn Press, 1932), 75, quoted in Martyn, 306.
25. Martyn, 307–308.
26. Paraphrase of analysis in Martyn, 307–308.
27. Bertensson and Leyda, 249–50.
28. Martyn, 312.
29. Letter signed by Sylvia Voorhees, a representative of Charles Foley, Inc., author's archival work in Annenberg Rare Book and Manuscript Library, University of Pennsylvania, July 11, 2006.
30. Martyn, 313.
31. M.A. Chekhov, Untitled, *Vospominaniia o Rakhmaninove*, ed. Z.A. Apetian, 5th ed. (Moscow: Muzyka, 1988), II: 290, trans. VZN.
32. Bertensson and Leyda, 355–56.
33. Ibid., paraphrase of 356.
34. Jack McCarthy, "Rachmaninoff's Philadelphia," Historical Society of Pennsylvania, March 14, 2017, https://hsp.org/blogs/fondly-pennsylvania/rachmaninoff%E2%80%99s-philadelphia.
35. Kovaleva-Ogorodnova, II: 138–39, paraphrase, trans. VZN.
36. Ibid., II: 139, trans. VZN.
37. Chekhov, untitled, in Apetian, II: 291, trans. VZN.
38. A.A. Gromyko, *Pamiatnoe*, Moscow: Izd. Politicheskoi literatury, 1988, 1: 146–48. V. I. Antipov encountered the detail that General Secretary of the USSR Joseph Stalin had promised Rachmaninoff an automobile, large apartment, and perhaps some other privileges in Moscow in order to entice him to return to his homeland.
39. It is noteworthy that Rachmaninoff had filed a Declaration of Intention to apply for U.S. citizenship on January 11, 1939. Because of his continued strong ties to his homeland, the most plausible explanations for this application would be personal and financial, that is, concerns for his family's financial security. The document can be viewed on the Rachmaninoff Network: https://www.rachmaninoff.org/articles/archive/147-sergei-rachmaninoff-application-for-american-citizenship-1939, accessed on September 13, 2021.
40. Bertensson and Leyda, 357.
41. Olin Downes, "Recital is Given by Rachmaninoff; Carnegie Hall is Crowded for Program of the Masters by Pianist in Afternoon," *New York Herald Tribune*, November 8, 1942.
42. Kovaleva-Ogorodnova, II: 160–61, trans. VZN.
43. The auditorium was renovated in 2003, but fortunately the renovation retained the architectural elements of the original performance space. Hence the visitor to this place can reasonably accurately reconstruct how Rachmaninoff may have looked in performance on this stage.
44. Jack Neely, "Gay Street's Wallflower: The Andrew Johnson Hotel," Knoxville History Project, https://knoxvillehistoryproject.org/andrew-johnson-hotel/, accessed December 25, 2020.

45. Bertensson and Leyda, paraphrase of 377–84.

46. Personal interview, Alexandre Rachmaninoff, Senar, Weggis, Switzerland, September 3, 2004.

47. A.B. Golitzyn, "The Illness and Death of S.V. Rakhmaninov," in *Vospominaniia o Rakhmaninove,* ed. Z.A. Apetian, 5th ed. (Moscow: Muzyka, 1988), II: 422–23, trans. VZN.

48. N.A. Rakhmaninova, "S.V. Rakhmaninov," in Apetian, II: 330, trans. VZN.

49. Kovaleva-Ogorodnova, II: 167, trans. VZN.

50. Benno Moiseiwitsch, "Reminiscences of Rachmaninoff," *Music Journal* 21 (January 1963), 68, quoted in Rimm, 149–50.

51. Anne McLean, "Rachmaninoff: The Bohemian," *Studies in Music from the University of Western Ontario* 15 (1995): 105–106.

52. Rakhmaninova, in Apetian, II: 331–32 paraphrase, trans. VZN.

53. Ibid., paraphrase, trans. VZN.

54. By an accident of fate I visited Rachmaninoff's grave (for the third time) on the day after (May 28, 2005) Ruth Laredo was buried. I strolled along the by-now familiar pathways near his gravesite, and just below the curve of a hill nearby I saw the rise of freshly packed dirt indicating a recent grave. It was Laredo's, located indeed just a short walk from Rachmaninoff's.

55. Lawrence B. Johnson, "Famed pianist left mark on chamber festival," *The Detroit News,* Saturday, May 28, 2005, 2.

56. Phone interview, Lena Donnelly, Kensico Cemetery, Valhalla, NY, June 4, 2004. Donnelly was 86 years old at the time of the interview; she was present at Kensico during the time of Rachmaninoff's funeral.

57. Personal interview, Judith C. Mitchell, Kensico Cemetery, Valhalla, New York, June 3, 2004.

58. Matushevski, 25.

59. After Alexandre Rachmaninoff's death the fate of Senar hung in the air between 2012 and 2021. It had been willed to the management of the Rachmaninoff Foundation (which he had established). On December 6, 2021, the parliament of the Canton of Lucerne approved the purchase of the villa. In the future it may be considered for the World Heritage List of UNESCO. See "Breaking News: Parliament Canton Lucerne Supports Purchase Villa Senar," Rachmaninoff Network, December 6, 2021, https://rachmaninoff.org/articles/news/199-breaking-news-parliament-canton-lucerne-supports-purchase-villa-senar.

60. Personal interview, B. S. Nikitin, Moscow, June 13, 2007.

Afterword

Rachmaninoff's Legacy in the Twenty-First Century

Rachmaninoff's legacy can be considered in terms of the growth and flourishing of his reputation as a musician in general and of the reception history of his works. He has remained one of Russia's most important composers, the heir mainly to Tchaikovsky, but also to some degree (as he acknowledged) to Rimsky-Korsakov. Performed regularly, his music is a secure part of the classical canon, both through the curriculum of the Moscow Conservatory and through the dazzling standard Rachmaninoff set for pianism, which endures in the powerful Russian Piano School.[1] During the six-week-long White Nights Festival in St. Petersburg coordinated by its artistic director Valery Gergiev, which brings to Russia many of the world's finest musicians, Rachmaninoff's music of all genres occupies a prominent position. His art songs, which are not performed outside Russia frequently, are noted on citywide billboards and performed almost every day of the festival. In Europe, especially in the United Kingdom and the Netherlands, Rachmaninoff's music is generally admired by critics and audiences; his position in musical programming is central. The UK Rachmaninoff Society, which was organized in the 1990s and dissolved in 2013, brought together at its annual conferences Rachmaninoff's surviving relatives (grandson Alexandre Conius Rachmaninoff and great-granddaughter Natalie Wanamaker Javier) and Rachmaninoff scholars/pianists from the United States, Europe, and Russia. Alexandre Rachmaninoff (who died in 2012) maintained the Rachmaninoff Foundation, which funded major performances by world-class orchestras of his grandfather's music, while Natalie Wanamaker Javier has sponsored Rachmaninoff piano competitions at the Novgorod Music School named for Rachmaninoff.[2] The Rachmaninoff Society in 2013 reorganized itself, becoming the Rachmaninoff Network.

U.S. audiences have an abiding love for Rachmaninoff's music; in the orchestral repertoire his Piano Concerto No. 2 in C minor was considered anecdotally the most-performed concerto of the twentieth century. The popularity of this work promises to continue, along with that of his Piano Concerto No. 3 in E minor and *Rhapsody on a Theme of Paganini*. By contrast, among professional musicologists Rachmaninoff's music (along with that of Tchaikovsky, Arensky, Taneev, Medtner, and other Romantics and Late Romantics) has received less attention than the works of Modernist Russian composers, such as Scriabin, Stravinsky, Prokofiev, and Shostakovich. The explanation for this tendency may simply lie in an American predilection for Modernism in general. What is certain, however, is that the critical reception of Rachmaninoff worldwide is constantly being revised upwards. An increasing number of doctoral dissertations are being produced by young scholars, especially in the Anglophone countries and Russia. Rachmaninoff's musical innovations, connections to American jazz, and positive influences on American standards in pianism are all being viewed in more appreciative terms. These contexts of his popularity have been taken up by professors of colleges and universities, making Rachmaninoff a visible figure in the presentation of the Russian musical landscape to students of world music.

The reception history of Rachmaninoff's music in the West is full of quirky twists and turns, many of which have little or nothing to do with the actual music of the composer. Few composers of the twentieth century have had as much nonsense written about them as Rachmaninoff. Thus some remarks concerning this mixed appreciation of Rachmaninoff's music in the West may help to explain the disconnect between the beauty and masterful craftsmanship of his music, and the negative attitudes American critics maintained toward his work in the 1920s and 1930s. In 1937 a *Call-Bulletin* reporter asked him if he considered himself mainly a pianist, conductor, or composer. Rachmaninoff answered somewhat tongue-in-cheek that he did not know:

And the critics don't help me. . . .
No, the critics are not helpful. When my first symphony was first played they said that it was so-so. Then when my second was played they said that the first was good, but that the second was so-so. Now that my third has been played—just this fall—they say my first and second are good but that my—oh, well, you see how it is.[3]

After Rachmaninoff was forced to leave Russia in 1917—when he had virtually all of Europe at his feet, composing and performing one masterpiece after another in the major capitals—he had to recreate himself in a Western culture completely alien to what he had known in his homeland. Whereas Europe represented a fairly similar set of cultural features to those of Russia, and Rachmaninoff was fluent in two of its major languages (French and German), American culture and the English language were truly foreign to him. Critics in the United States rarely paused to realize that this was a musician who was well-educated, had suffered extreme personal and professional trauma, and was speaking to them in the fourth language he had learned. Rachmaninoff's simple statements in English with a paucity of vocabulary vastly underrepresented the wit, sparkle, and intellectual breadth manifested when he spoke in the other three languages he knew; his interactions in his native Russian must be the final judge of how his inner world should be viewed.

American critical reviews starting in Rachmaninoff's first season of concerts in exile in 1919 and continuing through the 1920s were condescending and insulting; no doubt they temporarily crippled his creative forces. Paul Rosenfeld in *The New Republic* wrote on March 15, 1919:

> But there is an essential that his music wants. It wants the imprint of a decided and important individuality. . . . Nor is the music of M. Rachmaninoff ever quite completely new-minted. Has it a melodic line quite properly its own? . . . Nor can one discover in this music a distinctly original sense of either rhythm or harmony or tone-color. . . . In all the music of M. Rachmaninoff there is something strangely twice-told. From it there flows the sadness distilled by all things that are a little useless.[4]

Several years later, on September 20, 1924, Edward Sackville West, after a performance of the Second Symphony at a Promenade concert, commented in *The Spectator*:

> Few artists have proved to be ultimately negligible on so large a scale as Rachmaninoff. . . . Metaphorically speaking, Rachmaninoff shut himself up in a dark room, frightened himself to death, and then translated his soul-storm into the language of music. . . . I look forward to the time when people will be ashamed to listen to Scriabin, Tchaikovsky, Rachmaninoff, *Tod und Verklärung*, and the symphonies of Gustav Mahler.[5]

It is worth remembering that the period of 1914–1929 included the early years of World War I and beginning of the financial disasters set forth by the Wall Street Crash in the fall of the last year of the so-called Roaring Twenties. Rachmaninoff during these years was not only reeling from the events taking place in Western Europe and America but also suffering internally about the terrible circumstances in which his close friends, music colleagues, and family members (such as his mother) found themselves in Russia—with the Bolshevik government increasingly imposing limits on travel, communication, and artistic expression. Specifically, if one cites the events in question, with each one representing a major cataclysm for millions of people—World War I, the Bolshevik Revolution of 1917, Civil War of 1918–1922, famines throughout Russia in the early 1920s, and the seizure of power by Joseph Stalin in 1928—it is easier to understand the complex and troubled state of mind of the Russian émigrés, including Rachmaninoff, in these years in Europe and America. Rachmaninoff and his family experienced these events personally and were affected by them personally. He could talk about and reach some level of understanding with his fellow compatriots, but among Americans he largely remained silent. After all, how many Americans had even heard of Novgorod, Tambov, or Saratov?

The reasons for such dismissive and even vitriolic attacks on his music stem from the critics' views that his compositions were out of date, Romantic in an age of Modernism, and driven by the contours of his inner world, rather than by new theories of atonal and serial music. Rachmaninoff intensely disliked atonal music and in some interviews made cautious yet clear statements about it. He noted, "Melody is music and the foundation of all music. . . . I do not appreciate composers who abandon melody and harmony for an orgy of noises and dissonances as an end in itself."[6] He reflected further on audiences and various trends in music and art:

> Audiences learn that it is fashionable to admire certain phases of what is called futurism. They like the pose of being "modern," "up-to-date," and they affect to like the works that no human being with a rational mind could possibly enjoy. Such a public rarely thinks for itself; it is much more comfortable for them to accept a fashion that others applaud, even if that fashion is altogether hideous. Human nature is odd in this respect. Time, however, decides between the permanent and the artificial, and inevitably preserves the good, the true, and the beautiful.[7]

While some critics may have dismissed Rachmaninoff's compositions with harsh criticism, for the most part the audiences greeted each new work of his with warmth and enthusiastic appreciation. After his concert in Philadelphia on December 5, 1931, Sergei and Natalia Rachmaninoff met the Swans, who recollected comments he made while in very good spirits: "The musicians and critics were always waiting to devour me. One would say: 'Rachmaninoff is not a composer, but a pianist!' and another: 'He is primarily a conductor.' But the public—I love it. Everywhere and at all times it has treated me wonderfully."[8] It is fortunate that during this difficult period he had the sustained support of musician friends and admirers, such as Josef Hofmann, Fritz Kreisler, Vladimir Horowitz, and Abram Chasins.

Serious critical work on the music and life of Rachmaninoff was carried out in England in the 1940s and 1950s, and in Russia especially after Stalin's death in 1953. One must assign a distinguished place to the pioneering work of Zarui Apetian in the 1950s and 1960s of compiling the letters of Rachmaninoff and laying the foundation for future Rachmaninoff studies. In the United States the important critical biography by Sergei Bertensson and Jay Leyda, *Sergei Rachmaninoff: A Lifetime in Music* (1956) provided a starting point for the legitimization and appreciation of the composer's music, because it took into account the Russian contexts in which Rachmaninoff's creative identity was forged. The 1960s and 1970s saw a re-examination of previously published studies of Rachmaninoff, but little new work was undertaken. Following in the footsteps of the Bertensson and Leyda book is the tour de force musicological biography by the Australian Barrie Martyn, *Rachmaninoff: Composer, Pianist, Conductor* (2000).

Vera Briantseva's *S.V. Rachmaninoff* (1976) and Catherine Poivre D'Arvor's *Rachmaninoff ou la passion au bout des doigts* (1986) represent a perspective that takes into account both the composer's public and private spaces. Similarly, the publication of Maria Biesold's *Sergej Rachmaninoff, 1873–1943: Zwischen Moskau und New York: eine Künstlerbiographie* (1991) in Germany marked an important event in Rachmaninoff biographical studies. Liudmila Kovaleva-Ogorodnova's comprehensive two-volume *Sergei Rachmaninov* (2015) also deserves special mention. Biography in particular is a genre that can be affected by gender—of the more than thirty-five biographies of Rachmaninoff that have appeared since the 1940s, the overwhelming majority has been written by men. Women may examine the same evidence in different terms or may uncover what has not yet been revealed, and yet this thought does not at all invalidate or disparage the fine biographies on Rachmaninoff produced by men. Even the question of what is revealed to an interviewer by the interviewee hangs in the balance: the selection process of which information a person being interviewed may disclose, say, to a young woman or to a man roughly the same age as the interviewer surely is at work in this regard.

In Russia in the 1980s and 1990s study of the composer's music began to blossom; conferences that produced insightful articles and essays expanded the boundaries of Rachmaninoff research. All-Rachmaninoff music celebrations are exemplified by a program of his music at Emory University on February 22, 2003, involving performances by internationally renowned musicians—pianist Alexei Gryniuk and cellist Dmitry Kouzov. Smith College marked the centennial of Rachmaninoff's association with it in a conference on November 4–5, 2009, with Rachmaninoff specialists Francis Crociata and Vladimir Tropp participating.[9] In the United States on October 21–23, 2005, a major international conference devoted solely to Rachmaninoff took place at Rhodes College; this was the first of its kind in this country. The conference brought together scholars and musicians from five countries: Russia, England, Canada, Italy, and the United States. It boasted superb performances of Rachmaninoff's piano music by Vladimir Leyetchkiss (one of the last students of Heinrich Neuhaus), Sandro Russo, and Brian Ray, as well as of several movements of his choral work *All-Night Vigil* conducted by Tim Sharp. Clearly, Russian and English have established themselves as the preeminent languages of Rachmaninoff research; however, scholars in Anglophone countries who ignore the original Russian sources will be unable to access the genuine identity of the composer.

A historic scholarly publication on Rachmaninoff's music appeared in the early years of the twenty-first century: the inaugural volume of *The Critical Edition of the Complete Works of Sergei Vasilievich Rachmaninoff* was published in October 2005. Under the directorship of D. A. Dmitriev, the series is being produced by Russian Music Publishing in Moscow—which has continuously published musical scores since 1909 (moving from Moscow to Paris to the United Kingdom and returning to Moscow). Founded by Sergei and Natalia Koussevitzky, as well as Rachmaninoff, Russian Music Publishing has a distinguished history of collaborative work among major musicians and specialists. The editorial board for this important project has included, most notably, V. I. Antipov, as well as other scholars from Russia, the United Kingdom, United States, and Germany. This bilingual project, funded for several years by the Russian government and by donations from Alexandre Rachmaninoff, produced the volumes of the complete solo piano music; many more are being planned. These volumes have been welcomed by individual performers and orchestras alike, for they contain the urtext editions of the composer's works scrupulously evaluated by distinguished Rachmaninoff specialists, as well as critical assessments of his music.

Rachmaninoff studies in Russia and England are well-developed, with much fine scholarship produced on his compositions and a clearly articulated high esteem of his contributions to classical music. In the United States a well-informed understanding of Rachmaninoff's musical works is lacking, which stems from misconceptions about Russian culture and Russian Orthodoxy in general, and Russian music in particular. To be sure, American orchestras regularly include many of his instrumental works in their concert seasons, and his music is widely admired by audiences across the country. His solo piano and orchestral works in formal and thematic terms can stand alongside the best compositions in those genres, but some of his finest contributions to world music are also found in his choral music (sacred and secular) and art songs (*романсы*)—which rely on the knowledge of modern Russian or Church Slavonic.

In college and university musicology courses Rachmaninoff's compositions are not always included in the mainstream of the masters of Western classical music; they are either reduced to a minor category of European music or relegated to the ethnic category of "Russian music." Compositions by Rachmaninoff that are studied in such courses are usually the instrumental ones. The question arises as to whether Rachmaninoff's compositions (such as his symphonies) should be evaluated according to the specific features of Russian music, or whether they should be measured by the characteristics of Western classical music. Max Harrison provides important insights on this question:

> Rachmaninoff's symphonies have been widely discussed, often dismissed, as if they ought dutifully to have followed Austro-German models, whereas in most Russian symphonies it is not so much large-scale harmonic patterns but the emotive power of specific motifs that fuels the fluctuating tensions. Examples include Balakiref, Tchaikovsky, Borodin, Taneieff and in more recent times Prokofief and Shostakovich. It is against this background that Rachmaninoff's symphonies should be assessed, not in relation to precepts derived from Beethoven, Brahms, etc. With Rachmaninoff different types of thematic material and musical processes, of moods and feelings, are brought into varying degrees of conflict and finally resolved in ways that are personal and formally satisfying. Logically sustained argument has its role but an instinctive drama of the emotions is this music's chief thrust, its final import being a struggle between the representations of the forces of life and death.[10]

Rachmaninoff's art songs, operas, and choral music are not performed in the United States very often, due to the perceived difficulty of having to perform them in Russian. While classical music programs in academe regularly include performances of French, German, and Italian vocal music, they less often spotlight Russian art songs and operas. It is an open question whether or not the International Phonetic Alphabet (IPA), whose sounds are rendered in Latin letters, adequately represents the sounds in the Slavic languages (singers of Rachmaninoff's songs who are not trained in Russian must to some extent rely on the IPA system). As a consequence, Rachmaninoff's art songs have remained among the least familiar of that repertoire to American audiences. Several reasons account for this circumstance: Americans do not speak or understand Russian; the songs themselves are demanding to perform both for the vocalist and pianist; and the genre itself does not occupy a major place on the stages of U.S. concert halls. This last can be at least partially explained by a misinterpretation of the music and content of art songs as "sentimental," a term that rings negative to the American ear. To be sure, art songs from Beethoven to Schubert to Tchaikovsky to Rachmaninoff are by definition emotional—they capture a heightened moment in miniature form—but they are not cloying. And yet, despite the obstacles facing the performance of Russian art songs in America, recent evidence suggests that they are becoming more prominent in the United States' major centers of cultural production.

This rise in interest in Russian *романсы* can be attributed to the activities of Russian émigrés in the United States of the 1990s to the present, many of whom are accomplished professional musicians. Some settled in major cities such as New York and Chicago in order to continue their performance careers, while others found positions at top colleges and universities. In collaboration with native-born Americans, the Russian musicians quite naturally incorporated the *романсы* into their course syllabi and performing repertoires. The genre caught on: undergraduate and graduate music majors began training in the art song, and soon the Russian *романс* found its rightful place beside the German *Lied* and French *mélodie* in their recitals. A typical example is that of émigré and graduate of the Kiev Conservatory Galina Ivannikova, a sought-after opera singer based in Memphis, Tennessee, and who has performed Rachmaninoff's art songs in many cities. At the Rhodes College International Rachmaninoff Conference, Carole Blankenship performed several of Rachmaninoff's art songs from his opus 4 cycle to the piano accompaniment of Thomas Bryant.

Concerning the dearth of publications on Rachmaninoff in the West, a possible reason has to do with his direct engagement of intense human emotion in his work, a function of his Russian Orthodox sensibilities. Byzantine-Russian Orthodoxy has not problematized the body, the physical self, in the ways in which the body and the passions are treated in Western Christianity. Rachmaninoff's music with its distinct idiom and vocabulary portrays the full range of *being* (the intellectual, spiritual, and physical), engaging the full "body" of the piano—the farthest reaches of the lower register and ethereal heights of the upper one. The West, with its tradition of Gregorian chant (which has no connection to Byzantine chant), organum, the Reformation, and Puritanism in early American history, is still evolving adequate criteria for examining Russian music.[11] As a fuller understanding of Orthodox sensibilities, as well as the mysticism and philosophy of the Russian tradition, is developed in the West, so will the appreciation of Rachmaninoff's music on its own terms take firmer root. After all, Russians and the Russian Orthodox are more deeply a part of both European and American history than is commonly assumed, and it is time for the histories of these parts of the world to acknowledge that Russians need not be treated as the "other" because they themselves form part of the cultural fabric of what is termed The West. It will be up to both Europe and Russia themselves to determine whether civilizationally Russia is part of European culture or something else entirely distinct.

Aleksandra Gennadievna Kostina, professor of Russian Studies, grew up in Novgorod during the transition period of the 1980s as the Soviet Union as a political unit was dissolved and its fifteen constituent republics once again became sovereign states. She recalls the ways in which the legacy of Rachmaninoff and his music was kept alive during those years:

Novgorodians have always been very proud of their region being Rachmaninoff's *malaia rodina* (native land, birthplace). In the 1980s, when I was going through schooling, everyone was expected to know our famous *zemliaki* (countrymen), Rachmaninoff being the first among them. He was and still is considered a national treasure. One of the several music schools in Novgorod is named after him; and, being located inside the Novgorod Kremlin, it is one of the prominent spots in the city's landscape. After the fall of the Soviet Union, it was possible for Rachmaninoff's heirs who lived abroad to visit their famous relative's native parts; their visits always received the widest coverage in local news. A beautiful monument to Rachmaninov created by artist Leonid Stepanov stands in the city center and was unveiled on September 30, 2003; Rachmaninoff's music can be heard from loudspeakers around the clock at the square where the monument stands. Tour guides always mention Rachmaninov's association with Novgorod and how proud Novgorod is to be the birthplace of the famous composer. Rachmaninoff's mother is buried at Rozhdestvensky Cemetery in Novgorod; the inscription on her grave, which is taken care of by the locals, reads: "To the mother who has given a genius to the world" (Матери, подарившей миру гения).[12]

The reception of Rachmaninoff in Asian countries has also grown rapidly in the last thirty years, as gifted pianists discover the enchantment of many works of Western classical and Russian music. It does not hurt, either, that Russia and China share a long geographical boundary and immensely friendly relations; and that South Korea is located nearby. Even though the entire musical idiom and aesthetics of, say, Chinese opera differ markedly from accepted styles and conventions of Western opera, it may be that the exoticism of the "other" as well as its different kind of beauty serve as drawing forces. Chinese, Japanese, and South Korean musicians are indisputably drawn to the performance and conducting of Rachmaninoff's music. The internationally known pianists Lang Lang and Yuja Wang, as well as South Korean Music Director of the Lubbock Symphony Orchestra David Cho serve as representative examples. As for Japan, close cultural ties with Russia have existed for many decades, nurtured by the filmic collaborations between the countries especially in the incomparable works of Akira Kurosawa, who famously admired the novels of Dostoevsky. Japanese pianists such as Kyohei Sorita and Nobuyuki Tsujii make their particular contribution to the presence of Rachmaninoff's music on the world stage.

The received identity of Rachmaninoff and his works sometimes feeds on the inaccurate stereotype of a gloomy, humorless musician who remained aloof from the world. Any "melancholy" or introversion on his part stemmed from the facts that he was uncomfortable in American culture and unsure of himself when expressing himself in English. His letters in the original demonstrate abundantly that this image of him was false. A sensitive translation of his letters needs to be undertaken in order to reveal his witty and compassionate personality to the West. The letters are lively, full of humorous and self-deprecating anecdotes, span a broad range of emotions, and are packed with colorful accounts that reveal the richness of the writer's personality and the turbulent times in which he lived. His cousin Sofia Aleksandrovna Satina remarked that he answered every letter he received, while one peasant woman confirmed that he spent enormous amounts of time occupied with answering the stacks of letters on his desk.

The impeccable compositional skills evident in Rachmaninoff's music merit performance and serious study; the composer's work stands up well to close inspection. Many music societies comprised of scholars and serious listeners have developed scholarly journals, such as those of the Liszt and Scriabin societies. Although a website for the Rachmaninoff Network exists in Europe and provides a basic database for information about the composer, it does not yet have a sustained venue for scholarship. The Rachmaninoff Network is building a close relationship with the Museum-Estate Senar in Switzerland, and this connection seems promising. In 2015–2017 Senar was declared an international center for research on the life and music of Sergei Rachmaninoff. More work needs to be done not only to incorporate into Western scholarship well-established Russian composers such as Tchaikovsky and Mussorgsky but also to advance research on Russian luminaries less well-represented in this scholarship, such as Balakirev, Lyadov, Medtner, and Taneev, among others. Study of these composers, who are important in their own right, will additionally yield valuable information about the national context in which Rachmaninoff developed as a musician.

In Russia, Europe, and the United States, many music and arts communities are finding ways to keep the name of Rachmaninoff visible to the public. A major way in which knowledge of his life and works is disseminated occurs through courses at colleges and universities. In 2004 Nicolas Schidlovsky taught an entire course on Rachmaninoff's choral music at Westminster Choir College in Princeton, New Jersey. A hybrid course at Rhodes College on aesthetics explores connections among religious philosopher Vladimir Soloviev, poet Aleksandr Blok, and composer-pianist Sergei Rachmaninoff. A fine body of statuary has been established honoring the composer: one can admire statues of him in Moscow, Novgorod, Ivanovka, Weggis (Switzerland), and Knoxville, Tennessee. Music schools have been named in his honor, such as in Tambov, Novgorod, and Paris (the Sergei Rachmaninoff Russian Conservatory). Professional Russian musicians in their live performances and recordings preserve the historic features of the performance of his music; among them are Vladimir Ashkenazy, Yury Temirkanov, Nikolai Lugansky, Galina Vishnevskaya, Evgeny Nesterenko, Denis Matsuev, Anna Netrebko, and the late Dmitry Hvorostovsky. Even in the world of off-Broadway productions Rachmaninoff makes an appearance:

David Malloy's 2015 "musical fantasia" *Preludes* explores the difficulties of writer's block supposedly experienced by the composer in the late 1890s and early 1900s, which led to his counseling sessions with Dr. Nikolay Dahl. The Rachmaninoff Museum-Estate Ivanovka has evolved into a research, conference, and special activities center associated with the music of the composer. From a beautiful country estate completely restored with all its outbuildings, according to Sofia Aleksandrovna Satina's meticulous drawings, but without accommodations for visitors or researchers (on my first visit there in 2003, I slept on a sofa in a small room with tall windows thrown open to the fragrant night air[13]), the estate now can house visitors more comfortably. On January 25, 2020, President Vladimir Putin signed a federal decree designating 2023 in Russia as the Year of Rachmaninoff. The year represents a major one in two ways: it will celebrate the 150th anniversary of his birth and 80th anniversary of his death.

In the final analysis, it is Rachmaninoff's music and its essence of musical integrity, steeped in Russia's Orthodox liturgical tradition and containing haunting, memorable melodies, that will ensure the durability of his reputation. Nikolai Medtner wrote about Rachmaninoff's distinctive sound and overall contribution to Russian musical art, which lay at the heart of this enduring reputation:

> It is precisely because of his fame that it is difficult to speak of Rachmaninoff. This fame is more than his: it is the glory of our [Russian] art. This unbroken contact of his entire being with art itself can be sensed each time his touch produces sound. This sound, in score or keyboard, is never neutral, impersonal, empty. It is as distinct from other sounds as a bell is different from street noises; it is the result of incomparable intensity, flame, and the saturation of beauty.[14]

Uttered by an uncompromising fellow composer-pianist and dear friend of Rachmaninoff's, these words underscore the power and integrity associated with Rachmaninoff's art.

In addition to his triple, brilliant career as composer, conductor, and virtuoso pianist (unparalleled in the twentieth century), Rachmaninoff was a humanitarian and philanthropist of the Russian Orthodox Church Abroad. He remained to the end of his life a loyal son of his homeland. His musical artistry was appreciated by his peers and audiences and led to his worldwide fame during his lifetime. If the efforts of the aforementioned forms of activism and dedication to Rachmaninoff's life and music bear fruit, it is certain that the twenty-first century will unfurl a golden age for the study of this musician of international stature.

NOTES

1. See Valeria Z. Nollan, "piano performance, Russian/Soviet (Russkaia fortepiannaia shkola)," in *The Encyclopedia of Contemporary Russian Culture*, eds. Karen Evans-Romaine, Helena Goscilo, and Tatiana Smorodinskaya (NY: Routledge, 2007), 463–64.

2. Two major events sponsored by the Rachmaninoff Foundation are the performance of the St. Petersburg Philharmonic under the baton of Yury Temirkanov at Lucerne (Summer 2007); and the Rachmaninoff concert at the Ravinia Festival that featured the Chicago Symphony (July 2004). The author of this biography attended both of these events as the guest of Alexandre Rachmaninoff.

3. Sergei Bertensson and Jay Leyda, *Sergei Rachmaninoff: A Lifetime in Music* (Bloomington, IN: Indiana UP, 2001; originally published in New York: New York UP, 1956), 328.

4. Paul Rosenfeld, Review, *The New Republic*, March 15, 1919, n.p.

5. Bertensson and Leyda, 218–19.

6. Richard Anthony Leonard, *A History of Russian Music* (New York: Macmillan, 1957), 253; quoted in Robert Rimm, *The Composer-Pianists: Hamelin and The Eight* (Portland, OR: Amadeus Press, 2002), 156.

7. Sergei Rachmaninov, "New lights on the art of the piano," *Etude* (April 1923), 223, quoted in Robert Rimm, 156. Rachmaninoff's words are strikingly similar to Philippians 4:8—"whatsoever things are true, whatsoever things are honest, whatsoever things are just, whatsoever things are pure, whatsoever things are lovely, whatsoever things are of good report; if there be any virtue, and if there be any praise, think on these things." *King James Version (KJV)*. This famous passage is referred to at least once each year in the Russian Orthodox liturgical cycle of services; thus Rachmaninoff would have heard it many times.

8. Bertensson and Leyda, 279.

9. Clifton J. Noble, Jr., "Rachmaninoff Centennial" (excerpts from program essay), https://www.smith.edu/rachmaninoff/about.php, accessed June 5, 2022.

10. Max Harrison, *Rachmaninoff: Life, Works, Recordings* (New York: Continuum, 2005), 136.

11. See Truman Bullard, "An Introduction to Russian Music," in *Russia and Western Civilization*, ed. Russell Bova (Armonk, NY: Routledge, 2003), 210–40.

12. A. G. Kostina is a professor of Russian Studies at Rhodes College, Memphis, TN. Her recollection was sent to the author by email, October 1, 2021. Information about the monument to Rachmaninoff can be found at https://pravoslavie.ru/7731.html, accessed on October 3, 2021.

13. The previous guest at Ivanovka who had stayed in that same room not long before me was Mikhail Pletnev.

14. Nikolai Medtner, *The Muse and the Fashion*, trans. Alfred J. Swan (Haverford, PA: Haverford College Bookstore, 1951), reprinted in John L. Holmes, *Composers on Composers* (Westport, CT: Greenwood Press, 1990), 115, quoted in Rimm, 143.

Appendix I
Twists and Turns of a Mystery

In recent years in the critical literature concerning Sergei Rachmaninoff's creative work the name of Elena Dahl has begun to appear increasingly more often. During the years 2003–2004 specialists and admirers of Rachmaninoff's music encountered speculation of a long-lasting connection between Rachmaninoff and this unknown woman. A startling account of this hitherto-unknown personage was initiated by the composer's grandson Alexandre Borisovich (Conius) Rachmaninoff in various conversations with several persons, including myself. Because of the extraordinary international fame and activities of Sergei Rachmaninoff, the introduction of a new person, possibly a beloved, into the pantheon of those who mattered to him must be considered seriously even as a hypothesis.

MEETINGS AND CONVERSATIONS WITH ALEXANDRE BORISOVICH (CONIUS) RACHMANINOFF

In 2003 Alexandre Rachmaninoff began telling various persons an account of Sergei Rachmaninoff's connection with one Elena Dahl. He related to me an account of a beloved with whom the composer remained in active contact throughout his life. He learned about this relationship from his grandmother Natalia Aleksandrovna several days before her death on January 17, 1951. Apparently she told no one but her eighteen-year-old grandson about this relationship, and, according to his account, spent about two hours in an agitated state describing to him her late husband's lifelong connection with another woman.

Natalia Aleksandrovna spoke of this woman to her grandson Alexandre in what he termed a "deathbed" confession. According to this narrative, Rachmaninoff's wife felt guilty about the harsh conditions she imposed on her husband in exchange for his being "allowed" to maintain the relationship with Elena Dahl. She insisted that Rachmaninoff maintain the story of his being treated and healed of his depression after the failed première of his first symphony. This story would serve to camouflage the real reason why Rachmaninoff visited the musician and therapist Nikolai Dahl. Evidently Natalia Aleksandrovna felt the matter weighing heavily enough on her mind to share it with her grandson. Furthermore, she was concerned enough about the potential effects of her revelation that she extracted from him the promise not to share it with anyone—with the world—for a period of fifty years. In presenting to me the circumstances of the narrative that he planned to divulge, Alexandre also assumed the role of a dutiful grandson who did not break his promise to his grandmother.

I undertook the major project of writing a new biography of Rachmaninoff in 2002, supported by colleagues in Russia, the United States, and Europe. During the first years of my research, I had become acquainted with a cohort of Rachmaninoff scholars and musicologists in Moscow and Tambov, and I was given the contact information for the composer-pianist's grandson Alexandre Rachmaninoff. Upon my return to the United States, for an issue of *Rhodes*,[1] the namesake magazine of the institution at which I at that time had been a professor for seventeen years, I recounted some autobiographical details that explained my abiding connection with Rachmaninoff's music and desire to carry out major research on his life. After the magazine was published in Spring 2003 I mailed a copy of it to Mr. Rachmaninoff on June 10, 2003, along with a formal letter in Russian in which I introduced myself and my project concerning his famous grandfather.

Approximately two weeks later my phone rang, and when I answered it the voice on the other end immediately said in Russian, "When can you come to Switzerland?" Somehow I knew it was Alexandre Rachmaninoff. Collecting myself, I thanked him for the phone call and we made plans for me to visit the Rachmaninoff villa Senar in Weggis on Lake Lucerne. Alexandre Borisovich, as by Russian practice I would refer to him, offered to pay all my expenses except for the flights. I petitioned the dean of my college for an extraordinary travel grant, and my request was generously approved. When I arrived at the Zurich airport, Alexandre Borisovich had arranged for me to be met by a taxi to take me on the hourlong drive to the beautiful Park Hotel Weggis at 34 Hertensteinstrasse. This hotel was located only a few miles from Zinnenstrasse, the street on which Senar was located—at the top of a cliff overlooking the enormous lake. I stayed at Weggis for four days between

July 11 and 14, 2003, spending all my time with him, either at Senar, or driving around the lake, or enjoying a meal and long conversation at one of the local restaurants. When at Senar, I played the original Steinway concert piano in Rachmaninoff's studio for hours at a time, or strolled through the acres of gardens and pine trees. Alexandre Borisovich and I spoke only in Russian, and we talked of many things.

The account that follows is one that Alexandre Rachmaninoff related to me over the course of those several days that I spent with him at the villa Senar and touring various sites in the Weggis area with him. His grandmother allegedly told him in the last days of her life that her husband remained in touch with another woman who was dear to him throughout his life. This woman, named Elena Dahl (sometimes referred to as "Lana" Dahl), did not marry and stayed near Rachmaninoff wherever he lived. Alexandre Borisovich did not know if she had a formal occupation or how she spent her time; he also did not know how she was able to leave Soviet Russia, but he speculated that she may have left through Siberia and eventually China. This would have made her departure part of the White emigration from Russia into Harbin, which became a center for Russian refugees in the 1920s. At any rate, she and Rachmaninoff stayed in contact with each other, although (as Alexandre Borisovich recounted) there were periods of years at a time when they lost touch, but they were always able to find each other again. This was not difficult in the Russian emigration worldwide during those turbulent times. When Elena was able to attend one of Rachmaninoff's concerts he would obtain for her a seat in the tenth row, where he would be able to see her. In the 1930s she settled somewhere across Lake Lucerne not far from Senar. Natalia Aleksandrovna asked her husband not to bring Elena to Senar. If Elena's brother was Anton-Louis Morisovich Dahl, a talented Russian pianist who ended up in Los Angeles, this could lend credence to the alleged details that Elena as well settled in that city and that Natalia Aleksandrovna allowed her to say goodbye to Rachmaninoff during the last stages of his final illness.

I asked Alexandre Borisovich at one point how he would characterize his grandmother, suggesting the attributes of "warmhearted?" "kind?" or "reserved?" He replied right away that she was not warmhearted; I inferred from his tone of voice that he did not have a positive memory of her. He also added that he thought she remained with her husband out of the "prestige" of being married to such a famous and wealthy man. Even at that time it struck me that this could not be accurate, for the accounts of Natalia Aleksandrovna's contemporaries, her own memoir of her life with her husband, and the sum total of her devotion to him through extremely difficult circumstances both in wealth and limited financial means—all of this evidence would fly in the face of the claim that she sought prestige in marrying and remaining with her husband.

After these meetings with Alexandre Borisovich I flew from Switzerland to Moscow in mid-July 2003 to convey these startling new admissions to my colleagues in Russia. My relating to Valentin Ivanovich Antipov, Aleksandr Sergeevich Bazikov, Dmitry Aleksandrovich Dmitriev, Aleksei Aleksandrovich Naumov, and Boris Semenovich Nikitin of the contents of my discussions with Rachmaninoff's grandson marks *the first time* these distinguished Rachmaninoff scholars had heard the name of Elena Dahl. While researching Rachmaninoff's compositions that summer, I was studying the master score of his Piano Concerto No. 2 in C Minor at the Russian National Museum of Music. On the title page, written in the composer's own hand, I noticed a second dedicatory line that was heavily crossed out. The moment was extraordinary and slightly comical: the noted Rachmaninoff specialists V. A. Antipov and A. A. Naumov were standing with me. We all pulled out our magnifying glasses as if planned in advance in order to examine the line. It was evident that Sergei Vasilievich wanted to dedicate this composition not only to N. V. Dahl, but also to a second person, possibly a female relative of the psychotherapist. It is unclear why Rachmaninoff changed his mind and crossed out the name of this second dedicatee. If one peers closely at the blacked-out line, one can discern the faint outlines of several letters of the family name "Dahl"—it is impossible to make out all the letters of the name, because in all likelihood Rachmaninoff wanted to achieve precisely this effect. A. A. Naumov subsequently researched the genealogy of the Dahl family, and through the name and birth/death dates of Anton-Louis Morisovich Dahl as well as the cryptic "Delmo" of one of Rachmaninoff's compositions without an opus number he posited the patronymic of Morisovna for the mystery woman. Thus Elena Morisovna Dahl.

I was to meet with Rachmaninoff's grandson two additional times for several days each in Weggis in the years that followed, staying either at the Park Hotel or Gerbi Hotel at 48 Hertensteinstrasse on the lake. During one of my visits to Weggis I was his guest at a concert of Rachmaninoff's music in Lucerne given by the visiting St. Petersburg Philharmonic Orchestra conducted by the renowned Yuri Temirkanov, to whom Alexandre Borisovich introduced me before the concert began. This concert was sponsored by the Rachmaninoff Foundation, which Alexandre Borisovich had established in order to promote the music of his grandfather. In addition, I spoke with Alexandre Borisovich at length at the Rachmaninoff Society Conference at Pendrell Hall in Wolverhampton, England, on April 9, 2004. Finally, Alexandre Borisovich invited me, my husband, and our son to be his guests and sit in his cordoned-off box at the outdoor Ravinia Festival of the Arts in Highland Park (north of Chicago), Illinois, on July 10, 2004.

Appendix I 351

IMPRESSIONS AND CONCLUSIONS ABOUT THE POSSIBILITY OF A BELOVED

These various meetings with their sustained conversations provided me with an overall impression of Rachmaninoff's grandson's personality, with its generous and open side, its quirks, and its frustrations. His was a complex inner world, and it became clear to me early on that he enjoyed the element of surprise, and was both weary of living in the shadow of his grandfather and yet dedicated to preserving a robust legacy of his grandfather's identity and compositions. In considering an unusual account of such explosive information that challenged a well-established narrative—that Rachmaninoff was happily married and led a relatively untroubled inner life—one has to decide if the narrator is reliable and whether or not he has a motive for what he is relating. And one has to ideally corroborate a verbal account of an alleged memory with other types of credible evidence.

I have thought a great deal about these issues over a period of many years. They have stayed in my mind across countries and continents, at conferences and in conversations with specialists, during my sojourns at the Rachmaninoff estate of Ivanovka, and during visits to the villa Senar. The fact that I heard the narrative of the memory directly from the source, without mediation, and that my Russian colleagues (some of whom had met Alexandre Borisovich and had known him for many years) were inclined to believe him, added to my instinct to believe him. But the fact that to date not a single document verifying even the existence of such a woman has come to light creates doubt in the scholarly part of my mind. I also know, however, that a person can create a fiction about his / her life and come to believe that fiction; this is a mysterious element of the human condition. The truth can even lie somewhere in the middle: Elena Dahl existed and knew Rachmaninoff, but the nature of their relationship was exaggerated in Alexandre Borisovich's account.

Did Rachmaninoff's grandson have a motive for disseminating this alleged memory of his grandmother's "deathbed" confession? It is not difficult to find one, and it emerges directly from his grandmother's alleged remarks to him. He related to me that he wanted to make a film out of revenge against his grandmother, for he was saddened at the conditions she imposed on her married life with Rachmaninoff. The film was tentatively titled *The Diabolical Triangle*, taking as its subject matter a married man, his wife, and his beloved. Alexandre Borisovich told me that he had hired a director and a scriptwriter from Hollywood—but the project would subsequently fall through for various reasons. Alexandre Borisovich was especially angered about the fact that his grandfather was forced to live the "lie" that he suffered from mental illness and depression when the reality was that this condition was not the case. Clearly he considered that to attach mental illness to his grandfather's reputation was a stigma and undeserved. He also was convinced that his grandfather would have performed and concertized even more if he was not emotionally constrained by these circumstances. And yet, considering how active Rachmaninoff was internationally as a recitalist, it is hard to imagine that he could have added more dates to his very full schedule.

Another peculiar detail exists concerning the last name of the mystery woman: In one of my last meetings with B. S. Nikitin, he stated almost in passing that Elena's family name was not "Dahl," that it was either "Kostritskaia" or "Mystritskaia," and that Alexandre Borisovich had told him this himself. Initially I was stunned at this possibility, but on further reflection it could be plausible. Boris Semenovich Nikitin and Alexandre Borisovich Conius-Rachmaninoff were contemporaries and had known each other for a long time. Nikitin was an extremely serious and thorough musicologist and biographer of musical artists. While Alexandre Borisovich had possible motives for embellishing the narrative of a beloved in his grandfather's life, Boris Semenovich had no motives at all—only the desire for accuracy and truth. What emerged from Nikitin's statement, interestingly, shifted the focus from the *existence* of the woman herself to the implication that she existed but had changed her name. Her existence was assumed. To my regret, there was not enough time for me to question Nikitin further on this new detail, but I recorded the two possible family names.[2]

The family name changed from "Dahl" does not necessarily undermine the rest of the account that Alexandre Borisovich supposedly heard from his grandmother. During the time period in question—the turn of the twentieth century and political turbulence that developed in Russia between 1905 and 1922—it was not unusual for persons living in the Slavic countries to change their last names. This was done most commonly for political reasons, for at a time when sands were shifting under the feet and ideological or political party loyalties could be a matter of life and death, one could in principle register a name change at a regional office. Ongoing violence and destruction of government property often brought about the disappearance of official documents. Thus to any person living at that time, or to those studying the changing landscape that was the consolidation of Bolshevik power to form the Soviet Union, this would not be an unheard-of act. If one accepts that pianist Anton-Luis Dahl was a brother or close relative of Elena's, since he had performed at the court of Tsar Nicholas II, his life by association would have been in danger. He and his relative Elena could both have changed their last names out of fear for their personal safety. Another, perhaps unintended, outcome of the name change would be to make it more difficult for others in the music world to trace a connection between Elena and Sergei Rachmaninoff. The last name of "Dahl" would confer some legitimacy and even provide "cover" for the meetings between the two—since Rachmaninoff would maintain a warm relationship with therapist/musician N. V. Dahl well into the 1930s. This changing of the last name would produce the following: Elena Morisovna Kostritskaia / Mystritskaia (Dahl) and Anton-Luis Morisovich Kostritskii / Mystritskii (Dahl).

Can I comment authoritatively one way or the other concerning the authenticity of a beloved in Rachmaninoff's life? I will leave the matter hanging in the air, but consider it significant enough to record here to the best of my ability. It will be left for future researchers into Rachmaninoff's art and life to either flesh out further the existence of this woman and her importance for Rachmaninoff's art or to disprove this hypothesis entirely. What makes it such a compelling yet thorny issue is that Rachmaninoff's grandson—who carried within himself much of his family's shared knowledge and culture—was the sole bearer of this narrative. This fact alone makes it worthy of the attention it has received from serious scholars and in popular, romanticized stories of Rachmaninoff's cross rhythms of the soul.

NOTES

1. Valerie Zarin Nollan, "Nollan Plays Rachmaninoff," Rhodes 10, no. 2 (Spring 2003), 28–32, Rhodes College Digital Archives, https://dlynx.rhodes.edu/jspui/bitstream/10267/7381/1/2003_spring_rhodes_magazine_150_dpi.pdf.

2. Personal interview, Moscow, June 13, 2007.

Appendix II

List of Works

1880–1889

Scherzo in F major, orchestra	February 1887
Romance in A minor, violin and piano	1880s?
Étude in F sharp minor, piano	1886?
Tchaikovsky: *Manfred* Symphony arranged for piano duet	1886 (lost)
Lento in D minor, piano	1887?
Scherzo in D minor, orchestra	1887–February 1888?
Four Pieces, piano (Romance, Prelude, Mélodie, Gavotte)	1887
Three Nocturnes, piano	1887–1888
Concerto in C minor, sketches of a planned concerto for piano and orchestra	November 1889
String Quartet No. 1	1889

Note: *Esmeralda*, fragments of an opera based on Victor Hugo's *Notre Dame de Paris* (October 1888), was previously thought to belong to Rachmaninoff, but it is not his composition. It was composed by Leo Conius. V. I. Antipov made this discovery while working in the archives of the Russian National Museum of Music named for Glinka in Moscow.

1890–1899

"Again You Are Bestirred, My Heart," voice and piano	1890 or 1893
"At the Gates of the Holy Cloister," voice and piano	April 1890
"I'll tell you nothing," voice and piano	May 1890
Deus Meus, six-part unaccompanied mixed chorus	1890
Romance, cello, and piano	August 1890
Mélodie on a Theme of Rachmaninoff, violin or cello and piano	1890?
Piano Concerto No. 1 in F sharp minor Op. 1 (original version)	1890–1891
Tchaikovsky: *Sleeping Beauty*, arranged for piano duet	1890–1891
Two Pieces, piano six hands (Valse [Aug. 1890], Romance [Sept. 1891])	1890–1891
Piece (Canon) in D minor, piano	1890–1891
Manfred, unfinished symphonic work	1890–1891 (lost)
Two fragments based on the play *Boris Godunov* by Pushkin, voice and piano	1891
Fugue in D minor, piano	1891
Suite in D minor, piano reduction (from lost composition for orchestra)	Summer, 1891
Russian Rhapsody in E minor, two pianos	January 1891
"C'était en avril," voice and piano	April 1891
"Dusk has fallen," voice and piano	April 1891
Prelude in F major, piano	July 1891
Symphonic Movement in D minor, orchestra	September 1891
Prince Rostislav, symphonic poem, orchestra	December 1891
Prélude et Danse orientale Op. 2, cello and piano	1891–1892
Trio élégiaque in G minor	January 1892
Cinq Morceaux de Fantaisie Op. 3, piano	autumn 1892
Aleko, opera in one act	1892
Six Songs Op. 4	1893
"Song of the Disenchanted," voice and piano	1893
"Do you Remember the Evening?" voice and piano	1893
"The Flower Died," voice and piano	1893
O Mother of God Perpetually Praying, unaccompanied mixed chorus	1893
Fantaisie Tableaux (Suite No. 1) Op. 5, two pianos	1893
Deux Morceaux de Salon Op. 6, violin and piano	1893
The Rock, symphonic poem Op. 7, orchestra	summer 1893
Six Songs Op. 8	1893
Trio élégiaque in D minor Op. 9	October–December 1893

Sept *Morceaux de Salon* Op. 10	1893–1894
Two *Don Juan* Episodes, orchestra	1894 (lost)
Romance in G major, piano duet	1894?
Six Morceaux Op. 11, piano duet	April 1894
Capriccio Bohémien Op. 12, orchestra	1892 and 1894
Chorus of Spirits, unaccompanied mixed chorus	1894?
Song of the Nightingale, four-part mixed chorus and piano	1894?
Symphony No. 1 in D minor Op. 13, orchestra	1895
Twelve Songs Op. 14	1894–1896
Six Choruses for Women's or Children's Voices Op. 15	1895–1896
String Quartet No. 2	1896?
Six Moments Musicaux op. 16, piano	1896
Glazunov: Symphony No. 6 arranged for piano duet	1896
Morceau de Fantaisie in G minor, piano	January 1899
Fughetta in F major, piano	February 1899
"Were You Hiccupping?" voice and piano	May 1899
Pantelei the Healer, unaccompanied mixed chorus	1899

1900–1909

"Night," voice and piano	1900
Bizet: Minuet from *L'Arlésienne*, transcribed for piano	1900 (revised 1922)
Suite No. 2 Op. 17, two pianos	December 1900 / April 1901
Piano Concerto No. 2 in C minor Op. 18	autumn 1900 / April 1901
Sonata in G minor Op. 19, cello and piano	1901
Spring Cantata Op. 20, baritone, chorus, orchestra	1902
Twelve Songs Op. 21	1900 and 1902
Chopin Variations Op. 22, piano	1902–1903
Ten Preludes Op. 23, piano	1901 and 1903
The Miserly Knight Op. 24, opera	1903–1905
Francesca da Rimini Op. 25, opera	1904–1905
Fifteen Songs Op. 26	1906
Polka Italienne, piano duet	1906?
Salammbô, opera project	1906–
Monna Vanna, opera	1906–1908 (unfinished)
Symphony No. 2 in E minor Op. 27, orchestra	1906–1907
Sonata No. 1 in D minor Op. 28, piano	1907
"Letter to Stanislavsky," voice and piano	October 1908

Isle of the Dead Op. 29, symphonic poem, orchestra	1909
Piano Concerto No. 3 in D minor Op. 30	1909

1910–1919

Liturgy of St. John Chrysostom Op. 31, unaccompanied mixed chorus	1910
Thirteen Preludes Op. 32, piano	1910
Polka de V. R., piano	March 1911
Six Études-Tableaux Op. 33, piano	1911
Fourteen Songs Op. 34	1900 and 1912
The Bells Op. 35, soloists, chorus, orchestra	January / April 1913
Sonata No. 2 in B flat minor Op. 36, piano (original version)	1913
All-Night Vigil Op. 37, unaccompanied mixed chorus	1915
From the Gospel of St. John, voice and piano	February 1915
Six Songs Op. 38	1916
"Prayer," voice and piano	1916
Nine Études-Tableaux Op. 39, piano	1916–1917
Piano Concerto No. 1 in F sharp minor Op. 1 (revised edition)	1917
Three pieces, piano (Prelude in D minor, *Oriental Sketch, Fragments*)	1917
Liszt: Hungarian Rhapsody No. 2—cadenza	1919

1920–1929

Kreisler: *Liebesleid* transcribed for piano	1921
Mussorgsky: Gopak from *Sorochintsy Fair* transcribed for piano	1924
Schubert: *Wohin?* D795/2 transcribed for piano	1925
Kreisler: *Liebesfreud* for piano	1925
Piano Concerto No. 4 in G minor Op. 40 (original version)	1926–
Trois Chansons Russes Op. 41, chorus and orchestra	1926
Rimsky-Korsakov: *The Flight of the Bumblebee* transcribed for piano	1929

Appendix II

1930–1939

Variations on a Theme of Corelli (*LaFolia*) Op. 42, piano	1931
Sonata No. 2 in B flat minor Op. 36, piano (revised version)	1931
Mendelssohn: *A Midsummer Night's Dream* Scherzo transcribed for piano	1933
Bach: Movements from Partita No. 6 in E major for unaccompanied violin BWV10006, transcribed for piano	1933
Rhapsody on a Theme of Paganini Op. 43, piano and orchestra	1934
Symphony No. 3 Op. 44, orchestra	1935–36

1940–1943

Symphonic Dances Op. 45, orchestra	1940
Tchaikovsky: Lullaby transcribed for piano	1941

I accessed the following sources for assembling a chronology of Rachmaninoff's compositions: the extensive Rachmaninoff archives at the Russian National Museum of Music in Moscow; Sergei Bertensson and Jay Leyda, *Sergei Rachmaninoff: A Lifetime in Music* (New York: New York UP, 1956; repr., Bloomington, IN: Indiana UP, 2001), 402–19; Max Harrison, *Rachmaninoff: Life, Works, Recordings* (London: Continuum, 2005), 382–84; Barrie Martyn, *Rachmaninoff: Composer, Pianist, Conductor* (Burlington, VT: Ashgate, 1990), 19–21; Liudmila Kovaleva-Ogorodnova, *Sergei Rakhmaninov* (Sankt-Peterburg: Vita Nova, 2015), 2: 321–67; and the publications of Russian Music Publishing (Moscow). The late V. I. Antipov made extraordinary discoveries in the Rachmaninoff archive of the Russian National Museum of Music named for Glinka that will lead to a revision of the dating / cataloguing of Rachmaninoff's works especially of the Moscow Conservatory period of his compositions, 1887-1892. See also n.a., "Zakonomernaia sensatsiia: Naideny ranee ne izvestnye proizvedeniia Rakhmaninova," *Muzykal'noe obozrenie* 1 (241) 2004, 8–9. I thank D. A. Dmitriev, director of Russian Music Publishing, for conversations in Moscow in September 2019 about the revision of chronological dating of Rachmaninoff's works.

Selected Discography

I list the CD recordings below in chronological order by date of release (from earliest to most recent). Some of them are historic performances and as such were recorded at an earlier date. My main principle of selection is the quality of the performance itself, rather than the technical features of the mode of reproduction. Dazzling performances will transcend any considerations of technology. The modest list below includes some of the finest interpreters of Rachmaninoff's music, including the composer himself, across the generations. Several items in the list include music of Rachmaninoff's contemporaries by important pianists, to provide an impression of his era and influences. Note: the term "romances" signifies "art songs."

Rachmaninov: Piano Concertos Nos. 2 & 3: Walter Gieseking, Willem Mengelberg, Concertgebouw Orchestra (Music & Arts 250, recorded 1940, released 1987)
"The Immortal Fritz Kreisler" (includes Rachmaninoff as pianist for Beethoven"s Sonata in G, Op. 30, No. 3, recorded 1928): Fritz Kreisler, Sergei Rachmaninoff et al (RCA Red Seal 5910-2-RC, 1987)
Rachmaninov: Suites #1 and #2 for Two Pianos: John Ogdon, Brenda Lucas (Academy Sound and Vision, Ltd. DCA 636, 1988)
"Horowitz Plays Rachmaninoff": Vladimir Horowitz, Fritz Reiner, RCA Victor Symphony Orchestra, (RCA Gold Seal 7754-2 RG, 1989)
"Rachmaninoff Plays Rachmaninoff: The Ampico Piano Recordings": Sergei Rachmaninoff (Decca 425 964-2, recorded 1919-29, released 1990)
"Rachmaninov, Tcherepnine: Mélodies": Nicolai Gedda, Alexis Weissenberg (EMI 102573, 1990)
"Rachmaninoff: *Monna Vanna*, Piano Concerto No. 4": Sherrill Milnes, Seth McCoy, Icelandic Opera Chorus, Iceland Symphony Orchestra, conductor Igor Buketoff (Chandos 8987, 1991)

"Rachmaninov: The Three Operas": Soloists and Orchestra of the Bolshoi Theatre, conductor Andrey Chistiakov (Saison Russe CMX 388053, 1992-1993)

"Ruth Laredo Plays Rachmaninoff": The Complete Solo Piano Music, Vol. 4 of 5": Ruth Laredo (Sony SMK 48-471, 1993)

"Rachmaninoff: The Four Piano Concertos; *Rhapsody on a Theme of Paganini*": Sergei Rachmaninoff, Eugene Ormandy, Leopold Stokowski, The Philadelphia Orchestra (RCA Gold Seal, recorded 1929, released 1993)

"Rachmaninov: Songs": Elisabeth Söderström, Vladimir Ashkenazy (Decca 436 920-2, 1993)

"Tchaikovsky, Rachmaninov: Romances": Evgeni Nesterenko, Evgeni Shenderovich (Russian Disc 11 372, 1994)

"Rachmaninov: The Symphonies": Vladimir Ashkenazy, Concertgebouw Orchestra (Decca 455 798-2, 1994)

Rachmaninov: Piano Concerto No. 3 / Tchaikovsky: Piano Concerto No. 1: Sviatoslav Richter, Herbert von Karajan, Wiener Symphoniker, Stanislaw Wislocki, Warsaw National Philharmonic Orchestra (Deutsche Grammophon 447 420-2, recorded 1959, 1963, released 1995)

Rachmaninoff: *Symphonic Dances, Rhapsody on a Theme of Paganini, Aleko* Overture: Yuri Temirkanov, St. Petersburg Philharmonic Orchestra, Dmitri Alexeev (RCA Victor Red Seal 09026-62710-2, 1995)

"Rachmaninov: The Three Operas: *Aleko, The Miserly Knight, Francesca da Rimini*": Andrey Chistiakov, The Russian State Choir, Orchestra of the Bolshoi Theatre (Harmonia Mundi, 1996)

"Rachmaninov Plays and Conducts: Piano Concerto No. 3, Symphony No. 3": Sergei Rachmaninov, Eugene Ormandy, Philadelphia Orchestra (Vista Vera 00028, recorded 1939-40, released 2000)

Rachmaninov: Symphony No. 2: conductor Alexander Anissimov, National Symphony Orchestra of Ireland (Naxos 8.554230, 2001)

Rachmaninoff: *Études-tableaux, Preludes* (complete): Nikolai Lugansky, Maria Petkova (Brilliant 6368, 1992, 2002)

"Serge Rachmaninoff: Chopin": Sergei Rachmaninoff (Dante HPC053, recorded 1920-35, released 1996)

"Rachmaninov: The Symphonies" (also *Isle of the Dead, The Bells, Symphonic Dances*): Vladimir Ashkenazy, Concertgebouw Orchestra and Chorus, Natalia Troitskaya, Ryszard Karcykowski, Tom Krause (Decca, 1998)

"Russia and Feodor Ivanovich Shalyapin: Romances of Russian Composers" (Kanon, recorded 1902-31, released 1999)

"Sergei Rachmaninoff: Piano Sonata No. 2": Mark Gurovsky (Sonora S022595, 2000)

Rachmaninov: *Preludes, Moments musicaux*: Nikolai Lugansky (Erato Disques 8573-85770-2, 2001)

Sergei Rakhmaninov: *Vsenoshchnoye Bdenie* [All-Night Vigil], Male Choir "Soglasiye" of St. Petersburg, dir. Alexander Govorov (Soglasiye, 2001)

"Rachmaninov Plays and Conducts: Schubert, Schumann, Mendelssohn, Debussy": Sergei Rachmaninoff (Vista Vera 00039, 2003)

Rachmaninov: Piano Concerto No. 2; Rhapsody on a Theme of Paganini: Prelude in G Minor, Op. 23, No. 5: Lang Lang, Valery Gergiev, Mariinsky Orchestra (Deutsche Grammophon, 2005)

"Rachmaninoff Plays Chopin": Sergei Rachmaninoff (Past Classics, recorded 1919-35, released 2009)

Rachmaninov: Piano Concerto No. 2 in C Minor and Rhapsody on a Theme of Paganini: Yuja Wang, Claudio Abbado, Mahler Chamber Orchestra (Deutsche Grammophon B004KD5TPY, 2011)

"Rachmaninov: Complete Piano Concertos": Leif Ove Andsnes, Antonio Pappano, London Symphony Orchestra, Berliner Philharmoniker (Warner Classics, 2012)

"Art of Irina Arkhipova": Art Songs of Tchaikovsky, Rachmaninoff, Mussorgsky: Irina Arkhipova, John Wustman, Igor Guselnikov (Melodiya, 2014)

"Rachmaninov: Solo Piano Works": Sandro Russo (Steinway & Sons 30077, 2017)

Rachmaninoff: Piano Concerto No. 2 in C Minor, Op. 18 & Piano Concerto No. 3 in D Minor: Khatia Buniatishvili, Paavo Järvi, Czech Philharmonic Orchestra (Sony Music Canada 47427818, 2017)

Rachmannoff: Symphony No. 2: Sir Simon Rattle, London Symphony Orchestra (LSO Live B08SPFDS71, 2021)

Selected Bibliography

SOURCES IN ENGLISH

Album Notes. *Rachmaninov Symphony no. 1 in D Minor*, Op. 13, U.S.S.R. Symphony Orchestra. Conducted by Yevgeny Svetlanov. Recorded by Melodiya. Printed by EMI Records, Great Britain, ASD 2471, 1967.

"Anton L Dahl (unknown-1932)." Find A Grave. https://www.findagave.com/memorial/137984530/anton-l-dahl#source. Accessed September 13, 2021.

"Anton Luis Dahl: One-Time Pianist to Czar Dies on Los Angeles Street Corner." *The New York Times*, November 1, 1932, 21. https://www.nytimes.com/1932/11/01/archives/anton-luis-dahl-onetime-pianist-to-czar-dies-on-los-angeles-street.html.

Bambarger, Bradley. "Sergei Rachmaninoff." https://www.steinway.com/artists/sergei-rachmaninoff. Accessed August 11, 2021.

Barber, Charles F. *Lost in the Stars: The Forgotten Musical Life of Alexander Siloti.* Lanham, MD: Scarecrow Press, 2002.

Bazhanov, Nikolai. *Rachmaninov*. Translated by Andrew Bromfield. Moscow: Raduga, 1983.

Berdyaev, Nicolas. *The Russian Revolution*. Translated by R.M. French. Ann Arbor, MI: University of Michigan Press, 1961. Originally published by London: Sheed and Ward, 1931.

Berdyaev, Nikolai. "Salvation and Creativity." Translated by Fr. Stephen Janos. *Put'* 2 (January 1926): 26–46.

Bertensson, Sergei, and Jay Leyda. *Sergei Rachmaninoff: A Lifetime in Music.* New York: New York University Press, 1956. Reprint, Bloomington, IN: Indiana University Press, 2001.

Bird, The Revd Norman. "Letters: The Misappliance of Science." *The Guardian*, November 18, 2001. https://www.theguardian.com/news/2001/nov/18/letters.theobserver.

Borovsky, Victor, *Chaliapin: A Critical Biography.* New York: Alfred A. Knopf, 1988.

Bowen, Catherine Drinker. *Beloved Friend: The Story of Tchaikowsky and Nadejda von Meck.* Mineola, NY: Dover Publications, 1946. Reprint, Westport, CT: Greenwood, 1975.

Brower, Harriette. "'Beware of the Indifferent Piano Teacher,' Warns Rachmaninoff." *Musician* 30 (February 1925): 11–12.

Bullard, Truman. "An Introduction to Russian Music." In *Russia and Western Civilization: Cultural and Historical Encounters*, edited by Russell Bova, 210–38. New York: Routledge, 2003.

Campbell, Stuart, ed. *Russians on Russian Music: 1880-1917.* Cambridge, MA: Cambridge University Press, 2003.

Chaplin, Charlie. *My Autobiography.* New York: Simon & Schuster, 1964.

Cohen, Steve. "The Stokowski Story: Rachmaninoff." Audio interview, WHYY-FM, Philadelphia, 1968. https://www.stokowski.org/sitebuilderfiles/stokowski_story_1968_rachmaninoff.mp3. Accessed December 29, 2020.

Dexter, Benning. "Rachmaninoff in the Flesh: Two Eyewitness Accounts." Newsletter of the Rachmaninoff Society, 2004.

Dostoevsky, Fyodor. *The Brothers Karamazov.* Trans. Constance Garnett. New York: Norton, 1976.

Downes, Olin. "Recital is Given by Rachmaninoff; Carnegie Hall is Crowded for Program of the Masters by Pianist in Afternoon." *New York Herald Tribune*, November 8, 1942.

Evans-Romain, Karen, Helena Goscilo, and Tatiana Smorodinskaya, eds. *The Encyclopedia of Contemporary Russian Culture.* London: Routledge Ltd., 2007.

Fedotov, Georgy. *The Russian Religious Mind.* New York: Harper, 1960.

Gerich, George. "Sergei Jaroff and the Don Cossack Choir." December 1, 2015. https://orthochristian.com/88292.html.

"The Grand Hall of the Moscow Conservatory." https://www.mosconsv.ru/museum/english/bzk.html. Accessed June 14, 2022.

Haldey, Olga. *Mamontov's Private Opera: The Search for Modernism in Russian Theatre.* Bloomington, IN: Indiana University Press, 2010.

Harrison, Max. *Rachmaninoff: Life, Works, Recordings.* London: Continuum, 2005.

Haylock, Julian. *Sergei Rachmaninov.* London: Pavilion Books, 1996.

Holcman, Jan. "Hidden Treasures of Rachmaninoff." *Saturday Review* 41 (August 30, 1958): 31–33.

Holmes, John L. *Composers on Composers.* Westport, CT: Greenwood Press, 1990.

Hosking, Geoffrey. *The First Socialist Society.* Cambridge, MA: Harvard University Press, 1985.

Huth, Andrew. "Sergei Rachmaninov: man of steel and gold." In *Rachmaninov: Orchestral Works*, conductor Mariss Jansons, St. Petersburg Philharmonic Orchestra. 6 CD set. France: EMI, 2002, 14.

Jakim, Boris and Robert Bird, eds. and trans. *On Spiritual Unity: A Slavophile Reader.* Hudson, NY: Lindisfarne Books, 1998.

"John Chrysostom." https://orthodoxwiki.org/John_Chrysostom. Accessed July 21, 2021.

Johnson, Lawrence B. "Famed pianist left mark on chamber festival." *The Detroit News*, May 28, 2005, 2.

Klevantseva, Tatyana. "Prominent Russians: Ekaterina Dashkova." https://russiapedia.rt.com/prominent-russians/history-and-mythology/ekaterina-dashkova/. Accessed June 14, 2022.

Laciar, Samuel L. Review. *Public Ledger*, November 7, 1936.

"Lauter." Antique Piano Shop. https://antiquepianoshop.com/online-museum/lauter/. Accessed on October 1, 2021.

Lazor, Very Reverend Paul. "Introduction." *Holy Friday Matins*. Yonkers, NY: St. Vladimir's Seminary Press, 1980: 5–20.

Liebling, Leonard. "Variations." *The Musical Courier* 127 (April 5, 1943): 17.

Martyn, Barrie, *Rachmaninoff: Composer, Pianist, Conductor*. Burlington, VT: Ashgate, 2000.

Matushevski, Voytek. "Rachmaninoff's Last Tour." *Clavier* (March 1993): 20.

McAfee, Annalena. "Symphony for a True Survivor." *Evening Standard* (March 25, 1993).

McCarthy, Jack. "Rachmaninoff's Philadelphia." *Historical Society of Pennsylvania*, March 14, 2017, https://hsp.org/blogs/fondly-pennsylvania/rachmaninoff%E2%80%99s-philadelphia.

McLean, Anne. "Rachmaninoff: The Bohemian." *Studies in Music from the University of Western Ontario* 15 (1995): 95–106.

Meltzer, Ken. "Program Notes: Sergei Rachmaninoff, Symphony No. 2 in E Minor, Opus 27." 2020. https://fwsymphony.org/program-notes/rachmaninoff-sergei-symphony-no-2-in-e-minor-opus-27.

Miller, Matthew Lee. *The American YMCA and Russian Culture*. New York: Lexington Books, 2013.

Monsaingeon, Bruno. *Sviatoslav Richter: Notebooks and Conversations*. Trans. Stewart Spencer. Princeton, NJ: Princeton University Press, 2001.

Morosan, Vladimir, ed. *Sergei Rachmaninoff: The Complete Choral Works*. Bilingual edition. Madison, CT: Musica Russica, 1994, Series IX.

Neely, Jack. "Gay Street's Wallflower: The Andrew Johnson Hotel." Knoxville History Project. https://knoxvillehistoryproject.org/andrew-johnson-hotel/. Accessed December 25, 2020.

Newmarch, Rosa Harriet. *Tchaikovsky: His Life and Work*. New York: Greenwood Press, 1969.

Nikitin, B.S. Unpublished, untitled article on Rachmaninoff, Ivanovka, and Tambov. Given to
author on June 13, 2007.

Nikolsky, Y. Liner Notes. *Rachmaninoff Plays and Conducts*. Vista Vera-00039 (2003), Compact Disc.

Noble, Jr., Clifton J. "Rachmaninoff Centennial." https://www.smith.edu/rachmaninoff/about.php. Accessed June 5, 2022.

Nollan, Valeria Z. "Rachmaninoff's Music and Khomiakov's Poetry." In *A.S. Khomiakov: Poet, Philosopher, Theologian*, edited by Vladimir Tsurikov, 174–95. Jordanville, NY: Holy Trinity Seminary Press, 2004.

Nollan, Valerie Zarin. "Nollan Plays Rachmaninoff." *Rhodes* 10, no. 2 (Spring 2003), 28–32. Rhodes College Digital Archives. https://dlynx.rhodes.edu/jspui/bitstream/10267/7381/1/2003_spring_rhodes_magazine_150_dpi.pdf.

Norris, Geoffrey. *Rachmaninoff*, 2nd ed. New York: Oxford University Press, 2001; First published in 1994.

Ormandy, Eugene. Interview with Morris Henken. Philadelphia, PA (1973). Annenberg Rare Book & Manuscript Library, University of Pennsylvania. WorldCat record id: 155901926.

Ostrom, Natalia. Untitled liner notes. *Rachmaninov Plays and Conducts*. Vista Vera VVCD-00023 (1999) Vol. 2: 6. Compact Disc.

Paperno, Dmitry. *Notes of a Moscow Pianist*. Portland, OR: Amadeus Press, 1998.

Petro, Nicolai N. *The Rebirth of Russian Democracy: An Interpretation of Political Culture*. Cambridge, MA: Harvard University Press, 1997.

Piggott, Patrick. *Rachmaninov*. London: Faber and Faber, 1978.

———. *Rachmaninov: Orchestral Music*. Seattle: University of Washington Press, 1974.

Polkinghorne, John, ed. *The Work of Love: Creation as Kenosis*. Grand Rapids, MI: William B. Eerdmans, 2001.

Prokhorov, Vadim. "Oldies and Oddities: Sikorsky's Piano Man." *Air&Space/Smithsonian*, November 2002, https://www.smithsonianmag.com/air-space-magazine/oldies-amp-oddities-sikorskys-piano-man-36005729/.

Rachmaninoff Network. "Breaking News: Parliament Canton Lucerne Supports Purchase Villa Senar," December 6, 2021. https://rachmaninoff.org/articles/news/199-breaking-news-parliament-canton-lucerne-supports-purchase-villa-senar.

Rachmaninoff, Sergei. "Declaration of Intention." January 11, 1939. Rachmaninoff Network: https://www.rachmaninoff.org/articles/archive/147-sergei-rachmaninoff-application-for-american-citizenship-1939. Accessed September 13, 2021.

Rachmaninoff, Sergei. Letter to Frank C. Page, April 18, 1922. Section B1: Correspondence of Sergei Rachmaninoff, "A," Music Division, Library of Congress.

Rachmaninoff, Sergei. Letter to Ralph M. Easley, January 27, 1931. Section B1: Correspondence of Sergei Rachmaninoff, "A," Music Division, Library of Congress.

Rachmaninoff, Sergei. "Rachmaninoff Assails 'Heartless' Moderns; Music of Present Must Return to Fundamentals, He Says—'Color and Rhythm' Not Enough." *New York Times*. February 25, 1932.

Rachmaninoff, S.V. "Ten Important Attributes of Beautiful Pianoforte Playing," *The Etude* (March 1910).

Randall, Don Michael ed. *The Harvard Dictionary of Music*, 4th ed. Cambridge, MA: The Belknap Press of Harvard University Press, 2003.

Ray, Brian. Program Notes. Piano recital at Rhodes College. September 22, 2014.

Rimm, Robert. *The Composer-Pianists: Hamelin and the Eight*. Portland, OR: Amadeus Press, 2002.

Robinson, Harlow. *Russians in Hollywood, Hollywood's Russians*. Lebanon, NH: Northeastern University Press, 2007.

Roosevelt, Priscilla. *Life on the Russian Country Estate: A Social and Cultural History* New Haven: Yale University Press, 1995.

Rosen, Charles. *Piano Notes: The World of the Pianist*. New York: The Free Press, 2002.

Rosenfeld, Paul. "Rachmaninoff." *The New Republic* 18 (March 15, 1919): 208–10.

Roy, Basanta Koomar. "Rachmaninoff is Reminiscent." *Musical Observer* 26 (May 1927): 16. https://www.pianostreet.com/smf/index.php?topic=17183.0.

"Ruth Laredo, 1937-2005: Renowned Performer of Rachmaninoff and Scriabin." *Clavier*, July/August 2005.

Samson, Jim. *Virtuosity and the Musical Work: The Transcendental Studies of Liszt*. Cambridge, MA: Cambridge University Press, 2003.

Satin, Sophia Vladimirovna. *A 20th Century Life: The Memoirs of Sophia Satin*. London: The Rachmaninoff Society, 1997.

Satina, Sophia. "Conversations with Sophia Vladimirovna Satina about Her Uncle Sergei Vasilyevich Rachmaninoff." Ed. Harold Tillek. Unpublished memoir.

Savikovskaya, Yulia. "Villa Senar: A Magical Place Supported by Rachmaninoff Foundation." Interview with Ettore F. Volontieri, May 28, 2021. https://www.russianartandculture.com/villa-senar-a-magical-place-supported-by-rachmaninoff-foundation/.

Schiff, Stacy. *Véra (Mrs. Vladimir Nabokov)*. New York: Random House, 1999.

Schloss, Edwin. Review. *Philadelphia Record*, November 7, 1936.

Schonberg, Harold. *The Great Pianists: From Mozart to the Present*. New York: Simon & Schuster, 1987.

Soloviev, Vladimir. *The Heart of Reality: Essays on Beauty, Love, and Ethics*. Trans. Vladimir Wozniuk. Notre Dame, IN: University of Notre Dame Press, 2003.

Soloukhin, Vladimir. *A Time to Gather Stones*. Translated by Valerie Z. Nollan. Evanston, IL: Northwestern University Press, 1993.

"Dr. Sophia Alexandrovna Satina: 1879-1975." Find a Grave. https://www.findagrave.com/memorial/104618748/sophia-alexandrovna-satina. Accessed June 20, 2022.

Steinberg, Michael. *The Concerto: A Listener's Guide*. New York: Oxford University Press, 1998.

Stokes, Martin, ed. *Ethnicity, Identity, and Music: The Musical Construction of Place*. Providence, RI: Berg Publishers, 1994.

Sylvester, Richard D. *Rachmaninoff's Complete Songs*. Bloomington: Indiana University Press, 2014.

———. *Tchaikovsky's Complete Songs*. Bloomington: Indiana University Press, 2002.

Tarkovsky, Andrey. *Sculpting in Time*. Translated by Kitty Hunter-Blair. Austin, TX: University of Texas Press, 1987.

"Theophany: The Sacramentality of Matter." *Go Forth* 17, no. 3 (January 21, 2007). Publication
of the Orthodox Church in America.

Volkov, Solomon. *From Russia to the West: the Musical Memoirs and Reminiscences of Nathan Milstein*. Translated by Antonina W. Bouis. New York: Henry Holt, 1990.

Voorhees, Sylvia. Letter representing Charles Foley, Inc. Archival work in Annenberg Rare Book and Manuscript Library, University of Pennsylvania.

———. *Shostakovich and Stalin: The Extraordinary Relationship between the Great Composer and the Brutal Dictator.* New York: Alfred A. Knopf, 2004.

Walker, Robert. *Rachmaninoff: His Life and Times,* 2nd ed. Neptune City, NJ: Paganiniana Publications, Inc., 1981.

West, Krista M. *The Garments of Salvation: Orthodox Christian Liturgical Vesture.* Yonkers, NY: St. Vladimir's Seminary Press, 2013.

Wheeler, Nicholas. "Meeting Report: The Russian Influence on American Music." Washington, DC: Kennan Institute, 2003, XX: 11.

Williams, Robert. "The Russian Revolution and the End of Time, 1900-1940." *Jahrbücher für Geschichte Osteuropas* 43, no. 3 (1995): 364–401.

Yasser, Joseph. "The Opening Theme of Rachmaninoff's Third Piano Concerto and Its Liturgical Prototype." *The Musical Quarterly* LV, no. 3 (July 1969): 313–28.

SOURCES IN RUSSIAN

(cited according to Library of Congress transliteration system)

Apetian, Z.A., ed. *N.K. Medtner. Vospominaniia. Stat'i. Materialy.* Moscow: Sovetskii kompozitor, 1981.

———. *S. Rakhmaninov. Literaturnoe nasledie.* 3 vols. Moscow: Sovetskii kompozitor, 1978, 1980.

———. *S.V. Rakhmaninov: Pis'ma.* Moscow: Gos. muz. izd., 1955.

———. *Vospominaniia o Rakhmaninove.* 2 vols., 5th ed. Moscow: Muzyka, 1988.

Beschetnova, Alina Iosifovna. *Sviatoi Ioann Prigorovskii.* Pavlovskaia: Poligrafika, 2018.

Chaliapin, F.I. *Maska i dusha: Moi sorok let na teatrakh.* Moscow: Moskovskii rabochii, 1989.

Chinaev, Vladimir. "Stil' modern i pianism Rakhmaninova." *Muzykal'naia akademiia* 2 (1993): 202.

Demidov, V.V. "Tak gde zhe rodilsia Rakhmaninov?" Unpublished article, March 9, 2003.

Dmitr'evskaia, E., and V. Dmitr'evskii. *Rakhmaninov v Moskve.* Moscow: Moskovskii rabochii, 1993.

Dobuzhinskii, M.V., ed. *Pamiati Rakhmaninova.* New York: Publication of S.A. Satina, 1946.

Ermakov, A.I. *Sergei Rakhmaninov. Istoki.* Ivanovka: Muzei-usad'ba S.V. Rakhmaninova, 2003.

Ermakov, A.I., and A.V. Zhogov, comp. *Ivanovka: Vremena. Sobytiya. Sud'by.* Moscow: Irina Arkhipova Foundation, 2003.

———. *Znamenskoe: Raxmaninovskie mesta Tambovskoi oblasti* Tambov: TOGUP, 2004.

Gromyko, A.A. *Pamiatnoe.* Moscow: Izd. politicheskoi literatury, 1988, 2 vols.

Ivanov, Aleksandr. "Istoriia moskovskoi konservatorii." April 20, 2016. http://moscowwalks.ru/2016/04/20/moscow-conservatorium/.

Klenov, Viktor. *I.A. Ilyin: Pro et Contra. Lichnost i tvorchestvo Ivana Ilyina v vospominaniiakh, dokumentakh, i otsenkakh russkikh myslitelei i issledovatelei*. Russkii put' Series. St. Petersburg: Izd. russkogo Khristiianskogo gumanitarnogo instituta, 2004.

Klimkova, M.A., ed. *Tvorchestvo S.V. Rakhmaninova v kontekste mirovoi muzykal'noi kul'tury*. Tambov: Izd. Tambovskogo gosudarstvennogo tekhnicheskogo universiteta, 2003).

Kovalyova-Ogorodnova, L.L. *Rakhmaninov v Sankt-Peterburge*. St. Petersburg: Predpriiatie S.-Peterburgskogo coiuza khudozhnikov, 1997.

———. *Sergei Rakhmaninov: Biografiia*. Sankt-Peterburg: Vita Nova, 2015. 2 vols.

Medvedeva, I.A., ed. *Novoe o Rakhmaninove*. Moscow: Deka-BC, 2006.

Nikitin, B.S.. *Sergei Rakhmaninov: Dve zhizni*. Revised and expanded edition. Moscow: Klassika-XXI, 2008.

———. *Sergei Rakhmaninov: Dve zhizni*. Moscow: Znanie, 1993.

———. *Sergei Rakhmaninov. Feodor Shaliapin*. Moscow: OTiSS, 1998.

Rachmaninoff, Sergei. Letter to Metropolitan Evlogii, January 3, 1929. Section B1: Correspondence of Sergei Rachmaninoff, "A," Music Division, Library of Congress.

Rachmaninoff, Sergei. Letter to Nikolai Avierino, November 11, 1933. Section B1: Correspondence of Sergei Rachmaninoff, "A," Music Division, Library of Congress.

Rachmaninoff, Sergei. Letter to Nina Koshetz, July 5, 1919. Section B1: Correspondence of Sergei Rachmaninoff, "A," Music Division, Library of Congress.

Rakhmaninov, Ivan Ivanovich, and N. Vasilenko, eds. *Istoricheskie svedeniia o rode dvorian Rakhmaninovykh*. Kiev: G.T. Korchak-Novitskii, 1895.

Rakhmaninova, N.A. "S.V. Rakhmaninov." In *Vospominaniia o Rakhmaninove*, edited by Z.A. Apetian, 5th ed. Vol. II: 292–332. Moscow: Muzyka, 1988.

Riesemann, Oskar von, *Sergei Rakhmaninov: Vospominaniia zapisannye Oskarom fon Rizemanom*. Translated by V.N. Chemberdzhi. Moscow: Raduga, 1992. Originally published in English as *Rachmaninoff's recollections, told to Oskar von Riesemann*. London: The Macmillan Company, 1934.

Satin, Sophie [S.A. Satina], ed. *Pamiati Rakhmaninova*. New York: Grenich Printing Corp., 1946.

Savenko, S.I. *Sergei Ivanovich Taneev*. Moscow: Muzyka, 1984.

Strel'nikov, B.N. "Iz vospominaniy N.M. Strel'nikova." Senar.ru, 2006-2022. https://senar.ru/memoirs/Strelnikov/.

Vanovskaia, I.N., ed. *S.V. Rakhmaninov: Natsional'naia pamiat' Rossii*. Tambov: Iulis, 2008.

———. *S.V. Rakhmaninov i Tambovskii krai v aspekte razvitiia regional'noi kul'tury: Materialy dokladov*. III *Rakhmaninovskie chteniia*, Nov. 30, 2006. Tambov: Tambovskoe gosudarstvennoe muzykal'no-pedagogicheskii institut imeni Rakhmaninova, 2007.

Vostokova, Natal'ia and Tat'iana Gamazkova. "S.V. Rakhmaninov. Brasovo, Leto 1911." *Muzeinyi listok, Prilozhenie k Rossiiskoi muzykal'noi gazete*, 40, no. 4 (November 2003).

Yasser, I.S. Untitled. In *Pamiati Rakhmaninova*. S.A. Satina, ed. New York: Grenich Printing Corporation, 1946: 150–75.

Zvereva, S.G., ed. *Aleksandr Kastal'skii. Stat'i, Materialy, Vospominaniia, Perepiska*. Russkaia dukhovnaia muzyka v dokumentakh I materialakh V. Moscow: Znak, 2006.

SOURCES IN OTHER LANGUAGES

Biesold, Maria, *Sergej Rachmaninoff, 1873-1943: Zwischen Moskau und New York: eine Kunstlerbiographie*. Weinheim: Beltz/Quadriga, 1991.

D'Antoni, Claudio A., *Rachmaninov. Personalità e poetica* (Roma: Bardi Editore, 2002).

———. *Dinamica rappresentativa del 'suono-parola': La "drammaturgia compressa" delle Romanze di Rachmaninov*. Roma: Cromografica, 2009.

Guccini, Gerardo. "Spettacolo e visione nella drammaturgia di Arrigo Boito." *Mefistofele*. Teatro alla Scala, Program (February 20 – March 18, 1995): 47–48.

Poivre D'Arvor, Catherine, *Rachmaninoff: la passion au bout des doigts*. Monte Carlo: Le Rocher, 1986.

Séroff, Victor. *Rachmaninoff*. Translated by Michel Bourdet-Pleville. Paris: Robert Laffont, 1954.

Further Reading

SOURCES IN ENGLISH

Ardoin, John, ed., *The Philadelphia Orchestra: A Century of Music*. Philadelphia, PA: Temple University Press, 1999.

Bullock, Phillip, ed. *Rachmaninoff and His World*. Chicago, IL: University of Chicago Press, 2022.

Cross, Jonathan. *Igor Stravinsky*. London: Reaktion Books, 2015.

Cunningham, Robert E., Jr. *Sergei Rachmaninoff: A Bio-Bibliography*. Westport, CT: Greenwood Press, 2001.

Emerson, Caryl. *The life of Musorgsky*. Cambridge: Cambridge University Press, 1999.

Gosden, Stephen John. "Rachmaninoff's Middle-Period Orchestral Music: Style, Structure, and Genre." Ph.D. dissertation. Yale University, 2012.

Isacoff, Stuart. *Temperament: How Music Became a Battleground for the Great Minds of Civilization*. New York: Vintage Books, 2003.

Kramer, Lawrence. *Why Classical Music Still Matters*. Berkeley, CA: University of California Press, 2007.

Ledkovsky, Marina and Vladimir von Tsurikov, eds. *Russian Liturgical Music Revival in the Diaspora*. Jordanville, New York: Foundation of Russian History, 2012.

Maes, Francis. *A History of Russian Music*. Trans. Arnold J. Pomerans and Erica Pomerans. Los Angeles, CA: University of California Press, 2006.

Marullo, Thomas Gaiton. *Ivan Bunin: The Twilight of Emigré Russia, 1934-1953*. Chicago: Ivan R. Dee, 2002.

Mitchell, Rebecca. "In Search of Russia: Sergei Rachmaninov and the Politics of Musical Memory." *Slavonic and East European Review*, 97 (2019): n.p.

Mitchell, Rebecca. *Sergei Rachmaninoff*. London: Reaktion Books, 2022.

Palmieri, Robert. *Sergei Vasil'evich Rachmaninoff: A Guide to Research*. New York: Garland, 1985.

Plaskin, Glenn, *Horowitz: A Biography of Vladimir Horowitz.* New York: William Morrow & Co., 1983.
Reder, Ewald, *Sergej Rachmaninow, Leben und Werk (1873- 1943): Biografie* Gelnhausen: TRIGA, 2001.
Rego, John Anthony. "Skryabin, Rakhmaninov, and Prokofiev as Composer-Pianists: The Russian Piano Tradition, Aesthetics, and Performance Practices." Ph.D. dissertation. Princeton University, 2012.
Robinson, Harlow. *Sergei Prokofiev: A Biography.* Boston: Northeastern University Press, 2002.
———, ed. *Selected Letters of Sergei Prokofiev.* Boston: Northeastern University Press, 1998.
———. *Sergei Prokofiev: A Biography.* New York: Viking, 1987.
See, Truman. "Hear My Desire: Rachmaninoff's Orphic Voice and Musicology's Trouble with Eurydice." *19th-Century Music* 44, no. 3 (2021): n.p.
Steinway, Theodore E. *People and Pianos: A Century of Service to Music.* New York: Steinway, 1961.
Strunk, Oliver. *Essays on Music in the Byzantine World.* New York: Norton, 1977.
Taruskin, Richard. *Defining Russia Musically.* Princeton, NJ: Princeton University Press, 1997.
Threlfall, Robert. *Sergei Rachmaninoff; His Life and Music.* London: Boosey and Hawkes, 1973.
Timofeev, Alexandru. "The Great Russian Piano Tradition: Selected Repertoire by Tchaikovsky, Rachmaninoff, and Prokofiev." Ph.D. dissertation. University of Maryland, 2012.

SOURCES IN RUSSIAN

(cited according to Library of Congress transliteration system)

Briantseva, V.N. *S.V. Rakhmaninov.* Moscow: Sovetskii kompozitor, 1976.
———. "Tvorcheskoe svoeobrazie khudozhnika." [Creative originality of the artist] *Sovetskaia muzyka* 1 (1965): 35–40.
Kalashnikov, D.V. and O.A. Kaz'min. *"V Ivanovku ia vsegda stremilsia . . ."* Voronezh: Tsentr dukhovnogo vozrozhdeniia Chernozemskogo kraia, 2003.
Poltoratzkii, N.P. *I.A. Il'in i polemika vokrug ego idei o soprotivlenii zlu siloi.* London: Zaria, 1975.

Index

Page numbers followed with "n" refer to endnotes.

Albrecht, Konstantin Karlovich, 64
Aleko (Rachmaninoff), 11, 71–72, 82, 129, 166
Aleksandr II, 25, 78, 117, 232
Aleksandr III, 25
Aleksandrova, Nadezhda Aleksandrovna, 112
Aleksandrovich, Arkady, 33, 34
All-Night Vigil (Rachmaninoff), 206–8, 219, 319, 340
Altani, Ippolit, 84–85
American jazz, 305–6, 319
Antipov, Valentin Ivanovich, 190, 340, 350
Arensky, A. S., 56, 61–63, 68, 69
Arkadievna, Varvara, 146, 148, 152, 155–56, 159, 161, 163, 216, 223–26, 266
Arkadievna, Yulia, 33, 35
Artemova, Anna Pavlovna, 264
Asafiev, Boris Vladimirovich, 202
Avierino, Nikolai Konstantinovich, 252, 273

Bagrinovsky, Mikhail, 85
Balakirev, Mily, 60
Bamberger, Bradley, 256–57
baptism, 15
Barclay, Dagmar Rybner, 289

Bazikov, Aleksandr Sergeevich, 277
beauty, 185
Beketova, N. V., 184
The Bells (Rachmaninoff), 209–11, 296–97
"bended" note (jazz), 307
Berdyaev, Nikolai, 181, 228
Berman, Lazar, 250
Bertensson, Sergei, 237, 308, 339
Bird, Robert, 183
Blok, Aleksandr, 35
"The Blue Bird" (Maeterlinck), 178
blues, 306, 307
Blues Scale, 307
Böcklin, Arnold, 209
Bohemian Club, 239, 240
Boito, Arrigo, 87, 92
Bokarov, Viktor, 330
Bolsheviks, 192, 229–32, 234, 274; Revolution of 1917, 4, 119, 127, 129, 167, 208, 227, 232, 290
Bolshoi Theatre, 84, 85
Boris Godunov (Pushkin), 78
Borodin, Aleksandr, 60
Borovsky, Victor, 77, 88, 92
Brandt, Irina Aleksandrovna, 118, 119, 147, 148, 154, 157, 159, 180, 200–201, 216, 223

Brandukov, Anatoly, 158, 159, 163
Bullard, Truman, 109, 304
Bunin, Ivan, 130
Butakov, P. I., 17
Butakova, Sofia Aleksandrovna, 15–17, 23, 24, 27, 199, 200
Byzantine-Russian Orthodoxy, 342

Catherine II (the Great), 31
Certificate of the Tambov Meeting of Deputies of the Nobility, 30
Chaliapin, Boris Feodorovich, 217, 325, 326
Chaliapin, Feodor Ivanovich, 77, 82, 84, 85, 125, 130, 164, 166, 173–74, 177, 178, 188, 206, 247, 248, 259, 292, 304, 308, 309, 315, 320; music tour: (to Varazze, 87–93; to Yalta, 86–87); and Rachmaninoff, 76, 78–81, 87–93
Chaplin, Charlie, 308
Chasins, Abram, 185
Chekhov, Anton, 87
Chekhov, Mikhail, 279–80, 321
Chinaev, Vladimir, 257–58
Chopin, Frédéric François, 249; B flat minor Sonata, 249, 258, 324, 331
Chopin Variations (Rachmaninoff), 164, 294
Conius, Boris, 293
Conius, Olga Nikolaevna, 324
conscious counterfeit, 207
contractual agreement, 238
Corelli Variations (Rachmaninoff), 164, 285, 286, 294
The Covetous Knight (Rachmaninoff), 166
creativity, 181–82
The Critical Edition of the Complete Works of Sergei Vasilievich Rachmaninoff (Antipov), 340
Cross, Gustav, 26
Cui, César, 60
culminating point, 180, 247

Dahl, Anton-Luis, 127, 349, 350, 352
Dahl, Elena (Lana), 90, 126–34, 157, 293, 325, 347–52

Dahl, Nikolai, 125–26, 128, 130–33, 348, 350, 353
Dahl family, 126, 130, 350
Danilin, Nikolay, 205–7
Davydov, K. Yu., 26
Defert, Madame, 20
Delius, Frederick, 187
Demiansky, Vladimir Vasilievich, 26–27
Demidov, Valery Vasilievich, 37n10
Dexter, Benning, 244
Dies irae, 115, 177, 209–10, 226–27, 286, 298, 319
The Divine Comedy (Dante), 90
Donnelly, Lena, 329
Dostoevsky, Fyodor, 134

ecclesiology, 217
Ellis, Charles, 238
Ellis, George, 184
emigration, 265, 274
Engel, Yury, 85
equal temperament, 174
Ermakov, Aleksander Ivanovich, 134, 145, 263
estate culture, 28
estate of Ivanovka, 51, 67, 98, 99, 224–26
eternal themes, 109
Études-Tableaux (Rachmaninoff), 188, 191–92, 226–27

Farrar, Geraldine, 312
Faust (Goethe), 91, 177–78
Fedotov, Georgy Petrovich, 181, 214, 274
Findeisen, Nikolay Fyodorovich, 115
The Firebird (Stravinsky), 253
Foley, Charles, 238, 310, 312, 315, 323, 328
Francesca da Rimini (Rachmaninoff), 128, 129, 132, 166
Francesca da Rimini (Tchaikovsky), 90

Ganzburg, Grigory, 187–88
Gieseking, Walter, 169, 243, 244

Glagolev, Sergei Mikhailovich, 276–77
Glazunov, Aleksandr, 115, 218
Glinka, Mikhail, 174
Goldenweiser, A. B., 141, 297
Golenishchev-Kutuzov, A., 118
Golitsyn, Aleksandr, 325, 326
Greiner, A.V., 291
Gromyko, Andrei, 321
gypsies, 43–44
gypsy women, 44

Harrison, Max, 47, 115, 135, 162, 212, 215, 309, 341
Henderson, W. J., 249
Henken, Morris, 295
Herzog, Sigmund, 240
Hirst, Arthur, 323
Hitler, 276, 299, 300, 318–19
Hofmann, Josef, 237, 243, 314
Holcman, Jan, 249
Holy Friday Matins, 213
homosexuality/homosexual, 47, 50, 284
Horowitz, Vladimir, 169, 243, 244, 320
Huth, Andrew, 305

Ilyin, Ivan Aleksandrovich, 274–75
Inferno (Dante), 90
instability, 224–26
Institute of Music Pedagogy, 276, 277
integral approach to art, 186–87
International Phonetic Alphabet (IPA), 341
Isle of the Dead (Rachmaninoff), 166, 186, 209–10
Ivanova, Maria (Marina) Aleksandrovna, 102, 117–21, 148, 158

Jaroff, Serge, 205–6
jazz, 305–7, 319

Kamenka, Boris Abramovich, 236
Kashkin, N. D., 57
Kastalsky, Aleksandr, 206, 207, 212
kenotic love, 184
Khomiakov, Aleksei Stepanovich, 183

Kievan-Pechersk Russian Orthodox chant, 186
Komissarzhevskaia, Vera Fedorovna, 34–35
Koshetz, Nina, 191, 192
Kostina, Aleksandra Gennadievna, 342
Kovaleva-Ogorodnova, Liudmila, 130
Kreisler, Fritz, 237, 238, 285–86, 310, 312, 328

Laciar, Samuel L., 298–99
land decree of October 26, 1917, 227
Laredo, Ruth, 244, 328
La Scala. *See* Teatro alla Scala
Lenin, Vladimir, 228
"Letter to K.S. Stanislavsky" (Rachmaninoff), 178
Leyda, Jay, 237, 339
Lied, 306–7
Liszt, Franz, 34, 42, 61, 63, 66, 69, 191, 245
liturgy, 198, 204
Liturgy of St. John Chrysostom (Rachmaninoff), 204–5, 212
Lodyzhenskaia, Anna, 90, 102, 111–17, 120, 132, 158
Lodyzhensky, Petr Viktorovich, 111–13
love and orthodox kenosis, 184

Maeterlinck, Maurice, 178
Maksimov, Leonid, 42, 43, 49, 50, 61
Malatesta, Paolo, 90
Mamontov, Savva Ivanovich, 76–78, 82, 84; Private Opera Company, 76–78, 84, 86, 87, 92, 93
Mandrovsky, Nikolay, 276
Manfred (Byron), 78, 105
Martyn, Barrie, 136, 138, 140, 141, 158, 164, 169, 177, 189, 215, 226, 314, 316
McLean, Anne, 239, 285, 286
Medtner, Nikolai Karlovich, 142, 250–52, 259, 272, 313, 314, 345
Mefistofele (Boito), 87, 103
Meltzer, Ken, 175
Mikhailovna, Anna, 272

Moiseiwitsch, Benno, 327–28
monarchy, 232
Monna Vanna (Rachmaninoff), 129, 166, 178
Morceau de Fantaisie in G minor (Rachmaninoff), 90, 128, 131
Morosan, Vladimir, 203, 208
Morozov, Nikita Semenovich, 88, 163, 167, 175, 205, 267, 313
Moscow Art Theatre, 308, 309
Moscow Conservatory, 42, 52, 55–57, 59, 62; curriculum of, 61; Orthodox liturgical music, 63
Moscow Synodal Choir, 202, 203, 206, 208, 211–12
Moscow Synodal School, 202, 203, 208
Mussorgsky, Modest, 60

National Civic Federation (NCF), 273
Naumov, Aleksei Aleksandrovich, 90, 350
NCF. *See* National Civic Federation (NCF)
Nemirovich-Danchenko, Vladimir, 71
Nezhdanova, Antonina, 190
Nicholas II, 156, 192, 211, 232, 237
Nikitin, Boris Semenovich, 48, 51, 100, 104, 113, 119, 134, 136, 139, 255, 268, 274, 277, 291, 330, 352
Nikolsky, Y., 245
Nollan, Alex, 332n11
Norris, Geoffrey, 68, 204, 211

Obolensky, 283
O Mother of God, Perpetually Praying (Rachmaninoff), 203, 215
Ormandy, Eugene, 295–96, 317–19
Ornatskaia, Anna Dmitrievna, 20, 26
Orthodox: Christianity, 6, 197–98, 201–2, 209, 213; Church, 197–98, 204, 207, 212, 218, 219; faithful, 202, 213–16; liturgical music, 205, 219; parishioner, 213; piety, 214; religiosity, 214; theology, 213, 217–18
Orthodox Divine Liturgy, 204

orthodox kenosis, love and, 184
Orthodox Pascha (Easter), 203–4
Ostrom, Natalia, 269
Ostromyslensky, Ivan, 273

Pabst, Pavel, 64, 146, 153
Paganini, Niccoló, 245
Panteley-Utselitel (Panteley the Healer, Rachmaninoff), 92, 215
Parker, H. T., 240
Pavlovna, Anna, 58
peasant revolt against the Bolshevik regime, 228
Peer Gynt Suite (Grieg), 85
Peter I (the Great), 31, 60
Petrovna, Elizabeth, 31
Philadelphia Orchestra, 169, 170, 190, 295, 296, 298, 299, 317
Piggott, Patrick, 168, 176
Platonic aesthetics, 185
Plevitskaia, Nadezhda, 316
Poe, Edgar Allan, 210–11
poetry, 181, 183
political turmoil, 224
Pressman, Matvey, 42, 43, 45, 50, 61
Pribytkova, Zoya, 170
Prokofiev, Sergei, 191, 223, 238, 319
Pushkin, Aleksandr, 28, 50
Putin, Vladimir, 345

Rachmaninoff, Aleksandr Gerasimovich, 32, 33
Rachmaninoff, Alexandre, 8, 127–30, 134–35, 293, 300, 330, 351–52; meetings and conversations with, 347–50
Rachmaninoff, Fyodor Ievlievich, 31
Rachmaninoff, Gerasim Ievlievich, 31
Rachmaninoff, Liubov Petrovna (Butakova), 17–26, 35, 41–42, 156, 159–61, 200, 266–67
Rachmaninoff, Maria Arkadievna, 32–33
Rachmaninoff, Sergei Vasilievich, 7, 55, 56, 58, 60, 61, 82, 84–86, 97–100, 127–30, 134; activities

with their corresponding dates (1890s to 1900s), 131–32, 139; aesthetics, 173–93; agony of exile, 256; American critical reviews, 337; American tours, 304; archive, 9–10; aristocratic background, 29; art songs, 306–7, 341; attitude toward performing on stage, 255; baptism, 15; beauty in the classical sense, 185; Beethoven's ninth symphony, 253; benefit recitals for the Soviet Red Army, 276; biographies of, 339; birth, 13–15; and Brandukov, Anatoly, 158–59; cancer diagnosis, 325–26; Chaliapin, Feodor and, 76, 78–81, 87–93; character of, 157–58; Chopin's B flat minor Sonata, 249, 258, 324, 331; church practices of family, 200, 201; church-related activities of, 201; clan, 27–32; college and university musicology courses, 340–41; compassion of, 264, 270; composing the set of ten preludes (1903), 165; concerns to support the family, 236; concert in America (1919-1925), 313; Concerto No. 1, 67–70, 132, 318; Concerto No. 2, 70, 126, 128, 140, 142, 158, 187–90, 303, 308, 314, 336; Concerto No. 3, 166–69, 186, 314, 318; Concerto No. 4, 285, 303, 313–16, 318, 319; concert season of 1933-1934, 294; concert tour of the United States, 237–40; conducting of Grieg's *Peer Gynt Suite*, 85; content of music courses, 62–63; creative life, 185; critics on, 169–70, 188, 240, 314, 338–39; (Symphony No. 3, 298–99); culminating point, 180; as a dazzling pianist and musician, 244; death and burial service, 326–30; dedication of Opus 38 to Koshetz, Nina, 191; deep intimacy with Skalon, Natalia, 162; depth of personality, 133; donation of money, 219, 270, 319; early musical education, 41–52; as "easygoing agnostic," 212; emotional world, 136, 138; empathy for others, 265; *The Etude* interview, 179, 181; European and Russian music, 70; examination grade of "5 plus," 62; expansive style of playing, 245; failure of the Symphony No. 1, 126, 131, 134; familial lineage, 29, 31; family name Rachmanin, 32; fear of death, 210; final concert tour, 323; financial assistance: (to Avierino, Nikolai, 273; to Fedotov, Georgy, 274; to Ilyin, Ivan Aleksandrovich, 275; to Medtner, Nikolai Karlovich, 272; to Russia, 267–69; to Sikorsky Aircraft Corporation, 270–71; to TAIR publishing house, 271); *Folia* and *Dies irae* themes, 286; French and German fluency, 337; gravesite, 328–30; Grieg concerto, 69; gypsy culture, 71–72; historic scholarly publication on music, 340; as humanitarian, 4–5, 263–80; initial impressions of Zverev, Nikolay, 46–47; integral approach to art, 186–87; jazz and, 305, 306; and Koshetz, Nina, 191; leaving the Russia, 228, 230, 231, 233, 252, 336; legacy, 335–45; as legendary virtuoso pianist, 243–59; letter of protest, signing the, 30; letter to: (Morozov, Nikita, 167–68, 175; Natalia (Tatusha) Skalon, 161–62; Skalon, Liudmila, 77; Skalon, Natalia, 76, 104–7, 152, 161–62; Slonov, Mikhail Akimovich, 68); love and orthodox kenosis, 184–85; marriage of daughters, 284, 293; memorial plaster statue, 330; meta-authorial position of control, 187–93; meta-level of control, 247; missing letters, 10–11; money help to Russian Orthodox church, 271–72; moral and ethical man, 133; music, 3–4, 11; (celebrations, 339; as ocean of passion, 187–88; in the West, 336); musical heritage, 26, 32–33, 36; musical influence, 256–57; musical presentation of Russian Paschal bells, 204; musical training/education for, 26–27; musical works, examples of, 70; music education with Zverev, Nikolay, 42–45; music study: (with Arensky, Taneev and Siloti, 63; at Moscow Conservatory, 42, 52; at St. Petersburg Conservatory, 26; two majors, piano and special theory, 63, 66; music tour: to Varazze, 87–93; to Yalta, 86–87); New York program for the first concert, 317–18; noble heritage, 29; November 26 concert, 318; October 27, 1901 concerto, 141; opinion on modern music, 192; Orthodox music, 197, 203, 208; Orthodox piety, 197; penniless and jobless conditions, 235–36; performance in the White House, 313; performance style, 250; Piano Sonata No. 1, 166, 177; Piano Sonata No. 2, 189; poetry and music collaboration, 181, 183; prelude in E flat major, 165; prodigious talents in instrumental and choral, 51; purchase of a house at 610 North Elm Drive, 320; purchasing the land, 287–89; quality and color of the sound, 250; quarrel with Zverev, Nikolay, 47–49, 63, 154–55; recording methods, 309–10; rehearsal work, 85; relationship with: (Chaliapin, Feodor, 76, 190; Mamontov, Savva Ivanovich, 76; Satina, Natalia Aleksandrovna, 4); religiosity, 197–219; romantic style of performance, 257–58; Russianness, 7; Russian Orthodox religiosity, 5; Russian patriotism, 269; sacred choral music, 197, 200, 202–9, 215, 217, 218; and Satina, Natalia Aleksandrovna, 155–56; (dedication of two songs to Satina, 156–57; engagement plan, 153–54; harmonious relations, 159; marriage, 145–70; memoir, 151–52; opposition to the marriage, 156; wedding trip in Europe, 163, 164); Scandinavian tour, 233–34; self-criticism, 182; sense of stage presence, 247; socio-political status of highest ranks, 32; Sofia's emotional intimacy with, 148–49; sonata, 176–77; state of depression, 134; Steinberg's assessment of, 169; studies in Russia and England, 340; support to: (American anti-Bolshevik, 272–73; the large extended family of, 266); Symphony No. 1, 106, 111, 114–16, 126, 131, 164, 274; Symphony No. 2, 128, 166, 175–76, 245; Symphony No. 3, 128, 297–99, 305; Tchaikovsky as mentor to, 75; tonal compositions, 252; tone poem, 71; transcendent pianism, 188; twelve songs of Opus 21, 135–39; U.S. citizenship, 322, 333n39; views of monarchy, 232; women in life, 3, 9, 158; (Dahl, Elena, 126–33, 135; Ivanova, Maria (Marina) Aleksandrovna, 117–21; Lodyzhenskaia, Anna, 111–17, 120; Skalon, Vera Dmitrievna, 100–111, 120); working method of, 189–90; Youth Symphony of 1891, 175

Rachmaninoff, Tatiana, 151, 165, 201, 239, 285, 292, 293, 299, 300, 319, 323, 324, 329

Rachmaninoff, Vasily Arkadievich, 17–19, 21–23, 25, 30, 33, 35, 41, 71, 154, 161, 216

Rachmaninoff Cycle, 317

Rachmaninoff Foundation, 335

Rachmaninoff Network, 344

"The Raising of Lazarus" (Khomiakov), 183–84

RCA Victor, 306, 310, 318

Red Army, 265, 275, 276, 319

Red Cross, 275–76
Red Terror, 228
religious philosophy, 186
Rhapsody on a Theme of Paganini (Rachmaninoff), 164, 245, 285, 286, 294, 295, 299, 305, 318, 336
Richter, Sviatoslav, 191
Riesemann, Oskar von, 44, 46, 48, 288
Rimsky-Korsakov, Nikolay, 52, 60, 69, 108, 117, 164
RMS. *See* Russian Musical Society (RMS)
Robinson, Harlow, 278
Romanticism, 184, 257–58
Rosen, Charles, 258–59
Rosenfeld, Paul, 337
Ross, Alex, 259
Rostovtsova, Liudmila, 106, 132
Rubinstein, Anton, 57–61, 64, 158, 304
Rubinstein, Arthur, 243
Rubinstein, Nikolay, 57–61
Rusalka (The mermaid, Dargomyzhsky), 84
Russian: art songs, 107–10; church bells, 198–200; estates, 28–29; monarchy, 30; nobility, 27–31; Orthodox Church, 14; Orthodox religiosity, 28, 200; Paschal bells, 204; prisoners of war (POW), 275–76; religious philosophy, 181; symphony, 297–98
Russian Musical Society (RMS), 52, 57, 58
Russia's imperial heritage, 229
Rybner, Dagmar, 238–39, 266

Sabaneev, L. L., 125
Sackville West, Edward, 337
sacred choral music, 197, 200, 202–8, 215
Safonov, Vasily, 55, 61, 63–67; personality differences between Siloti and, 66
Sakhnovsky, Yury Sergeeevich, 112
Samson, Jim, 245

Sanborn, Pitts, 314
Satina, Natalia Aleksandrovna, 4, 9–10, 23, 76, 90, 99, 104, 106–8, 110, 111, 120, 126, 127, 129, 132, 133, 135, 139, 140, 145, 149, 150, 216, 217, 236, 239, 240, 250, 253, 256, 266, 267, 285, 293, 294, 308, 320, 322, 324–26, 328–30, 347–49; characteristics and interests, 146; facing the series of difficult final examinations, 152–53; and Ivanova, Maria (Marina), 148; protectiveness, 147; unstable and turbulent childhood, 154
Satina, Sofia Aleksandrovna, 1, 8, 10, 33, 112, 139, 147, 199, 200, 233, 266, 292, 326, 330, 344–45; characterization of her husband in memoir, 151; emotional intimacy with Rachmaninoff, 148–49; protection of Rachmaninoff, 150–51; recollection of Trubnikova, Anna, 151; as a scientist, 149–50
Satina, Sophia, 263, 283, 284, 293, 300
Satina, Varvara Arkadievna, 33, 216
Savenko, S. I., 57
Schidlovsky, Nicolas, 344
Schloss, Edwin, 298
Schonberg, Harold, 246, 250, 256
Scriabin, Alexander, 248
self-criticism, 182
Sergei Zharov. *See* Jaroff, Serge
Serkin, Rudolf, 328
Seroff, Victor, 114
Shaginian, Marietta, 189, 191, 210, 232, 248, 306
Shchepkina-Kupernik, T. L., 268
Sheffield Festival, 296–97
Sikorsky, Igor, 270–71
Sikorsky Aircraft Corporation, 270
Siloti, Aleksandr Ilyich, 29, 34, 42, 49, 61, 63–67, 69, 84, 163, 164, 229, 233, 244, 245; personality differences between Safonov, Vasily and, 66

Skalon, Liudmila Dmitrievna, 102, 105, 106, 110, 111
Skalon, Natalia Dmitrievna, 102–7, 110, 111; Rachmaninoff's letter to, 76, 104–7, 152, 161–62
Skalon, Vera Dmitrievna, 10, 100–111, 120, 157
Skavronskaia, Ekaterina, 31
Slonov, Mikhail Akimovich, 67, 68, 112, 117
Smolensky, Stepan, 63
Soloviev, Vladimir, 181, 186
Somov, Evgeny, 133, 266, 294
Sorabji, Kaikhosru Shapurji, 303, 314
Soviet Embassy, 4, 269, 273, 275, 319
Spalding, Charles, 238
Spring (Rachmaninoff), 163
Stanislavsky, Konstantin, 81
Stasov, Vladimir, 56, 78
Stefan IV, 31, 32
Steinberg, Michael, 141, 169
Steinway, Henry Ziegler, 133, 256
St. Nicholas Cathedral, 237
Stokes, Martin, 229
Stokowski, Leopold, 190, 308, 314, 315, 318, 319
St. Panteley, 215–16
St. Petersburg Conservatory, 26, 52, 56–60; curriculum of, 61
Stravinsky, Igor, 130, 253
Strelnikov, Nikolay Mikhailovich, 15, 16
St. Sergius Orthodox Theological Institute, 218
subconscious counterfeit, 207, 221n25
Svetlanov, Yevgeny, 116
Swartz, Anne, 304
Sylvester, Richard D., 110, 138
Symphonic Dances (Rachmaninoffs), 305, 318–19

TAIR publishing house, 285
Tambov Rebellion, 228
Taneyev, Sergei Ivanovich, 56, 61–66, 68, 140–41

Tarkovsky, Andrei, 210, 229
Tchaikovsky, Petr Ilyich, 50, 52, 57–65, 68–69, 108; death of, 75–76
Teatro alla Scala, 63, 87, 89–93
Teliakovsky, Vladimir, 82, 84
"Ten Important Attributes of Beautiful Pianoforte Playing," 179
Three Russian Songs (Rachmaninoff), 313–16
Threlfall, Robert, 187, 294
Tillek, Harold, 293
Tiuneev, Boris, 189
Tolbuzin, Sergei Petrovich, 106
Tolstoy, Alexei, 215
Tolstoy, Leo, 114, 173, 182
"To My Children" (Khomiakov), 183–84
Toscanini, Arturo, 87
transcendent pianism, 188
Trio élégiaque (Rachmaninoff), 76
tripartite musical identity, 182
Trubnikova, Anna, 132, 151, 154, 200
tsar's rule, 25

UK Rachmaninoff Society, 335

Variations on a Theme of Corelli (Rachmaninoff), 164, 285–86, 305
Variations on the Theme of Chopin's Prelude in C minor (Rachmaninoffs), 164
Vasilievich, Vladimir, 78
Velimirovic, Milos, 212
Vespers service, 219, 220n22
Vigil service, 220n22
Villa Senar, 287–94, 297, 299, 300, 344
Volkonsky, Petr Prince, 283–85. *See also* Wolkonsky, Petr Prince
Volontieri, Ettore F., 287, 289

Walker, Robert, 297–98
Waller, "Fats", 306
Walt Disney, 307–8
Western musical education, 61

Whiteman, Paul, 305–6
Wolkonsky, Irina, 151, 165, 201, 238, 271, 280, 283–84, 299, 315, 323, 326, 329–30
Wolkonsky, Petr Prince, 283–85
Wolkonsky, Sophia, 285, 293–94, 299, 330
Wood, Henry Sir, 296–97
World War I, 17, 119, 192, 208, 218, 223–25, 235, 237, 265
World War II, 7, 116, 265, 269, 275, 276

Yasser, Joseph, 186, 207, 286
Year of Rachmaninoff, 345
Youth Symphony of 1891, 175
Yuzefovich, Igor, 304

Zhukovskaia, Elena, 146, 153, 154
Zverev, Nikolay Sergeevich, 42–45, 49–52, 61, 72, 158; piano teaching, 46; quarrel between Rachmaninoff and, 47–49, 63; Rachmaninoff's impressions of, 46–47; rumor as homosexual, 47; teaching method, 47

About the Author and Principal Research Colleagues

Valeria Z. Nollan is professor emerita of Russian Studies at Rhodes College. She is active as a scholar, poet, and musician. She was born in Hamburg, West Germany; she and her parents were Russian refugees displaced by World War II. From 1985 to the present, she has made over thirty extended research trips to Europe, the Soviet Union, and Russia. She has lectured widely in such world cities as Havana, San Juan, London, Rome, Moscow, and St. Petersburg. She also has given piano and voice recitals of Rachmaninoff's music in the United States, Europe, and Russia. Her book-length publications include *Bakhtin: Ethics and Mechanics* (2004), a translation of Vladimir Soloviev's *Philosophical Principles of Integral Knowledge* (2008), the co-edited *Greece, Rome, Russia, America: Essays in Eastern Christianity* (2016), and the poetry collection *Holocaust of the Noble Beasts* (2020). *Sergei Rachmaninoff: Cross Rhythms of the Soul* is her latest book.

PRINCIPAL RESEARCH COLLEAGUES

Valentin Ivanovich Antipov

Preeminent Rachmaninoff specialist; General Editor and Director of the Board of Researchers, *S. Rachmaninoff. Critical Edition of the Complete Collected Works* (Russian Music Publishing, Moscow); educated at the Gnessin State Musical College in Moscow (piano performance and music theory) and the Moscow Conservatory (Ph.D. in musicology); in 1997 was honored for his achievements in the field of music by the Ministry of Culture of the Russian Federation; author of many articles on musical text analysis and aesthetics, Mussorgsky, and Rachmaninoff; participant in numerous conferences worldwide.

Aleksandr Sergeevich Bazikov

Distinguished music scholar, administrator, and specialist in the bayan. Graduate of the Saratov State Conservatory named for L. V. Sobinov (folkloric instruments, especially the bayan); 1996–2010 Rector of the Tambov State Institute of Music Pedagogy named for Rachmaninoff; areas of specialization: music education in contemporary Russia, psychology of music education, the role of the emotions in music learning, and curricular development in music in higher education; author of over forty-five scholarly works, including monographs; 2010–present Provost of the Gnessin State Musical College in Moscow, 2016–present Chair of the Department of National Instruments of the Peoples of Russia, Gnessin State Musical College; Honored Artist of the Russian Federation.

Dmitrii Aleksandrovich Dmitriev

Director and Chairman of the Board of Russian Music Publishing in Moscow (2005–present); prime mover of the *S. Rachmaninoff. Critical Edition of the Complete Collected Works*; specialist in Rachmaninoff, music administration and publishing, and archival discoveries in music; active in international music publishing initiatives; business entrepreneur in Moscow.

Aleksei Aleksandrovich Naumov

Musicologist and Senior Research Associate of the Russian National Museum of Music in Moscow; eminent scholar of Rachmaninoff specializing in choral and liturgical music; published many articles based on discoveries resulting from his music archival work; attended a conference at Senar in Switzerland and met Alexandre Borisovich (Conius) Rachmaninoff; numerous presentations at scholarly conferences in Russia.

Boris Semenovich Nikitin

Well-known Moscow musicologist and biographer; many publications include biographies of Rachmaninoff, Chaliapin, and Tchaikovsky; his methodology involves comparative analyses of lives of major composers and nuanced psychological studies connecting composers' identities with their music; personally acquainted with Rachmaninoff's grandson Alexandre Borisovich (Conius) Rachmaninoff, and with Marina Koshetz, daughter of the singer Nina Koshetz. Nikitin traveled widely in Europe, the United States, and Russia for his research.

www.ingramcontent.com/pod-product-compliance
Lightning Source LLC
Chambersburg PA
CBHW051249300426
44114CB00011B/953